DOCUMENTS ON CONSERVATIVE FOREIGN POLICY, 1852–1878

DOCUMENTS ON CONSERVATIVE FOREIGN POLICY, 1852–1878

edited by
GEOFFREY HICKS, JOHN CHARMLEY, AND
BENDOR GROSVENOR

CAMDEN FIFTH SERIES
Volume 41

CAMBRIDGE
UNIVERSITY PRESS

FOR THE ROYAL HISTORICAL SOCIETY
University College London, Gower Street, London WC1 6BT
2012

Published by the Press Syndicate of the University of Cambridge
The Edinburgh Building, Cambridge CB2 8RU, United Kingdom
32 Avenue of the Americas, New York, NY 10013-2473, USA
477 Williamstown Road, Port Melbourne, VIC 3207, Australia
C/Orense, 4, Planta 13, 28020 Madrid, Spain
Lower Ground Floor, Nautica Building, The Water Club, Beach Road,
Granger Bay, 8005 Cape Town, South Africa

First published 2012

A catalogue record for this book is available from the British Library

ISBN 9781107035928 hardback

SUBSCRIPTIONS. The serial publications of the Royal Historical Society, *Royal Historical Society Transactions* (ISSN 0080-4401) and Camden Fifth Series (ISSN 0960-1163) volumes, may be purchased together on annual subscription. The 2012 subscription price, which includes print and electronic access (but not VAT), is £130 (US $218 in the USA, Canada, and Mexico) and includes Camden Fifth Series, volumes 41 and 42 (published in September and November) and Transactions Sixth Series, volume 22 (published in December). Japanese prices are available from Kinokuniya Company Ltd, P.O. Box 55, Chitose, Tokyo 156, Japan. EU subscribers (outside the UK) who are not registered for VAT should add VAT at their country's rate. VAT registered subscribers should provide their VAT registration number. Prices include delivery by air.

Subscription orders, which must be accompanied by payment, may be sent to a bookseller, subscription agent, or direct to the publisher: Cambridge University Press, The Edinburgh Building, Shaftesbury Road, Cambridge CB2 8RU, UK; or in the USA, Canada, and Mexico: Cambridge University Press, Journals Fulfillment Department, 100 Brook Hill Drive, West Nyack, New York, 10994-2133, USA.

SINGLE VOLUMES AND BACK VOLUMES. A list of Royal Historical Society volumes available from Cambridge University Press may be obtained from the Humanities Marketing Department at the address above.

Printed in the UK by MPG Books Ltd

CONTENTS

ABBREVIATIONS

This list provides abbreviations that are used for all printed sources and archival collections to which frequent reference is made.

BDL	M.G. Wiebe, J.B. Conacher, J. Matthews, and M.S. Millar (eds), *Benjamin Disraeli Letters*, vol. V (Toronto, 1993)
	M.G. Wiebe, M.S. Millar, and A.P. Robson (eds), *Benjamin Disraeli Letters*, vol. VI (Toronto, 1997)
Cairns Papers	Papers of the first Earl Cairns, The National Archives, Kew
Carnarvon Papers	Papers of the fourth Earl of Carnarvon, British Library
Cecil	Lady Gwendolen Cecil, *Life of Robert, Marquis of Salisbury*, 4 vols (London, 1921–1932); particular reference is made to vol. II (London, 1921)
Cowley MSS	Papers of the first Earl Cowley, The National Archives, Kew
Cranbrook Papers	Papers of G. Gathorne Hardy, first Earl of Cranbrook, Suffolk Record Office, Ipswich; also a smaller deposit at the British Library
Cross Papers	Papers of R.A. Cross, first Viscount Cross, British Library
DD	J.R. Vincent (ed.), *A Selection from the Diaries of Edward Henry Stanley, 15th Earl of Derby (1826–93) between September 1869 and March 1878* (London, 1994)
DDCP	J.R. Vincent (ed.), *Disraeli, Derby and the Conservative Party: Journals and Memoirs of Edward Henry, Lord Stanley, 1849–1869* (Hassocks, Sussex, 1978)
Dep. Hughenden	Papers of Benjamin Disraeli, first Earl of Beaconsfield, Hughenden Deposit, Bodleian Library, Oxford
DGH	N.E. Johnson (ed.), *The Diary of Gathorne Hardy, Later Lord Cranbrook, 1866–1892: political selections* (Oxford, 1981)
DP	Papers of the fourteenth and fifteenth Earls of Derby, Liverpool City Record Office

Goodwood MSS	Papers of the sixth Duke of Richmond, West Sussex Record Office, Chichester
IP	Papers of Sir Stafford Northcote, first Earl of Iddesleigh, British Library
LP	Papers of A.H. Layard, British Library
LQV	A.C. Benson and Viscount Esher (eds), *The Letters of Queen Victoria, 1837–1861* (first series), 3 vols (London, 1907)
	G.E. Buckle (ed.), *The Letters of Queen Victoria, Second Series*, 2 vols (London, 1926)
M&B	W.F. Monypenny and G.E. Buckle, *The Life of Benjamin Disraeli, Earl of Beaconsfield*, 6 vols (London, 1910–1920)
Memoirs	Earl of Malmesbury, *Memoirs of an Ex-Minister*, 2 vols (London, 1884)
MP	Papers of the third Earl of Malmesbury, Hampshire Record Office, Winchester
Parl. Deb.	*Hansard's Parliamentary Debates*, 3rd Series
SP	Papers of the third Marquis of Salisbury, Hatfield House, Hertfordshire
TNA	The National Archives, Kew, London

ACKNOWLEDGEMENTS

This volume was originally conceived in a research seminar at the University of East Anglia nearly a decade ago and has taken some years to produce. In the process of collating and editing the material we have accumulated a number of debts. I am very grateful for a British Academy Small Research Grant, without which it would have been impossible to have carried out much of the collation and checking of material. The Royal Historical Society patiently awaited the manuscript, while its Literary Director, Arthur Burns, was understanding and extremely helpful in his advice. A number of archivists and librarians across the country assisted us in the research, but particular thanks are due to Paul Webster at Liverpool Record Office for his help in the summer of 2011. We are grateful to Daniel Pearce, Gwenda Edwards, and Paul Gibb of Cambridge University Press for their hard work on the volume, to our copy-editor, Hester Higton, who has been eagle-eyed, helping us to avoid a number of pitfalls, and to Meg Davies for her skilful work on the index. Our thanks to Roy Bridge and Thomas Otte for helping us track down Count Montgelas, to Angus Hawkins for advice about the fourteenth Earl of Derby's handwriting, to Jennifer Davey for taking time out from her own research to check references and for advice regarding Lady Derby, and to Laurence Guymer for his assistance with the Danubian Principalities. We would like to thank the Marquess of Salisbury, the Earl of Malmesbury, the British Library, The National Archives, and Hampshire Record Office for kindly permitting us to use primary material. We are grateful to the Earl of Derby for depositing the Derby Papers at Liverpool Record Office, and to the National Trust for its deposit of the Hughenden Papers at the Bodleian Library. If we have inadvertently failed to acknowledge anyone's copyright, we would be grateful if they would contact us at the publishers so that any oversight can be corrected.

Finally, I must express my gratitude to my fellow-editors, John Charmley and Bendor Grosvenor, who have been unfailingly supportive, assisting with all kinds of obscure questions and tracking down elusive information. Bendor Grosvenor's work gathering material for Chapter Four, in particular, was invaluable. This volume is the joint result of our labours, and we hope others find the material as interesting as we do.

Geoffrey Hicks
June 2012

INTRODUCTION

Conservative foreign policy

The Conservative Party served four terms in government between 1846 and 1880. It did so three times in a parliamentary minority under Edward Geoffrey Stanley, the fourteenth Earl of Derby, and then with a substantial majority from 1874 until 1880 under Benjamin Disraeli, later the Earl of Beaconsfield (for ease of reference, referred to here as Disraeli throughout). During that time, foreign policy was dominated by the Stanleys: Derby closely monitored that of his governments, in the first two of which the Foreign Secretary was his close lieutenant, the third Earl of Malmesbury; thereafter, Derby's son, Lord Stanley, served as his father's Foreign Secretary from 1866 to 1868, then as Disraeli's in 1868 and between 1874 and 1878, by the last period having succeeded to his father's title as the fifteenth Earl of Derby.

This volume is designed to assist those seeking to explore the histories of both Conservatism and foreign policy. The historiographical moment is opportune; the political history of the nineteenth century has been reshaped in the last thirty years. However, while ever more sophisticated views of nineteenth-century Liberalism have emerged, it is only recently that the Conservative Party of 1846–1868 has received sustained attention from historians. In the last few years, the publication of Angus Hawkins's two-volume biography of the fourteenth Earl of Derby, the first for fifty years, has galvanized the process of reassessing mid-Victorian Conservatism.[1] In parallel developments, historians of Liberalism – notably Jonathan Parry and David Brown – have placed foreign policy firmly centre-stage, while another group of historians (mainly based at the University of East Anglia in Norwich) have started to reconsider the role of the Conservatives in foreign policy.[2] Recent research has also begun to challenge what might be described as the 'orthodox' narrative of

[1] Angus Hawkins, *The Forgotten Prime Minister: the 14th Earl of Derby*, 2 vols (Oxford, 2007–2008).

[2] See, e.g., John Charmley, *Splendid Isolation? Britain and the balance of power, 1874–1914* (London, 1999); David Brown, *Palmerston and the Politics of Foreign Policy, 1846–55* (Manchester, 2002); Jonathan Parry, *The Politics of Patriotism: English Liberalism, national identity and Europe, 1830–1886* (Cambridge, 2006); Geoffrey Hicks, *Peace, War and Party Politics: the Conservatives and Europe, 1846–59* (Manchester, 2007); David Brown, *Palmerston: a biography* (New Haven

foreign policy in the 1870s. In this, perpetuated by historians from the 1930s to the late twentieth century, the fifteenth Earl of Derby presided over a policy of drift, from the 'War-in-Sight' crisis of 1875 to the Treaty of San Stefano in 1878, despite Disraeli's attempts to provide firm leadership.[3] While the orthodox account still has its adherents, among whom might be included T.G. Otte and Miloš Ković, this view has been challenged by others.[4] Derby's tenure as Foreign Secretary represents an area of increasing debate.

Until recently, Disraeli's victory over Derby in the policy disputes of 1878 had led to a version of events being constructed by the winners. Before the 1950s, the fourteenth Earl of Derby had no serious biographer;[5] his foreign secretaries – his son and Malmesbury – still await theirs. Although the crises of 1874–1878 have more readily attracted historians, they are still considered within a framework designed by Disraeli's first biographers, W.F. Monypenny and G.E. Buckle, whose work casts a long shadow.[6] Their forensic examination of Disraeli's papers enabled them to produce a coherent narrative of his life and career, with verisimilitude provided by primary material. Their thorough editing, supported by judicious admission of some of Disraeli's errors, created a picture in which the line of perspective was guided always to his triumph at the Congress of Berlin in 1878, when the Prime Minister collaborated with Bismarck and Austria to outfox the Russians. The extent to which he undermined his Foreign Secretary during the Great Eastern Crisis was obscured. A chain of evidence was constructed to give Disraeli's analysis of foreign policy a coherence that it rarely possessed at the time, and sometimes placed him at the centre of events in which he had played a subsidiary role or none at all. Only recently have historians started to challenge these conclusions about his role.

Academic fashion has played its part. The study of a Conservative Party dominated by aristocrats, like the history of diplomacy, was

and London, 2010); Geoffrey Hicks (ed.), *Conservatism and British Foreign Policy, 1820–1920: the Derbys and their world* (Farnham, 2011).

[3] See e.g., R.W. Seton-Watson, *Disraeli, Gladstone and the Eastern Question: a study in diplomacy and party politics* (London, 1935, 1962); Richard Millman, *Britain and the Eastern Question, 1875–1878* (Oxford, 1979).

[4] See, e.g., T.G. Otte, '"Only wants quiet riding"?: Disraeli, the fifteenth Earl of Derby and the "War-in-Sight" Crisis', in Hicks, *Conservatism and British Foreign Policy*, pp. 99–127; Miloš Ković, *Disraeli and the Eastern Question* (Oxford, 2011). For alternative views, see, e.g., Charmley, *Splendid Isolation?*; Bendor Grosvenor, 'Britain's "most isolationist Foreign Secretary": the fifteenth Earl and the Eastern Crisis, 1876–1878', in Hicks, *Conservatism and British Foreign Policy*, pp. 129–168.

[5] Until W.D. Jones, *Lord Derby and Victorian Conservatism* (Oxford, 1956).

[6] W.F. Monypenny and G.E. Buckle, *The Life of Benjamin Disraeli, Earl of Beaconsfield*, 6 vols (London, 1910–1920).

all but washed away in the historiographical tsunami of the 1960s and 1970s. Disraeli survived, because his cultural, literary, and racial identity made him different, exotic, more recognizably 'modern', and, compared with his aristocratic colleagues, a much more attractive subject for new forms of historical enquiry: social, cultural, ethnographic, and interdisciplinary. This process emphasized his centrality and meant that Conservatism was seen through a Disraelian kaleidoscope. Meanwhile, the study of foreign policy became a niche interest unless it was determinedly of a twentieth-century nature and could help explain the causes of wars.

There was, however, another reason for posterity's neglect. Any student of nineteenth-century Conservatism has been hampered by the limited availability of source material. The papers of the earls of Derby and Malmesbury were not readily accessible to scholars until the 1980s. The diaries of the fifteenth Earl were only discovered in the late 1970s, and his papers have been awaiting full cataloguing ever since. On the Liberal side of British politics, not only have papers been available for many years, but a slew of primary material has been published, including the multi-volume editions of Gladstone's diaries and Cobden's letters.[7] The published documents include much valuable material on foreign relations. Fascinating insights into the construction of Liberal policy are provided by the Kimberley letters and diary, and by Agatha Ramm's edition of the Gladstone–Granville correspondence.[8] Much less has been forthcoming on the Conservative side. For example, barely a letter of the fourteenth Earl of Derby's has appeared in print since Monypenny and Buckle reproduced some of his correspondence with Disraeli.

That said, two very significant sets of Conservative documents have been published. The Disraeli Letters project at Queen's University, Toronto and John Vincent's editions of the Derby diaries have presented invaluable material.[9] Given the enormous extent of the

[7]M.R.D. Foot and H.C.G. Matthew, *The Gladstone Diaries*, 14 vols (Oxford, 1968–1994); A.C. Howe's edition of *The Letters of Richard Cobden* is projected to extend to four volumes, two of which have been published thus far (Oxford, 2007 and 2010).

[8]John Powell (ed.), *Liberal by Principle: The Politics of John Wodehouse, 1st Earl of Kimberley, 1843–1902* (London, 1996); Angus Hawkins and John Powell (eds), *The Journal of John Wodehouse, First Earl of Kimberley, 1862–1902* (Cambridge, 1997); Agatha Ramm (ed.), *The Political Correspondence of Mr Gladstone and Lord Granville, 1868–76*, 2 vols (London, 1952).

[9]Eight volumes of the *Benjamin Disraeli Letters* (hereafter *BDL*) have so far been published (Toronto, 1982–2009), with a number of editors, principally M.G. Wiebe, John Matthews, J.B. Conacher, and Mary S. Millar; the ninth volume, anticipated in 2012, will go up to 1867 and constitute the halfway point of the projected publication; J.R. Vincent (ed.), *Disraeli, Derby and the Conservative Party: Journals and Memoirs of Edward Henry, Lord Stanley, 1849–1869* (Hassocks, Sussex, 1978) (hereafter *DDCP*); *A Selection from the Diaries of Edward Henry Stanley, 15th Earl of Derby (1826–93) between September 1869 and March 1878* (London, 1994) (hereafter

former task, however, it may be decades before we see all of Disraeli's letters in print, particularly from his later career. And, vital though that work is, it inevitably emphasizes his role at the expense of his colleagues'. The Derby diaries give us another important Conservative perspective and essential context for the policy-making process, but were of course not themselves part of it; policy was constructed in a process of discussion and correspondence. The lack of published correspondence is not for want of material: in the record offices of Liverpool and Winchester there are significant numbers of letters written by Malmesbury and the elder Derby, while in a range of archives the debates of 1876–1878 have left their mark in hundreds of letters. The huge value for scholars of the Disraeli letters and the Derby diaries underlines the importance of more such material being collected, edited, and made widely available.

The case for producing a volume of this kind becomes all the more pressing when one considers the momentous nature of the events that embroiled the Conservative governments of 1852, 1858–1859, 1866–1868, and 1874–1880. These include the declaration of the French Second Empire, the first of the wars of Italian unification, the crises that followed the Austro-Prussian War, and, of course, the Great Eastern Crisis of 1876–1878, which left Ottoman power propped up for another forty years. With the publication of documents on topics such as these, the part played by Conservative ministries can be the better examined, considered, and re-inserted in the historical narrative.

The documents

This book does not purport to be a comprehensive collection of all that was written on foreign policy even by the principal members of those governments. Such a work would be enormous, and would contain a great deal of material that would be either trivial or unnecessarily obscure. To make the collection both coherent and useful, the editing process has been guided by certain principles. It was decided to end with the fifteenth Earl of Derby's resignation from the office of Foreign Secretary on 28 March 1878 (to be replaced by the third Marquis of Salisbury), when a consistent strand of policy also came to an end. Geographically, the correspondence contained in this volume relates to Britain's European and Near Eastern policy. Much of it concerns relations with the four 'great powers': Austria (Austria-Hungary from 1867), France, Prussia (Germany from 1871), and Russia. From 1861

DD); *The Diaries of Edward Henry Stanley, 15th Earl of Derby (1826–93) between 1878 and 1893* (Oxford, 2003).

Italy took its place in the first rank of geopolitics and was accordingly the subject of intense interest. The Ottoman Empire, and the problem of managing its decline – the so-called 'Eastern Question' – takes up a similarly large place in the collection, particularly in the chapter dealing with the second Disraeli government. But almost all territories that constituted political nations on the European continent (and several that did not) are the subject of correspondence reproduced here.

The editorial decision to focus on European and Near Eastern policy is not intended to diminish the significance of other material. In the archival collections on which this edition draws, the papers on foreign policy also include material dealing with imperial affairs, relations with America, and the minutiae of diplomatic appointments. All three warrant separate consideration. To maintain the coherence of the collection, and to make it manageable (no small consideration, given the hundreds of documents examined), we have largely excluded material falling into those three categories. This being an art and not a science, our principles have occasionally had to be set aside when material has been found relevant to the broader themes of the collection.

One other exclusion, which the aficionado of the Great Eastern Crisis will immediately note, is the Constantinople Conference of late 1876 and early 1877, the gathering of great powers that was held to consider the deteriorating situation in the Near East, but which failed to prevent the Russo-Turkish war of 1877. Salisbury attended as Britain's representative; accordingly, there is in the Salisbury, Derby, and Disraeli papers a great deal of correspondence relating to its proceedings. After some consideration, it was decided to exclude documents dealing with the detailed discussions at Constantinople, which are worthy of collection in a separate volume. To include them here, in bowdlerized form given the confines of space, would not have done the conference justice either as a separate diplomatic episode or for its place in Salisbury's career. The natural home for material generated by the conference is with other documents relating to Salisbury's contribution. Given the conclusion of this collection in March 1878, when he succeeded to the Foreign Office, the exclusion of the earlier Salisbury endeavour seemed logical, and it enabled us to include other unpublished material. In the broader narrative of the Eastern Question, the caesura is not significant: the failure of the conference meant that the unfolding crisis in the Near East went unresolved and events careered on regardless.

In the first three chapters, the correspondence is overwhelmingly that generated by a small group of ministers. In Chapter One, it is all but a bilateral exchange between the elder Derby and Malmesbury; in Chapter Two, their letters still form the bulk of the collection, although their correspondence with and about Disraeli takes on a greater significance. In these two chapters, however, we have the immense advantage of being able to examine documents alongside those published in the Disraeli Letters, which have not been reproduced here, being already in the public domain in very fine editions. In Chapter Two, we have added a number of extracts from the unpublished diary of the Earl of Malmesbury, which he used as the basis for memoirs that were published in 1884. Unfortunately, only snippets of the diary survive in his papers. What little remains from 1852 is almost identical to the published memoirs, but that from 1858–1859, while brief, is rather different from what was published and, we hope, illuminates contemporary events. In Chapters Three and Four, dealing with a period for which the Toronto editors have not yet completed their labours, Disraeli's correspondence takes a more significant place than in the earlier sections. Chapter Three is, for the most part, a three-way exchange between Derby, Stanley, and Disraeli.

We make no apology for the limited number of correspondents in the first three chapters. It is an accurate reflection of their contributions to policy-making. In foreign policy, a small number of ministers guided, decided, and occasionally collided. In the first three Derby governments, the rest of the Cabinet were kept informed as much as was necessary, which for the most part meant not very much. Their contribution to policy was limited to commenting after the event or in Cabinet, where unfortunately no record was kept. Of course, many Conservative politicians, both in Cabinet and out, did discuss foreign policy in Parliament. That material, too, is under-utilized by historians, but not for want of opportunity, given all the volumes of *Hansard's Parliamentary Debates* (now collectively present on the Internet). Nevertheless, while speeches in Parliament presented policy and debate for public consumption, the private correspondence published here was generated in the substantive process of policy-making.

In its range of material, Chapter Four is different. For the first time in the nineteenth century, a Conservative Cabinet was filled with men with strong views about foreign policy and a readiness to express them. Such had often been the case with Whig and Liberal Cabinets, and Viscount Palmerston had long had to deal with incursions into his departmental territory, but Conservative ministers (the Duke of Wellington and Disraeli aside) had meekly deferred to their leaders and foreign secretaries. By contrast, Disraeli's Cabinet was full of armchair foreign-policy experts. The problem for Disraeli and Derby was that the armchairs were in departments of state, and the experts could not be so easily dismissed as could commentators in the press or Parliament. The Cabinet nearly shattered over foreign policy in 1877, and the range of interlocutors reflects the complexity of debate about the Eastern Question.

Others who played a significant role in foreign policy included Queen Victoria (and, before 1861, her husband, Prince Albert) and, of course, British officials at home and in foreign postings. Where royal contributions affected policy-making or illuminated policy-makers' intentions, material relating to them has been retained; but, in the Queen's case, it cannot be said that she has suffered from the neglect of posterity, nor that there is a paucity of primary material available for the historian. Her contribution has been amply served by the nine collections of her letters and the six subsequent volumes publishing her correspondence with her eldest daughter. For the Eastern Crisis of 1876–1878, the Buckle volumes also provide a wealth of material from Disraeli's exchanges with the Queen. But these publications have played their part in distorting our view of British foreign policy. While much heat was generated from Windsor, Balmoral, and Osborne, there was little light. The monarch's *influence* was significant, and when she could frustrate, delay, and harass ministers, as she made it her constitutional duty to do, she did. In 1876–1878, of course, she also took the opportunity of Cabinet divisions to intervene, as the fifteenth Earl of Derby recognized and deplored but could do little to stop. As the correspondence in this volume demonstrates, however, the Queen did not have *power*: she neither initiated nor directed policy, even if it suited Disraeli's purpose to foster the illusion that she did. For that reason, this work treats the monarch as one of several 'noises off'.

Britain's diplomatic representatives, as the agents of foreign policy on the ground, are a continuous presence in this book. The contributions of various ambassadors, ministers, consuls, and other officials were vital; they were the instruments of day-to-day policy, and their role excited comment, approbation, and disapproval. Like the Queen, however, they did not direct policy. Some, notably Lord Cowley in Paris, were given a great deal of latitude by virtue of seniority and experience. Others, such as successive representatives in Constantinople, were so far away that they sometimes had to act before directions could be received from London. But they were the agents, not the instigators, of policy. In 1858, for example, Cowley played a vital role in mollifying Napoleon III after a series of difficulties, but he did not determine policy. While diplomats might bemoan the political leadership they received, particularly if they were not of the same political hue as their masters, they could do little about it. Notable exceptions to this rule were Austen Henry Layard, who acted as much as Disraeli's agent in 1877 and 1878 as he did Britain's ambassador in Constantinople, and Colonel Frederick Wellesley, who played a similar (if more junior) role for Disraeli in Russia. Documents illustrating their contributions are therefore incorporated. Broadly speaking, however, this book treats the periphery as peripheral. It provides the correspondence of those at the centre of power. All of the documents in this collection would usefully be augmented with material from other archives, but this volume incorporates the 'core' of policy debate and decision.

The Derby governments of 1852, 1858–1859, and 1866–1868

The problems with which Conservative governments wrestled may be divided roughly in two. The principal concerns of the fourteenth Earl of Derby's three minority governments, and Disraeli's first, were generated by French revisionism on the European continent. By contrast, the second Disraeli government of 1874–1880 faced problems that lay as much outside Europe, and that blew up within a political landscape defined by Bismarckian conservatism.

While both Italian and German nationalism acted as catalysts, the Conservatives' major foreign-policy difficulties between 1852 and 1868 were caused by Napoleon III's foreign policy. In 1852, both over Belgium at the beginning of the first Derby government's period in office, and over the Second Empire at its end, France generated the most concern. The great powers feared that France was about to invade Belgium in early 1852, and were troubled by the potential consequences of Louis Napoleon Bonaparte's declaration of his new empire (and himself as Napoleon III) in December 1852. In both cases, the Conservative government played a key role in resolving the crises. In 1858, the first weeks in office were spent mending relations with France. These efforts followed the political row that had brought down Palmerston's government, after French refugees in Britain were revealed to have been involved in the Orsini plot to assassinate Napoleon at the beginning of the year. Palmerston had been heavily criticized in Britain for bowing to French pressure and bringing in a Conspiracy to Murder Bill; the Conservatives had to mollify both French and British opinion. The summer of 1858 was overshadowed by French naval expansion; 1859 was dominated by French intervention in Italy. At Plombières in 1858, Napoleon had conspired with Count Cavour of Piedmont-Sardinia to provoke Austria into a war in which France would support Piedmont. This duly came to pass in the spring of 1859, and, as the diplomatic situation deteriorated in the prelude to war, the Conservative government tried to mediate. Caught between France (Britain's liberal ally from the Crimea) and Austria and Prussia (with whose desire for stability it sympathized), Derby's government failed in its efforts, but maintained British neutrality.

France was not, however, the originator of difficulties in the first month or so of the 1866–1868 government, which was dominated by the Austro-Prussian War. The Prussians won comprehensively and took advantage of their victory to create a North German state, embodying a greater Prussia. The conflict itself was over so quickly that it barely required a British reaction. Derby and his son (for simplicity in this section referred to as Stanley) were determined to keep Britain out of the diplomatic manoeuvres that surrounded its conclusion. Much greater difficulties stemmed from Napoleon's desire to secure compensation for the expansion of Prussia. He sought his recompense for wounded French pride by precipitating a row with Prussia over the contested territory of Luxembourg. Ultimately, the only way in which the crisis could be resolved was for Britain to take the lead in mediating at a conference and, with great reluctance on Stanley's part, to agree to a European guarantee of the grand duchy. In keeping with their non-interventionist instincts, the Foreign Secretary and his father then did their best to draw back from that commitment in Parliament.

In the period covered by the first three chapters, there were also several minor difficulties that generated a disproportionate amount of publicity. In 1852, for example, the opposition made hay with the fact that the Conservatives mishandled the case of a young Englishman, Erskine Mather, who was injured in a scuffle with an Austrian soldier in Tuscany. The northern Italian duchy was one of a series of Austrian puppet states in the region, so first the Conservatives had to address the question of who was the proper power with whom to negotiate for compensation for Mather (the Whigs having made very little progress with Austria). While the Government resolved this successfully, two British diplomats in Florence, Scarlett and Barron, then accepted an ill-advised settlement, which Malmesbury and Derby did not check thoroughly, but which – when revealed to the public – gave their opponents ammunition to accuse them of abandoning British interests. This left them open to unflattering comparisons with Palmerston's bravado over the Don Pacifico affair in 1850. The Conservatives faced similar dangers in 1858 over the case of two British sailors, Watt and Park, captured by the Neapolitans aboard a Sardinian ship, the *Cagliari*, that had been engaged in piracy. Over this, however, they negotiated much more effectively, successfully mediating between Sardinia and Naples and obtaining the release of the sailors, with compensation. This was in stark contrast to their Whig predecessors, who had failed to produce a settlement before losing office in 1858.

One of the most important questions raised by this volume is whether, in dealing with problems of any kind, there was an identifiable 'Conservative' foreign policy. Although others may draw different conclusions, it is certainly our contention that there was. Examining the way in which Conservative administrations handled business prior to 1868, certain patterns emerge. The fourteenth Earl of Derby and Malmesbury in 1852 and 1858–1859, and Derby and Stanley in 1866–1868, appear to have deployed four guiding principles: to pursue good relations with all states regardless of systems of government; to resist being drawn in to any of the great continental struggles of the day; to mediate in international disputes; and to contain and underplay differences between states.

In relations with the great powers, they sought to mend fences and avoid disputes with both the autocrats and Bonapartist France. In 1852, overtures were made to Austria and Russia after Palmerston and his Foreign Secretary, the second Earl Granville, had left relations in a fragile state. Russia was consistently seen as a partner, for example over the Belgian crisis in 1852 and the Italian crisis in 1859. In 1866–1868, Stanley was still trying to take opportunities to appease the Russian court, especially if a cheap benefit could be obtained by, for example, giving the Tsar the Garter that he desired. While the Liberals, too, had of course sought good relations with France, Malmesbury went to great lengths to woo Napoleon in 1852, and was publicly criticized for doing so. In 1858, during a war scare, the Conservatives mended relations with France, while at the same time seeking to augment Britain's defences. In relations with the minor powers, a similar placatory approach was adopted. With Tuscany over the Mather case in 1852, Conservative policy-makers rejected the unsuccessful Liberal method of doing business with Austria. In 1859, Derby and his ministers sought to mend fences with Naples; they deplored an earlier Liberal decision to break off relations, given the problems that it had caused for them in resolving the question of the *Cagliari*. In 1852, a secret mission had also been sent to see if diplomatic relations could be established with the Vatican. Although they were unsuccessful in restoring diplomatic links with either court, their attempt was characteristic of a pragmatic, almost technocratic approach to foreign policy, in which instinctive cultural reflexes were ignored or set aside.

Throughout the correspondence in the first three chapters, one may perceive a deep concern about the extent to which Britain might be drawn into the political struggles of the European continent. In 1859, over the Italian crisis, while Derby and Malmesbury were happy to intervene as peacemakers, there was a frustration with French dabbling, Piedmontese ambition, and Austria's reluctance to embrace moderate reform. Once war had broken out, that frustration was replaced by a desire to wash Britain's hands of all the participants. The letters betray no sense of the fellow feeling exhibited by British Liberals for Italian nationalism, but neither was there any support for Austrian reaction, as contemporaries suspected there was. Meanwhile, a suspicion of the Palmerstonian commitment to Belgium – and the problems that it might create for Britain – manifested itself at regular intervals, as did a general contempt for that nation, for Greece, and for other smaller powers. In 1866–1868, Stanley and Derby rebuffed all efforts to involve Britain in the struggles between Prussia, Austria, France, and Italy. Indeed, it was only with great reluctance that Stanley was persuaded to involve himself in the Luxembourg dispute, which ran counter to all his Conservative instincts. Despite raising historians' eyebrows, the parliamentary statements that Derby and Stanley made about Luxembourg – in which they appeared to evade the commitment they had made – appear far less odd when one considers the *mentalité* revealed in this correspondence.

While the Conservatives were deeply reluctant to be embroiled in continental struggles, and contemplated military intervention only *in extremis*, they did seek to intervene diplomatically in order to keep the peace and resolve European disputes. So in 1852 (over the disputed canton of Neuchâtel in Switzerland, over a Greek succession crisis, and on the question of the Second Empire), in 1858, over the case of the *Cagliari* and another ship, the *Charles et Georges* (the subject of a dispute between Portugal and France), in 1859 (at the outset of the Italian war), and in 1867 (over Luxembourg), Derby and his foreign secretaries spent a great deal of time and political capital in pouring oil on troubled waters. In all but the Italian war, they were successful. There was also a desire to avoid confrontational grandstanding in the manner of Palmerston. Thus, in the cases of Mather in 1852 and several British subjects who ran into difficulties with the Austrian authorities, and in the case of the *Cagliari*, Malmesbury and Derby worked to resolve disputes as quietly as possible. Indeed, so little did they seem to defend British interests over the Mather case that their solution backfired badly. Examining their private correspondence enables the historian to obtain a more coherent sense of their conduct than either parliamentary exchanges or the published 'Blue Books' permit. It also allows such cases to be seen as part of a broader approach to policy.

Conservative policy stemmed from a clear desire to maintain the European status quo, and this desire permeates all the correspondence in the first three chapters. The Conservatives acted on the (mostly) unspoken assumption that the existing order in Europe and the Near East favoured Britain and provided the best conditions for economic expansion. Effort was thus best expended preserving that happy situation. Britain had no need to tie itself up in foreign difficulties;

non-intervention was the obvious policy to pursue. This was not so very different from many Liberal analyses – leaving aside more radical visions such as Richard Cobden's – and to some extent it was born of British certainty about constitutional and economic progress. As Jonathan Parry has suggested, talk of non-intervention in the 1860s resulted from a 'complacent and insular confidence that the world was naturally moving Britain's way: not the end of arrogance but its zenith'.[10] Sometimes, there was minimal difference between the parties. It is quite possible to imagine Palmerston resolving the Greek and Swiss problems of 1852 much as the Conservatives did, while they cheerfully concluded his Schleswig-Holstein negotiations. Leaving aside the question of public presentation, important though it was, there is nothing to suggest that the Liberals would not have reached the same basic agreement over Luxembourg in 1867, especially given Gladstone's intervention three years later over Belgium. Where Conservatives and Liberals divided most obviously was over direct challenges to the existing order.

'Ye shall know them by their fruits', and it was in the response to crises and problems that Conservative policy can be seen most clearly. Faced with nationalist assaults, Derby, Malmesbury, and Stanley drew the conclusion that change should be as minimal and conservative as was necessary to maintain stability. By contrast, and unsurprisingly, their opponents favoured prodding Europe in a more liberal direction, which men such as Palmerston, Lord John Russell, and Gladstone all agreed (in their different ways) would help maintain order, stability, and the wellbeing of the people, as it had in Britain. From Malmesbury's point of view in 1859, merely moderate Italian reform by the Austrians would resolve the difficulties in that region. His analysis was very different from that of his political opponents, who were attracted to the notion of a liberal Italian state. He was wrong about the potential for reform, and so were they in assuming that an Italian state would always be a natural British ally. But Conservative policy was pragmatic. Once Austrian power had drained away, the Conservatives were quite happy for Bismarck to deliver the *coup de grâce*, in order that a balance of power might be preserved to prevent Russian or French expansion. This superseded any desire to prop up Austria, as might have been the Conservative instinct fifteen years before.

For all governments, foreign policy has a tendency to be a fire-fighting exercise, but this was even more pronounced in the case of the Conservative ministries, which saw foreign policy almost entirely as a reactive process. Given that the shape of Europe and much

[10] Parry, *Politics of Patriotism*, p. 238.

of the world beyond had been defined in international agreements by which Britain had gained, the principal objective was to deflect threats when they emerged. There were no higher goals. Distilled, Conservative political philosophy was *survival*, in both domestic and foreign policy. In the Near East, where any threat to stability might have led to a Russian expansion or a great power free-for-all, Derby, Malmesbury, and Stanley were happy to embrace any solution that maintained the status quo. The Serbs, Montenegrins, Greeks, and Rumanians were regarded with disdain, and the problems thrown up by them as irritations to be resolved and dismissed as quickly as possible. Once the Cretan revolt had broken out in 1866, Derby's and Stanley's profound wish was for it to be extinguished swiftly. In these areas as in others, what emerges from all the letters is a sense of foreign policy as pragmatic conservatism, not for the pursuit of grand ideological visions, the garnering of prestige, or high-flown rhetoric. Distracted by elections and reform at home, the Conservatives' focus was in any case a domestic one, and foreign policy was to be kept at bay. Perhaps the Salisburian metaphor of foreign policy putting out the occasional boathook as it moved downstream might be best applied to the mid-Victorian Conservatives.

Out of power, the party leadership – though not always the rank-and-file MPs – monitored foreign policy and sought to moderate what they saw as Palmerstonian excesses or Aberdonian weakness, choosing particular moments of vulnerability to press home an attack. During the prelude to the Crimean War, for example, Malmesbury – the only living former Foreign Secretary not in Aberdeen's coalition – was one of the principal critics of the Government. He and Derby took the lead in condemning British policy in China in 1857, while the party also took advantage of Liberal weakness over the Orsini affair in 1858 and the Schleswig-Holstein imbroglio of 1863–1864. Gladstone's ineffectual response to German unification was one of many factors exploited by the party prior to its election victory in 1874.

But the Derby–Malmesbury–Stanley model of Conservatism did not go uncontested. One of the advantages of reading the correspondence across twenty-five years is that it is possible to contextualize the tensions in the upper reaches of the party that almost pulled the Cabinet apart in 1877 and 1878. Over twenty years, Disraeli's desire for Britain to seize opportunities in Europe periodically clashed with what might loosely be called the 'Derbyite' policy of limited, peaceful intervention and peace with all the powers (though one must enter the caveat that there were sub-variants of this even within the Conservative Party). Correspondence dealing with Disraeli's earlier interventions in foreign policy has been published before, albeit in edited form. However, in collections that take

Disraeli as their central subject, his interventions appear only as part of a Disraelian narrative, the frustrations of a dynamic minister confounded by the timidity of colleagues such as Malmesbury and Stanley. His earlier commentary on foreign policy thus underscores the classic narrative of the Great Eastern Crisis; these early signs of his dynamism and decisiveness point to the great victory at Berlin in 1878. This collection similarly enables us to see the development of Disraeli's persona in foreign policy, but in rather different ways: unfocused in its objectives and out of tune with Conservative orthodoxy.

The events of 1877–1878 make rather more sense when seen as the destructive struggle of different philosophies of foreign policy whose roots went back much further than the 1870s. Appearing here as merely one element in ministerial exchanges, Disraeli's contributions were rather insignificant in contemporary terms; they were dismissed by Malmesbury and Derby in 1859 and ignored by Stanley in 1867. When one reads the correspondence in this volume it is clearer why. Both in 1859 over Italy and in 1867 in more general terms, Disraeli came up with amorphous suggestions for grand gestures; for Britain to seize the diplomatic initiative and re-orient relations between the great powers. As he explained to Stanley in 1867, it was time 'to dictate a little to Europe', which would give the Foreign Secretary the chance to 'turn out a regular Chatham'.[11] It was never wholly clear precisely what he was trying to achieve – other than the enhancing of British prestige – and the impracticality or vagueness of his proposals evidently left his colleagues nonplussed. What *was* clear in 1859 and 1867 was that he was at odds with the Conservative foreign-policy norm. But in the 1850s and 1860s, Disraeli did not have sufficient power to undermine his colleagues or challenge their policies. However one may view those policy-makers and their conclusions, it was not they who were eccentric in foreign policy, although accounts of the later government would have us believe that Stanley was. Historians will disagree over what Conservative foreign policy was in 1852, 1858–1859, and 1866–1868, and we hope that this volume will give them much evidence to fuel debate. Whatever it was, though, it was not Disraeli's, and the policy he faced down in 1878 was one that had a much longer history.

The second Disraeli government

The Conservative victory at the General Election of 1874 was unexpected; the first since 1841, it also gave Disraeli a parliamentary majority for the first time. The victory dashed the hopes of those

[11] Letter **241**.

Conservatives who found him an uncongenial and incongruous leader of their party, and it put such men, of whom the third Marquis of Salisbury was the best example, in an awkward situation: should they swallow their objections and serve under a man whom they did not respect; or should they stick to their principles and perhaps find themselves excluded from future Conservative governments? For Salisbury, and others, the existence of Stanley, by now the fifteenth Earl of Derby, was crucial to resolving their dilemma. As the third Marquis explained to his former stepmother, Mary, now Countess of Derby, he had great respect for Lord Derby's intellect and character and would have been happy to have served under him; and he was reassured by Derby's advice that the best way to restrain Disraeli's odd propensities was to be a part of the Cabinet. There can seldom have been a Cabinet in which so many ministers saw it as part of their task to keep the Prime Minister from doing something dangerous; and there has rarely been one in which such a resolve was more necessary.

Derby's return to the Foreign Office was a foregone conclusion. The most important man in the Government after the Premier, he commanded far more confidence among the party faithful. Derby had all the qualities required of a nineteenth-century Prime Minister: immensely rich and of ancient lineage, he was also possessed of a social conscience, an interest in the 'march of mind', and a commitment to public service, which, as he himself deplored, was becoming less common in his class. His political power derived from the same source as his wealth – the ownership of much of Lancashire; it was he, rather than his nephew the seventeenth Earl, who was the 'last king of Lancashire'. His influence on the formation of the Cabinet was considerable: he played a major part in persuading Salisbury to join it; he also kept Gathorne Hardy out of the Home Office, which went to his own Lancashire protégé, Richard Assheton Cross; his brother and heir, Frederick Arthur Stanley, became Financial Secretary at the War Office. One of Disraeli's few intimates, Derby possessed the power that went with that – and with the fact that he was clearly marked out as his successor. That the Prime Minister's health was visibly failing added even more weight to his position. The political augurs expected Derby to become the next Conservative Prime Minister; but across this roseate prospect, some shadows could be discerned by those with eyes to see them.

Derby had served in every Conservative government since 1852, but his commitment, both to the party and to politics, was open to doubt: as early as 1855, Palmerston had tried to coax him into a Liberal government; in 1866, the prospect had been raised of his being the leader in the Commons of a coalition of moderates headed by Lord Clarendon; in 1872, those Tories dissatisfied with Disraeli's lacklustre performance in opposition had seen him as the obvious replacement. The object of the political calculations of others, Derby's own were of a more complex nature. He saw politics as the public service owed by men of his class to the State; an effective and diligent minister, he disliked precisely those elements of politics that so enthralled Disraeli – the plotting, the manoeuvring, the cut and thrust of parliamentary conflict; the prospect of the highest office was not one that held much appeal for him. Changes in his private life did nothing to help: in 1870 he married the dowager Marchioness of Salisbury – an event whose consequences for his career require some comment.

Lady Mary Catherine Sackville-West had been twenty-two when she married the widower second Marquis of Salisbury in 1847; she inherited five stepchildren, including Robert, later the third Marquis, who was only six years her junior. She established Hatfield as the great Tory salon of the 1850s and 1860s; a highly political woman, she seems to have formed an affectionate attachment to the slightly younger Lord Stanley sometime in 1855. The question of whether Lady Salisbury and the future fifteenth Earl had a full-blown affair is one that naturally occurs to the modern mind, whose prurience will have to remain unsatisfied since evidence is wanting. Certainly, Stanley continued to be a regular, honoured guest at Hatfield.

Salisbury's death in 1868 cleared the way for the couple to wed. It was not, however, until after the death of the fourteenth Earl of Derby in 1869 that the couple finally married. The marriage brought the new Earl of Derby deep domestic satisfaction: a naturally uxorious figure, he arranged his affairs to spend the maximum amount of time with his new wife; this took him out of the social round that was Disraeli's natural medium, and further distanced him from his old friend. The Conservative victory that brought him back to the Foreign Office posed questions about his future commitment to politics to which Derby had no simple answers. He resumed his duties out of a sense of public obligation – but without much enthusiasm. One of the biggest beasts in the political jungle, he was not even sure he wished to be part of it.

The documents in this selection challenge the orthodox dismissal of Derby as an oddball and an isolationist. He was no odder than most politicians (and a good deal less so than his chief), and his foreign policy was firmly in the mould of previous Conservative governments; any differences were in fact the result of what Disraeli called the 'German Revolution'. For all his addiction to hyperbole, Disraeli was right in his assessment of the impact of Bismarck's new German empire. Most of the rules under which the great diplomatic game had been played required serious readjustment, not least because Bismarck spent the period after the Franco-Prussian war creating a new system of alliances and arrangements that secured German gains and isolated France. Derby, who took a less histrionic view than Disraeli, distrusted Bismarck and was prepared to act against him if the risk was small and the price not too high; but he remained anxious to work with what might loosely be called 'the Concert of Europe', when it would work with him. Lacking in glamour and excitement, such an approach was the antithesis of the one that Disraeli hankered after; where Derby strove for effectiveness, Disraeli wanted to win prestige. This difference between them was one that Derby recognized from early on, and it would be the root of the separation between the two old friends.

Derby's approach was exemplified in the 'War-in-Sight' crisis of 1875. For a time it seemed as though Bismarck might be about to launch a pre-emptive war against a revived French Republic, which had been expanding its army since the Franco-Prussian War. An officially inspired headline in the Berlin *Post* of 8 April 1875 asked 'Is war in sight?', and European statesmen feared that Bismarck's answer might be 'Yes'. Unlike Disraeli, Derby had not thought war very likely, but in May 1875 he joined with the Russian Chancellor, Prince Gorchakov, in warning against such a pre-emptive strike. Derby was happy enough to gain a diplomatic success at so low a price. Approaches from Bismarck in 1875 hinting at a possible alliance were politely, but firmly, declined. Derby saw in them only the intention of pulling Britain into Bismarck's orbit, and the creation of bad blood with France; he had no intention of playing such a game, preferring, instead, to retain a freedom to act with whichever partners happened to present themselves as and when Britain needed them. Disraeli's views on these matters were, of course, less pragmatic and more dramatic. He regarded the formation of the *Dreikaiserbund* (League of the Three Emperors) of Germany, Austria-Hungary, and Russia in 1873 as the recreation of the old 'Holy Alliance', seeing in the new alignment a diplomatic bloc that both isolated France and condemned Britain to irrelevance in continental affairs; for a Prime Minister who had criticized Gladstone for failing to maintain the prestige of Britain and her empire, this was hardly a satisfactory situation.

While an opportunity to rectify it took some time to appear, Disraeli found other ways to assert Britain's place in the world. One was the Royal Titles Act of 1876, by which the Queen was made Empress of India, and about which much has been written. The gloss he placed on the purchase of shares in the Suez Canal was another. In both cases, Disraeli acted in a manner designed to maximize the public impact of his preferred policies. Derby, as befits his rather negative caricature, is usually presented as having opposed purchasing the reversion of the Khedive's shares, but – as these documents demonstrate – he was in favour of the scheme. Like the rest of the Cabinet, once it was clear that the Khedive was willing to sell, he was persuaded that the danger of another power purchasing the shares was too great a risk to allow.[12] The belief that the initiative was solely Disraeli's arises largely from the flamboyant manner in which the Prime Minister conveyed the news to the Queen. Disraeli was focused primarily on the political impact of the purchase, and he ensured that it was presented in such a manner as to delight both monarch and public opinion. Derby was mystified and somewhat disturbed by the excitement. But he failed to appreciate, as he would so often, the power of such symbolic acts. Disraeli recognized, as few others did at the time, that the grand gesture was what mattered; British prestige was asserted, honour satisfied, and the electorate entertained. He sought the same advantages when the 'Eastern Question' erupted.

The Balkan uprisings against the Ottoman Empire that began in Bosnia and Herzegovina in 1875 posed challenges to the Bismarckian diplomatic system, and to the assumptions that underlay British policy in the Levant; it also provided Disraeli with an irresistible opportunity to play a hand in the 'great game' of diplomacy. All these aspects are reflected in the documents that we have selected.

Britain's interest in the 'Eastern Question' went back to the 1770s, and from Palmerston's day it had been a matter of consensus that the Ottoman Empire should be preserved. The precise meaning and modalities of this were open to debate; the end was not. Britain's interests in the Mediterranean, the Persian Gulf, and northern India made it useful to have a buffer zone between its spheres of interest and those of the Russian Empire. Successive Russian victories over the Ottomans between 1774 and 1829 had eroded this zone, and the Crimean War of 1854–1856 was, in part, an attempt to secure it through an Anglo-French-Ottoman alliance. The allies' victory over Russia in the Crimea and the resulting Treaty of Paris in 1856 had slowed down the Russians' advance for a generation, but by the 1870s they were on the borders of Afghanistan, looking ever more of a threat to British India. Britain could expect no help from the other great powers in dealing with this, but Russia's place in the Bismarckian system offered the chance of assistance – in the right circumstances.

The Achilles' heel of Bismarck's diplomacy lay in the conflict of interest in the Balkans between his two allies, Austria-Hungary and Russia. The Habsburg Empire was content to support the status quo with regard to the Ottoman Empire and did not want the Slav peoples within its own borders to get ideas about independence.

---

[12] For a detailed exploration of the share purchase and Derby's role in it, see, e.g., Geoffrey Hicks, 'Disraeli, Derby and the Suez Canal, 1875: some myths reassessed', *History*, 97 (2012), pp. 182–203.

The Romanovs, who saw themselves as the champions of Orthodox Christianity and Pan-Slavism, were happy to support those who wished to follow Greece in securing independence from Ottoman rule. They also saw the opportunity for influence over any successor states. Bismarck's main demand of the Balkans was that the area would stay quiet and cause no problems. He was frustrated by the revolts of 1875 and 1876; his desire thereafter was to prevent his two allies from going to war with each other – and asking him to choose between them. He therefore happily promoted any scheme that worked towards this end. By the spring of 1876, he and his allies had agreed upon what came to be known as the Berlin Memorandum: it called for an armistice and new negotiations between the insurgents and the Ottomans, based on five points, which required a significant number of concessions from the Turks. If hostilities continued after the armistice, then the great powers would arrange unspecified 'measures' accordingly. The British were not consulted over the terms of the Memorandum, but were asked to adhere to it in May 1876.

Derby's and Disraeli's differing reactions to the Memorandum revealed much about the different ways in which the two men regarded foreign policy. Derby disliked it because he felt that it would be ineffective – being, in effect, a licence to the insurgents to reject the proposals and hold out for better ones from the powers – and would bind Britain to further intervention. It would, he thought, have been better simply to have sought an armistice in the fighting. Disraeli cared little for whatever merits the plan might – or might not – have had; his objections to it lay elsewhere. He was irked by the assumption that Britain was expected to assent to a policy in whose formulation it had taken no part; he also saw an opportunity to disrupt the *Dreikaiserbund*. Vastly different though their reasoning was, the Prime Minister and the Foreign Secretary were agreed that the Memorandum should be rejected.

From Seymer Thompson's *Public Opinion and Lord Beaconsfield*, which was published in 1886, through R.W. Seton-Watson's magisterial *Disraeli, Gladstone and the Eastern Question* (1938), to Millman's *Britain and the Eastern Question* (1979), there has been a consensus that, in refusing to join the Bismarckian overture to the Porte, Britain ensured that no action would be taken at Constantinople and effectively colluded in the 'Bulgarian Atrocities' that followed. This reflects the contemporary charge recorded by Derby when he told a delegation of working men that: 'there are a great many people in England who fancy that Lord Beaconsfield is the Sultan and that I am the Grand Vizier'.[13]

---

[13] T.H. Sanderson and E.S. Roscoe, *Speeches and Addresses of Edward Henry, XVIth Earl of Derby*, I (London, 1894), p. 296.

Underlying such criticisms of Disraeli and Derby, then and now, is a set of 'Orientalist' assumptions. It is assumed that the 'Grand Turk' was effete, in decline, and entirely a creature of whichever European power sat on him last; thirty years after Said's *Orientalism* is certainly not too soon to jettison such views.[14] The new Turkish Sultan, Abdul Hamid II, had to contend with a real, and powerful, internal hostility to the attempts of the Christian powers to dictate to the one Islamic great power, and the notion that he, or his regime, was some sort of *tabula rasa* upon which a Westernizing agenda could be written is one that fails to stand up to any real scrutiny. Lacking this Orientalist perspective, Disraeli and Derby were more willing to see the Porte as an autonomous actor in its own drama; by holding aloof from the attempts to bully it, they simultaneously won its support and avoided the danger that Canning incurred in 1826 when he allied with Russia and France, which was that, in the event of Ottoman obduracy, the Tsar would be able to declare war on Turkey as Europe's mandatory. Unfortunately for them, any gains made from this line of policy were immediately imperilled by the reaction of British public opinion to the news of the 'Bulgarian Atrocities'.

Of all Victorian politicians, Disraeli was the least well equipped to deal with the public's response to the news that Turkish troops had massacred thousands of Christians in the Balkans. Sceptical of such stories, Disraeli allowed his cynicism public airing when he referred to them as coffee-house 'babble'; and his inability to empathize with the suffering Christians simply reminded his critics of his Judaic origins. In the face of massive public demonstrations demanding that action should be taken against the Turks, and with Gladstone's return from 'retirement' to help lead the agitation in September, giving it a fresh lease of life, Disraeli not only found it impossible to support the Turks but found himself facing increasing dissent from within his own Cabinet. He would have liked to have assured the Turks that he would not allow the Russians to attack them; he would have liked to have warned the Russians off; but he could do neither, not least because leading (and more religiously minded) members of the Cabinet began to take an increasingly anti-Turk and, by extension, pro-Russian line. The documents reveal the growing desire of the Cabinet to be involved in foreign affairs and the extent to which, at this point, Disraeli was reliant upon Derby. His stolid calm reassured the Prime Minister and acted as a brake on their Cabinet colleagues, almost all of whom were alarmed by the public outcry. So weakened had Disraeli become by the end of the 'Atrocities' campaign, that all he could do was keep his head down, encourage Cabinet members

[14] Edward Said, *Orientalism* (London, 1978).

to hold their nerve, and agree to the conference of the great powers that met in Constantinople in December 1876 to discuss reforming the Ottoman Empire. The decision to nominate Salisbury as Britain's representative brought him on to the European stage for the first time. It was a shrewd move. Salisbury had a reputation as no Philoturk, was known to oppose Disraeli's tendencies in that direction, and would be unable to complain about the failure of the conference if he was actually there.

Throughout 1876, the continuing Balkan upheavals further threatened the stability of Europe. The British refusal to sign the Berlin Memorandum drove the continental powers to make shift for themselves. That summer, the Russians and the Austrians reached a secret agreement at Reichstadt, which provided for the creation of spheres of influence in the event of a break-up of the Ottoman Empire. When the Constantinople Conference concluded in January without the Turks agreeing to its demands for reform, the two empires renewed their agreement – which prepared the way for a Russian declaration of war on the Porte. The documents in our selection show the attempts of the Conservative government to find a continental partner – and its helplessness in the absence of one. Disraeli's desperate wooing of Vienna was based upon his ignorance of the terms of Reichstadt, which Derby, by contrast, had long suspected. Disraeli's failure to win a European ally drove him back to the need for unilateral British action; it was here that the scale of his disagreement with Derby and others in the Cabinet finally became clear. As so often with Disraeli, rhetoric failed to keep pace with reality. His desire to 'do something' was difficult to translate into a policy; nor did it command the assent of his Cabinet.

The documents illustrate the way in which Cabinet government really worked in the high Victorian era. Disraeli, for all the bombast in his own letters, was no autocrat; the Cabinet needed to be wooed, persuaded, and cajoled; senior ministers – what a later generation would call the 'big beasts' – appear almost as independent potentates with whom careful negotiations needed to be conducted. The personal dynamic between the leading members of the Cabinet is therefore vital to understanding how the crisis ruptured the continuity between the Conservative foreign policy favoured by the House of Stanley and that popularized by Disraeli and his later admirers.

The reader can follow, sometimes on a day-by-day basis, Disraeli's attempts to convince, browbeat, and threaten his colleagues into agreeing to his preferences. What needs commenting on here are two aspects of it. The first is the initial weakness of Disraeli's own support in Cabinet: he had no unconditional supporters, with the exception of his old friend, Lord John Manners (by late 1876, the only other veteran of all the mid-Victorian Conservative governments). The second is the normative nature of Derby's preferences.

On the first of these, the documents chosen cast fresh light on Disraeli's famous claim that there were six or seven 'parties' in the Cabinet: for war (Gathorne Hardy, John Manners, Sir Michael Hicks Beach); for war if the Russians reached Constantinople (Lord Cairns, R.A. Cross, W.H. Smith, the Duke of Richmond); for war if they refused to leave it afterwards (Salisbury); for peace at any price (Derby); for an appeal to the other European powers (Sir Stafford Northcote); for Russian acquisition of Constantinople (the Earl of Carnarvon); for reconciling all the parties (Disraeli and the Queen).[15] At one level, that is far too few; on another, far too many. It is far too few because there is a sense in which every minister had his own view, even if many of them were ill-informed ones; it is too many in so far as not all views were of equal significance. Of those who regularly expressed their views, by far the most important were Disraeli himself, Derby, and Salisbury; to some extent all other views were subordinate to those expressed by these three, and the dynamic of the Cabinet meant that other ministers tended to cluster around them. Disraeli's last 'party', in any case, was disingenuous: he belonged variously in one of the first two, while the Queen was determinedly in the war party. Until December 1877, the High Church, anti-Russian Salisbury and the non-interventionist, pacific Derby appeared to be on the same side, and neither of them agreed with Disraeli. But this was not in fact quite the case; the documents here allow the reader to see more clearly. What they reveal is that Disraeli's bellicose policy alarmed almost everyone except Manners, Hardy, and Richmond; they show that Derby's caution was, for much of the crisis, a more attractive option for most ministers; but they also show the importance of contingency in politics. After the climax of the crisis it was easy to portray Derby as vacillating; but it was only at the end that most colleagues came to that conclusion. For much of the crisis, he enjoyed a good deal of support and approval, and that was because his policy was entirely in line with that of previous Conservative governments – to work with the 'Concert of Europe' to avoid war. The Derby of 1877 was the Stanley of 1866–1868, who had only reluctantly accepted a guarantee of Luxembourg, and his policy was that of his father in the 1850s.

During the most dangerous phase of the crisis – that is, between May 1877 and February 1878 – Derby tried to avoid the war that he feared Disraeli's bellicosity might bring. His close contacts with the Russian ambassador, Count Pyotr Shuvalov, were critical. Shuvalov,

---

[15]Disraeli to Queen Victoria, M&B, VI, p. 194. The story varied slightly depending on the audience: see, for example, *DD*, 21 October 1877, p. 446.

like Derby, had his own home-grown hotheads whose love of 'prestige' threatened to bring the two countries into conflict again, and the two men were at one in trying to lower the diplomatic temperature. Derby's policy of trying to secure British interests while avoiding a repeat of the mistakes that had led to the Crimean War commanded majority support in Cabinet throughout 1877 and, to Disraeli's frustration, into 1878. It was, as is the way of successful diplomacy in such situations, lacking in showmanship and any public profile. By the time the Turkish redoubt of Plevna fell in December 1877 and the Russians were at the gates of Constantinople, public opinion was beginning to demand some dramatic demonstration of British power. To this clamour, Derby remained deaf.

Famously, in the novels of Jane Austen, the Napoleonic Wars appear only as noises off; in these letters, something of the same is true of the diplomatic crisis of 1877–1878. Given that the detail of the crisis is obscured by the political manoeuvring foregrounded in these documents, some brief account of it may be welcome to the reader.

After the failure of the Constantinople Conference, the spring of 1877 was replete with attempts to avoid a Russo-Ottoman war and, as that became increasingly impossible, to contain the damage it might do. In May, with war inevitable, Russia agreed to demands designed to safeguard British interests: Russia would not threaten the Suez Canal; it would not attack or occupy Egypt; it denied any imputation of a desire to acquire Constantinople and agreed that, were the city to be threatened, its status would be a matter for international negotiation; and it accepted that rights of passage through the Bosphorus and the Straits of the Dardanelles would be preserved in a manner satisfactory to all interested parties. Few thought that this was more than papering over the cracks. The key questions seemed to be how swiftly Russia would win the war, and what would happen if its demands were excessive in the eyes of Britain and Austria.

Wars seldom follow the expectations of those who launch them. Far from winning a swift war, the Russians found themselves bogged down on the way to Constantinople, with an Ottoman General, Osman Pasha, mounting an heroic defence of the fortress of Plevna. Always apt to spring to the defence of gallant little foreigners defending themselves against a great empire (provided, of course, that that empire was not British), British public opinion took Osman to its heart; that tide which had flowed so strongly against the Turks in 1876 now began to flow in their favour, strengthened by the growing anxiety that the Russians would seize Constantinople. All of this presented Disraeli and his colleagues with problems. News from the war zone was slow, intermittent, and sometimes contradictory; nonetheless, ministers were expected to react to it.

The documents that we have selected illustrate the flexibility of Disraeli's responses as he pursued – with increasing frustration – a more 'active' policy resisted principally by Derby, Salisbury, and Carnarvon, as well as tracing out the lineaments of the divisions within his Cabinet. Upon one issue, however, the Prime Minister was clear: the political and diplomatic consequences of the fall of Constantinople would be fatal to his Government, and therefore that event must be prevented. The question of how best to secure this essential desideratum allowed of some degree of manoeuvre; but this should not obscure from the reader Disraeli's determination to stop the Russians from occupying Constantinople. Here, Derby's position was critical.

By June, Disraeli was quite ready to contemplate the resignation of Salisbury and other ministers who felt unable to defend Constantinople from Russian attack; but without Derby's support he could not to take the decisive action he desired. Not for the last time, Disraeli would appeal to their old friendship; and, not for the last time, Derby would be deaf to his entreaties. He was guided by his sense of public duty, nothing more. Derby was convinced that middle-class opinion was firmly against the war; Disraeli, who always despised the middle class, told him that 'the upper and working classes were united against Russia'.[16] The selections from Disraeli's secret correspondence with the British ambassador to the Porte, Austen Layard, provide an insight into exactly how bellicose Disraeli was prepared to be at this juncture, and the extent to which he was prepared to bypass the Cabinet. Writing to Layard on 6 August, in a letter his biographers chose not to publish, Disraeli appeared to be contemplating the British occupation of Armenia and Tiflis – a policy that would certainly have caused war.[17] He also stressed the importance of Turkish resistance being such as to secure another Russian campaign, which would present Britain with a *casus belli*. The extraordinary episode in which he and the Queen entrusted Colonel Wellesley, the British military attaché to the Tsar, with a 'secret mission', warning that Britain would not stay neutral in the event of a second campaign, is more comprehensible when placed in this context, but its risks are also more apparent. Disraeli had sent Wellesley to threaten the Tsar over the potential consequences of a Russian campaign that he was at the same time trying to provoke via Layard. Buckle's comment – that the mission was a 'questionable proceeding' – remains an unbeatable example of English understatement.[18]

[16]*DD*, 30 June 1877, p. 413.
[17]Letter **448**.
[18]M&B, VI, p. 148.

The question of what to do should the Russians menace Constantinople was, as Derby admitted to his diary on 31 July, one that caused him to 'move, as it were, with my resignation in my hands'; nor, as the crisis wore on, was he the only one.[19] Between July and December, Disraeli made repeated attempts to force his colleagues to take the line he wanted on this issue – namely to threaten war if the Russians threatened Constantinople. Thanks to Derby, these attempts ended in failure. The documents enable the reader to make a full assessment of the Disraelian version of events. Derby's role can be fully traced, as can the persistent concern exhibited by Carnarvon and Salisbury. It also becomes clear that there was, as Northcote's letter to Corry of 15 August 1877 shows, some dissatisfaction with the manner in which Disraeli conducted Cabinet business.[20] The notion that Derby was, in some way, an isolated figure fails to survive close scrutiny. Such a conclusion does, however, invite a fresh question: why, in that case, was it Derby who ended up resigning in 1878?

This is not an absurd question – even if the Disraelian mythology might make it appear as such; the fact that it was Derby who resigned should not blind us to the fact that, at the time, other possibilities existed. The 'policy' that Disraeli outlined to the Tsar through Wellesley was never that of his Cabinet – which was why he used such an unorthodox and irregular route to promote it. Disraeli's conviction that the threat of British intervention would deter Russia from occupying Constantinople was not shared by enough of his colleagues for him to make it official British policy. By the time that Plevna fell to the Russians in early December, the Cabinet was as divided as it had been in the summer; however, with public opinion now in full cry, the time and space that had allowed the luxury of such debate was contracting. On the stage of the London music halls, the 'Great' MacDermott sang

> We don't want to fight,
> but by Jingo if we do,
> we've got the ships,
> we've got the men,
> we've got the money too

before declaring 'The Russians shall not have Constantinople!'

Disraeli looked to the 'Jingoes' for support; he found little in his own Cabinet. As the pressure from public opinion increased, and as rumours abounded that the Russians were in the suburbs of Constantinople, Disraeli pressed his colleagues to agree with him – but

[19] *DD*, 31 July 1877, p. 426.
[20] Letter **449**.

to little positive effect. Even at a supposedly decisive meeting of the Cabinet on 17 December 1877, where he pressed for an immediate summoning of Parliament, increased defence preparations, and British pressure on Russia to make peace, Salisbury, Carnarvon, and Derby would not move. It was Disraeli who had to threaten to resign, and even then his opponents were not persuaded. What followed showed how close things were. For what was the final time, on 18 December 1877, Disraeli made another personal appeal to Derby; with the help of Cairns and Salisbury, a compromise was reached at Cabinet later the same day.[21] This postponed the summoning of Parliament to a date later than originally proposed and deferred the question of increased defence expenditure.

Contemplating future policy, however, Disraeli recognized that he could not be sure of achieving either his ends or Cabinet unity by such uncertain means. Shortly before Christmas 1877, he insured his position by seeking to win Salisbury's support.[22] He recognized that he needed to split Derby and Salisbury; the weaker, less well-respected Carnarvon could be more easily picked off. It was to Salisbury, therefore, that he let slip two secrets: that of the Wellesley mission, and his fears that the 'leaks' of Cabinet secrets came from Lady Derby herself. That Disraeli should have chosen to impute an act of betrayal to her in his letter to her former stepson, who may have suspected her of betraying his father, may simply have been a coincidence; but it put the relationship between the two men on a new footing. As far back as 14 July 1877, Derby, as the record here shows, had denied that the notes he made of Cabinet meetings could be the source of any leakages of information; only his wife and his private secretary, Thomas Sanderson, had access to those notes.[23] This, as the research of Bendor Grosvenor has shown, was not the reassurance that Derby imagined.[24]

Grosvenor's work has demonstrated the lengths to which Mary Derby was prepared to go to get access to the notes that her husband made of Cabinet meetings. Derby's notes (which have all disappeared save for one copy found by Jennifer Davey) were kept securely locked in his desk; only Derby and Sanderson had keys to unlock the drawer. But what Derby did not know was that his wife had access to the papers through Sanderson's agency. Sanderson seems to have nursed a tenderness for Mary Derby's youngest daughter, Margaret, and it

---

[21] *DD*, 18 December 1877, pp. 465–466.
[22] Letter **497**.
[23] Letter **440**.
[24] B.G. Grosvenor, 'Lord Derby and the Eastern Crisis' (unpublished PhD thesis, University of East Anglia, 2009), ch. 8.

may be that that, or the formidable personality of Lady Derby, made him give her the key when she asked for it. The extent to which this made her the author of the information that Shuvalov then apparently passed to his government about Cabinet divisions is, however, unclear. Anyone who moved in London society, as the suave and amiable ambassador did, could scarcely have avoided hearing the anecdotes that dropped so readily from the lips of the Prime Minister himself. The Duke of Richmond had warned Lord Cairns in July 1876 of the dangers of the 'Chief's' love of gossip.[25]

The role of Lady Derby has recently been examined in great detail by Jennifer Davey, whose work shows the extent to which she should be seen not as some exotic interloper in a male world but as a 'female politician' in the mould of Trollope's Lady Glencora Palliser.[26] The part played by aristocratic women in British political life is worthy of much further study. We are aware that this volume is open to the charge of perpetuating the separation of 'male' and 'female' spheres by excluding most of Lady Derby's correspondence. That is far from our intention; rather, we hope that the letters here will be used as a starting point for further scholarship in this area, as in others. To have hastily added Lady Derby's letters, many of which have only recently been discovered or received attention, would have done a disservice to scholarship, while the detailed further work of historians such as Davey is ongoing.

Even as Disraeli was beginning to poison the wells of their friendship, Derby was taking the higher ground. His letter to Salisbury written on 23 December 1877 stands as the most lucid expression of the Conservative tradition of which he was heir: 'prestige' was all very well for those who, like Disraeli, seemed to be blinded by it, but this was not the way in which the British aristocracy ran things.[27] However, Derby's confident appeal to aristocratic solidarity was misplaced. For reasons that have been variously explained, Salisbury chose to side with Disraeli, and when Derby for the first time decided to resign, on 23 January 1878, Salisbury was the obvious choice to succeed him. Derby was undermined by widespread rumours as to his incapacity; Grosvenor has shown the way in which sources close to Disraeli disseminated stories about Derby's addiction to drink and the nature of his wife's relationship with Shuvalov.[28] In the 'Jingo' atmosphere created by the possibility of Russia occupying Constantinople, it was

---

[25] Letter **338**.
[26] J. Davey, 'The invisible politician: the political career of Lady Mary Derby, latterly the Countess of Derby (1824–1900)' (unpublished PhD thesis, University of East Anglia, 2012).
[27] Letter **496**.
[28] See, e.g., Grosvenor, 'Britain's "most isolationist Foreign Secretary"', pp. 159–160.

easy enough to portray Derby as at best a weak vacillator, and at worst a drunken cuckold unable to come to grips with events. Aware that there were rumours, Derby fastidiously regarded them as further evidence that public opinion was not a fit barometer of foreign policy.[29] Despite everything that had passed, however, Disraeli was forced to take Derby back into the Government when it became clear, first, that the Turks were going to make peace with Russia anyway and, secondly, that the rumours had not quite done their work and Conservative backbenchers were not prepared to lose Derby.

Derby's refusal to countenance any formal threat to Russia was based upon two considerations: the first was that Britain could not act without an ally, and he did not think that the Austrians would fill that position if it came to war; the second was that the Russians would make a moderate peace settlement, probably along the lines of whatever they and the Austrians had concocted at Reichstadt in the summer of 1876. These two propositions hung together, and they hung on the reassurances of Shuvalov. Unfortunately for Derby, and fortunately for Disraeli, Shuvalov was not in the loop when it came to the negotiations being carried on by the Grand Duke Nicholas with the Ottomans. For the Pan-Slavs in the Livadia Palace (the Tsar's Crimean base), the time had come to seize their maximum gains, while Chancellor Gorchakov, like Shuvalov, wanted a more modest settlement that would not unite the old Crimean coalition against Russia. It would only become apparent which side had the Tsar's ear when the terms being negotiated at San Stefano were known.

When the news of the treaty eventually concluded between Russia and the Ottomans at San Stefano on 3 March 1878 became public, it was clear that, despite Shuvalov's assurances, it was a 'Pan-Slav' peace. The product of the thinking of the Russian military rather than its diplomats, San Stefano created a 'Big Bulgaria', which seemed destined to be a Russian client state, giving its patron access to an Aegean Sea port. This changed everything. A harder-line policy was now clearly needed, and with Austria-Hungary furious at what its foreign minister, Count Gyula Andrássy, took to be a blatant disregard of Reichstadt, the ally to help enforce such a line now became available. Presented with Disraeli's determination to annex some portion of Ottoman territory as part of a policy of confronting Russia, Derby again resigned from the Government on 28 March 1878 – when our collection of documents ends.

This collection ends there because that was the point at which the line of policy long accepted by the majority of Conservatives – and led by the House of Stanley since the 1840s – went into eclipse.

[29] DD, 9 February 1878, pp. 504–505.

Salisbury, who had for so long seemed to agree with Derby, succeeded to his position at the Foreign Office. Tiring of what he had come to see as the constant negativity of Derby's position, he seems to have decided that even Disraeli's policy was better than not having one at all – which is what, increasingly, the Cabinet felt that Derby's position constituted.[30] Austrian resentment over San Stefano gave him the ally Derby had never had, while Bismarck's fears of an Austro-Russian war gave him an 'honest broker' to bring the two sides together in Berlin in June to undo San Stefano's more objectionable provisions.

At San Stefano the Russians had effectively destroyed Ottoman influence on the European side of the Bosphorus, replacing it with their own through a series of what looked to the other powers like client states; the mission of the powers at Berlin was to reverse this as far as it could be done, but without giving the Ottomans any real compensation. The Treaty of Berlin, signed on 13 July 1878, allowed Serbia, Montenegro, and Rumania to keep the independence conceded by the Ottomans at San Stefano, though not the exact borders; but the same was not true of the 'Big Bulgaria'. A new kingdom ruled by a Russian protégé which included the whole of Macedonia and which had a coastline on the Aegean was the sort of thing that only the Pan-Slavs who had negotiated San Stefano could have imagined would have been acceptable to the other powers; Berlin saw it dismantled. It was first bisected, with most of Macedonia and Thrace being returned to the Ottomans, and then divided into two: a smaller Bulgarian Principality, which was independent, and an autonomous Eastern Rumelia, which remained under Ottoman suzerainty. The Austrians got their pound of flesh in the form of a protectorate over Bosnia-Herzegovina and the right to garrison the Sanjak of Novi-Pazar. Russian influence in the Balkans was curtailed, and the results of the Congress were easily portrayed by Disraeli and a friendly press as a huge success, although within a generation it would become clear, as Salisbury would admit in 1886, that they had 'backed the wrong horse' in thinking that the 'Big Bulgaria' would have been a Russian client state.

All of that lay nearly a decade away from the summer of 1878, when Disraeli and Salisbury returned in triumph from Berlin declaring that they brought 'peace with honour'; sixty years later another Prime Minister would use those words in Downing Street. A delighted Queen Victoria rewarded both her ministers with the Order of the Garter, and they basked in public acclaim. Everyone agreed that it was a notable British diplomatic triumph. One dissident voice was that of Derby, whose only contribution to the general gaiety was to explain to the

[30]See, e.g., letter **482**.

Lords the reasons behind his resignation. This led to his being accused
by Salisbury of both leaking and falsifying Cabinet discussions, and
being likened to Titus Oates, the seventeenth-century perjurer who
had made a series of allegations about Roman Catholic plots. The
breach between the two men was complete. Salisbury remained as
Foreign Secretary until the Government's defeat at the general election
of 1880, eventually succeeding Disraeli as leader and becoming Prime
Minister in 1885. By that time Derby had completed his detachment
from the Conservative Party by accepting office in Gladstone's Liberal
Cabinet. Where Salisbury became a prominent figure in the history
of the Conservative Party, Derby was all but forgotten. This collection
is a contribution to excavating the role that he, and his father, played
in that history.

Easy and tempting though it is to suggest that Disraeli's triumph
marked the complete eclipse of the Derbyite position in Conservative
foreign policy, there are grounds for proceeding with more caution.
The exact nature of the relationship between Disraeli and Salisbury
at the Foreign Office after 1878 suggests that the showmanship of the
former was of limited use for a defined period of time, the *réclame*
of Berlin and of Disraeli's posthumous reputation notwithstanding.
Since history deals in continuities as well as change, it might be
that further study of Salisbury's diplomacy will reveal its similarities
with that traced in this collection, raising the question (which we
cannot answer here) of the real legacy bequeathed to the Conservative
Party by Disraeli. The notions of continuity and bipartisanship
in British foreign policy have created the impression of a golden
thread running from Canning, through Palmerston and Disraeli, to
Churchill, Thatcher, and Blair, in which a concern for British prestige
and an activism on its behalf have been the dominant themes. This
collection suggests the existence of other continuities; in place of the
'golden thread' we can discern something more complex. When Paul
Kennedy and Paul Schroeder wrote about the persistence of a policy
of 'appeasement', they were, in part, stumbling over the prostrate
remains of the Conservative tradition traced in these documents. But
labelling it 'appeasement' was to continue a tradition (already a long
one by the 1970s) of reading British foreign policy backwards.[31]

Beginning with Gooch and Temperley's documents on the origins
of the Great War and continuing with the volumes on British policy
leading to the Second World War, edited by Sir Llewellyn Woodward,
published collections of documents on British foreign policy have

---

[31] For a detailed exploration of the 'tradition' of appeasement, see Geoffrey Hicks,
'"Appeasement" or consistent Conservatism? British foreign policy, party politics and the
guarantees of 1867 and 1939', *Historical Research*, 84 (2011), pp. 513–534.

focused on the twentieth century and on the origins of wars. There is an obvious place for both, but too great a concentration on the latter is, to diplomatic history, what autopsies in cases of sudden death are to forensic pathology; if we drew our knowledge of pathology solely from studying sudden death, we might end up supposing such a state of affairs to be natural – when it is not. Equally, a concentration on the twentieth century can lead us to neglect the long-term continuities that underlie British foreign policy. Many years ago, Rab Butler commented that it was impossible for a global empire to have one 'simple traditional policy', because British interests 'and the world itself' are too complicated to enable us to follow any one high road'.[32] We hope that the documents that follow offer ample evidence of that assertion – and sources from which further studies may proceed.

[32] Trinity College, Cambridge, R.A. Butler MSS, Butler to Ian Black, 21 April 1938, RAB G/9/13.

EDITORIAL NOTE

Biographical details

For individuals mentioned in more than one document, an asterisk * at first appearance denotes an entry in the biographical appendix. Biographical details are supplied for other individuals as and when they appear.

Undated letters

The vast majority of documents left undated by their authors have been placed in chronological order by context, inference, or other information. In the Malmesbury papers, however, a few letters remain without an obvious chronological location. In those instances, we have been guided by folio order.

Addresses of correspondents

Where the author of the letter gave an address, or it is identifiable from the letterhead, the address is given. Otherwise, no address is listed.

Glossary

Some terms were regularly used by correspondents, but require explanation:

F.O.: Foreign Office
H.M.: His/Her Majesty
HMG: Her Majesty's Government
Lord B/Ld B [from 1876]: Lord Beaconsfield (Disraeli)[1]
L.N./L. Nap: Louis Napoleon, i.e. Emperor Napoleon III
Pam: Lord Palmerston

[1] Although Disraeli was created the Earl of Beaconsfield in 1876, in editorial notes he is referred to as Disraeli throughout.

R.C.: Roman Catholic
Schou: Count Shuvalov, the Russian ambassador
Servia: Serbia
tel: telegram

Where the 'powers' or 'great powers' are referred to collectively in notes, those powers are Austria (later Austria-Hungary), France, Prussia (later Germany), and Russia.

Spelling/punctuation

The spelling from the original documents has been retained; so, too, has the punctuation, except where it has occasionally been necessary to assume a mark for the sake of clarity. Malmesbury, in particular, used an all-purpose dash of his pen, thus – to represent commas, full stops, colons, and semi-colons. These dashes have been retained, and the reader may decide which was intended. The correspondents were erratic in their use of punctuation, spelling, and diacritics (for example, Brunnöw might appear with or without an umlaut even in the same letter, as in letter **9**). In all cases, the form has been retained as in the original letters.

Ellipses and paragraph breaks

All editorial omissions are indicated by ellipses in square brackets, thus: [. . .]. All paragraph breaks follow those in the original letters.

Contractions

Contracted words have been expanded, except for common words whose meaning is clear. In case of any doubt, these are as follows:

cd/c^d: could
Govt/gov^t: government
Ld/L^d: Lord
shd/sh^d: should
wd/w^d: would
wh:/w^h: which
yr/y^r: your

TIMELINE

23 February 1852	14th Earl of Derby forms his first minority administration. 3rd Earl of Malmesbury Foreign Secretary; Disraeli Chancellor of the Exchequer.
8 May 1852	Treaty of London (regarding Danish succession).
20 November 1852	Treaty on Greek succession signed in London.
2 December 1852	Declaration of the French Second Empire, recognized by Britain.
17 December 1852	Fall of the 14th Earl of Derby's first administration.
28 March 1854	Britain, in alliance with France, enters the Crimean War against Russia.
30 March 1856	Treaty of Paris ends the Crimean War.
20 February 1858	14th Earl of Derby forms his second minority administration. Malmesbury again Foreign Secretary; Disraeli Chancellor of the Exchequer.
12 July 1858	Pact of Plombières between Napoleon III and Count Cavour of Piedmont-Sardinia.
29 April 1859	Outbreak of Second Italian War of Independence.
4 June 1859	Franco-Sardinian victory against Austria at the Battle of Magenta.
11 June 1859	Fall of 14th Earl of Derby's second administration.
24 June 1859	Franco-Sardinian victory against Austria at the Battle of Solferino.
11 July 1859	Preliminary Treaty of Villafranca ends Italian war.
14 June 1866	Outbreak of the Austro-Prussian War.
28 June 1866	14th Earl of Derby's third administration. His son, Lord Stanley, is Foreign Secretary; Disraeli again Chancellor.
26 July 1866	Armistice and Preliminary Treaty of Nikolsburg ends Austro-Prussian hostilities.
23 August 1866	Peace of Prague formally ends the Austro-Prussian War.

11 May 1867	Treaty of London guarantees the neutrality of Luxembourg.
25 February 1868	Derby resigns as Prime Minister, succeeded by Disraeli. Stanley remains Foreign Secretary.
1 December 1868	Fall of Disraeli's first administration.
2 September 1870	Napoleon III captured at the Battle of Sedan. Second Empire falls two days later.
18 January 1871	Wilhelm I declared Emperor of United Germany at Versailles.
6 June 1873	Treaty between Austria and Russia, joined by Germany on 22 October 1873, creating *Dreikaiserbund* (League of the Three Emperors).
18 February 1874	Disraeli becomes Prime Minister for the second time, this time with a Conservative majority. 15th Earl of Derby is again Foreign Secretary.
July 1875	Uprising against Turkish rule begins in Herzegovina.
4 January 1876	Britain receives the 'Andrássy Note'.
13 May 1876	The Berlin Memorandum is presented to Britain, but rejected.
May 1876	Turkish irregular troops commit the 'Bulgarian Horrors'.
30 June 1876	Serbia and Montenegro declare war on Turkey.
8 July 1876	Alexander II and Franz Josef meet at Reichstadt in Austria. The agreement between Russia and Austria is secret, but plays a significant role in the Eastern Crisis.
23 December 1876	Constantinople Conference opens. Its recommendations are rejected by Turkey.
20 January 1877	Conclusion of Constantinople Conference.
24 April 1877	Russia declares war on Turkey.
10 December 1877	Plevna falls. The 'road to Constantinople' lies open to Russia.
23 January 1878	15th Earl of Derby's first resignation from the Cabinet.
3 March 1878	Treaty of San Stefano between Russia and Turkey is published.
27 March 1878	15th Earl of Derby resigns for the second and final time, and is replaced by 3rd Marquis of Salisbury.
13 July 1878	Treaty of Berlin.

CONSERVATIVE CABINETS, 1852–1880

1852

Prime Minister	14th Earl of Derby
Lord Chancellor	Lord St Leonards
Lord President of the Council	2nd Earl of Lonsdale
Lord Privy Seal	2nd Marquis of Salisbury
Chancellor of the Exchequer	Benjamin Disraeli
Home Secretary	Spencer Horatio Walpole
Foreign Secretary	3rd Earl of Malmesbury
Colonial Secretary	Sir John Pakington
First Lord of the Admiralty	4th Duke of Northumberland
President of the Board of Control	J.C. Herries
President of the Board of Trade	J.W. Henley
Commissioner of Woods and Forests	Lord John Manners
Postmaster-General	4th Earl of Hardwicke

1858–1859

Prime Minister	14th Earl of Derby
Lord Chancellor	Lord Chelmsford
Lord President of the Council	2nd Marquis of Salisbury
Lord Privy Seal	4th Earl of Hardwicke
Chancellor of the Exchequer	Benjamin Disraeli
Home Secretary	Spencer Horatio Walpole; Thomas Sotheron Estcourt (from 3 March 1859)
Foreign Secretary	3rd Earl of Malmesbury
Colonial Secretary	Lord Stanley; Sir Edward Bulwer Lytton (from 5 June 1858)
Secretary of State for War	General Jonathan Peel
India Secretary	Lord Stanley (from 12 September 1858)
First Lord of the Admiralty	Sir John Pakington
President of the Board of Control	Earl of Ellenborough (until 5 June 1858); Lord Stanley (until 2 August 1858). *Thereafter, post abolished.*
President of the Board of Trade	J.W. Henley; 4th Earl of Donoughmore (from 3 March 1859)
First Commissioner of Works and Public Buildings	Lord John Manners

1866–1868

Prime Minister	14th Earl of Derby; Benjamin Disraeli (from 25 February 1868)
Lord Chancellor	Lord Chelmsford
Lord President of the Council	3rd Duke of Buckingham; 7th Duke of Marlborough (from 8 March 1867)
Lord Privy Seal	3rd Earl of Malmesbury
Chancellor of the Exchequer	Benjamin Disraeli; George Ward Hunt (from 29 February 1868)
Home Secretary	Spencer Horatio Walpole; Gathorne Gathorne Hardy (from 17 May 1867)
Foreign Secretary	Lord Stanley
Colonial Secretary	4th Earl of Carnarvon; 3rd Duke of Buckingham (from 8 March 1867)
Secretary of State for War	General Jonathan Peel; Sir John Pakington (from 8 March 1867)
India Secretary	Viscount Cranborne; Sir Stafford Northcote (from 8 March 1867)
First Lord of the Admiralty	Sir John Pakington; Henry Lowry-Corry (from 8 March 1867)
President of the Board of Trade	Sir Stafford Northcote; 6th Duke of Richmond (from 8 March 1867)
First Commissioner of Works	Lord John Manners
Chief Secretary for Ireland	Lord Naas (succeeded as 6th Earl of Mayo, 1867). *Mayo left the Cabinet at the same time as Derby's retirement, to take up his post as Viceroy of India. His successor did not sit in Cabinet.*
President of the Poor Law Board	Gathorne Gathorne Hardy (until 17 May 1867). *His successor did not sit in Cabinet.*
Minister without office	Spencer Horatio Walpole (from 17 May 1867)

1874–1880

Prime Minister	Benjamin Disraeli (created Earl of Beaconsfield, 1876)
Lord Chancellor	Lord Cairns (created Earl Cairns, 1878)
Lord President of the Council	6th Duke of Richmond

Lord Privy Seal	3rd Earl of Malmesbury; Earl of Beaconsfield (from August 1876); 6th Duke of Northumberland (from 4 February 1878)
Chancellor of the Exchequer	Sir Stafford Northcote
Home Secretary	R.A. Cross
Foreign Secretary	15th Earl of Derby; 3rd Marquis of Salisbury (from 2 April 1878)
Colonial Secretary	4th Earl of Carnarvon; Sir Michael Hicks Beach (from 4 February 1878)
Secretary of State for War	Gathorne Gathorne Hardy (created Viscount Cranbrook, 1878); Frederick Stanley (from 2 April 1878)
India Secretary	3rd Marquis of Salisbury; Viscount Cranbrook (from 2 April 1878)
First Lord of the Admiralty	George Ward Hunt; W.H. Smith (from August 1877)
Postmaster-General	Lord John Manners
Chief Secretary for Ireland	Sir Michael Hicks Beach (until 4 February 1878). *Entered Cabinet, February 1877; his successor did not sit in Cabinet.*
President of the Board of Trade	Viscount Sandon. *Entered Cabinet, 4 April 1878.*

LIST OF AMBASSADORS

Representatives of the European Great Powers in Britain

(Dates of presentation of credentials, where known, in brackets).

1852

Austria
Count Karl Ferdinand Buol-Schauenstein (1851)
Count Francis de Colloredo-Wallsee (May 1852)

France
Comte Alexandre Colonna Walewski (1851)

Prussia
Chevalier Christian von Bunsen (1842)

Russia
Filip Ivanovich, Baron Brünnow (1840)

Turkey
Constantine, Musurus Bey (1851)

1858–1859

Austria
Rudolf, Graf Apponyi von Nagy-Apponyi (27 May 1856)

France
Jean Gilbert Victor Fialin, comte de Persigny (1 June 1855)
Aimable Jean Jacques Pélissier, duc de Malakoff (16 April 1858)
Jean Gilbert Victor Fialin, comte de Persigny (18 May 1859)

Prussia
Albrecht, Count von Bernstorff (17 July 1854)

Russia
Filip Ivanovich, Baron Brünnow (22 March 1858)

Turkey
Constantine, Musurus Bey (see above; ambassador, 30 January 1856)

1866–1868

Austria (afterwards Austria-Hungary)
Rudolf, Count Apponyi von Nagy-Apponyi (ambassador, 8 December 1860)

France
Henri Godefroy Bernard Alphonse, prince de la Tour d'Auvergne-Lauraguais (2 December 1863)

Prussia
Albrecht, Count von Bernstorff (ambassador, 1862)

Russia
Filip Ivanovich, Baron Brünnow (see above; ambassador, 4 February 1861)

Turkey
Constantine, Musurus Pasha (see above)

1874–1878

Austria-Hungary
Friedrich Ferdinand, Count Beust (21 December 1871)

France
George, marquis d'Harcourt (28 June 1875)

Germany
Count Georg zu Münster-Ledenburg (26 June 1873)

Russia
Count Pyotr Shuvalov (September 1874)

Turkey
Constantine, Musurus Pasha (see above)

British representatives in the capitals of the European great powers

(Date of appointment listed in brackets. Note that the date of appointment was not necessarily the date when a post was taken up: outgoing representatives or their senior staff might occupy a post for a period after the formal appointment of successors.)

1852

Austria
John Fane, eleventh Earl of Westmorland (27 January 1851)

France
Henry Richard Charles Wellesley, Lord Cowley (3 February 1852); created first Earl Cowley, 1857

Prussia
John Arthur Douglas Bloomfield, Baron Bloomfield (28 April 1851)

Russia
Sir (George) Hamilton Seymour (28 April 1851)

Turkey
Stratford Canning (19 October 1841, for the second time); created Viscount Stratford de Redcliffe, 1852

1858–1859

Austria
Lord Augustus Loftus (31 March 1858)

France
Henry Richard Charles Wellesley, first Earl Cowley (see above)

Prussia
John Arthur Douglas Bloomfield, Baron Bloomfield (see above)

Russia
John Wodehouse, Lord Wodehouse (4 May 1856)
Sir John Crampton (31 March 1858)

Turkey
Stratford Canning, Viscount Stratford de Redcliffe (see above)
Sir Henry Bulwer (10 May 1858)

1866–1868

Austria (afterwards Austria-Hungary)
John Arthur Douglas Bloomfield, Baron Bloomfield (22 November 1862)

France
Henry Richard Charles Wellesley, first Earl Cowley (see above)
Richard Beckerton Pemell Lyons, second Baron Lyons (6 July 1867)

Italy
Sir Henry Elliot (12 September 1863)
Sir Augustus Paget (6 July 1867)

Prussia (afterwards North German Confederation)
Lord Augustus Loftus (to Prussia, 19 January 1866; to North German Confederation, 24 February 1868)

Russia
Sir Andrew Buchanan (15 September 1864)

Turkey
Richard Beckerton Pemell Lyons, second Baron Lyons (10 August 1865)
Sir Henry Elliot (6 July 1867)

1874–1878

Austria-Hungary
Sir Andrew Buchanan (16 October 1871)
Sir Henry Elliot (31 December 1877)

France
Richard Beckerton Pemell Lyons, second Baron Lyons (see above)

Germany
Lord Odo Russell (16 October 1871)

Italy
Sir Augustus Paget (see above)

Russia
Lord Augustus Loftus (16 October 1871)

Turkey
Sir Henry Elliot (see above)
Sir Austen Henry Layard (special ambassador at Constantinople *ad interim*, 31 March 1877; ambassador, 31 December 1877)

CHAPTER 1
THE FIRST DERBY GOVERNMENT,
FEBRUARY–DECEMBER 1852

1

14th Earl of Derby* to 3rd Earl of Malmesbury,* MP 9M73/451/1/1
29 February 1852
St James's Square

Together with Lord Cowley's* despatches, I send you a note I have just received from the Queen.* I have told Her Majesty that I agree in her opinions, but fear we cannot <u>effectively</u> interfere as Austria is acting in concert with France, Russia will not recognise Switzerland, & Prussia will make no objection.[1] We are to have another Council on Friday at 3 – in case you have any business to be done there. [...]

[Enclosure: Queen Victoria to Derby, 29 February 1852, MP 9M73/451/1/2]

The Queen returns the enclosed despatches to Lord Derby & hopes that he will give his fullest consideration to the pretensions which France now puts forward with regard to Switzerland. The Queen cannot consider them in any other light than as establishing an entirely new principle of international law, which if admitted, will put an end to the independence of all smaller states, to which it may in turn be applied, as in fact it will make their internal government dependent upon the momentary interests & arbitrary demands of their more powerful neighbours. There is nothing M. Turgot* says of the inconvenience to France of the internal state of Switzerland which Europe at large might not have applied with greater justice to France herself ever since 1848.

---

[1] Louis Napoleon's government in France was irritated by Swiss protection of refugees from the Bonapartist regime and discrimination against French Jews at Basle. France had restricted visas for Swiss passport-holders and, in an ultimatum sent to the Swiss Federal Council on 24 January 1852, had demanded that the Swiss promise to expel French refugees as and when France demanded. Malmesbury was attempting to negotiate a compromise. See also **2** and **3**.

2

Malmesbury to Derby, DP 920 DER (14) 144/1
29 February 1852

Since the Queen saw Ld Cowley[']s despatch to w^h she alludes one has arrived from McGinnis [*sic*]^2 at Berne stating the Federal Gov^t. to be more tractable.

The dispatches today from Russia declare Nesselrode* to be most anxious for our reconciliation with Austria — Tomorrow I see the for[eign] ministers & I w^d not do so till I had got hold of the points.

I can't help thinking that if we are in long enough we shall get our old friends right. —

Just arrived
Vienna dispatches
nothing^3

[Note added at end of letter:]

Berlin

The D[uke]. of Augustenberg* [*sic*] has refused the pecuniary compensation from Denmark (w^h opens that question again)^4 but the Court of Prussia^5 will do her best to persuade him to do so —

---

^{2}Arthur Charles Magenis (1801–1867), British minister in Switzerland, 1851–April 1852.

^{3}This note is laid out in this form, after the main body of text.

^{4}The great powers were attempting to resolve outstanding questions about the duchies of Schleswig, Holstein, and Lauenburg, and their relationship to the Danish king who ruled over them. In 1848 the duchies had revolted against Denmark. Augustenburg, head of the secondary branch of the Danish royal family, had helped lead the revolt. The childless King Frederick VII of Denmark intended to settle the succession on Christian of Glücksburg, whose branch of the family was junior to that of Augustenburg. All the other claimants renounced their claims and Augustenburg was offered significant compensation for the loss of his estates following the revolt, providing he renounced his claims to the throne. In a letter forwarded to Earl Granville on 18 February, Augustenburg had written to Prince Albert, informing him that he had refused compensation. Granville Papers, TNA, PRO 30/29/20/1, fos 55–57. Persuading Augustenburg to co-operate was one of the key preliminaries to the Treaty of London, which appeared to resolve the Schleswig-Holstein question and was signed by Malmesbury on 8 May 1852. See below, **16**.

^{5}Prussia was acting as mediator between Augustenburg and the Danish government.

3

Malmesbury to Derby, DP 920 DER (14) 144/1
'Monday' [1 March 1852][6]
Foreign Office

I have had my levée — I am to see Walewski* tomorrow as the Swiss question is the most pressing[7] — I wish to know under the present circumstances whether it w^d not be well to suggest that we might consent to the President[']s demand as regards certain French refugées [*sic*] at <u>this moment</u> obnoxious to him if he will on his part consent to waive that portion of his demand as to <u>all future refugees</u>[8] — I think all Europe except perhaps <u>Austria</u> w^d oppose this latter assertion of power —

[P.S.] I shall see Buol* & Van de Weyer* tomorrow.—
What '<u>reparation</u>' do you think ought to satisfy M^r. Mather?[9] It was a blunder of Granville* not to hold the Tuscan Gov^t. entirely responsible from the beginning —

4

Malmesbury to Derby, DP 920 DER (14) 144/1
'Wednesday' [3 March 1852][10]

I have taken a copy of yr paper[11] w^h is admirable —
I think it will be as well to see Buol tomorrow — We sh^d not look too much in a hurry, but if you think otherwise I will send for him sooner.

---

[6]Date appended.
[7]See above, **1**.
[8]Derby's note appended: 'Seen & ans[were]^d. We must not concede so much to L.N. as to recognise his <u>principle</u>.' Malmesbury's proposed solution was successfully adopted.
[9]A young Englishman, Erskine Mather, had been injured by an Austrian soldier while on holiday in Florence, in the Habsburg puppet state of Tuscany. Granville had been demanding compensation from the Austrians. See also **19, 21, 22, 23, 24, 29, 32, 33**.
[10]Date appended.
[11]Presumably the draft of a paper to be read to Buol on the subject of refugees from the Habsburg empire, as referred to in letter **5**.

5

Derby to Malmesbury, DP 920 DER (14) 180/1, fos 21–22[12]
4 March 1852

The Queen has not sent back the draft[13] and till she has, I think you had better avoid, if possible, reading the draft to Buol, or if you do, read it as a 'mere sketch' subject to alteration, but merely prepared as a basis, on which you may be prepared privately to negotiate with him for the removal of a vexatious obstacle to a good understanding. But you must not show your hand without making him show his also: and he must give you satisfactory explanations and conclude in civiller terms than the language of P. Schwarzenberg's* despatch,[14] or he can have nothing from us. [. . .]

6

Derby to Queen Victoria, DP 920 DER (14) 179/2, fos 60–63
11 March 1852

Lord D[erby] &c – submits to Y[our].M[ajesty]. two despatches received yesterday by Count Buol & communicated by him to L[d]. Malmesbury & himself after post-time yest[erda][y]. under date of the 5th inst. from Vienna. L[d] D trusts that the communication of these despatches will be as satisfactory to Y.M. as he cannot but admit they have been to him, appearing, as they do, to indicate on the part of the Court of Vienna an anxious desire to renew with Y.M.'s Govt. those friendly relations, which of late years have been unfortunately exchanged for a position of mutual distrust & alienation. The despatch No. 2 appears to L[d] D peculiarly significant; & plainly to intimate that while circumstances have driven Austria into an unusually close alliance with France, she is quite aware of the danger of that alliance, & is even looking forward to certain 'eventualités' in which it would be necessary for her to have secured a good understanding with the other great powers against the pretensions

---

[12]Copy in Derby's letter book. Original not found.

[13]On the question of refugees from the Austrian empire sheltering in Britain, about whose conduct Austria had been conducting an acrimonious correspondence with Lord John Russell's government.

[14]That of 4 February 1852 to Buol (for his transmission to the Whig government), reprinted in Parliamentary Papers, 'Further correspondence respecting the foreign refugees in London' (presented to Parliament 29 March 1852), document 1, pp. 1–2.

of France herself. Ld D. thinks that the answer to these despatches, but especially the second, will not be very easy; for while it will of course be necessary to accept with cordiality, & warmly to reciprocate the friendly professions of Austria it will be hardly less important to avoid drawing too broad a line of demarcation between the policy of Y.M.'s late & present servants, or giving encouragement to the idea which Prince Schwarzenberg appears desirous of inculcating, that henceforth Austria & England are under the same banner, & engaged in a common cause for the general promotion of 'order' throughout the world.[15] It will be necessary, as it seems to L^d. D. to imply at least, & that so clearly as to leave no possibility of misapprehension, that we draw a broad distinction between abstaining from giving support, physical or moral, to those who are seeking to overthrow the institutions of their own country, & joining with Austria in the maintenance of arbitrary principles of government, & the subversion, through Europe, of constitutional rights. Against any inference of such an understanding between the two powers, which L^d. D. cannot help thinking that Prince Schwarzenberg would desire to insinuate, Y.M.'s Govt. cannot too cautiously guard themselves, & any such union, L^d. D. hopes he need hardly say, would not be more repugnant to the feelings of L^d. Palmerston* than they would be to his own. But, this reserve apart, L^d. D. cannot but feel that in the altered tone of these despatches there is a fresh security for the maintenance of the peace of Europe, & he understands that the instructions sent to the Austrian minister at Paris will have led to a very much altered tone of his communications with the French Govt, who will henceforth have no pretence for saying that Austria is <u>driving</u> them into violent measures. [. . .]

[15]This should be read in conjunction with Derby's letter to Malmesbury, reproduced in Malmesbury's autobiography, *Memoirs of an Ex-Minister*, 2 vols (London, 1884), I, p. 312, in which Derby also warned of the danger of appearing too close to Austria: 'I have no idea of committing the Government to another Holy Alliance.' That letter was dated 'March 1852' in the *Memoirs*, but was clearly written late in the evening of 10 March. It has not been found in Malmesbury's or Derby's papers.

7

Derby to Malmesbury, MP 9M73/451/2
'Sunday night' [?14 March 1852][16]
St James's Square

I have read your private instructions with great interest — they
are <u>excellent</u> – terse, clear, and admirably expressed – If all my
young soldiers show as well, we shall exhibit a formidable line of
battle. [. . .]

8

Malmesbury to Derby, DP 920 DER (14) 144/1
27 March [1852]

Do not think me lazy for sending you back this despatch, I am
ready to answer it tho' I sh^d do it less well – but you will see at
the end that it is to be <u>read</u> to <u>you</u> & that the reply must be made
accordingly.[17]

If I am to answer I conclude that I am to accept the very safe &
natural proposal made with reference to Belgium calling a conference
of the guaranteeing powers in case of being threatened[18] – but should
we not ask Russia what she w^d do if L. Nap acted <u>without notice</u>,[19]
& should we say that <u>we</u> could not submit to see <u>the Scheldt</u> in
the hands of France. This last eventuality I suppose w^d be war with
England —

[16]The date appended is 15 March. This was a Monday, however, so was perhaps the date
of receipt, not despatch.

[17]At the top of this letter, Derby noted, 'I have drafted the desp. D.' The draft seems likely
to have been that of TNA, FO 181/268, either no. 30 or no. 31 to Seymour, 29 March 1852.
The drafts were both initialled by Derby, TNA, FO 65/404.

[18]France had presented a list of demands to Belgium about curtailing anti-French
agitation, which was widely interpreted as the precursor to an attack on the kingdom.
This raised the prospect of joint action by the other four great powers to protect Belgium,
in accordance with the guarantee of 19 April 1839.

[19]Britain had for some time been attempting to clarify what Russia would do if it became
necessary to act quickly. See, e.g., TNA, FO 65/404, no. 59, Granville to Seymour, draft, 18
February 1852.

9

Derby to Malmesbury, MP 9M73/451/4
28 March 1852
St James's Square

I have just had a long conversation with Brünnow.* I think he <u>is</u> possessed of the powers to which I refer in the last paragraph of the draft I left with you last night,[20] but he will not say so, unless we are prepared now to enter into negotiations as to the naval assistance which we would afford in the event of an invasion of Belgium. This of course I told him I was not prepared to do; and indeed it might depend materially on the amount of cooperation which we might expect from other powers. I told him the nature of the despatch which he was about to receive; but he wished (and said that it would be more in accordance with diplomatic usage) that it should be addressed, not to him, but to Sir Hamilton Seymour.* Will you therefore throw it into that form. It will not require much alteration – and the enquiry with which it concludes is more fitly addressed through him to Count Nesselrode, than to Brünnow himself. I believe you send a courier off tomorrow – Brunnow wishes to send his despatches by the same messenger.

10

Derby to Malmesbury, MP 9M73/451/6
'Wednesday' [undated]

Brünnow[']s confidential despatch to Nesselrode, which he will show you is very skilful, and very friendly.[21] He has not at all exaggerated my views, and has availed himself of the situation to withdraw the Emperor quietly from a too pertinacious adherence to the letter of former treaties which might be embarrassing. He inserted, at my suggestion words limiting the 'intime union' near the end of the despatch, to a 'système défensif' – I think you will be quite satisfied with his language —

---

[20] See above, **8**.
[21] Explanatory note appended: 'Alluding to invasion of Belgium by France'.

11

Derby to Malmesbury, MP 9M73/451/8/1–2
13 April 1852
St James's Square

Bunsen* has been with me again this morning, and I think it is right you should know the language he holds.[22] He began by saying that the French Government, as indeed we know from Cowley, would not make any objection to recognizing the claims of Prussia upon Neufchâtel; and he says that Walewski declares that the French Article of 'unanimity' was only inserted from jealousy of another Power (of course Austria) and he seems even to think that it would not be insisted on – but he adds that the French Government declare that the real obstacle is the English Cabinet – and that we are determined to do nothing in the matter. He then went on with much apparent fussiness, to speak of the ulterior views with which he desires a joint note to be addressed to the Swiss Government in support of the Prussian claims. He adverted to the difficulty which I had suggested of the uselessness of a joint note, which the parties presenting it had bound themselves by a previous convention not to support, or allow to be supported by coercive measures. He admitted that in his opinion the Swiss Government would refuse; and although he attempted to account for the recent election[23] in various ways, he evidently is convinced that the feelings of the population in the aggregate are not with Prussia — Indeed he went so far as to say that a representation of this kind made & rejected would be the best way of 'shelving' the question. On my saying something about the question being 'settled', he again, in a marked way, used the word 'shelved'; and added, that after having recognized the rights of Prussia, and having failed in obtaining from Switzerland a consent to their reestablishment, we

---

[22] About the Swiss canton of Neuchâtel. This was an integral part of Switzerland, but the arrangements in the Vienna settlement of 1815 provided for it simultaneously to remain as a Prussian principality, with the Prussian king as head of state. In 1848, the Neuchâtel republicans had overthrown the royalists and produced a new, republican constitution. Previous attempts to negotiate a settlement with Prussia about the canton's status had failed. Malmesbury was conscious of Britain's favourable relationship with Switzerland, and of Swiss vulnerability to criticism from other great powers. He was therefore exploring how a great-power protocol might be concluded that would be a sop to the Prussians (whose support was separately needed on the Schleswig-Holstein question) and theoretically provide the basis for a settlement, but which would avoid antagonizing the Swiss and in practice leave open the option of deferring any conference to conclude such a settlement. See also letters **12**, **15**, **44**, **49**, and **50**.

[23] Elections in Neuchâtel at the end of March 1852 had produced a clear victory for the republicans.

might then address our advice to Prussia to recede from pressing her rights, and that in such advice the K[ing]. of Prussia*[24] would find the easiest solution of the difficulty, and the best answer to his adherents in Neufchâtel. He offered to pledge me his honor [*sic*], that if the rights were recognized, and a representation made by the Great Powers to Switzerland unsuccessful, the K[ing] of Prussia would take no steps in support of his claims. This certainly places the case in a different light; but I cannot help thinking there would be considerable awkwardness in engaging the Great Powers to make a representation to Switzerland, inviting a refusal. It may be that Prussia thinks that the signature of a Convention would lead to a proposal for a mediation, and to a surrender of her claim, on the part of Prussia, for a consideration which the Swiss Government would in that case agree to give. One thing is clear to me, that Prussia feels the question a very embarrassing one, and would be glad to retreat, if she saw how to do so with dignity, or even so as to save appearances. Bunsen will see you on your return to Town; but I thought it as well that you should receive the report of his language while it was fresh in my recollection, that you might be prepared for the line he will take with you. I should add that he told me he had conversed with Aberdeen,* wh[i]c[h] led me to infer that he approved the proposed course, though he evidently had given no encouragement to any resumption of authority by Prussia.

I said a few words to him on the Danish question,[25] but he has no instructions, and chooses to be censé[26] to have nothing to do with it.

He believes in the President's peaceable intentions for the present – but that sooner or later he means to be Emperor, and that what may happen after that he hardly knows himself.

I sent your letter on to the Queen this morning.

We were well received at the Lord Mayor's yesterday, when all went off well —

12

Malmesbury to Derby, DP 920 DER (14) 144/1
16 April 1852
Foreign Office

[. . .] I cannot see what advantage we are to gain by Bunsen's plan.[27] The claim on Neufchatel is perfectly acknowledged by us & I don't

---

[24]Friedrich Wilhelm IV.
[25]Schleswig-Holstein. See above, **2**.
[26]'supposed'.
[27]See above, **11**.

see the use of christening Prussia over again as an empty honour —
In fact we are to eat dirt to keep up Prussia's dignity. — We stand
well with the Swiss now – & I am quite against throwing away our
credit by inviting a preconcerted refusal, w^h they (the Swiss) not being
behind the scenes would boast of giving —

I sent Ch[arles] Murray's[28] last despatch[29] to the D[uke]. of
North[umberland],* as it was urgent his orders to strengthen the
Mediterranean fleet should go tomorrow. He sends two ships from
Lisbon & Hotham[30] will go by the Vixen & we keep the Dauntless. —

The Duke who knows the Med[iterranean] Sea well says the
account respecting settlements there is nonsense —

The orders to the two ships sent to Alexandria are to remonstrate
against any hostilities between the two Turks until reference is made
to the great powers, as also with the French if they attempt to land
troops – but not to fire – in fact to put in a protest. [. . .]

13

Derby to Malmesbury, MP 9M73/451/9
[Undated] '¼ past 1'

I have this moment received the enclosed from Brünnow.[31] I have
told him he shall have an answer in an hour or two. When you have
made what use you think fit of his despatch, send it me back in a large
cover (I have none here large enough) unsealed that I may return it to
him. I think his report of what passed in conversation is substantially
correct.

[PS] It would be useful that you should look up our old treaty
obligations, that we may see whether we should rest on them, or
whether it would be expedient to establish any new basis.

[28] Charles Augustus Murray (1806–1895), consul-general in Egypt from 1846 to 1853.
There he secured Britain's first hippopotamus; he later wrote a memoir of Mehmet Ali.

[29] Murray had written to Stratford Canning on 27 March, concerned about French
intrigues to gain influence in the Near East and about a potential 'coup-de-main' by
the Porte, supported by France, to assert the Sultan's authority over the viceroy in Egypt.
He requested 'one or two English men-of-war in the Harbour of Alexandria'. TNA, FO
78/916, no. 6, fo. 7. See also Malmesbury to Murray, 8 April 1852, *Memoirs*, I, pp. 326–327.

[30] Sir Charles Hotham (1806–1855) was taking up a diplomatic mission to South America.

[31] Explanatory note: 'Alluding to efforts made by Northern Powers to force us to an
alliance'. This initiative was later referred to by Disraeli in his notes for unpublished
memoirs: 'Shortly after the formation of this government, Baron Brunnow, the Russian
Ambassador, proposed to Lord Derby an alliance between England and Russia, offensive
& defensive. Lord Derby at once rejected the proposition.' Helen M. Swartz and Marvin
Swartz (eds), *Disraeli's Reminiscences* (London, 1975), p. 93.

14

Derby to Malmesbury, MP 9M73/451/10
'Monday' [?26 April or 3 May 1852][32]
St James's Square

Read the enclosed and bring it with you to the Council.[33] The Queen's, or rather the Prince's*,[34] meddling in this matter will give us much trouble if we do not mind.

15

Malmesbury to Derby, DP 920 DER (14) 144/1
29 April [1852]

You will see that there is a hitch about Neufchatel at Paris & that Bunsen lied as usual when he said they put the refusal on our shoulders.[35] Walewski assured me it was false. I think we had better stave it off. It can do us no good to go & <u>bark</u> at Switzerland & at this moment when she is of her own accord returning to a Conservative form of gov^t. — I wait yr orders & only give my opinion w^h you know was always against this move. —

I do not want to praise myself but I must say for Walewski that the solution of the Swiss question & the line France has taken on the Tanzimat[36] is entirely attributable to him & to our discussions. Turgot was dead against me on both at first —

[32]If this letter is accurately placed in chronological order in the bundle, it ought to have been one of the Mondays between 13 April and 8 May. Malmesbury's explanatory note: 'Alludes to Danish Treaty of Succession wh I carried through without offending the Court'. A conference on the Schleswig-Holstein question, chaired by Britain, began on 28 April. Its culmination would be the Treaty of London. See below, **16**. If this letter was connected with the conference proceedings, it was probably written on either Monday 26 April or Monday 3 May.

[33]The Privy Council. The enclosed is enclosed no longer.

[34]i.e. Prince Albert.

[35]The great powers were negotiating a protocol that would be signed on 24 May. For the background to this comment, see above, **11**.

[36]The Tanzimat-ı Hayriye or 'auspicious reorderings', the programme of reform pursued by successive Ottoman rulers between 1839 and 1876, supported by Britain. Turkey sought to impose the Tanzimat in Egypt, the politics of which had drawn in France and Britain.

16

Derby to Malmesbury, MP 9M73/451/11
[8 May 1852] '4.35'[37]
Downing Street

I am just come away from the Palace – an hour & a half, and not a word about Denmark — Sign away —[38]

17

Derby to Malmesbury, MP 9M73/451/14
[Undated]

You have only sent back half my paper[39] – bring the other with you to the Levée. I should not be in a hurry – Radetzky's[40] report is most unsatisfactory, and will require to be answered in detail & firmly. How did it come to you?

18

Malmesbury to Derby, DP 920 DER (14) 144/1
22 May [1852]

I believe the writer of the letter you send me to take a perfectly correct view of the case & I agree in all he says.[41]

I was going to propose to you that we should make this case of Murray[42] the opportunity for establishing diplomatic relations with

---

[37] Explanatory note: 'Danish Treaty of Succession signed this day.'

[38] The Augustenburg claim to the Danish throne having been renounced, the Treaty of London of 8 May 1852, signed by all the great powers, stipulated: (1) in default of male issue from the direct line of Frederick III, the Danish crown would pass to Christian of Glücksburg; (2) the rights of Denmark and the Germanic Confederation in Holstein and Lauenburg were unaffected. The treaty therefore reaffirmed the status quo and allowed for Christian to rule in the duchies when he succeeded Frederick.

[39] Explanatory note: 'Relating to the Mather case'.

[40] Joseph Wenzel, Graf Radetzky von Radetz (1766–1858), Austrian marshal; commander of the Austrian army in the occupied territory of Lombardo-Venetia, 1831–1857.

[41] Correspondence not found.

[42] Edward Murray was a British citizen who had been inspector of police in Ancona, central Italy, which fell within the territories of the Papal States. He was condemned to death for having committed a murder during the revolutionary occupation of Rome in 1848–1849. Malmesbury and Stanley succeeded in having his sentence commuted to life imprisonment later in 1852. See Disraeli to Stanley, *BDL*, VI, no. 2422.

Rome by placing Bulwer* in the position formerly intended for him[43]
— The Pope*[44] w^d accept him pro tempore[45] & that is sine die.[46] But I
would not advise this till after the elections.

19

Derby to Malmesbury, MP 9M73/451/16
'Wednesday' [?26 May 1852][47]
St James's Square

I have forwarded your Box to the Queen – but I cannot say I like the
course of conduct pursued by the French Gov[ernmen]^t. It appears
to me shuffling and evasive.[48] [. . .]
I send you a letter from Scarlett* – I will speak to you about the
answer at the Cabinet. The Mather case is dead and buried, and
producing papers about it now would be absurd.[49]

[43] Lord John Russell's Whig government (1846–1852) had been trying to make diplomatic
contact with Rome, formally or informally, in order to attempt to obtain its support in
calming the situation in Ireland. In November 1851, Bulwer had been nominated as minister
in Tuscany, with the intention that he should go on a mission to Rome. For the same domestic
reasons, Malmesbury and Derby intended to pursue this. See also **23**, **24**, **26**, **27**, **35**, **53**,
58, **61**, **62**.

[44] Pope Pius IX.

[45] 'for the time being'.

[46] 'indefinitely'.

[47] Given Derby's rejection of the idea of publishing the Mather papers, this letter was
clearly written before he and Malmesbury realized the extent of the furore that the case
would generate. This places it prior to the end of May. It must have been written after
17 May, when the initial details of the settlement were received and the matter appeared
resolved. This leaves two possibilities – 19 or 26 May – and, given its place in the bundle
and the French reference similar to **20**, the latter seems most likely.

[48] It is unclear to what this refers, though it may be to the same matters discussed below,
20.

[49] In March 1852, Malmesbury had asked the father of Erskine Mather to name an
amount as suitable compensation for his son's injuries. He had suggested £5,000, but
Malmesbury advised Scarlett, the British representative in Florence, to seek £1,000 instead.
On 5 May, an ailing Scarlett had accepted the rather lower sum of 1,000 *francesconi* from the
Tuscans – about £222 – and the release of some other British prisoners, the Stratfords. See
'Correspondence respecting the assault committed on Mr. Erskine Mather at Florence',
Parliamentary Papers, 1852 session, LV. Derby was wrong in his assessment; the case was
about to cause a significant political row. See below, **21**.

20

Malmesbury to Derby, DP 920 DER (14) 144/1
28 May [1852]

We have a very up-hill game to fight in a certain quarter,[50] where
they have also some crude ideas about France.

It would not cost Louis Nap[oleon] any thing to <u>promise</u> what
is desired[51] — I am trying to bring him to the more practical act
of proving his pacific intentions by a reduction of his army & navy
whenever he assumes the imperial crown — [. . .]

21

Malmesbury to Derby, DP 920 DER (14) 144/1
'Sunday' [30 May 1852][52]
Heron Court

I have received a letter from Disraeli in a tremendous stew about
the Mather case of which he as yet knows nothing.[53]

I have ordered the correspondence to be printed & (with the
exception of three letters w[h] I have sent you up to be added) you
will receive it tomorrow —

Scarlett has done far worse than I at first believed. By M[r] Barron[']s*
letter[54] of the 9th ins[t]. we were led to believe that £222 & the release

---

[50] The Court.

[51] Malmesbury's scepticism related to concerns raised by the Queen with Derby on 27 May.
She had suggested how to handle the anticipated declaration of a new French empire: 'All
the Foreign Powers have to be careful about is to receive an assurance that the *Empire* does
not mean a *return to the policy of the Empire*, but that the existing Treaties will be acknowledged
and adhered to.' *LQV*, first series, II, p. 390. Derby had either forwarded this letter to
Malmesbury or had communicated its contents to him. How Malmesbury was pursuing
the reductions is unclear.

[52] Date appended.

[53] Disraeli's letter to Malmesbury has not been found, but his letters of 29 May to Derby
and Stanley survive (*BDL*, VI, nos 2296 and 2297). The Mather case (see above, letters **3** and
19) was producing a political storm. Questions about the settlement accepted by Scarlett
had been asked in the House of Lords on 27 and 28 May. On 28 May, the father of the
injured man had written an indignant letter to *The Times*, criticizing Malmesbury's handling
of the affair, and the newspaper followed this up with an editorial on 29 May. That day,
Malmesbury rescinded his acceptance of Scarlett's settlement with Tuscany.

[54] Barron had reported Scarlett's settlement with Tuscany when the latter fell ill.
Malmesbury held him in part responsible for the problems the case generated.

of the Stratfords[55] had been offered & accepted as a legal & fair demand & compensation for M[r] Mather's injury — Absurd as this was[56] there was no serious harm in it, & I wrote to Bulwer[57] on the 21st. to recognise Scarlett[']s act – but on the 22nd there comes another batch of despatches stating that Scarlett had formerly waived the principle of Tuscan responsibility, & not only that, but accepted a note, w[h] you will see, from the D[uke]. of Casigliano[58] in which the £222 is ostentatiously put forward as an act of generosity! not to be used as a precedent —

It is clear that Scarlett must have been non compos, for he quotes my despatch of the 9th of April as his excuse w[h] despatch is the strongest of all in its instructions to maintain Tuscan responsibility & independence.—

He has now got us into a complete mess, because if he had asserted the principle of forcing Tuscany to do justice as an independent power, we might have made light of the actual sum paid, but as the case stands, we have ended by taking charity & that in the most humiliating manner —

I cannot stand this & hope you will approve of a despatch I have written to Bulwer to close the mission if the principle of protection to our subjects is not recognised by the Tuscan Gov[t]. & the insulting language of Casigliano's note altered — It is our only way out of the scrape w[h] that hothead has got us into. — [. . .]

22

Malmesbury to Derby, DP 920 DER (14) 144/1
30 May 1852
Heron Court

I wrote to you early this morning to save the messenger as I was anxious you should know how completely Scarlett had stultified all our policy respecting Tuscan disputes & Austrian influence at Florence — As we stand now we have not even got one expression of regret for Mather's injury but on the contrary an insolent note accompanying

---

[55]The Stratfords were British citizens imprisoned in Tuscany for possession of a private printing press and using it to produce material critical of the Tuscan government. In fact, their release had already been separately agreed before the Mather case had been resolved.

[56]On 24 May, Henry Addington had written (on Malmesbury's instructions) to Mather senior, accepting that the compensation was inadequate but urging him to accept it anyway.

[57]Bulwer had succeeded Scarlett as Britain's representative in Tuscany at the beginning of May.

[58]The duc de Casigliano, Tuscan foreign minister.

the payment & treating it as a generous allowance not a legal redress. — Swartzenberg [*sic*] & Buol have both publicly stated their friendly sentiments & sorrow for the accident but not one word has the Italian uttered w^h approaches an apology. I see nothing left for us, even if it were not our duty, than to write in the sense I have done to Bulwer & as it is a despatch of some consequence, I should be much obliged to you, if you approve of the substance, to touch up the diction.

On Thursday Dudley Stuart[59] will move for the papers, & I wish them to be laid before the House as soon as [is] convenient but I sh^d not like the discussion & perhaps the hostile motion they will induce to take place there long before I can tell my story in the Lords, which do not sit for any business this week.[60] I shd propose therefore that Edward*[61] sh^d present them tomorrow week.

23

Malmesbury to Derby, DP 920 DER (14) 144/1
31 May 1852
Heron Court

I send you a letter from Bulwer in which you will find a graphic confirmation of the extent of Scarlett's folly. — That Bulwer (who never thinks of anything but Bulwer) should recommend us not to make him 'break his shins' over this obstacle, is natural enough, but sh^d we not act as I proposed to you, it is my shins if not those of the entire Gov[ernmen]^t. that will be kicked by the House of Commons, if indeed they do not kick some other part of our persons. —

In looking over the papers you will see that Barron's first despatch[62] simply announcing the settlement of the question & the amount to be paid in money & prisoners, reached the F.O. on the 17th. & that I wrote to Bulwer on the 21st to recognise Scarlett[']s act the extent of which I had no idea of. On the 22. the second batch[63] arrived at the F.O. with the details of his absolute concessions of principle & dignity but as the 23rd was Sunday these despatches did not reach me till Monday the 24th, & were not read by me till Tuesday the 25th.[64]

---

[59] Lord Dudley Coutts Stuart (1803–1854), Liberal MP for Marylebone.
[60] The Commons debate on the Mather case was on 14 June, the Lords debate on 21 June.
[61] Edward, Lord Stanley.
[62] That of 9 May.
[63] Despatches of 11 and 14 May 1852.
[64] Malmesbury told the Lords that he had read them on 24 May 1852. See *Parl. Deb.*, 21 June 1852, CXXII, col. 1036. In fact, it is unclear whether he read them on either date. He

after I had instructed Addington* to write to Mather to inform him (on the strength of the <u>first</u> despatch from Barron) that the affair was concluded. —

Referring to another part of Bulwer's letter w^h treats of his negotiations with Rome I should be much obliged to you to put down the instructions he requires as to what we want the Pope to do or not to do.[65] If we could get him to help us in Ireland at the elections or even to make his people abstain from hostility it would be a great victory, but I am so absolutely ignorant of Irish politics & you are so completely experienced in them that I cannot do otherwise than require y[ou]r instructions for Bulwer in detail.

We must leave their execution to him & his judgement, w^h I suppose is good as every body says so —

He is certainly sharp enough in his own interest.— M^r. Hudson* must settle it with him for keeping M^r. Barron against the rules of the service & of all civility. —

24

Derby to Malmesbury, MP 9M73/451/18
1 June 1852
St James's Square

I think your answer to M^r. Mather will do very well. The question about Bulwer is more difficult, but I think your notion of letting him <u>retire</u> to Rome, in no official character is a good one. He might there at all events see Cardinal Antonelli,* who is the real director of every thing, and endeavour to find out the real mind of Rome as to English & Irish affairs. It is difficult to say what he is to urge the Pope to do or not to do, because what we really want is to abridge his own power and that of the Priesthood his agents – in which he is not likely to assist us, especially as we have no quid pro quo to offer him, and no threat effectually to alarm him. <u>Just at present</u> the great object would be to restrain the R.C. clergy from making religious questions prominent at the elections – a course of proceeding which will infallibly kindle into tenfold fury the Protestant feeling which is already burning so fiercely[66] – but even were His Holiness disposed to act towards us in a friendly spirit, which I doubt, his orders could hardly be received in

told the Lords on 27 and 28 May that the matter was concluded; despatches repudiating the settlement were not sent until 29 May.

[65] See above, **18**.

[66] Not least because of the agitation of the Tenant League and the Roman Catholic priesthood's active involvement in politics. Tension was high on both sides of the sectarian

time to influence the present elections. I should like however to talk to you about these matters. Could you come to me in D[ownin]^g S^t a little before 5?

25

Derby to Malmesbury, MP 9M73/451/17
[?2 June 1852] '10 P.M.'[67]
St James's Square

I wish you would come down here as soon as you can get away, without attracting observation, from your dinner. The Queen is in a great fuss about the proposal – and I must write to H.M. tonight — I wish to have the latest intelligence, and to be able to assure H.M. that you have thrown, not cold, but iced, water on the proposition.[68]

26

Malmesbury to Derby, DP 920 DER (14) 144/1
20 June [1852]

The contradiction that Bulwer alludes to between my private letter & public despatch to him he ought to have understood, because in my public instructions I of course desired him if he closed the embassy to repair to Parma or Modena to w^h courts he is also accredited – & I cd not allude to Rome – whilst in my private letter I tell him that he might make the rupture with Tuscany an opportunity for going to Rome —[69]

Pray, if you can, send me the documents he required to shew Antonelli before the middle of the week —

---

divide. K.T. Hoppen has described the 1852 general election as 'one of the most violent of all nineteenth-century Irish elections.': K.T. Hoppen, *Elections, Politics, and Society in Ireland, 1832–1885* (Oxford, 1984), p. 397.

[67]Malmesbury's explanatory note: 'Rec[eive]^d at dinner at Walewski's'. Malmesbury's *Memoirs*, I, p. 336, refer to a dinner at the Walewskis on 2 June. Given the letter's proximity in the bundle to letters from June, this seems the likeliest date.

[68]Malmesbury's explanatory note: 'Proposal made was from the Emperor to marry the Princess Hohenlohe. M[almesbury].'

[69]See above, **23, 24**.

27

Derby to Malmesbury, MP 9M73/451/20
24 June 1852
St James's Square

I send you back the papers furnished by Naas.* [. . .] An abstract however of the Tenant League Bill[70] might be desirable. I have not time to prepare <u>instructions</u> to Bulwer, but I send him a long private letter, which, if it meets your concurrence, I will thank you to send over to Talbot[71] to have copied, and then despatch it by your messenger. I wish you would have a copy made, to go with it, of the R.C M.P's oath; and of the declarations made by the R.C. bishops & clergy before the passing of the Relief Bill.

28

Derby to Malmesbury, MP 9M73/451/21
25 June 1852

I think Sir H[enry] B[ulwer].'s course sh^d be entirely approved, and the immaterial concession made on which the Grand Duke[72] lays so much stress.[73] Regret for the past, and acknowledged responsibility for the future are all that we can require[.]

29

Derby to Malmesbury, MP 9M73/451/23
28 June 1852

I should think the conciliatory tone more likely to effect the object, but on that point Sir H[enry].B[ulwer] must have better means of judging than either you or I.[74]

---

[70] Ireland's Tenant League was agitating for 'the three Fs': fixity of tenure, free sale, and fair rent; Naas was attempting to calm that agitation with his Tenant Right (Ireland) Bill, which he had introduced in May.

[71] Sir (Wellington) Patrick Manvers Chetwynd-Talbot (1817–1898), Derby's private secretary, 1852; House of Lords serjeant-at-arms, 1858–1859; married Lady Emma Stanley (Derby's daughter), 1860.

[72] Leopold II (1797–1870), Grand Duke of Tuscany, 1824–1859.

[73] Explanatory note: 'Alludes to Mather case & its settlement.' This letter is clearly a response, on the same piece of paper, to another note (presumably from Malmesbury or Addington): 'There is an opportunity for writing to Florence, this, Friday, evening. F.O. June 25/52'.

[74] Explanatory note: 'Alludes to Murray the murderer at Ancona'. Derby's note was appended to the original query from Malmesbury: 'What instructions shall I give Bulwer

30

Derby to Malmesbury, MP 9M73/451/26
[Undated]

I think we may accept the reparation offered,[75] though it is not very satisfactory; but our forbearance here may strengthen our hands in Mather's case.

31

Derby to Malmesbury, MP 9M73/451/43/1
'Friday night' [16 July 1852][76]
[Osborne House][77]

I shall take this letter over with me tomorrow; but as I shall only pass through London, I write to say that the Queen in a long and most free conversation on the part of Her Majesty this morning, expressed some surprise at not having heard from you of the arrival of Lord Howden[78] or of Lord Stratford* (or as she always calls him Lord Stuart) de Redcliffe.[79] She said, very good-humouredly, that she supposed you imagined that being at Osborne she would not wish to be troubled with Audiences – but that she wished on the contrary to know of the arrival of any foreign ministers, and she would always find means, if it was inconvenient to her to receive them, of putting them off – but in the present instance I think it clear that she wishes to see both one and

– My own opinion is that Mr Murray's character is not such as to justify us in a tone of "menace"?' See above, **18**.

[75]Malmesbury's explanatory note: 'Outrage on British corporal of Firebrand at Leghorn.' A corporal of marines from the *Firebrand* had gone ashore and ended up offending a Tuscan gendarme, who had beaten and imprisoned him. *Parl. Deb.*, 18 March 1852, CXIX, cols 1224–1225.

[76]Date appended: 'August 1852'. But clearly this letter was written before 9 August, a Monday, a date which was to follow both the envisaged trip 'next week' and the opportunity for a reception 'the following week'. The only Friday in August prior to that was 6 August, which could not have allowed for those events by 9 August. The Court Circular confirms that Derby left London for Osborne on Thursday 15 July (see *The Times*, 16 July 1852). He was back in St Leonards by 19 July (see below, **33**).

[77]No address is given, but Derby had arrived at Osborne on Thursday 15 July, and the rest of the letter describes a drive from Osborne that Derby had taken with the Queen and Prince Albert on the Friday.

[78]John Hobart Caradoc, second Baron Howden (1799–1873), minister in Spain, 1850–1858.

[79]The Queen was confusing Lord Stratford de Redcliffe with Lord Stuart de Rothesay (1779–1845).

the other.[80] Next week she is going on a short cruise in the Channel for three or four days beginning with Monday; and I should therefore suppose that the following week will suit her for receiving them.[81] I understand another cruise is meditated for about the 9th of August.[82] I have arranged with Her Majesty that you should accompany her to Scotland on the 30th [83] and that I should relieve guard about the 10th.[84] She was very civil about you, and her tone altogether most friendly & confidential. [. . .]

32

Malmesbury to Derby, DP 920 DER (14) 144/1
17 July [1852]
Foreign Office

I found your letter on my return here & also Colloredo* whose despatches I send you to read. We are not to copy. I don't much like the one about Mather & Tuscany. Should it be answered or treated as a brutum fulmen[85] – Colloredo said it was necessary for Austria to say this as she had a treaty with Tuscany but that he did not wish to open the question & as the paper is not to be copied no record of it will remain here[.]

33

Derby to Malmesbury, 9M73/451/29
19 July 1852
St Leonards

I agree with you in not much approving Buol's tone about Tuscany,[86] though I think it is chiefly to be taken as an indication of the stiff manner of the man, rather than of an unfriendly spirit. I think however

---

[80] According to his *Memoirs*, I, p. 341, Malmesbury held a dinner for Stratford and Howden on 17 July.

[81] From 19 to 23 July the royal family went on a Channel cruise around locations in the south-west. Malmesbury's *Memoirs*, I, p. 343, record that he visited Osborne on 27 July, having been 'the other day' with Stratford and Howden.

[82] The Queen arrived in Belgium on 11 August, and returned to Osborne on 17 August.

[83] August.

[84] September. Malmesbury's *Memoirs*, I, p. 347, corroborate this, recording his return from Balmoral to Achnacarry on that date.

[85] 'an empty threat'.

[86] Given **32**, this clearly refers to the Mather case.

that you cannot allow the despatch to remain altogether unanswered: nor to appear to concede the principle for which he contends of recognising Austrian responsibility for acts done in Tuscany: and I am the more inclined to this opinion, because Count Boul rests his case in great measure on a treaty between Austria & Tuscany, which has never been communicated, as I believe, and which I do not wish should be, to this country; and to which, as being a secret treaty, or at least containing a secret article, he has, as I should think, no diplomatic right to refer. On this point however I may be mistaken; but I think, while deprecating discussion, you should reaffirm the responsibility, as coincident with the independence, of Tuscany. [. . .]

34

Derby to Malmesbury, MP 9M73/451/31
'Friday ev^g.' [Undated][87]
St Leonards

I return your proposed answer to the Duke of Augustenburg,[88] which I think is quite right — I see no reason why you should show it to the Queen. I hope you observe his signature on the article[89] Duke of <u>Holstein</u>.

35

Derby to Malmesbury, MP 9M73/451/33
'Sunday' [Undated]
St James's Square

I have sent, both through Walpole* and Naas[,] to get materials for our representation as to the state of the R.C. clergy in Ireland, and I will forward them the moment I get them, but I fear they will hardly be in time to do any good for the elections — You shall have your draft in the 'Empire' case tomorrow.

[87]Date appended: 'July 1852'.

[88]Augustenburg was in London, and met the Queen (with Malmesbury) at the end of June.

[89]The editors were divided on the correct reading of this word, which might also be interpreted as 'outside'.

36

Malmesbury to Derby, DP 920 DER (14) 144/1
25 July [1852]

I had a long talk with Brunnow yesterday about the Greek succession[90] & found him quite of our mind & ready to revise the treaty of 1832 & substitute Adelbert[91] the Greek for Luitpold[92] the Roman assuming always that the latter is ready to renounce his rights.

B. will open upon you on this subject at Goodwood[93] but do not tell him that Cowley had pressed it upon me from Thouvenel* as I treated it as a subject which we originated to him Brunnow officially[94] — I shall now address Cowley officially to know the opinion of France, & then ascertain officially from Bavaria the disposition of the two princes —

37

Malmesbury to Derby, DP 920 DER (14) 144/1
30 July [1852]
Foreign Office

[. . .] I sent for Colloredo yesterday (Bunsen was out of the question) to ask him whether there was any truth in the convention signed by

[90]The question of the Greek succession was pressing by the summer of 1852. The treaty of 7 May 1832 between Britain, France, Russia, and Bavaria had established Otto of Bavaria as King of Greece. His heir was his brother, Luitpold. The Greek constitution of 1844 had specified that every successor to the Greek throne should be of the Orthodox religion, but Luitpold had made it clear that he would remain a Roman Catholic and raise his children in that faith. The Foreign Office was concerned that tension between the treaty and the constitution might result in instability in an area of strategic significance to Britain. See also **49, 51, 59,** and **70**.

[91]Prince Adalbert of Bavaria (1828–1875), youngest son of King Ludwig I and brother of King Otto of Greece.

[92]Prince Luitpold of Bavaria (1821–1912), later Prince Regent of Bavaria; third son of King Ludwig I and brother of King Otto of Greece.

[93]The Derbys were visiting the Duke of Richmond (and the races) at Goodwood, 25–29 July.

[94]In Malmesbury's *Memoirs*, I, pp. 351–352, a letter from Derby to Malmesbury, addressed 'Goodwood', is included with other material relating to Greek affairs, all of which dates from October 1852. The original has not been found in Malmesbury's papers. The published letter is undated ('Thursday'), but, given the content, it is clearly a response to **36** and it is reasonable to suppose it was written on Thursday 29 July, despite its location in the *Memoirs*. Derby had indeed seen Brünnow, and had arranged with him that Malmesbury 'should write to Petersburg and Paris, sending a *résumé* of the case, suggesting the necessity for a revision of the Greek treaty, so as to bring it into harmony with the Constitution, and proposing to call jointly on the King of Bavaria to state the intentions of his sons with regard to the acceptance of the Greek religion or the renunciation of the rights of succession'.

the Great Powers w^h appeared in the Chronicle & Times[95] — I said that if it was true it did not concern us beyond the fact that they had made overtures to us which meant nothing[96] — Colloredo said that it was only a confused invention founded upon the fact of those overtures w^h somehow or other had leaked out & that no convention had been signed — I cannot say however I was satisfied for he looked what is vulgarly called 'foolish', but it may be that he suspected such a convention has been signed without his knowledge. — If it is so the overture to us was made merely to ascertain our intentions & is a low trick out of wh they get nothing – & if such a treaty be not a dead letter it will be the origin of a European war hereafter —

In the meantime L. N. won't be pleased & will [be][97] more civil than ever to us —

38

Derby to Malmesbury, DP 920 DER (14) 180/2, fos 183–184[98]
31 July 1852

With the draft of your despatch to Lord Cowley, I send you a letter which I received last night from the Queen, and a copy of my answer, which will I hope be in accordance with your views. I had a few words with Brunnow yesterday and he will no doubt see you. He evidently wishes that you should write to Petersburgh [sic] as well as to Paris and to have the appearance of making a simultaneous suggestion to both Courts.[99] Before I saw him, I had, as you will see, in some degree altered the terms of your draft, so that you should not seem to say to the French Government that you had arranged everything with Russia before consulting them. I know the reverse is the case; but the public despatch, on the face of it, would have that appearance. I shall be at the office till 5 or later if you want to see me.

[95] On 29 July, *The Times* had published terms of a treaty it said had been signed on 20 May. Russia, Austria, and Prussia had allegedly agreed to refuse to recognize Louis Napoleon as hereditary emperor if he claimed to be such, and to consult 'as to the ulterior measures which they may think it necessary to take'. If Louis Napoleon died or was overthrown, they would assist the restoration of the Bourbon heir.

[96] In June, Russia, Austria, and Prussia had sent almost identical notes to Britain, in which they offered to waive their objections to a Bonaparte on the French throne, on the grounds of his services to the cause of order, and proposed a 'mutual system of defensive policy'. Malmesbury rejected this overture. See e.g., TNA, FO 181/272, no. 10, Malmesbury to Seymour, 29 June 1852.

[97] Word missing in original.

[98] Copy in Derby's letter book. Original not found.

[99] Presumably about the Greek succession.

39

Derby to Malmesbury, MP 9M73/451/35
11 August 1852
St Leonards

I enclose you an acceptance of Walewski's invitation which I will thank you to forward, if you are satisfied that we should dine there.[100] The only point which raises the least doubt in my mind is the note 'en uniforme' – which gives the whole affair a more formal & official character than would otherwise belong to it. I think however we ought to accept, subject to an assurance, which I have no doubt Walewski will give you, that nothing shall be said or done to give to the dinner any political significance, and especially nothing as regards the Imperial title.

[. . .] I am writing to Her Majesty today, and shall tell her the view we take of the French Dinner – it is just as well to name these little matters. [. . .]

40

Derby to Malmesbury, MP 9M73/451/36
17 August 1852
St Leonards

Buol's note,[101] which I had last night[,] is outrageous, and must be very seriously taken up – I think I had better see Colloredo. I wish you would bring it down with you in the train tomorrow, and with it the statement of Mr Newton. We can talk it over on our way.[102] [. . .]

---

[100]It seems likely that this was a dinner on 15 August, the festival of the Virgin Mary and the anniversary of the first Emperor Napoleon's birth, marked by feasts and parades in France.

[101]Malmesbury's explanatory note: 'Alludes to violence offered to Mr Newton at Verona & journey to Osborne.' Henry Robert Newton, an architect, had been arrested, manhandled, and imprisoned overnight by the Austrian authorities in Verona in June 1852, while apparently making a sketch of the fortifications there. His father had written to Malmesbury on 16 July, asking him to seek redress. The Government subsequently obtained 'a full and ample expression of regret' from Austria, as Stanley outlined on 16 November 1852. *Parl. Deb.*, CXXIII, cols 198–200. See also **41, 42, 43**.

[102]They would be on the way to Osborne for a Privy Council meeting on 18 August.

41

Derby to Malmesbury, MP 9M73/451/37/1–2
20 August 1852
10 Downing Street

These papers which Walpole sends on to you through me, are any thing but agreeable. The refugees in Jersey want looking after closely; and I must say that the collection of a large number of them in such immediate proximity to the French coast, together with the language they are reported to hold, is calculated to give just cause of umbrage to France. We must keep a sharp look out over these fellows; and I do not think it would have a bad effect, and might supersede the employment by the French Government of unauthorised spies, if we were to follow up the precedent of the Exhibition, and on the very ground of the number of the refugees, and their supposed projects, invite the President to send over some of the French police to cooperate with ours. It is a step which would mark confidence, and would I think be justified by the circumstances. Hardinge,*[103] who I have just seen, is going over there in a few days, and I have asked him to keep his eyes & ears open.

Cowley has been with me, and, oddly enough, expressed <u>his</u> anxiety as to the state of these Channel Islands, and possible causes of difference with France, arising out of the conduct of the refugees. He wants to avoid taking his seat, and giving his proxy; but I think I have given him to understand that we shall expect it. He is to take a few days to consider what he will do. I have seen Colloredo, and have expressed to him strongly the painful impression produced upon your mind and my own by Buol's answer to Mr Howard* which I read to him.[104] I told him he must not be surprised if in answer to it we were compelled to use strong language, & that the tone of Buol's communication, independent of the substance, struck us as quite inconsistent with his professions of friendship, and fell short of ordinary courtesy. He protested of course that he was sure nothing was farther from Count Buol's wishes than to show any unfriendly feeling; but that he would write to him tonight, and let him know the impression produced upon us, and I told him that as Lord Westmorland* was returning to Vienna, and from a private letter which I had seen, there was some reason to hope that a further communication, in a different spirit, might yet be received from Vienna, we would postpone for a short time sending our official reply to his letter. I hope you will approve of this delay, which may do some good, and which we can afford, as Parliament is not sitting.

---

[103] See also below, **48**.
[104] Explanatory note: 'Alludes to Mr Newton's arrest at Verona'.

42

Malmesbury to Derby, DP 920 DER (14) 144/1
'Saturday ev^g.' [21 August 1852][105]
Heron Court

I have received yr papers & letter on the Jersey refugees since I sent off mine of this morning to ask you what Colloredo had said — I quite agree with you on both subjects – of course on the first as it was I who desired Sir R Mayne[106] to send over a detective. I had however intended to communicate the intentions of these persons to the President privately letting him know at the same time that I was aware of his own spies. It seemed to me that we should equally deserve the confidence of the French Govt without risking the outcry w^h will be made if we openly propose to them to join in a surveillance. The French Gov^t would certainly shew us up, but if the President were informed by some one viva voce the whole object w^d be obtained without any risk of a debate in the H[ouse] of Commons —
I talked to Cowley about it & he said he could find means of letting him know —
I will follow yr instructions on the Newton case[107] about w^h we have a fair excuse for delay inasmuch as the hero is not returned from abroad & that there is considerable discrepancy between his own story & his father['] s w^h obliges me to see him. — Considering the brutal nature of the Austrian soldiers & police, & the state of their country, & then the incurable snobbism of our young English travellers of the middle class, I see no end to these cases unless we openly say that if they choose to go for <u>pleasure</u> into a country so misgoverned we cannot go to war for the roughness they meet with.

43

Malmesbury to Derby, DP 920 DER (14) 144/1
21 August [1852]
Heron Court

As you are going to Osborne on Monday[108] I should be much obliged to you for a line to say what passed between you & Colloredo on the

---

[105] Date appended.
[106] Sir Richard Mayne (1796–1868), joint commissioner of the Metropolitan police.
[107] See above, **40**.
[108] According to the Court Circular in *The Times*, 24 August 1852, Derby left St Leonards for Osborne on Sunday 22 August.

subject of M^r. Newton.[109] — It appears to me that we must settle upon some definite course of policy as regards these cases w^h are sure to recur & to be taken up in the H[ouse]. of Commons & by the press with popular virulence. — I send you a translation of an article from the Gov^t. papers at Vienna w^h shews the feeling entertained against us by Palmerston's bluster & Haynau's case[110] — We shall get nothing from Austria & the more we write the more incapable of obliging her to repair injustice & the more ridiculous shall we appear —

Supposing Buol positively to refuse redress what can we do? The ultima ratio[111] w^d be to blockade Trieste & Venice & stop a trade w^h gives us a million sterling per ann[um]. — My opinion is if, as I expect he will, Buol maintains his present tone, that we should openly declare in Parl[iamen]^t. our inability to answer for the safety of our subjects upon Austrian territory & warn them accordingly that if they visit that country it is at their peril, that if they do so merely for pleasure they must take the consequences as they would in a barbarous land, altho' we are ready to protect our merchants vis et armis.[112] We may recall Westmorland or not at the same time. —

Edward will have told you what I heard from Cowley about Belgium & you will have seen Cowley yrself. — Whenever Austria is well with France she waxes insolent.

44

Malmesbury to Derby, DP 920 DER (14) 144/1
27 August [1852]
Foreign Office

[...] I am to see a Conseiler from Neufchatel tomorrow. It is the only question that I think may give us trouble —[113]

The President[114] is very angry at the difficulties thrown in the way of his marriage by Austria &c[.] The lady says she will have him & Walewski & Persigny* both agree that he never will forgive this interference.

---

[109] See above, **40**.

[110] The notorious manhandling of the Austrian general Julius Jacob von Haynau (1786–1853) by the London draymen in 1850.

[111] 'the final reckoning'.

[112] 'by force of arms'.

[113] The Prussians were antagonized by anti-royalist policies in the canton, and earlier that month had requested that Britain call a conference for mediation on the question of its status, as stipulated in the 1852 protocol. The request was rebuffed. See below, **46**, **49**, and **50**.

[114] The French President, Louis Napoleon Bonaparte.

45

Malmesbury to Derby, 920 DER (14) 144/1
2 September 1852
Balmoral

[...] My private secretary is about a mile off so it is not easy to carry on the business in an official manner & I must trust to Edward who is much more fit for the F[oreign].S[ecretaryshi]^p. than I am. [...] Nothing can be more amiable than the Queen & Prince are, & as far as you & I are concerned I am sure there is no personal prejudice –

46

Malmesbury to Derby, DP 920 DER (14) 144/1
2 September 1852
Balmoral

[...] Bulwer seems to be doing very well but his Austrian news corroborated unintentionally by Dawkin's[115] [*sic*] account of their studied rudeness to British travellers is very important as regards Italy, & I think we must finally play France against them. Russia w^d not help Austria in any ambitious views on Italy but only defend her from internal revolution. I may say en passant I had a very satisfactory conversation with Brunnow on Neufchatel before I left town & shall frame a despatch to Bloomfield* upon it soon — [...]
The Prince's mind is actively engaged in foreign politics & he shews on this subject as upon all others great information — In respect to Austria he is I think quite what he should be, & I agree with him that we can do her much more harm than she can do us —

47

Malmesbury to Derby, DP 920 DER (14) 144/1
3 September [1852]
Balmoral

[...] I wish you would ascertain that the Duke [of Northumberland] has sent a steamer to be permanently stationed at Jersey — Walpole is getting nervous about it — I am not if we show that we attend to the point — The Alderney forts sh^d not be starved. —

---

[115] Clinton Dawkins, British consul-general in Venice since 26 June 1846.

The President knows by this time from me the plots against him & that I am aware of his spies at Jersey as against us —

Walpole won't believe that he can buy at Paris a correct map of our works there & every where else whenever he likes – & I do not mind that, but if it be true that French Gov^t. agents are trying to debauch the loyalty of the people it is dangerous —

48

Derby to Malmesbury, DP 920 DER (14) 179/2, fos 190–191[116]
3 September 1852[117]

I inclose you a part of a letter which I have received from Walpole with the inclosures, which I quite agree with him in thinking that you should see. [. . .] You will be the best judge what course to take; but I think you should let Cowley have this information, & that some representation should be made, through him, to the French Govt. of the double part which their agents are acting. I do not know whether the laws of Jersey would allow our removing the refugees from a position the proximity of which to France affords some justification for the espionage practised by the French Government. If we can do it, we certainly ought. Meanwhile I hope the steamer we have ordered there will be of some service as a check on those gentry. I asked Hardinge to keep his eyes & ears open, & to give me, on his return, his political, as well as his military, opinion.[118] [. . .]

49

Malmesbury to Derby, DP 920 DER (14) 144/1
4 September [1852]
Balmoral

I send you a draft I have written on the Neufchatel question[.] I hope you will revise the language but approve of the sense – I am perfectly sure that if we go into this thorny question we shall upset your government & raise a storm in Europe.

Brunnow thinks the same & I am sure I can get the President to oppose it —

---

[116] Copy in Derby's letter book. Original not found.
[117] Not received until 5 September. See below, **50**.
[118] See above, **41**.

I also send a despatch from Brunnow upon Greece & Edward's comments upon his views – he gave E. a duplicate of the conversation he bestowed upon me last Sunday. We had better wait to see what Bavaria means. Her family compact is not officially announced but only told me by letter namely to substitute Adelbert for Luitpold who w^d not for himself or his children renounce their religion.

Whilst in the Highlands I shall not send you any rubbish of a routine nature —

[P.S.] Pray send the draft to Bloomfield on to the F.O. as the Queen has seen a duplicate w^h I sent her to hasten the course of business —

50

Malmesbury to Derby, DP 920 DER (14) 144/1
'Sunday morning' [5 September 1852][119]
Balmoral

I had last night a conversation with the Prince on Neufchatel & I found that among the many other objections to any interference with that canton you may add the royal displeasure at any such policy.

The Prince says it is entirely a 'marotte'[120] of the King's[121] w^h Austria & Russia work according to their wish to obtain any particular object from him — He said he w^d write himself to the King to tell him not to press the subject further —[122]

I have just got yr letters on Jersey — I wish you would get F. Somerset* to send for a battalion more to the island as the barracks w^d hold that, & I see no reason why we sh^d not fill them — I found him very averse to sending troops there & I do not know why. The idea of offending the French w^h he suggested is nonsense. I will send a copy of Sanders[']['] [123] report to Cowley with instructions to make a verbal

[119] Date appended.
[120] 'hobby' or 'craze'.
[121] Friedrich Wilhelm IV of Prussia.
[122] Prince Albert wrote to the king on 6 September 1852, advising him that 'the only way' to obtain a satisfactory solution to the Neuchâtel problem 'will be by way of negotiation and by convincing the Swiss Confederation, and proving to them the usefulness, and in fact the necessity, of arriving at a legal agreement with Your Majesty; whereas menaces would only raise fresh obstacles, and forcible measures would produce greater evils than could possibly arise if you could find it in your power to refrain from using force'. K. Jagow (ed.), *Letters of the Prince Consort 1831–1861* (London, 1938), p. 183.
[123] A Scotland Yard detective.

remonstrance. It will come very well after Harris'[124] conversation with the President[125] — [...]

51

Malmesbury to Derby, DP 920 DER (14) 144/1
9 September [1852]
Balmoral

[...] With respect to Greece I think we should be satisfied if Adelbert adopts the Greek faith <u>immediately</u> & promises it for his unhatched chickens —

If there is any truth in Milbanke's[126] suspicion that Russia wants the Emperor Nicholas' nephew to succeed we should have France with him, as the boy is cousin to the President & a Beauharnais, but I have found the F[rench].G[overnment]. very jealous of Russia on this question, & I therefore do not believe it. — You will learn a great deal of the private springs w^h influence German politics if you talk of them to the Prince. He has his crotchets, but he strikes me as a very clever man, & can be of use to us by giving us information w^h our ministers ought to give but never do. — He will shew you a copy of his letter to the K[ing]. of Prussia. [...]

My cousin's letter[127] contained nothing more respecting the Jersey conference with the President than what I sent you – I shall see him at Achnacarry & will send you more particulars. Meantime Cowley is to remonstrate against the three agitators. [...]

You will see that Buol continues to be bearish. I suspect he dislikes Howard[128] for his Whig connexions[129] —

[124]George Harris (1816–1857), Malmesbury's cousin and private secretary.
[125]Harris had seen Louis Napoleon on 31 August 1852, to let him know privately about the plots being hatched by refugees in the Channel Islands.
[126]Sir John Ralph Milbanke (1800–1868), British minister in Bavaria, 1843–1862.
[127]This can be seen in *Memoirs*, I, pp. 346–347.
[128]Henry George Howard at Vienna. See above, **41**.
[129]Howard's eldest brother, George, the seventh Earl of Carlisle, had sat in the Melbourne and Russell Cabinets, and would later serve as Palmerston's Lord Lieutenant of Ireland. Their father, the sixth Earl, had also been a Whig minister.

52

Malmesbury to Derby, DP 920 DER (14) 144/1
19 September [1852]
Achnacarry

I send you attached to these Neapolitan despatches Edward's & Addington's remarks & counter remarks on M^r. Hamilton's case —[130]

It is one w^h will make a great noise in the H[ouse]. of C[ommons]. & his memorandum here inclosed makes it worse than I at first thought —

I should propose acting simply in the same course we we [*sic*] have adopted till now namely.

Insist on the entrance being a breach of the treaty.

Admit that M^r. H. has no right to educate Neapolitan children if the Gov^t. objects —

Insist that he has a right to receive, take care of, & educate British children.

Demand compensation for M^r. H equivalent to the actual loss he has suffered by the closing of his school for a time.

My conversation with Prince Carini[131] induces me to believe that we can carry all this out, & I am very averse to any pottering about the treaty now — Addington was away when we began the dispute —

If you approve of this course pray write me a word to that effect & whilst the despatches are with the Queen I will give instructions to the F.O.

53

Malmesbury to Derby, DP 920 DER (14) 144/1
3 October 1852

The very important letters I send you from Bulwer cannot be answered by me without detailed instructions from you. If you are not overwhelmed with work they had better be answered by you in person —

---

[130] A case involving a dispute between a British citizen and the Neapolitan authorities over the education of children. Despite Malmesbury's worries, it was handled effectively and kept away from parliamentary and press attention.

[131] Prince de Carini, the London representative of the Kingdom of the Two Sicilies, had met with Malmesbury in early September. Carini had agreed that he would obtain an apology for Hamilton's treatment, but had requested that British subjects should ensure that they were complying with Neapolitan law.

That dated Sep 21 sent under flying seal thro' Cowley gives a resumé of Bulwer's work & of his questions. It appears that we are to give the Pope an opportunity of speaking for us in Ireland — Can you find any [word missing in original] in the course proposed? Is there such a bishop as he requires & who will play into our hands?

The subject is so important & the time so short before the 11th of November that I send you the letters straight from here. If you do not want to keep the principal ones or to send them to Naas or Eglinton* pray forward them to Edward —

54

Malmesbury to Derby, DP 920 DER (14) 144/1
8 October [1852]

You will see by this letter of L^d. Howard's[132] that Leopold* is frightened & our court also, for it must be from them that Leopold knows the Austrian & Russian answers to my questions about the Belgian press — I shall write to him that we cannot put on any such pressure as the King requires, as to be useful to him it must be public & to be public it w^d be fatal to any English gov^t. —

It is this gadfly of the Belgian press, w^h being in French, is stinging & working L.N. into a fever. I do not wonder at it, for it requires the public school education of an Englishman & his natural phlegm to stand the misrepresentations of an English & Belgian newspaper with indifference, especially when one begins at four & forty years of age like L.N.

55

Derby to Malmesbury, MP 9M73/2/255
'Friday E^{vg}.' [?8 or 15 October 1852][133]

I think it would be better not to volunteer printing any explanation of the private conversations which passed between Card^l. Antonelli & Bulwer, both on the general principle that they were private, and also because one explanation will lead to another, and we should have to disclose more of our case than would be convenient.

---

[132] Charles Augustus Ellis, sixth Baron Howard de Walden and second Baron Seaford (1799–1868), minister in Belgium, 1846–August 1868.
[133] Filed between letters of 2 October and 16 October.

56

Malmesbury to Cowley, Cowley MSS, TNA, FO 519/196, fos 173–174
15 October 1852
Foreign Office

In great haste I write you a line to beg of you to send me the best account you can of the French navy & of what they have been about lately in that department — All our newspapers talk of increased activity & you in your last letter use a similar phrase — Now the navy is the pulse we feel the President by — Without a navy he can do us no harm & a navy adapted for invasion.

[. . .] I see a presentiment in both countries almost universal that L.N. means mischief – Lord Derby gets letters every day to say so — I alone do not believe it as he studiously shuns every cause of offence to England – but still we must be ready[.]

57

Malmesbury to Derby, DP 920 DER (14) 144/1
15 October [1852]

Do you wish to see me before the Cabinet? Walewski comes to see me at 5 o['] clock. — These letters confirm what I think of the general opinion of L.N.'s views upon this country. If general opinion be right all we can do is de rester dans notre droit[134] & be prepared at the Admiralty.

58

Derby to Malmesbury, MP 9M73/451/47/1–3
17 October 1852
St Leonards

I return you a number of your private letters, of great interest, and which you ought to have had back earlier. I cannot however even now find time to give you the full explanation of my views which you wish for; still less to attempt to send instructions to Bulwer on the very important questions to which his letters refer. It would seem to be his opinion, and I agree with him, that at present it will not do to attempt

---

[134] Roughly translated, 'to stay within our rights'; presumably, avoiding provocation of France.

to establish formal diplomatic relations with Rome. Whenever we do attempt it, we ought to accredit a Minister there, without receiving one here in return. I think Eglinton ought to have Bulwer's two letters of the 21st. September; and if he can find a R.C. Bishop whom he can trust, he should employ him to write such a letter as Antonelli suggests. If he cannot find such a Bishop, Dean Meyler[135] I believe is one of the most moderate and trustworthy ecclesiastics. I confess however that I have not much faith in the sincerity of any desire on the part of Rome to repress that spirit of turbulence on the part of the Irish priesthood, which they see causes considerable annoyance to a Protestant – and in their eyes a liberal government. I will not believe that if they were in earnest, they would feel any delicacy at all about waiting to have their opinions asked, but would let their opinions be known in a way that could not be misunderstood. Even if, in answer to the letters of our ecclesiastic, we get a general exhortation to peace and good order, to avoid politics &c &c, unless it be directed to particular cases, and to particular persons, it will be taken by the Irish clergy just at its real worth, and will be treated with indifference accordingly – while on the other hand Rome will be able to appeal to this declaration of her views, as a proof of her moderation, and of her desire to restrain the spirit of disaffection at which she secretly connives. A declaration against the Tenant Law League would be something; an avowal that R. Catholics enjoyed full religious liberty, would of itself be of use; but that which is most desirable, is of course most difficult for the See of Rome to pronounce upon, namely the crusade instituted by the R.C. priesthood against the temporalities of the Established Church. And yet it is really in the interest of Catholics, well considered, that this crusade should be discouraged. I do not want that they should not consider, or avow that they consider, the Protestant Endowment as an injustice; but I do not understand how any body of clergy can take in their hands the oath required by the Relief Act to be taken by R.C. M.Ps, and bear in mind the circumstances under which that oath was imposed, and the advantages which they obtained in consideration of it, and then make the single qualification for their tumultuous support of any candidate, his declaration that in the teeth of that oath he will use his utmost endeavours to subvert that Establishment. I think the Pope must see that the contradiction between the obligation accepted, and the pledge required, is such as to justify the bulk of Protestants in the charge which is repelled by R. Catholics as calumnious, that it is an article of their belief that no faith is to be kept with heretics, and that the good of their Church justifies the violation of a solemn

[135]Dean Walter Meyler, Roman Catholic priest of St Andrews, Dublin; regarded as a moderate.

oath. It is this belief mainly which keeps alive the prevailing animosity. We Protestants have no desire to interfere with the religious belief or religious worship of R. Catholics. If there are any that have, they are a small minority, with whom the Government would have no difficulty in dealing – and I will venture to answer for it, that if the Church of Rome puts forth no pretensions to temporal power, inconsistent with the laws of the land, and if the mass of R. Catholics, content with the full enjoyment of religious freedom which it is admitted they possess, respect the settlement of property, and are content to have the Church of England in undisturbed possession of that which is legally hers, religious animosity would die away for want of food, and no government would be disposed to draw the slightest political distinction between Protestant & Catholic. But as long as the present system continues, and is not peremptorily checked by Rome, it will be believed to be secretly encouraged by Her – and the indignation of the Protestant public may be excited to such a pitch, as that no government can refrain from taking measures in accordance with the public will, for enforcing, at all hazards, the supremacy of the Law, and the security of the Church to which the great majority of the people belong. How far the Pope & Cardinal Antonelli may be inclined to go in imposing a real check upon the aggressive spirit of Irish Catholicism I know not; but according not to their professions, but to the reality of their efforts in that direction, I for one, and the country with me, will judge of the sincerity of the friendly feelings they profess.

59

Malmesbury to Derby, DP 920 DER (14) 144/1
'Monday ev^g.' [?18 October 1852][136]

I send my proposition to France & Russia for settling the Greek question – It gets rid of Cetto's[137] rigmarole w^h I inclose. — It also put an end to Brunnow's views of forcing a conversion immediately upon Adelbert. — Walewski[,] Brunnow & I met today in conference – They were rather startled at the simplicity of the plan[138] but adhered –

---

[136]Malmesbury's *Memoirs*, I, p. 358, recount a conference of the three on 18 October, though he describes Brunnow being 'startled' at his plan, originally, under the entry for 17 October. Nevertheless, 18 October was also a Monday and this date seems likeliest.

[137]August, Freiherr von Cetto (1794–1879), Bavarian minister in London, 1822–1833 and 1835–June 1867.

[138]Malmesbury's plan was simply to declare that Otto's successor would profess the Orthodox faith, and this was what was agreed by the 1852 treaty. In the long term, however, it did not resolve the question.

Walewski wanted Cetto to be present but we opposed it on the score of the protecting powers being on a higher footing than the protected, the creator [rather][139] than the creature — We shall therefore invite Greece & Bavaria to adhere to our works as was done in 1832 – & I hope this job is as good as settled —

60

Malmesbury to Derby, DP 920 DER (14) 144/1
19 October [1852]

I wish very much you w^d see Lavradio[140] before the Cabinet & I have told him to call at 1 o'clock — His acc[oun]^t of French projects & feeling coming from an intelligent man like him & a foreigner, & spontaneously offered to the Gov^t. are to be valued & respected under any circumstances, but still more at the moment when we are about to discuss our Budget. [. . .] It is a question in my opinion whether we should not increase our seamen & have 2000 more in hand.

Van de Weyer you must hear on the same theme but he is an interested party. Both however are to be listened to — The Empire, coronation, &c. will ensure us six months at least of peace & we sh^d not lose that time. I still adhere to my opinion that L.N. does not wish to fight us, but, I confess he may be [*sic*] have to choose between his own or our destruction.

61

Derby to Malmesbury, MP 9M73/451/50
'Sat[urda]^y.' [23 October 1852][141]
St Leonards

I have just received your letter by messenger, enclosing Eglinton's, which I return. If you will look back to a letter which I wrote you on the 17th [142] – you will find that in all the main points I concur with Eglinton, and have indeed anticipated much of what he has now said to you; especially as to the inutility, for our purposes, of such a letter as it is proposed that the Pope should write, if it be directed only to

---

[139] Word missing in original.
[140] Count Lavradio, Portuguese minister in London.
[141] According to his *Memoirs*, I, p. 359, Malmesbury arrived at St Leonards on Sunday 24 October.
[142] See above, **58**.

general, and not to specific, objects. I also agree with him, and have so
written, that such a letter would eminently serve the Pope's interests,
by giving a plausible ground for talking about his moderation &c –
and I have further expressed my utter disbelief, in which Eglinton
also agrees, of the sincerity of the Pope's pretext as to not liking to
volunteer interference. I have given myself a holiday from coming up
to Town today, to help me to get through more work here. Why should
not you come down to dine & sleep here tomorrow? and [*sic*] if you
will come in good time, we can talk over this important matter. I shall
be in Town in good time on Monday, but I have an appointment at
12, and our Cabinet is fixed for 1.

62

Malmesbury to Derby, DP 920 DER (14) 144/1
'Saturday' [23 October 1852][143]
Foreign Office

I sent yr letter of the 17th. to Eglinton with the other papers from
Bulwer. I conclude that as you <u>both</u> object to the course Bulwer
& Antonelli agreed upon (I understand you to have waived yours)
we must try some plan for establishing diplomatic relations like that
proposed by my Chelsea friend[144] whom you really ought to see some
day. — I will come down to see you tomorrow & be at S[t] Leonards by
½ past 3 but I am sorry to say I must return as I have 3 or 4 people to
dinner with me[.]

63

Malmesbury to Derby, DP 920 DER (14) 144/1
31 October [1852]

I send you some papers w[h] L[d] Raglan[145] brought me yesterday.
The information of the writer as to the French force is said to
be pretty correct — Their intentions are another thing & I utterly

[143] Another hand has appended 'Oct 24', but this seems to refer to the date of receipt,
rather than its despatch (given that Saturday was 23 October and 'tomorrow' was thus
Sunday 24 October). See above, **61**.

[144] Father Joseph J. Mahé, a Roman Catholic priest attached to St Mary's, Cadogan
Terrace, Sloane Street. He was a contact of Malmesbury's who was prepared to act as an
intermediary with the Catholic hierarchy.

[145] Formerly Lord FitzRoy Somerset. See above, **50**.

discredit a piratical expedition against us — It is however true that they have ordered their Meditteranean [*sic*] fleet to be composed entirely of steamers.

I trust you will ask for 2000 more seamen £24000 added to the £36000 voted for the reserve will pay them —

The Empire will be proclaimed the 20th prox.[146] & on this subject I think I ought to address the Cabinet as soon as possible — Recognise him we must, but as Napoleon the III I do not understand how we can, seeing that we acknowledged Charles X and Louis Philippe whilst Napoleon II was alive. [. . .]

64

Malmesbury to Cowley, Cowley MSS, TNA, FO 519/196, fos 183–184
2 November 1852
Foreign Office

I saw Walewski last night & in conversation he announced to me that L.N[.] would not take the titles of King of Algeria & Protecteur de leurs Saints but Nap[oleon] III he would have — I said I thought it would give rise to difficulties — With us? Yes even with us as I did not see how we were to stultify all our acts for the last 37 years — To recognise him as legitimate sovereign was illegitimatising retrospectively Louis 18th [and] Charles Xth whom we had recognised on the principles of hereditary right while the supposed Nap[oleon] II was alive as Duc de Reichstadt — that if we recognised L.N. it was upon the elective principle w^h we had followed since 1830 — If the subject is mooted to you you will hold the same language but state you have no instructions.— I have written to Vienna[,] Berlin & Petersburgh [*sic*] to ask what they mean to do. — We are anxious to prevent all difficulties but the President ought on his side to smooth the way as much as possible — [. . .]

65

Malmesbury to Derby, DP 920 DER (14) 144/1
3 November [1852]

The inclosed letter from M^r. Hudson is the history, for the 1000th time repeated of an Italian prince – Independent in early life as they

---

[146]'proximo' – next month.

advance in years they invariably fall into the hands of their bigotted wives[,] mistresses & confessors — I consider this King of Sardinia*[147] to be now rapidly descending to the degraded position of the Grand Duke of Tuscany — It is a caution to England how careful she must be committing herself in the defence of a race which will not defend itself. —

66

Derby to Malmesbury, MP 9M73/451/53
4 November 1852
Downing Street

I send you a letter received this morning from Mahon,[148] which corroborates alarmingly the reports we hear from all quarters of L. N.'s intentions. Van de Weyer has been with me also, and has shown me a very strong letter from Leopold. I can hardly bring myself to believe in such recklessness as would be indicated by any early move; but it behoves all your agents to be on the alert, and Cowley should be especially warned to have his eyes open, and not to neglect the means of obtaining such information which I presume he possesses.

67

Malmesbury to Cowley, Cowley MSS, TNA, FO 519/196, fos 189–192
5 November 1852
Foreign Office

Your letter is a very important one at this moment[,] the principal object w^h occupies me now being the subject of the numeral III w^h L.N. means to attach to his name. It is impossible not to see that it means so much, & is of such consequence to him & to the memory of his uncle that he cannot yield the point without losing ground in France — Before I discuss the subject further I must inform you that having dined on Tuesday with Walewski he was so full of the matter

---

[147] Victor Emmanuel II.

[148] It is unclear precisely to whom this refers. There are two possibilities. Philip Stanhope (1805–1875), Lord Mahon (later fifth Earl of Stanhope), was a Conservative peer with a lively interest in diplomacy who had briefly served as parliamentary under-secretary at the Foreign Office under Wellington, 1834–1835, though there is no reason to suppose he had particular information relating to France. Charles James Patrick Mahon (1800–1891), 'the O'Gorman Mahon', was an Irish Whig who had just lost his seat, and reportedly travelled to Paris. A former Orleanist adherent, he had a range of continental contacts, so is an equally plausible correspondent.

that he took me apart for an hour to the great offence of his company. He renewed the conversation[,] which I entered into freely but always guarding myself as giving private & friendly advice to the President thro' him & actuated by an earnest desire to smooth all difficulties in his path — When asked & replying that I believed the Great Powers would be most unwilling to recognise L.N's legitimate right to the throne w^h the numeral III inferred Walewski declared it did not mean that but was merely a designation that he was the 3rd of that name who had appeared on the stage. [. . .] He concluded by stating that we might glisser[149] over the word. [. . .] It appears to me that we must first be quite sure that the 3 Great Powers will oppose the numeral – but that we must after this one act of coalition separate ourselves as to the form of disapprobation – that whenever the title shall be announced to the Queen we shall, (before she replies to the letter of the new Emperor) inquire the meaning of the numeral III assuming that it does not infer, what it might be supposed to declare, the hereditary right of succession inchoate in the family of his uncle, a principle w^h we cd not recognise both for the sake of the past & the future, seeing that we had recognised the two last Bourbons on that principle & were now ready to recognise him on the opposite one[:] election.

There might be another course[:] namely to recognise the Emperor of the French with a protest against our recognition being misinterpreted for reasons as before stated.– The more he accompanies his announcement with assurances of respect for territorial rights & the more he puts forth the popular principles of his elective power the more easy it will be for us to slide easily over the numeral – but whether we accept it under protest or ask explanations as to its meaning, we must at all events comment upon its anomalous nature[.]

[P.S.] If you have any opportunity unofficially of using the contents of this letter as furnishing you with arguments or elements of advice you will employ them at yr own discretion —

68

Malmesbury to Cowley, Cowley MSS, TNA, FO 519/196, fos 193–194
6 November 1852
Foreign Office

I have just read y^r letter & the President[']s message to the Cabinet. Knowing as we do by your private information what the animus of the Empire is we cannot but be alarmed at the prospect of affairs —

[149] 'glide'.

Still we must act upon what is officially said & done & we read in the message a moral not a physical triumph as the actual sentiment expressed – 'conquetes du 89' evidently means popular liberties not territory as no territory was gained for France in that year — Such being the case we do not think this message as giving us an advantageous ground of protesting – but there is a better reason for yr remaining silent & that is that I have no positive assurances from the 3 Great Powers & if Prussia & Austria consult first with Russia I cannot receive any for a fortnight.— The feeling of the Gov^t is decidedly to oppose the recognition of the title of Nap[oleon] III because it infers a stultifying of our former acts & treaties.

You had better therefore at present continue on the best terms with the Gov^t. & to any questions reply that you have no instructions. If any thing urgent occurs send over immediately. — [. . .]

69

Derby to Malmesbury, MP 9M73/451/58/1
'Tuesday' [9 November 1852][150]

I have this moment received the enclosed. It is most inconvenient, as I have not yet taken my seat – but I mean to go down by the 10.40 train, and wish you would meet me at the Paddington Station at that time[.]

[Enclosure: Queen Victoria to Derby, 8 November 1852, 9M73/451/58/2]

The Queen has rec[eive]^d this even[in]^g. the draft wh: it is proposed to send to the different courts on the subject of the Imperial Title.[151] The matter it treats of is so important that the Queen does not wish to let it go without having had some verbal explanations about it from Ld Derby. She therefore w^d wish him to come down here tomorrow either with or without Ld Malmesbury, any time between 11 – & 3 – .

---

[150] Given the enclosure, it was clearly written on Tuesday 9 November.

[151] Derby's long, detailed memorandum on the subject of the imperial declaration had been drafted on 8 November, and would be sent to Austria, Prussia, and Russia on 9 November. See TNA, FO 120/270, no. 30, Malmesbury to Howard, 9 November 1852. The draft is in Derby's papers, DP 920 DER (14) 37/2.

70

Malmesbury to Derby, DP 920 DER (14) 144/1
12 November 1852

Here is a most important & agreeable letter from Cowley.[152]
Louis Nap renounces all claim to the throne from hereditary right
& on the score of legitimacy — We shall now in recognising him as the
de facto & elected emperor have merely to refer to these spontaneous
explanations & interpretations, & express our satisfaction at his having
thus saved us the necessity of asking for them. —
It was the thorniest subject I have yet had to deal with, & it was
with great hesitation I took the step of making our opinions known
to him <u>unofficially</u> & as an old friend, so I am glad I was right in my
decision.
We shall now save our honour without risk of a quarrel —
As to promises about treaties they do not affect <u>that</u> & in my opinion
are moonshine – The great powers have not their own hands clean
enough to handle the subject with advantage —
I want to see you for 5 min[utes] on an important matter before I
meet the 4 ministers on the Greek treaty at 3.

71

Malmesbury to Cowley, Cowley MSS, TNA, FO 519/196, fos 197–198
12 November 1852
Foreign Office

I have only time to beg of you to assure the President personally
from me & from Ld Derby that his explanation to you[153] of the numeral
attached to Napoleon gave us the greatest pleasure by removing a
difficulty which I explained to Walewski. We could not interpret
the title as retrospectively claiming a legitimate right to the throne
of France without entering into insuperable sophisms & altering
history —
Assure him that I have always <u>smoothed</u> difficulties for him & that it
is the earnest desire of both myself and the English Gov^t. to continue
our relations with him on the most friendly footing of alliance. — [. . .]

---

[152] TNA, FO 27/939, no. 627A, Cowley to Malmesbury, 11 November 1852. Louis Napoleon
assured Britain that his empire was not hereditary, because he did not call himself 'Napoleon
V' as he might have done (given that both Joseph and Louis Bonaparte had outlived
'Napoleon II'), he did not date his reign from the death of 'Napoleon II', and he had called
an election.
[153] See above, **70**.

72

Malmesbury to Derby, DP 920 DER (14) 144/1
17 November [1852]

I send you some papers from Brunnow upon Nap[oleon]. III. They
were written before my first despatch was addressed to Petersburgh
[*sic*] & therefore before yr memorandum w^h followed it a week later. —
Nesselrode therefore did not know our view of the matter & still less
L. Napoleon's present intention to declare himself an elected & not
hereditary sovereign.—

It is very satisfactory to a tyro like me to find that so old a statesman
recommends the same manner of turning the difficulty by a protest
w^h I submitted to the Cabinet. — Brunnow at the time was not
satisfied with this view of the subject & was inclined to go farther than
Nesselrode.

If the President[']s assurances to Cowley are officially given &
voluntarily expressed we should allude to them as rendering questions
unnecessary w^h w^d otherwise have been indispensible [*sic*] —

73

Derby to Malmesbury, MP 9M73/451/61
'Wednesday' [17 November 1852][154]
10 Downing Street

I return your Russian papers. It does not seem to me however that
Nesselrode & you are quite on the same tack – for while you propose to
recognise as Napoleon III under protest against the hereditary claim –
he declares distinctly that the Emperor 'reconnaitre l'Empereur du
Francais – mais, pour Napoleon III, il l'ignore'[.][155] We shall have
plenty of time however to talk this over tomorrow. [. . .]

---

[154]It seems reasonable to suppose that this letter was written on 17 November, given
that it is evidently a response to **72**, that Wednesday was the 17th, and that the Duke of
Wellington's funeral was the following day, thus allowing 'plenty of time' for discussion as
Derby suggested.
[155]The Tsar might 'recognize the Emperor of the French, but of Napoleon III, he is
unaware'. The editors are grateful to Angus Hawkins for his advice on Derby's handwriting
in this letter.

74

Malmesbury to Derby, DP 920 DER (14) 144/1
23 November 1852
Foreign Office

I shall be much obliged to you to return the papers which I send you to Prince Albert when you go to Windsor tomorrow —

They advert to improvements in our system of national defence & if you have not seen them they are well worth reading.

The D[uke]. of North[umberlan]^d. has been to me most anxious that the 1500 marines w^h he expected to have sh^d not be suppressed. He says he cannot carry out his plan without them. Whatever may be the supplementary vote you may finally determine to ask for there can be now no doubt that it will be supported by the Whig leaders & many of the Peelites – Ld John [Russell,]* Palmerston & S. Herbert[156] have declared this & wish you to know it. — It seems to me of vital importance to employ the next 4 months actively in our preparations. L.N. cannot attack England in winter even if he had not other domestic amusements in hand. These months are invaluable & are to us what the peace of Amiens was to Napoleon the 1st. when it gave him time to create his artillery. — My opinion still is that L.N. will avoid a war with us if he can, but I now know that he is preparing for it – M^r. Hamond[157] the Cherburgh [sic] consul has been to me today – 300 large cannon have arrived at S^t. Malo & 30 at Granville – There are four times the number of men employed in Cherburgh dockyard that there were in April last. Within a month a new class of steamer has been built 130 feet long with a screw & flat bottomed evidently made to carry & land troops in shallow water. They would not draw 5 feet being iron laid over wood so that men could jump out & walk ashore — The French pretend they are for the African & S. American rivers but that cannot be as they could not outlive the voyage with flat bottoms. They w^d be most formidable boats because as they need not be towed they w^d accompany without retarding the large steamers to effect a most instantaneous landing for the first detachments to obtain a footing — After M^r. Hamond I saw Walewski & held the language you instructed me to repeat to him respecting the title of Nap[oleon] III. — He appeared much annoyed at the difficulties to be expected from the great powers, but said he w^d hope to the last that

---

[156] Sidney Herbert, first Baron Herbert of Lea (1810–1861), prominent Peelite Conservative; Secretary at War (a post junior to that of the Secretary for War and the Colonies), 1845–1846 and 1852–1855; Secretary for War, 1859–1861.
[157] Horace Hamond, Consul at Cherbourg from 1 April 1852.

there w^d be no appearance of coalition between them & England –
that if there was[,] sooner or later it must occasion a war in w^h we
sh^d be left to pay the piper, that the President did not care for them
if we stood aloof for he knew they had neither the pluck nor power
to hurt him – that he would make all the explanations necessary to
save our credit & honour & that if we refused to recognise the numeral
all his friendly conduct would have been ungratefully received.— Here
he used the old arguments – I replied that we had determined nothing,
that if explanations were given they must be official & such as I could
repeat to Parl[iamen]^t.

The moral of all this is that I am convinced we should immediately
ask for 5000 seamen – 1000 marines & money for our seven steamers –
2000 artillerymen sh^d also be raised because they cannot be made
soldiers as quickly as infantry —

75

Malmesbury to Derby, DP 920 DER (14) 144/1
28 November [1852]

I send you the Russian despatches.[158] I have had a long conference
with Brunnow who says that my view is the best for England & that the
declaration I shall get from L.N. will be of the greatest use to the other
powers. He says also that nothing can have been more honorable [*sic*]
& friendly than our conduct to all of them, & he even added that ours
was the most practical & statesmanlike view of the subject —

I am glad our hands are free — I am writing a despatch for Cowley
to clinch the nail I want to drive into the French gov^t. & I will call on
you this afternoon to shew it you.

76

Malmesbury to Derby, DP 920 DER (14) 144/1
1 December [1852]

Will you have the goodness to send the inclosed letter to the Queen
when you have read it —

My opinion is that we must now obtain the recognition by D[rouyn]
de L['Huys].* of the memorandum as proposed by Cowley as all we

---

[158]Malmesbury's *Memoirs*, I, p. 369, noted in his entry for 27 November that 'Russian
despatches arrive of 20th'.

are likely to get, & that when we recognise the Empire I should announce it in my place in Parl[iamen]ᵗ. & state the objections we felt to the numeral & under what circumstances those objections were waived. This will bind the French <u>historically</u> as much as any thing they can give us on paper. I would <u>advise</u> holding out & writing a note which he <u>must</u> answer, but if he did so in the language Walewski used the other day & wʰ I shall notice at his court, it would lead to a wrangle —

This again I should not mind were I not persuaded that the H[ouse]. of Commons is too ignorant or too vulgar to see & appreciate the value of our objections to a cipher —

77

Malmesbury to Derby, DP 920 DER (14) 144/1
'Wednesday' [8 December 1852][159]

Many thanks for Guizot[']s[160] letter — There is a great deal of truth in it but he never was more wrong than in calling L.N. <u>indolent</u>. He never was a minute of his life unoccupied either with <u>violent</u> exercises or study. [. . .]

---

[159]Date appended. Explanatory note: 'On Mr Guizot's letter to Lord Aberdeen'.

[160](François Pierre) Guillaume Guizot (1787–1874), French foreign minister, 1840–1847; prime minister and foreign minister, 1847–1848. He had fled to Britain after the revolution in 1848.

CHAPTER 2
THE SECOND DERBY GOVERNMENT,
FEBRUARY 1858–JUNE 1859

78

Malmesbury to Derby, DP 920 DER (14) 144/2
[23 February 1858][1]

As I am anxious both from friendship & gratitude to be as useful
to you as possible at the F.O. I remind you how <u>indispensible</u> [*sic*] it
is that you shd give me a good <u>working</u> U[nder]. Sec[retary]. who
can both <u>write</u> & <u>speak</u> & above all that he sh^d be in the H[ouse] of
C[ommons].[2] — If the Premier is <u>there</u> as Palmerston was, he knows
all the business of the F.O. as well as the Sec[retary] of State because
it all passes under his eye, but it is impossible to <u>cram</u> a Chancellor of
the Exchequer with ready answers or even with the bearing, of a case
w^h may have gone thro' a dozen phases — Stanley was perfection & of
course I cannot expect to get so clever a fellow, but it is very important
that he shd be what & <u>where</u> I point out.

I think we shall have to move Cowley & certainly must send a good
man to Petersburgh [*sic*] — [. . .]

[1] Date in another hand.
[2] In the event, W.R.S. Vesey Fitzgerald was appointed.

79

Malmesbury's unpublished diary, MP 9M73/79

23 February 1858

[. . .] Clarendon* writes to beg me to see Persigny who is just come over[.] Excitement of French ag[ain]st us very great & the same on this side ag[ain]st the Emperor.[3]

25 February 1858

Went by Clarendon's invitation to see Persigny – Found him in good humour – suggested to him that after an answer to Walewski[']s despatch[4] we shd proceed with Palmerston[']s Bill.[5]

28 February 1858

Saw Persigny at my House – Very violent when I told him we could not proceed with the Refugee Bill[6] w[h] indeed we found impossible. Agreed to write a despatch to be submitted to him sub rosâ[7] & his answer d[itt]o [. . .]

80

Malmesbury to Derby, DP 920 DER (14) 144/2
1 March [1858]

[. . .] I shall see P[almerston] at 12. He wishes you not to state positively yr intentions on the Bill but to announce only yr answer to W[alewski]'s despatch & give 10 days to cool down — I don't think this a bad idea – <u>Time</u> is everything – & you may say that you will wait

---

[3] Palmerston's government had fallen over its alleged subservience to France, in the wake of the attempted assassination of Napoleon by Felice Orsini on 14 January 1858. The attack had been planned by French refugees in Britain, where the bomb was also made. As a measure to control the refugees, Palmerston had introduced the Conspiracy to Murder Bill. The occasion for the Government's defeat had been a Radical motion in the House of Commons, tabled during the second reading of the Bill, criticizing the Government's failure to reply to a critical despatch of Walewski's. Anglo-French relations in the wake of Palmerston's defeat were the poorest they had been for some years.

[4] See above, entry for 23 February. Walewski's despatch of 20 January was received by the Foreign Office on 21 January. The correspondence had been published on 6 February.

[5] The Conspiracy to Murder Bill.

[6] The Conspiracy to Murder Bill.

[7] 'secretly'; literally, 'under the rose'.

the result of the trial[8] before you renew the subject before the House, without saying how — At the same time you must express y'self ready to act &c &c[.] I wrote to Walewski last night a letter shewing our amicus & for the Emperor to see — [. . .]

81

Malmesbury's unpublished diary, MP 9M73/79

1 March 1858

The same hopeless conversation with Persigny – submitted a despatch w[h] he altered. Par[l][iamen][t] met & Derby made his statement in w[h] he pledged himself to nothing on the Bill but spoke well in the French sense — Our army and militia 103000 men in G[t] Britain – want of seamen.

2 March 1858

Persigny again pleased at the speech but a reaction in the evening when I met him at his own house — conversation with Claremont[9] — Both say they don't know how to appease the French people who will not understand the abandonment of the Bill —[10] [. . .]

6 March 1858

Persigny at 12[11] – Said I might send the despatch to his Gov[t] —[12]

[8]The trial of Dr Simon Bernard, one of the conspirators in the Orsini plot, who lived in London and would be tried and acquitted by a British court in April 1858.

[9]Lieutenant-Colonel Edward Stopford Claremont, military attaché at the British Embassy in Paris.

[10]These concerns were overcome. See below, entry for 6 March.

[11]Malmesbury told Cowley the same day that Persigny 'is now much more reasonable but I find that he considered he had some cause of offence with Disraeli whom, rightly or wrongly, he accuses of having promised him uninterrupted support of the Refugee Bill'. Cowley MSS, TNA, FO 519/196, fos 271–272.

[12]The despatch was sent off that day.

82

Derby to Malmesbury, MP 9M73/20/61
'Tuesday' [9 March 1858][13]
St James's Square

I return your box, and wish you joy — Look at the leading article in the Morning Post.[14] If the despatch from Walewski is as conciliatory as his language reported by Cowley all will be well, and I think it will be. Telegraph your satisfaction – but I think it would be well to telegraph also to Cowley, who is confidentially to see it, that we hope it will contain an explicit disclaimer of the meaning attached here to the despatch of Jan[uar]ʸ. 20 that the 'law' and 'legislation' of England designedly 'favoured' such offences, and 'sheltered' such criminals.[15] That is the real sore point with the public[.]

83

Derby to Malmesbury, MP 9M73/20/58
'Tuesday night' [9 March 1858] '11.30 PM'[16]

There is the d[evi]l to pay – I went to congratulate Persigny,[17] and found him profoundly ignorant of all that had taken place! My congratulations were received with a face like a thunder cloud – and my explanations were not better accepted. Enfin, he sends his démission[18] by telegraph tomorrow – he has been insulted – passed over – God knows what — I told him the Emperor knew too well the value of his services &c &c[.] Non, non, l'affaire est fini. Whether you can do any thing or not, I know not – but imagine having an

---

[13]As this letter must have been written before 12 March, when Malmesbury received Walewski's despatch, and given Cowley's news of Walewski's intention to respond positively to Malmesbury's overture, it was clearly sent on Tuesday 9 March.

[14]Its editorial declared that: 'We quite agree with Mr Disraeli that there has been great mismanagement in the conduct of our late transactions with the Government of France [. . .] Lord Malmesbury will merit the designation of a dexterous statesman, indeed, if he manages to write such a despatch and extract such a reply as shall at once make matters smooth with France.' *Morning Post*, 9 March 1858.

[15]Malmesbury followed Derby's instructions. See his messages to Cowley of 9 March 1858, TNA, FO 146/757.

[16]Given the meeting Derby describes and Malmesbury's diary entry for the same day, the date is clear.

[17]On the news of Walewski's positive response to Malmesbury's despatch, thus ending the dispute with France.

[18]'resignation'.

ambassador ignorant for 24 hours of such an arrangement as Cowley announces!

84

Malmesbury's unpublished diary, MP 9M73/79

9 March 1858

Cabinet on France – Hodges[19] [*sic*] – Cagliari[20] – Isthmus of Suez — Derby went to Persigny in evening – found him ignorant of Walewski[']s receipt of my despatch – Declares he will send in his resignation —

10 March 1858

Persigny still in London — Party at Ld Derby – all late Govt there but Pam[.][21] Saw Bernstorff*[22] on the Naples quarrel — [. . .]

12 March 1858

Gale kept back steamers – French answer to my despatch was only remitted to me at 3 0 clock by Persigny who was ill & sulky. — House of C[ommons]. hostile – Case of Cagliari put forward factiously[23] – We gave the papers —

---

[19]Hodge was a British citizen arrested in Sardinia for his alleged connection with the attack on Napoleon. France had attempted to extradite him, but the terms of the treaty meant that Sardinia required British permission, which was refused.

[20]In 1857, a Sardinian ship, the *Cagliari*, had been hijacked by Mazzinian revolutionaries, who took it to Ponza and freed inmates at the prison island. After the subsequent failure of the hijackers' attempt to storm the town of Sapri, the crew regained control and sailed for Naples, claiming that they were intending to report the incidents. For its previous piratical activities, the ship was seized en route by the navy of the Kingdom of the Two Sicilies. The Neapolitans imprisoned the crew, including its British engineers, Henry Watt and Charles Park. Prior to Palmerston's resignation, Clarendon had begun exploring legal options to resolve the matter and free the men, but to no avail. See below, **86, 87, 88, 89, 90, 91, 94, 95, 97, 98, 101, 102, 103, 104, 134.**

[21]Palmerston.

[22]Bernstorff's previous experience in Naples made him the logical intermediary while Britain had no formal diplomatic relations with Naples (see, e.g., entry for 13 March, below).

[23]See *Parl. Deb.*, CXLIX, cols 82–108.

13 March 1858

Cabinet – Disraeli as usual alarmed[24] – agree to refer the Cagliari case again to the Law Officers tho the last gave 3 decisions in favour of Naples.[25] — Saw Bernstorff who promised to use his offices at Naples for the release of the English engineers,[26] but after the decision of the Cabinet I thought it right to write to him & allow him to retract if he chose — Dined at Salisburys[27] – Society ag[ains]t us – Cambridge* family very hostile and mischievous.—

16 March 1858

Cabinet on a mem[orandum] by Prince Albert on the state of the navy. [...]

17 March 1858

Levee – Persigny in good humour but determined to resign.

20 March 1858

[...] At 6 with the Queen. [...] Deprecated the increasing wish of the H[ouse] of Commons to meddle with for[eign] affairs [...]

85

Malmesbury to Derby, DP 920 DER (14) 144/2
4 April 1858
Heron Court

[...] Bad appointments were so fatal to the last Gov^t. & w^d be so much more so to ours that I have taken great pains about them, & if you get the list you will see that I have observed seniority throughout

---

[24]Disraeli's alarm was presumably because of the hostility that he had encountered in the House of Commons the previous night. See, e.g., Disraeli to Queen Victoria, 12 March 1858, *BDL*, VII, no. 3055.

[25]A number of reports were delivered to Clarendon by the law officers in late 1857 and early 1858. Further details, including the law officers' reports, can be found in 'Correspondence respecting the "Cagliari"' and 'Further correspondence respecting the "Cagliari"', Parliamentary Papers, 1857–1858 session, LIX.

[26]Watt and Park were released shortly after, not because of Bernstorff's good offices but following the intervention of a special diplomatic mission to Naples. See below, **87**.

[27]James Brownlow William Cecil, second Marquis of Salisbury (1791–1868), Lord Privy Seal, 1852; Lord President of the Council, 1858–1859. His second wife, Mary, would go on to marry the fifteenth Earl of Derby.

excepting where there were cases like Walter[,][28] Edgecombe[29] & Barron[30] — The Queen too is very officious & knowing about the Dipl[omatic]. Corps — [. . .]

86

Malmesbury to Derby, DP 920 DER (14) 144/2
8 April [1858]

[. . .] Also a letter from Kelly[31] who says & I hear Cairns* agrees with him that the King [of Naples][32] has not a leg to stand upon — I will ask them to attend the Cabinet tomorrow. I am not sorry if we have the law on our side to recover our fiasco on India[33] by a popular piece on Naples[.]

87

Derby to Malmesbury, MP 9M73/20/4
12 April 1858
St James's Square

On my return from the House this evening, I found your box with the opinions of the Law Officers on the cases of the two engineers.[34] Although they all concur in saying that we are entitled to ask for

[28] Although Malmesbury crossed the 't', there was no 'Walter' in the diplomatic service. It seems likely that he meant Sir Thomas Wathen Waller, Secretary of Legation in Brussels, who was persuaded to retire in September 1858.

[29] The Hon. George Edgcumbe, Secretary of Legation in Hanover; in the service since 1821. On 29 February, Malmesbury had described him as 'poor Edgecombe', who was 'perfectly unfit for any European mission'. Malmesbury succeeded in pensioning him off in June 1859.

[30] See above, 21. While at Florence in 1852, Barron had particularly irritated Malmesbury over his handling of the Mather affair. Earlier in this letter, Malmesbury had described him as 'a very vulgar & stupid fellow' who 'bears a long reputation at the F.O.' He was moved to Lisbon.

[31] Sir Fitzroy Edward Kelly (1796–1880), Solicitor-General, 1845–1846 and 1852; Attorney-General, 1858–1859.

[32] Ferdinand II (1810–1859), King of Naples, 1830–May 1859.

[33] In dealing with the post-Mutiny reform of Indian government, it had become clear that the Conservatives' India Bill did not command sufficient support and would have to be withdrawn. A parliamentary compromise was being negotiated with Lord John Russell.

[34] The legal opinions addressed two questions, as the Government had required. Derby's letter refers to the first set of answers, formally communicated on 12 and 13 April, which dealt with the imprisonment of Watt and Park. That of 17 April would deal with the right of capture.

compensation, yet I must confess that the opinion, as a whole, is by no means satisfactory to me. You will have to use great caution in making it the basis of a demand on Naples. What strikes me most forcibly is that throughout the opinion the Law Officers never attempt to raise the question, which after all would be our best ground, that the offence with which they are charged, was not, according to international law, triable in Naples. In my judgement you must refuse to lay this opinion before Parliament; and while you follow the precise language of the opinion with reference to the ground on which you demand reparation, (which will be a sufficient parliamentary ground, as admitted by John Russell, for not producing the opinion itself) you must be careful not to narrow your ground as much as that opinion would do. If I might suggest to you the substance of a despatch,[35] I would begin by recognising the feelings of amity towards this country, and of humanity towards the prisoners, which, on the representations of Mr Lyons* as to the state of health, first of Watt, and next of Park,[36] had induced the King of the Two Sicilies to interpose his authority (if such authority was avowedly interposed) for their liberation, and for waiving further criminal proceedings which H.M. deemed justifiable according to Neapolitan and international law. But, you should say, the recognition of such motives on the part of the King, did not exempt us from the duty of examining, on the part of our countrymen, what plea of justification could be alleged, for their capture, detention, and subsequent trial. As to the result of that trial, I should express myself in terms which implied the impossibility, under any system of justice, of arriving at any conclusion, other than that of entire acquittal. But I should hold it necessary to discuss the merits of the whole case, in order to arrive at any conclusion. I would admit, that according to international law, after all that had occurred, the Neapolitan frigates were justified in boarding, and overhauling a vessel, which, under whatever circumstances, had notoriously been engaged in a piratical attack on Neapolitian territory; and although the gravest doubts might be raised, whether it was competent to the Neapolitan vessels to do more than ascertain the nationality of the vessel, and then to hand over the crew & passengers to be dealt with according to the law, and before the tribunals, of the country to which she belonged, yet that we should not, under the very peculiar circumstances of the case, have raised any objection on the score of a violation of the strictest principles of international law, in taking the vessel and her crew to

[35]Malmesbury clearly used this letter as the template for the despatch he sent to Naples. See Malmesbury to Lyons, 15 April 1858, covering Malmesbury to Carafa, 15 April 1858, TNA, FO 70/297.

[36]See above, **84**, entry for 9 March.

Naples, more especially as by the written testimony of the captain, it was his intention, had he not met the frigates, to have proceeded to Naples, with the consent of his crew. But, after waiving every point on which the slightest doubt can be raised, and admitting them all in favour of the Neapolitan Government – not contesting that is, for the sake of argument, the validity of the capture, however doubtful; not insisting on the utter illegality of <u>any</u> judicial proceedings in the courts of Naples, we are compelled to urge upon the Neapolitan Government the claims of our countrymen for compensation on the following grounds. <u>Then</u> I would set forth the view taken by the Law Officers; and in this way, while you avoid committing yourself to going all lengths with the Sardinian Government in demanding the restitution of the Cagliari, with which, properly speaking, we have nothing to do, and which our Law Advisers, as well as those of the late Government[,] consider at least a doubtful claim, you do not abandon a position which may be a matter of European interest, and by not insisting on what is in the least degree doubtful, strengthen your case for that which can hardly be disputed. Mental malady in one case, and broken health in the other, arising indisputably from long confinement on charges which could not be supported on even prima facie evidence, form a ground of claim for compensation which hardly could be, and which in the state of our relations with Naples hardly will be, resisted. I would not, in my despatch, intimate any amount of compensation; but I would say to Lyons (privately) that £1000 for each of the prisoners would be accepted as a reasonable and very moderate reparation. I think I would authorise him to intimate that the return of the Sardinian vessel, as an act of courtesy, waiving the question of the legality of the seizure, would be agreeable to H.M.'s Government, who would use their endeavours to have such a restitution accepted in the same spirit by the Sardinian Government, without, of course, abandoning <u>their</u> opinion as to the rights of the case.

The sooner we can get France to join us, on any plausible pretext, in renewing diplomatic relations with Naples, the better.[37] The truth is, that, in theory, our ground of rupture was absolutely indefensible; and, in practice, we never should have had these difficulties to contend with, had we had a resident minister at Naples.

[37] Palmerston's government had broken off relations with the Kingdom of the Two Sicilies in 1856.

88

Malmesbury's unpublished diary, MP 9M73/79

14 April 1858

Cabinet. Read my despatch[38] to Carafa[39] asking for compensation for Watt and Park —

89

Malmesbury to Disraeli, Dep. Hughenden, 99/2, fo. 5
15 April [1858]

Fitzgerald* is very much hurt at yr not letting him answer any questions & he says Graham[40] & others have chaffed him about it — If you take the Cagliari you can safely give him the others —

90

Malmesbury to Derby, DP 920 DER (14) 144/2
17 April [1858]

Here is an important letter[41] w^h ought I suppose to be read to the Cabinet or else it will be impossible to make them understand the position — With the great majority or the aggregate of legal opinions in favour of the captain of the Cagliari & the opinion at the same time given that her condemnation was illegal we cd easily join France in urging the Neapolitans to surrender the ship & the Sardinians to accept it as enough. The Emperor w^d then get out of his mess —

[P.S.] Pray keep the letter for the Cabinet.

---

[38] See above, **87**.

[39] The Neapolitan foreign minister.

[40] Sir James Robert George Graham (1792–1861), second baronet, prominent Peelite Conservative and former Whig; First Lord of the Admiralty in Earl Grey's Whig administration, 1830–1834, and in the Aberdeen coalition, 1852–1855; Conservative Home Secretary under Peel, 1841–1846.

[41] The second set of legal opinions, dealing with the capture of the *Cagliari*, was formally communicated on 17 April, and declared the vessel's confiscation illegal. See also above, **87**.

91

Derby to Malmesbury, MP 9M73/20/5
'Monday' [?19 April 1858][42]
Downing Street

We may, and I think should, support Sardinia, at all events by the expression of our strong opinion, so far as the restoration of the vessel,[43] illegally confiscated – but I doubt whether France will join us. I wish she may.

92

Derby to Malmesbury, MP 9M73/450/2
[24 April 1858][44]
St James's Square

I have just received from Cowley Walewski's letter to you, of which I heard from you a couple of hours ago.[45] It is overbearing in its tone; but being a strictly private letter, is less offensive than I had apprehended from your letter — In any event, it can not be made the basis of any public discussion: and, I hope, it may rather be considered as an attempt at bullying, on Walewski's part, than as the interpretation of the real intentions of the Emperor. Still I do not like it – It coincides, too nearly to be pleasant, with the account sent us by Chelsea[46] of Espinasse's[47] most unguarded language; and we must not allow ourselves to be deceived by Cowley's (possibly misplaced) confidence. The publication of Walewski's letter (or allowing its contents to be made known) would neutralise any and every other policy in this country; and though the language of France with respect to Sardinia (and the conduct of Sardinia, which I now attribute to French

---

[42]This is a difficult letter to date, but, given that it must have been written after the law officers' reports of 17 April (see above, **90**) and that it deals with the matters raised in letter **90**, this date seems more likely than any other. It could conceivably have been written on any of the Mondays between 17 April and 19 May (it seems unlikely to have been written after letter **98**), thus 19 or 26 April, or 3, 10, or 17 May.

[43]The question of compensation to Sardinia was not considered a matter for Britain to address.

[44]Date taken from Derby's out-book, DP 920 DER (14) 184/1.

[45]On 23 April, Malmesbury sent to Derby via Cowley a 'most insolent letter' from Walewski. Malmesbury's account of it to Derby has not been found. See Cowley MSS, TNA, FO 519/196, fo. 375.

[46]Henry Charles Cadogan, Viscount Chelsea, later fourth Earl of Cadogan (1812–1873), Secretary at the British Embassy in Paris.

[47]General Esprit Charles Marie Espinasse (1815–1859), French Minister of the Interior, 1858; killed at the battle of Magenta, 1859.

influence) is very suspicious, I cannot believe they would choose to break with us on such a ground. If they take up the Sardinian case with a view to embarrass us, they deprive themselves of all the advantage which they would have from the refugee question with the absolutist powers; and on the other hand Sardinian interests in the popular sense will be greatly injured by being connected with an insolent demand for an 'overt act' in support of the pretensions of France on the refugee question. The position is a critical one, but I do not think hopeless. I am glad that we have a Cabinet tomorrow, and that Cowley will be able to attend.

Meantime I send you not a pleasant letter from H.M. who objects to Bath[48] for the complimentary mission to Lisbon[49] – and on no ground alleged. I think we must make a stand on this – of the list she sends, I hardly know one who would accept unless it were old Westmoreland [sic] – and we cannot afford (nor can She) to give Bath such a slap in the face[.][50]

93

Malmesbury to Derby, DP 920 DER (14) 144/2
27 April [1858]

Ought not Lord Lyons[51] have secret orders to go to Tangiers if the French made a descent upon Morocco either by land or sea[?][52]

If this is likely to happen we ought to send an additional reg[imen]^{t}. to Gibraltar to send over to Tangier – with some artillery — Lord Clarendon told me that Louis Nap[oleon]. had offered to let us have Egypt if we w^{d} let him have Morocco,[53] but it is evident that if we agreed he would keep the gates at Tangier.

---

[48]John Alexander Thynne, fourth Marquess of Bath (1831–1896), a Conservative-supporting Anglo-Catholic.

[49]The special mission was in honour of the forthcoming wedding of King Pedro V and Princess Stephanie of Hohenzollern. Bath was due to take the Order of the Garter for the new queen.

[50]Derby got his way and Bath went to Lisbon.

[51]Vice-Admiral Edmund Lyons, Baron Lyons of Christchurch (1790–1858), temporarily promoted to Admiral while Commander-in-Chief of the Mediterranean fleet, which post he had taken up in 1857.

[52]British trade and strategic interests in north-west Africa were potentially affected by the deteriorating situation in Morocco, where resistance by the indigenous population was threatening Spanish fortresses. Britain feared that either Spain or France would intervene, and that British commerce would suffer in consequence. Spain finally went to war with Morocco in October 1859.

[53]The bargain finally agreed in the Entente of 1904.

94

Malmesbury to Derby, DP 920 DER (14) 144/2
23 April [1858][54]

The inclosures especially that from Hudson are important.[55] You
will get in an hour my despatch to Hudson the pith of w^h has been
telegraphed to him already, & w^h is the substance of a statement
I intend (with yr approval) to make tonight[56] in reply to Airlie's[57]
questions – a similar one to be made in the Commons — When you
have read the <u>despatch</u> pray send it back to <u>me</u> that Disraeli may read
it before it goes to Aldershot where the Queen is at present —
    I have a pleasant day before me – Pelissier[,]* Cowley[,] Bernstorff
& Azzeglio!*

95

Malmesbury's unpublished diary, MP 9M73/79

29 April 1858

[…] I make a speech on Cagliari – whole house concurs – many
mistakes in H[ouse] of Commons —

96

Malmesbury's unpublished diary, MP 9M73/79

2 May 1858

[…] Cancelled the despatch I had written to Cowley — Cabinet
alarmed at Emperor's conversation with him[58] — […]

---

[54]This letter is filed with letters from 1859, but the only relevant question of Airlie's was
in 1858, and concerned the *Cagliari*.
    [55]Not found.
    [56]Notice of Airlie's question was given on 23 April, when – as Malmesbury mentioned –
the Queen was indeed at Aldershot, but discussion was postponed until 29 April. See *Parl.
Deb.*, CXLIX, cols 1930–1935. Malmesbury referred to his rebuttal of Airlie's points in his
diary. See below, **95**.
    [57]David Graham Drummond Ogilvy (1826–1881), fifth Earl of Airlie (tenth if earlier
attainder disregarded); Scottish representative peer, 1850–1881.
    [58]Cowley had written to Malmesbury on 29 April, recounting a conversation with
Napoleon, in which he had seemed 'very much out of spirits about the alliance' and suggested
that 'something shd. be done' to strengthen Anglo-French relations. MP 9M73/6/49.

97

Malmesbury to Derby, DP 920 DER (14) 144/2
19 May [1858]

I am much obliged to you for having charmed L^d. S[tratford].[59] who
has actually written me a civil letter in consequence.[60] This looks as if
he thought your Gov^t w^d stand —

Pray send me the phrase you wish me to employ to the King of
Naples as regards our renouncing a cause of immediate reprisal, &
adopting the line of arbitration,[61] as you sketched it in our conversation
of yesterday. The <u>wording</u> is important & should be severe.

98

Derby to Malmesbury, MP 9M73/20/6
20 May 1858
Downing Street

I have had such a mass of work thrown upon me all at once this
morning, that I have hardly been able till now to look at the question
in your letter of yesterday.

The language which I think you should use would be that the
case appears so clear that we should be fully justified, as reparation
is refused us, in taking matters into our own hands, and enforcing
compliance with our just demands; but that desirous of giving to
Europe a practical proof of moderation, and of our adherence to
the principle recorded at our insistence in the Protocol of the Paris
conference,[62] we are willing to submit the question in dispute to the

Malmesbury had replied to Cowley on 1 May: 'It is for England & France to be seen arm
in arm upon every <u>public</u> question, however small.' He told Cowley to remind Napoleon
how they had worked together in 1852. Cowley MSS, TNA, FO 519/196, fos 385–387.

[59]Malmesbury had just appointed Sir Henry Bulwer as Stratford's replacement at
Constantinople.

[60]Stratford to Malmesbury, 12 May 1858, MP 9M73/15/34.

[61]The difference between 'arbitration' and 'mediation' was material. On 11 May,
Malmesbury had offered Britain's good offices to Sardinia in obtaining restitution of the
Cagliari and her crew. If that attempt were to fail, he offered the Sardinian prime minister,
Cavour, the choice of either mediation or arbitration by a neutral power. By telegram on 16
May (TNA, FO 70/298), Cavour had accepted the offer and indicated that, if the British
attempt failed, he would favour mediation by the Swedes. Malmesbury would have preferred
arbitration to resolve the matter, and his use of the term may not have been accidental. In
letter **98**, however, Derby refers to 'mediation'. See below, **101**.

[62]The 23rd Protocol of the Treaty of Paris, 14 April 1856, stipulated that states in dispute
with one another should resort to the mediation of another power.

mediations of a friendly Power; and we take this course the more readily, because the disproportion between the relative means of the two states is such as to preclude the possibility of any misconstruction as to our motives. We must make it a condition that the question of the Cagliari, in which we support the claims of Sardinia[,] shall be submitted to the same mediator, with the consent, of course, of Sardinia.[63]

99

Derby to Malmesbury, MP 9M73/20/7
20 May 1858

The accompanying letters[64] from L^d. Lyons are important and unpleasant, not to say alarming. I think you should send them to the War Office – and extracts at least from that of the 15th. to Cowley. Matters are very serious if a reinforced fleet is coming from Toulon to Cherbourgh – Should these letters be sent to H.M.? They will create great excitement, and bring on us heavy demands for increased expenditure.

100

Malmesbury to Derby, DP 920 DER (14) 144/2
24 May [1858]
Heron Court

I send you a disagreable [sic] letter from Cowley – but what he says of the Emperor[']s views of this country I look upon as much tainted by the disgust he feels at Pam's fiasco[65] on Friday night.— He (Cowley) is a most honest & able servant but has his political bias w^h is ag[ain]st us. —

The Montenegro part of Cowley's letter is settled since by telegraph & the limitation will take place without touching on Turkish

---

[63]Malmesbury followed Derby's instructions exactly, and phrases from this letter may be seen in his despatch of 25 May 1858, sent via Lyons to Carafa. TNA, FO 70/298, no. 2.

[64]Not found.

[65]The Opposition had introduced motions of censure in both houses of Parliament after Lord Ellenborough, the President of the Board of Control, had criticized a declaration by Viscount Canning, the Governor-General of India. Opposition unity, however, had collapsed and, on 21 May, the Commons motion had been publicly withdrawn, at Palmerston's request.

seigneurial rights.[66] We have succeeded in preventing the French &
Russians from making Montenegro independent, & Brunnow is very
sulky with me. — [...]

101

Derby to Malmesbury, MP 9M73/22/60
24 May 1858

Bernstorff has been with me, in your absence, and read to me,
but could not leave with me, a telegraphic dispatch from Berlin to
say that Naples would accept arbitration, providing it was that of a
great power, but not mediation. I told him I was sorry to hear it
– for that we were willing to accept mediation in the sense of the
Protocol of Paris,[67] but not arbitration on the part of any power. He
seemed surprised, and said that in conversation you had told him we
were ready to accept 'médiation ou arbitrage' and that he had so
written to his Government. I told him he must have mistaken you,
for I had had a conversation with you in the Cabinet on Saturday on
this very subject. I asked him whether he referred to our claim for
compensation, or to that of Sardinia for restitution of the Cagliari –
as I could not undertake to say whether as to the latter Sardinia
might be willing to accept arbitration. He said no, he referred to our
claim for compensation. I then said I was sorry to find there was any
misunderstanding, but that I would write to you immediately. To save
time, I do so by messenger. If Naples refuses to accept mediation, we
shall have to take stronger measures.

102

Malmesbury to Derby, DP 920 DER (14) 144/2
24 May [1858]
Heron Court

---

[66]Montenegro had declared itself independent of the Ottoman Empire and sought to
obtain Bosnian territory from the Turks. The territorial dispute had become increasingly
violent by the summer of 1858, and Malmesbury had proposed that a European commission
should settle the territorial limitations of Montenegro and Bosnia, but without dealing
with the delicate question of Ottoman sovereignty. Any discussion about sovereignty
would have presented France and Russia, which had threatened to proclaim Montenegrin
independence, with opportunities to undermine Turkey.
[67]See above, **98**.

I have just got yr note about Naples. There is no mistake & we must stick first to mediation — Bernstorff has no authority whatever to act in the matter — The longer we drag out the question the better – It ought not to be settled till Parl^t. gives way to grouse – & I hope to keep it open till then. — [...]

103

Malmesbury to Derby, DP 920 DER (14) 144/2
25 May 1858
Heron Court

I wrote you a hasty note last night [...]
What I told Bernstorff was that I had given Sardinia (with whom we were bound to a certain degree,) the choice of mediation or arbitration – & Bernstorff himself has nothing to do with the business unless he comes from the King of Naples — I prefer acting at once thro' Lyons — Sardinia has chosen mediation & to that we must now adhere — My draft is written offering Naples to take Sweden for mediator but is waiting for the legal answer to the 'argumentative reply' w^h must be embodied in it. —

The next step will be the reply of Naples whether she accepts a mediator, & what mediator – It won't do to have one of the Congress Powers, as there is controversy enough among them already. — If Naples refuses mediation or compensation we must take reprisals — If she accepts the next step will be to lay down the terms of mediation — Then comes the mediation itself & it will be strange if the Cagliari affair does not last till August.[68] — [...]

104

Malmesbury to Derby, DP 920 DER (14) 144/2
26 May [1858]

I hope you will not think this despatch[69] to Carafa too rough – It is written for the H[ouse] of Commons — The three lawyers go on plaguing me about mediation being unpopular, but I am sure it is the right line & that I have kept up an unbroken link between the injury,

---

[68] In fact, it was resolved somewhat earlier. See below, **104**.

[69] The despatch to Naples was sent on 3 June, claiming a £3,000 indemnity for the treatment of Watt and Park, and proposing mediation. On 8 June, the Neapolitans backed down, surrendering the *Cagliari* and her crew, and paying the compensation.

the demand, the refusal, the reference to mediation, & the ultima ratio.—[70]

105

Derby to Malmesbury, MP 9M73/20/8
15 June 1858
St James's Square

I quite approve of your proposed answer to Stratford.[71] It would never do to have him interfering with Bulwer in political matters. If he goes, and goes in good humour, he may be useful to us. [. . .]

106

Derby to Malmesbury, MP 9M73/450/5
[?30 July 1858][72]

I see Pakington* is gone down to Osborne, so the Queen will probably give him her own orders as to her event.[73] Old Sir C. Napier[74] called on me yesterday in a great state of mind as to our ships, none of which, he said, except the Royal Albert, were fit to put to sea; and our lubberly crews would only get laughed at by the French, whose ships & crews are in admirable order. If he is in any measure right, the smaller the event, the better.

---

[70] 'the final reckoning'.

[71] At the suggestion of the Queen, Lord Stratford was to be allowed to return to Constantinople on a complimentary mission, formally to take his leave of the Sultan. Derby and Malmesbury were careful to limit Stratford's remit to encouraging reform. Malmesbury wrote to Stratford on 15 June stressing the importance of not interfering with Bulwer's work. Stratford Canning MSS, TNA, FO 352/49(1), fos 25–26. Derby and Malmesbury remained unmoved by a series of letters from Stratford hinting that he would like to do more. See below, **115, 119, 120, 121, 122, 123**.

[72] Pencil note: 'with 14–7–58'. The Court Circular in *The Times* on 31 July recorded a visit by Pakington to the Queen at Osborne on 30 July. He returned the following day.

[73] The 'event' was presumably the Queen's forthcoming visit to meet with Napoleon at Cherbourg.

[74] Sir Charles Napier (1786–1860), retired vice-admiral, commander of the Baltic fleet in the Crimean War and of the Spanish constitutionalist fleet, 1833–1834; MP for Southwark, with radical views, from November 1855 until his death; campaigned on naval issues. He was a popular hero.

107

Malmesbury to Derby, DP 920 DER (14) 144/2
3 August 1858

I think we must try to get out of Sir B[aldwin]. Walker[75] whether any other work could safely be suspended if we appropriate 2 or 300 000 £ to converting sailing ships into screws until Par[liamen]^t. meets again. I cannot help fearing that the Emperor remembers the humiliation of <u>this</u> past <u>spring</u> when he was <u>not ready</u> to go to war, & that he is determined never to be so placed again as regards England.

Another attempt at assassination or rebellion emanating from our refugees w^d certainly try his peaceful resolve very hard, & this may happen any day. —

It appears to me that you should insist on your Naval Lord having <u>all the year round</u> a <u>complete</u> squadron of <u>6 sail of the line</u> with frigates &c in proportion in or near the Channel, & that they shd be considered as much a matter of course & necessity as are the Guards in London & Windsor. — This w^d be a nucleus of well trained ships w^h would prevent a surprise & which could be increased at need – We have now nothing, & our money is spent without producing what one may call our ordinary means of self defence — [. . .]

On 4 August 1858, Malmesbury accompanied the Queen and Prince Albert on their visit to Napoleon III at Cherbourg. He then travelled with them to Prussia. For the remainder of August, Derby took day-to-day charge of the Foreign Office.

108

Malmesbury to Derby, DP 920 DER (14) 144/2
13 August [1858]

I send you a letter from a man who has friends in the French Admiralty & we have generally found his information correct – Pray send it to Pakington and Disraeli[.]

[75] Sir Baldwin Wake Walker (1802–1876), rear-admiral; Surveyor of the Navy, 1848–1860.

109

Derby to Edmund Hammond,* MP 9M73/20/11
13 August 1858
Chevening

I forward an unsealed letter to Lord Cowley, which I will thank you to send on, having first sent a copy of it, and of the enclosure, to Lord Malmesbury.[76] I think his attention ought to be called to a matter, which may have no peculiar meaning, but which, together with many minor symptoms, exhibits a somewhat urgent anxiety on the part of the French Government to be in a state of more immediate readiness for military operations than is consistent with an entire determination to maintain friendly relations generally.

110

Malmesbury to Derby, DP 920 DER (14) 144/2
15 August 1858
Potsdam

[…] I find the Prince of Prussia*[77] reasonable on the Danish question.[78] — I have put in a good word for Bernstorff & altho' the Princess of Prussia[79] hates him I do not think he will be removed.[80] — I believe Manteuffel* will go as soon as the King dies & a moderate liberal gov[ernmen]t succeed to his —[81]

[76] This letter encloses two others: a copy of one from Derby to Cowley of the same date (fo. 12), drawing the latter's attention to the large French imports of saltpetre and sulphur from Britain, details of which had been supplied in a memorandum by the Treasury (copy also included by Derby, fo. 14); and a copy of one from General Peel of 12 August (fo. 13), describing the memorandum.

[77] Prince Wilhelm, shortly to become Prince Regent of Prussia. In October 1857, he had taken over royal duties on a 'temporary' basis, because his brother's physical and mental state had deteriorated.

[78] Malmesbury was attempting to defuse the growing tension between Denmark and the German Diet over the Schleswig-Holstein question. See below, **127**.

[79] Augusta, Princess of Sachsen-Weimar-Eisenbach (1811–1890); married the future Wilhelm I, 1829; Queen of Prussia, 1861–1871; Empress of Germany, 1871–1888.

[80] Malmesbury was right.

[81] In fact, Manteuffel was dismissed rather earlier; Wilhelm formally became regent in October 1858, and on 5 November appointed a liberal conservative government under Prince Karl Anton von Hohenzollern-Sigmaringen.

111

Derby to Malmesbury, MP 9M73/20/15
16 August 1858
Osterley Park

[. . .] The large purchase of timber which your correspondent notices coincides rather ominously with the intelligence I sent you (and Cowley) as to orders for saltpetre and sulphur; and though I do not believe our trusty ally has any hostile feelings or intentions at this moment, it is clear that he means to place himself in a position to make his power be felt, whenever it suits him that we should feel it. One of the papers had rather a good simile for him the other day when it said that he kept the gates of the Temple of Janus[82] neither open nor shut, but creaking day & night on rusty hinges, so that nobody could get a wink of sleep. Nevertheless, we were wonderfully amiable and cordial at Pelissier's dinner yesterday. He was in great force, and told all his after-dinner stories, with which you are familiar. He had the Turk[83] on his right at dinner, and on his left the Duke of Wellington[84] – not Brunnow – who sat next but one to Musurus,* with De La Warr[85] for a buffer. I was directly opposite to him, with Van de Weyer on one side and De Cetto on the other. The latter had taken a panic that the Conference at Paris had been occupying itself lately with the succession to the Throne of Greece. I thought I might venture to assure him such was not the case, and that Cowley, I knew, had strict orders as to the subjects which he was to entertain. [. . .] Neither Apponyi* nor Bernstorff present, but represented by their Chargés d'Affaires. The Turk was prodigal of his assurances of reparation for Djiddah,[86] and of the innocence of the Turks as to any of the late contests with the Montenegrins.[87] He expressed himself well satisfied with the result of the conferences,[88] and grateful for the assistance which Turkey had received from Cowley. [. . .]

---

[82] The Temple of Janus in the Forum in Rome. According to Plutarch's *Life of King Numa*, XX.1, the doors were closed in times of peace and open when Rome was at war.

[83] Constantine Musurus.

[84] Arthur Richard Wellesley, second Duke of Wellington (1807–1884), son of the victor of Waterloo.

[85] George John Sackville-West, fifth Earl De La Warr (1791–1869), Lord Chamberlain, 1858–1859. He had first held the post under Peel, 1841–1846.

[86] An anti-Western riot at Jeddah on the night of 15–16 June had left the British and French consuls dead.

[87] See above, **100**.

[88] Since May, a European conference at Paris had been considering the future status of the Ottoman Danubian Principalities of Moldavia and Wallachia, disputes over which had helped precipitate the Crimean War. The conference had concluded on 16 August.

112

Derby to Malmesbury, MP 9M73/20/22
19 August 1858
Downing Street

I send you a letter from Cowley, which you would have had a day earlier if I had come up to Town yesterday. I add one from him to me, with Claremont's explanation of the large French order for saltpetre. It seems at least plausible, and it is corroborated by the large estimate for blasting powder. But what a store of powder they have in hand! Enough for six Crimean wars! If they are equally well prepared with other warlike stores, we are sadly behind, especially if we have many such actions as Roebuck's and Lindsay's.[89] [...]

113

Derby to Malmesbury, MP 9M73/20/23
19 August 1858
10 Downing Street

Since I wrote to you an hour ago, Musurus has been with me in a great state of mind in consequence of Capt[ain]. Pullen,[90] in virtue of his first orders, having proceeded to bombard Djidda, before the arrival of the Turkish Troops.[91] It was unlucky that he should have done so, though of course no blame can be attached to him for acting on his orders; but it does not seem that the bombardment produced the desired effect, till the Sultan's orders were received. Musurus wished me to authorise him to write to his Government that

The Principalities, which would remain under Turkish suzerainty, would not be permitted political union (as Romania) sought by the French.

[89]John Arthur Roebuck (1802–1879), the outspoken independent MP for Sheffield, and William Schaw Lindsay (1816–1877), the shipowner and MP for Tynemouth and South Shields, had been among the British visitors to Cherbourg when the Queen was there. On 10 August at Tynemouth they had then delivered speeches lampooning the French navy.

[90]William John Samuel Pullen, Captain of the *Cyclops*, a steam frigate of the East Indies and China station. On 31 July 1858, in the wake of the riots (see above, **111**), he was appointed by Malmesbury as Britain's Commissioner for the Settlement of the Affairs at Jeddah.

[91]Pullen had bombarded Jeddah on 25–26 July as retaliation for the earlier riots (see above, **111**), having been sent on Malmesbury's orders to ensure punishment. He had not received a second telegram, which had directed him to await the arrival of the Turkish general, Ismail Pasha, sent by the Sultan to restore order and punish the leaders of the riots. It emerged that the Admiralty had strengthened Malmesbury's original instructions, precipitating the bombardment.

we regretted what had taken place. I begged him however to write nothing till he heard from you. I admitted to him that after hearing of the massacre the Porte had spontaneously done all it could; and I said it was unfortunate that Captain Pullen had sailed before receiving his second instructions: I need not say that his communication was strictly confidential and unofficial. He went so far as to tell me that he looked on this bombardment, in the face of all that the Porte was doing at the same time, with alarm chiefly on account of the precedent; for that France would be only too apt to profit by the example, and take a similar course whenever one of her agents should choose to fancy himself insulted. I ventured to hint to him that the massacre of a consul and a considerable number of Christians was not an every day [*sic*] proceeding, and to say the least, was an exceptional case – but in truth he has some foundation for his apprehension that bombardment is a weapon to which our friends across the water will be only too ready to have recourse, particularly if they can appeal to a precedent set by us. It would therefore I think be well, as the Turk has really behaved very well in the matter, that you should write something, not in the nature of an apology, but of regret that the second instructions had not reached Capt[ain]. Pullen in time to prevent him acting on his first.

114

Derby to Malmesbury, MP 9M73/20/24
20 August 1858
Osterley Park

[. . .] I return Cowley's letter — Our friend[92] is rather a bold man – and if he does not take care, he is likely, from your account, after the capture of the fort, to find allies willing to assist him in the occupation.[93] [. . .]

[92] The two men regularly used this term for Napoleon III.
[93] It is unclear to what this refers, but it may be to the news of Napoleon's meeting with Cavour at Plombières on 12 July, at which they had first hatched their secret scheme for provoking Austria into a war.

115

Malmesbury to Derby, DP 920 DER (14) 144/2
21 August 1858
Potsdam

I had anticipated your wishes respecting the bombardment of Jeddah by telegraphing to Bulwer – 'That we must support Capt[ain] Pullen but that he might express our regret that he had not waited rather longer or that Ismail Pasha had not made more haste' — Musurus is a comedian[,] has no weight with his Gov^t. & is never instructed till long after his instructions are of any use.—

He has been getting up the steam ag[ain]s^t Stratford's mission[94] but I told him that was not the line he ought to take when the Queen meant to pay the Sultan a comp^l[iment].

116

Malmesbury to Derby, DP 920 DER (14) 144/2
21 August 1858
Potsdam

[...] The Prince (ours I mean)[95] is up to his neck in German intrigue to get rid of this Gov^t.[96] A Nassau princess has been brought here to be looked at for the P. of Wales, but she is a very seedy article & will not do. — I have confined my eloquence with both Manteuffel & the Prince of Prussia to urging them to be one with Austria & the other German states as against the possibility of a war with France & I have held the same language to Koller[97] the Austrian minister — [...] As to France we must be in a better state to meet her in case of need – We are very deficient in materials of war & have not 100 000 muskets in the whole country so that our population is defenceless — The Whigs have ruined our navy by mismanagement & miscalculations – I fear the Commission for manning it is not a good one – My brother,[98] who while he was in Parl[iamen]^t, took a great interest & trouble about the question says it is composed of tartars well known & disliked by the

---

[94] See above, **105**.
[95] The Prince Consort.
[96] Manteuffel's, not Derby's.
[97] August, Freiherr von Koller (1805–1883), Austrian minister in Berlin, 1857–1859.
[98] Sir Edward Alfred John Harris (1808–1888), one of Malmesbury's younger brothers, formerly a captain in the Royal Navy, later an admiral; MP for Christchurch, 1844–1852. From 1852 he held a series of diplomatic posts, ending up as British minister in the Netherlands, from where he retired in 1877.

sailors as such, & who know nothing & care less for the altered feelings & circumstances of modern 'Jacks' who like all of us have progressed, perhaps without being better than our predecessors – that there ought to be younger officers on the Commission who have been employed in the manning of ships lately — This is the most important subject of all. [. . .]

117

Derby to Malmesbury, MP 9M73/20/26
23 August 1858
St James's Square

Karolyi[99] has just been with me to communicate a despatch from his Government to the effect that by the confession of the Montenegrins themselves they were the aggressors in the last affair of Kolashin,[100] and it is added that they have committed all sorts of atrocities, and carried off above 100 women. The Porte intends to demand reparation, and Austria is anxious to support the demand, and wishes us to do the same, and to induce France! to do so likewise. I told him that I had not seen our reports of this last affair, and that I could therefore express no opinion; but that the papers were probably gone to you, and that I was on the point of writing to you, and would report the communication he had made to me. We owe the Turk a good turn for our bombardment; but whether we or any one can persuade the Emperor that the Montenegrins can be in the wrong, or the Porte in the right, is more than I can undertake to say.

Cowley wrote to me on Saturday,[101] very uneasy at the state of feeling in France.[102] Roebuck & Lindsay have done no end of mischief.[103]

---

[99] Count Alajos Károlyi von Nagy-Károly (1825–1889), Austrian Secretary of Legation in London; Austro-Hungarian ambassador in London, 1878–1888.

[100] Initially there had been confusion as to whether the Turks or the Montenegrins were the perpetrators of a massacre in the Bosnian town of Kolašin.

[101] 20 August.

[102] Malmesbury replied to Cowley from Potsdam on 25 August, admitting that, although he 'never doubted' Napoleon's 'wish to keep well with us', he felt 'those presentiments w^h people are said to have before a storm'. He 'was not satisfied' with the conversation he and the emperor had had at Cherbourg. Cowley MSS, TNA, FO 519/196, fos 532–533.

[103] See above, **112**.

118

Malmesbury to Derby, DP 920 DER (14) 144/2
23 August 1858
Potsdam

I send you a proof of our friend Brunnow's treachery — I have met him as well as I could by writing to Bulwer & Crampton* from here but the latter has I find retarded his departure from London unknown to me for 3 weeks & is not expected in Russia till the 27th when he promised to be there the first week of this month. — The French I believe will not be humbugged by this misrepresentation of Brunnow's. [...]

I had a very satisfactory interview with the Neapolitan minister here (officieusement.) & I expect to receive fair overtures – & practical offers.[104] [...]

119

Malmesbury to Derby, DP 920 DER (14) 144/2
25 August 1858
Potsdam

[...] If Fitzgerald has not sent you some copies of despatches upon Montenegro written by Buol to his chargé d'affaires here, & my replies as described to Bulwer, pray ask for them. — To demand compensation from Montenegro for its raids, is asking for an impossibility, & w[d] only produce an envenomed correspondence.[105] The commiss[ione][rs]. are just going to Constantinople to explain & settle the boundaries[106] but that country must long resemble the old Scottish border. — All European politicians believe that if Napoleon breaks out it will be against the East — L[d] Stratford has been with Fitzgerald to say he would not be Bulwer[']s guest, & that he does not like his mission to be strictly complimentary – I cannot consent to any other arrangement. This was the one he accepted, & if not followed there would be two Kings of Brentford at Constantinople. I think he won't go after all. [...]

---

[104] In October, an overture from Naples would come via Bernstorff. See below, **133**.
[105] See above, **117**.
[106] See above, **100**.

120

Derby to Malmesbury, MP 9M73/20/27
25 August 1858
Downing Street

Lord Stratford has just been with me, and has shown me a letter which he has received from you, and also his answer. You know how touchy he is, and how difficult it is to talk over business with him, particularly of a personal character; and I was more than once tempted to tell him that it was to me a matter of perfect indifference whether he went to Constantinople or not. We have parted however very good friends. He wished to know, in consequence of some expressions in your letter, whether there were any change in the views of the Government, or whether he was to look on his former instructions as still in force in letter and in spirit. I told him I knew of no change – that his mission was of a purely complimentary character; but that before leaving Turkey it was desirable that he should take the opportunity of once more urging on the Sultan his old advice as to the policy towards his Christian subjects, and especially as to the Hatti Humayoun.[107] He talked about his stay in Constantinople, and wished to know if there was any desire to hurry him away – that he proposed to remain about a month, which would be required for the settlement of his affairs; but that he did not contemplate more than one (if one) private conversation with the Sultan, besides his audience of leave, in which latter he would officially (or semi-officially[)] urge on H.M. the views of his Gov^t. I said the only inconvenience attending so long a stay would be the way in which he would be watched by all foreign diplomatists, and the awkwardness of his position vis-à-vis Bulwer, whose guest, by the way, he positively refuses to be – and said he would prefer remaining on board, or going to the Inn! As I understand, he will occupy one of the Embassy houses, on his own account. He assured me however that he fully understood that he was to enter on no political question whatever – to give no opinion on passing events, on appointments, and in no respect interfere with Bulwer, farther than to give him any support in his power. I think I have given you the substance of what he said – the upshot of which was that if on account of the jealousy of other parties he was to be hurried away, he would rather not go at all – and a month is the time he names for his stay. I think you must let him have his way, but the time is rather unfavourable for

---

[107]The Hatt-ı Hümayun of 18 February 1856 was a decree issued by Sultan Abdülmejid I that dealt with the organizational reform of the Ottoman Empire. It proclaimed the equality of all Christian subjects and promised freedom of religion.

urging the claims of the Christians. I have had Musurus with me again, to deliver a despatch which Fitzgerald will have sent you by this messenger. I told him that before receiving it we had instructed Cowley to represent to the French Gov^t. our horror and indignation at the atrocities which had been committed,[108] and to invite them to join with us in reprobating them, and to use their influence with Prince Danilo* for their suppression.

121

Malmesbury to Derby, DP 920 DER (14) 144/2
27 August [1858]
Potsdam

You could not have spoken more to the purpose to Ld Stratford who had before been to Fitzgerald whose letter I inclose — My reply to F. was that I could not alter any thing that had been settled, that I understood him to be satisfied to be Bulwer's guest, Bulwer having written him a very handsome letter on the subject & that it w^d be very offensive to him to alter the arrangements now — It is much better he should not go at all under the present circumstances of the Porte, & if he refuses on the score of a personal quarrel with Bulwer it is his fault — Fitzgerald will send you my answer w^h he was to shew to L^d. S[tratford].
    If you still think he ought to have a separate palace assigned to him I will tell him so. [. . .] I shall not answer Musurus' circular till I know what the French mean to say but I think the Porte right in all but the pecuniary indemnity, & I have told Cowley to speak in that sense — The Prince of Prussia has promised not to act on Oriental questions without coming first to an understanding with us — I believe he is to be trusted w^h Manteuffel is not – & his asking me to write to him instead of Manteuffel shews that he will get rid of him as soon as he is regent —[109]

---

[108] See above, **117**. France was the only power with any influence over Montenegro. The Montenegrin Prince had a French adviser, and French was the language of his court.
    [109] See above, **110**.

122

Derby to Malmesbury, MP 9M73/20/29
30 August 1858
Knowsley

[. . .] Knowing what sort of man Stratford is, I think rather than give him an excuse for throwing up his mission, I should give way upon the question of his separate residence. Indeed I understand from him that he had given orders for some furniture to be placed in one of the palaces attached to the embassy. In his present frame of mind, and with his feelings towards Bulwer, I cannot conceive a more <u>agreeable</u> 'guest' to have for a month! Besides which, he takes his whole family, and I believe some friends, so that on the whole, separate maintenance will be the better plan. But if you think it not desirable that he should go at all, you have only to stand out on this point, and I think after all he will not go. It would however have the appearance of yielding to the jealousy which has been expressed by foreign courts. I am glad you have had an opportunity of seeing and conversing with the Prince of Prussia – I believe him to be thoroughly honest, and I should think he has character enough to be his own master, whenever he gets free from his present embarrassing position. [. . .]

123

Malmesbury to Derby, DP 920 DER (14) 144/2
1 September 1858
London

[. . .] Yesterday I saw L^d. Stratford — He shewed me a letter from Bulwer offering to place either palace at his disposal so I settled with him that he was to go to Pera & he solemnly promised to stay less than a month & to see the Sultan not oftener than twice. — He had lowered his tone very much w^h I attribute to his conversation with you [. . .] I send you a report from our spy of the information possessed by France of our navy – & also a letter from Cowley respecting the Emperor's conversation with Palmerston. [. . .]

124

Derby to Malmesbury, MP 9M73/20/30
2 September 1858
Knowsley

Cowley's report of Palmerston's conversation with the Emperor is more satisfactory than any thing we have heard lately, as to the state of H.M's disposition not only towards this country, but as to Russia, with regard to whose views I hope he is beginning to open his eyes. She has however, aided by the effect produced on his vanity by the flatteries of that demi-savage Danilo, completely made a catspaw of him in the Montenegrin affair: while his jealousy of Austria prejudices his views on Turkish questions. Palmerston's report confirms our view that his great military preparations have primary reference to Italy. I do not quite understand the second paper you have sent me and which I return.¹¹⁰ How much of it is the report to the Emperor, and how much a report on that report, made to you? Our navy looks more formidable on paper than I am afraid it is in reality. [. . .]

125

Malmesbury to Derby, DP 920 DER (14) 144/2
17 September 1858
Achnacarry

[. . .] I have written to the Queen to explain why she [has] not & will not get as many despatches as formerly – 1ˢᵗ Because there is complete tranquillity & no vexatious correspondence with any Power – 2ⁿᵈ Because for the next month almost all the principal ministers abroad & their representations here are absent on their holydays [*sic*], wʰ is also the case with HM. ministers <u>abroad</u> – 3ʳᵈ because I have reduced the messengers of wʰ Clarendon had got a useless army costing above £30 000 a year. [. . .]

126

Malmesbury to Derby, DP 920 DER (14) 144/2
18 September 1858
Achnacarry

[. . .] Palmerston has written me a letter wʰ I send you. [. . .]

[P.S.] In answering Palmerston I have rejected the Emperor[']s assertion that we ever promised to pass his Conspiracy Bill – This was Persigny's lie —

---

¹¹⁰Not found.

127

Malmesbury to Derby, DP 920 DER (14) 144/2
4 October [1858]
Achnacarry

[...] Elliott* [*sic*] at Copenhagen is very uneasy & tho his personal tendencies are German he says the Danes can do no more & deserve to be permitted to negotiate on the basis they offer.[111] He says the violent German party have spread a report that the Queen[']s visit to Prussia has made them safe & that in my conversations with Platen[112] at Hanover & the Prince of Prussia I promised not to interfere at all – They also say the Prince Consort did so – I believe this to be as untrue as the first — My language to all of them was this – that we recognised the jurisdiction of the Diet over the King of Denmark as regards Holstein & Lauenberg but not as regards Shleswig [*sic*] – If the latter point was unfortunately stirred that the Powers who signed the treaties must alone consider & settle any breach or infringement of the treaties to w^h they had been parties – That it was a fixed principle of British policy to maintain the integrity of the Danish monarchy & we shd insist on the succession as arranged by the Convention of 1852 — The Queen will send you my draft to Elliott [*sic*] & I shd not wonder if the Prince tried to alter it but altho' the Holstein question is a German one it may in five minutes become European if German troops enter Holstein, & I think we ought to tell them, what I believe to be just, namely that this last proposal of the Danes ought to be received with respect as a basis of negotiation — [...]

[111]Malmesbury was attempting to defuse the growing tension between Denmark and the German Diet over the 'common constitution' (affecting all Danish territories and Schleswig, Holstein, and Lauenburg in equal measure) that the Danish king had proclaimed in 1855, in breach of the 1852 Treaty of London. In May, the Diet had demanded a declaration of Danish intentions, claiming that the constitution could not legally be in effect in Holstein and Lauenburg. As a result of Malmesbury's pressure, Denmark had offered to suspend the constitution in Holstein and Lauenburg, but Elliot was concerned that the Danish tone was inflammatory. Eventually, the Diet did accept the Danish offer and in November Denmark actually abolished the constitution in so far as it applied to Holstein and Lauenburg. See also above, **2**, **14**, **16**.

[112]Adolf, Graf von Platen-Hallermund (1814–1889), Hanoverian foreign minister, 1855–1866.

128

Derby to Malmesbury, MP 9M73/20/35
6 October 1858
Knowsley

[...] I do not at all like the aspect of affairs between France
and Portugal.[113] The former refuses all reference to arbitration, and
sends two ships of war to enforce her demands. The quarrel is a
very awkward one, and I believe Portugal is in the right. She will
undoubtedly have the sympathies of England with her. There is no
denying the fact, that the transaction was essentially a slaving one,
even beyond the wide limits of free emigration claimed by France;
and the fact of a French Government agent having been on board so
implicates the Government itself, that they are compelled to brazen it
out. [...]

129

Malmesbury to Derby, DP 920 DER (14) 144/2
8 October 1858
Achnacarry

[...] I think that the informalities that took place at the beginning
of the French & Portuguese transaction will get us out of that difficulty
– but I have asked Pakington to send a couple of ships to the Tagus
for the protection of British subjects & to watch proceedings[114] — [...]

[113]Under the Whigs, Britain had encouraged Portugal to crack down on slave-traders, and
in November 1857 Portugal had seized a French ship, the *Charles et Georges*, off the coast of the
Portuguese colony of Mozambique. The labourers found on board declared that they had
been sold and were not 'free', as the French had claimed. On 13 August 1858 the ship had
arrived at Lisbon. France was challenging the legality of the capture, demanding the return
of the ship and an indemnity. Two French ships had arrived at the Tagus on 3 October, and
on 5 October Malmesbury had received a formal request from Portugal for Britain's good
offices in mediation. See also **129, 130, 131, 136, 137**.
[114]See above, **128**. On 6 October, Malmesbury had protested to France about its hostility
to Portugal, and agreed on 9 October to offer British mediation.

130

Derby to Malmesbury, MP 9M73/20/36
11 October 1858
Knowsley

[. . .] I do not like the turn things are taking about the Charles et Georges.[115] France will listen to nothing, and is determined, as you will see by Cowley's last telegram, to have the ship released by fair means or foul, and not in any way to menager the 'susceptibilité' of Portugal.[116] I suppose she will have to give way; but certainly Walewski is not making it very easy for her to do so. [. . .]

131

Derby to Malmesbury, MP 9M73/20/37
16 October 1858

[. . .] I do not at all like the aspect of the Charles et Georges affair.[117] Walewski's tone is so haughty and unaccommodating, as hardly to leave a loop-hole; and a quarrel with Portugal, and on such a subject, will not be favourably looked on here. We shall have plenty of people urging on us our treaty engagements;[118] and I should not wonder to see Palmerston take up this question to make political capital out of, if we can not get some fair settlement. However, we have been in worse difficulties; [. . .]

132

Malmesbury to Derby, DP 920 DER (14) 144/2
17 October 1858
Achnacarry

I have got two private telegrams from Bulwer to say that Stratford has been interfering, & advised the Sultan not to confirm the Montenegro boundary proposed by the C.C.[119] &

---

[115]See above, **128**. On 10 October, Cowley had conveyed the news of an unproductive meeting with Walewski on the subject.

[116]'to spare Portugal', or – more literally – to handle its sensitivities carefully.

[117]See above, **128**. Malmesbury had proposed a compromise on 15 October, but on legal grounds it proved impractical.

[118]Britain and Portugal were longstanding allies.

[119]The commissioners appointed to examine the boundary. See above, **100**.

R.R.[120] & that Ali Pasha[121] who had pledged the Porte to the agreement will resign. Thouvenel thinking it a trick of Bulwer writes to complain of him but I hope the telegraph by this time has set things right.— I have telegraphed to Stratford that the Curacoa[122] cannot be spared any longer & that I hope he will release her as soon as possible — [...]

133

Derby to Malmesbury, MP 9M73/20/38
25 October 1858
Knowsley

I have had a long conversation with Bernstorff today, at his request, on the subject of Naples, on which he says he had also spoken to you. I hope our language has been the same. He laid great stress on the concessions which the King of Naples had made to us in the matter of the Cagliari, and said that you had given him to understand that when that affair was settled, diplomatic relations would be renewed. I corrected him by saying that the language we had held was that while that affair remained unsettled, it was idle to talk about renewed relations; that the settlement of that question removed an additional obstacle, and replaced us where we were. I said we were still willing to consider any proposition which the K[ing]. of Naples might make, analogous to the previous proposal, which Clarendon had rejected, of a convention with the Argentine Republic. That convention had fallen to the ground, but some overt act upon the part of the King was necessary. I admitted to him that had I been in office, I should not have advised the demonstration which was made, nor the recall of the ministers; but it was a very different case sending them back again without having obtained any satisfaction on the subject on which we & France had made a joint demand. He then said we were not on the same line with France; that France required nothing but 'des phrases' – a mere explanation of the terms in which the demands of France, conjoinably with us, were answered – but without any intimation of any concession to her and our wishes. I said I did not know how that might be, though I thought he overrated the facility with which France would receive mere explanations of the tone of a reply; but that on the part of England I thought there would be great difficulty in renewing

---

[120] The great powers' representatives at Constantinople.
[121] The Turkish Grand Vizier.
[122] The naval frigate sent for Stratford's use.

friendly relations, as long as no step whatever was taken by Naples towards improving the condition of the political prisoners. He then read me letters from Carafa, and from the Prussian minister at Naples to Manteuffel, the substance of which was that the King of Naples was willing to take the initiative in sending back a minister, if assured that he would be well received, he could enter on no discussion as to the fate of the political prisoners; and that any attempt to introduce the subject would only eloigner[123] the chances of an accommodation. That he considered all offers on his part to have been set aside by Clarendon's rejection; and that although he had been ready to send them to the Argentine Republic, where the government would make due provision for their health, their morals, and their religion, he would not be justified in sending them to the United States, where they would have no one to attend to them, and where perhaps they would die of hunger! It was difficult to listen to this with a grave face – so I merely suggested that the prisoners themselves might be offered the choice of risking these formidable dangers, or remaining where they were! I then said that on the statement he made, it seemed to me that it would be worse than useless to continue the negotiation; that to us it was very immaterial whether we had a minister at Naples and they one here, or not; but that we should be very happy to renew our relations whenever the King would give us a reasonable ground for doing so, that we should of course cease to press for any modification of his system of government, or of his treatment of his own subjects; but that the most likely mode of reconciling the public mind in England to a renewal of diplomatic intercourse would be some signal act of grace and mercy taken spontaneously by himself – after which an explanation of any thing which might have been offensive in his language would have every chance of being favourably received by France and ourselves. In reply to an observation of Bernstorff's that the public mind was so prejudiced by exaggerated statements (and he referred particularly to Gladstone)* that any such act as I spoke of would have no effect, I said that I thought he was mistaken; that the people of England certainly thought the Government of Naples a detestable one; but that the best mode of mitigating such feelings would be to take some overt act which should place it in a more favourable light. At present I could only recommend that the subject should be dropped, as in the King's present temper I did not think further discussion could serve any useful purpose. I believe this is a very correct account of our conversation, which I hope was in accordance with your views.

[123]'postpone' or 'remove'.

134

Malmesbury to Derby, DP 920 DER (14) 144/2
26 October [1858]
Foreign Office

If I had been y^r parrot I cd not have spoken to & answered Bernstorff about Naples with verbatim identity more completely the same as yr conversation with him — I have sent the Queen some very interesting reports from 'our friend'[124] containing Ad[mira]^l La Graviere's plan for invasion drawn up in 1857![125] Among them is a statement that Louis Napoleon is unwilling to renew with Naples & I certainly have found no help from him to do so, & illwill in the Cagliari case. His game is to give hopes to the Italian liberals — [. . .]

135

Derby to Malmesbury, MP 9M73/20/39
27 October 1858
Knowsley

I am very glad to find that we have been so exactly on the same tack with Bernstorff in re Naples. He is evidently very sick of his vicarious duties;[126] and is the more anxious for a renewal of diplomatic relations which would have the effect of relieving him from them. I shall be glad to see the papers from 'our friend'[127] which you have sent to the Queen as soon as H.M. returns them. [. . .] I must say I am not quite easy about your friend the Emperor's preparations; and the plan of an invasion, drawn up in 1857, has an ugly look about it, when coupled with the particular description of armaments which he is strengthening. We must, at all hazards, keep up our naval strength. I only hope we may be able to effect such reductions in parts of the naval expenditure, where I am sure there is much waste, as may keep the estimates within reasonable compass.

---

[124] Probably a British agent.
[125] See *Memoirs*, II, p. 141, in which he included a letter to Cowley of the same date.
[126] See above, **84**.
[127] See n. 124, above.

136

Malmesbury to Derby, DP 920 DER (14) 144/2
27 October 1858
London

This Portuguese business[128] cannot I think be passed over in silence & I propose writing a despatch to Cowley expressing the regret of HMG that the French sh^d not have adopted the principle of the Paris Protocol[129] shewing the disquietude such summary proceedings occasion in Europe & the risk of the most fatal consequences[130] — If France had fired a shot at Lisbon we must have gone to war with her or broken our treaties with Portugal – & France ought to know this from our Gov^t. She was quite in the wrong as to the acts of her vessel the Charles & Georges, but Portugal when she found a French delegate on board ought not to have seized her but made a diplomatic complaint to the F[rench].G[overnment]. w^h by the presence of that official became the responsible party — It is requisite distinctly to know what France expects in regard to these emigration ships.

The moral of all this is that with such a neighbour & that neighbour so reckless, if we are to hold our own we must have more ships at our command in the Channel —

Every body [*sic*] is for strengthening our Navy & I am sure you may do what you like in that way — Had the casualty taken place at Lisbon to w^h I have alluded, France would have been mistress of the Channel at once.

137

Derby to Malmesbury, MP 9M73/20/41
28 October 1858
Knowsley

I concur with you that it will hardly be possible to avoid writing something to Cowley for communication to Walewski on the subject of the Charles et Georges[131] –but the despatch will require the most careful consideration, and I should like to see your proposed draft before you send it. I apprehend that our parliamentary line of defence for having allowed Portugal to be coerced must be that she made no

---

[128]See above, **128**. The *Charles et Georges* had been surrendered to France on 25 October.
[129]See above, **98**.
[130]Malmesbury duly sent such a despatch on 30 October. See below, **137**.
[131]See above, **128**, **136**.

application to us for protection – that had she done so, it would have been our duty to have examined into [*sic*] the merits of the case, and, if she proved to be in the right, to have afforded her our aid. But as she did not, we were exempted from the necessity of examining into the case, or pronouncing any opinion as between the conflicting statements. In writing therefore to Cowley I think you had better abstain from any discussion of the case, but only instruct him to point out to Walewski the serious complications which might result from such hasty and violent measures as France had resorted to, not to mention the perpetual risks attending the so-called free! emigration. It would also be better, I think, only to instruct Cowley to make verbal representations, and not to read, still less give a copy of your despatch.[132] In the Emperor's present temper we cannot answer for the character of his reply to a written communication, and it might be such as to lead to serious consequences. Much as I desire to maintain the French alliance, in which I am sure you agree with me, I confess, I am less sanguine about it than I was; and I am entirely of your opinion that we ought to lose no time in placing our navy on such a footing that a rupture, at all times possible, should not find us as ill prepared as I am afraid we are at this moment. For this reason we ought for the present to be doubly cautious to give no excuse for a <u>premature</u> quarrel.

138

Malmesbury to Derby, DP 920 DER (14) 144/2
17 December 1858
Wimpole[133]

[...] Disraeli[']s complaint as to the distribution of the patronage by some of our colleagues is just & well founded.[134]

[...] I can conscientiously say I have not <u>yet</u> named an attaché[,] a consul or a clerk whose belongings & godfathers are not of the right colour. In the upper grades of the diplomatic service I had no choice – they are <u>all</u> 'not of us.' — [...]

[132]Malmesbury clearly followed Derby's instructions in writing the despatch. See Malmesbury to Cowley, no. 60, 30 October 1858, TNA, FO 146/805.

[133]Wimpole Hall, the Cambridgeshire home of the Earl of Hardwicke, Malmesbury's Cabinet colleague.

[134]Disraeli was concerned about the way in which his colleagues were dispensing patronage. See, e.g., Disraeli to Pakington, 19 December 1858, *BDL*, VII, no. 3249, in which he noted 'that there is a great error, on the part of some of my Colleagues, on the subject of Patronage. They are too apt to deem the preferment at their disposal to be merely a personal privilege. In my opinion, it partakes of a corporate character.'

139

Malmesbury to Derby, DP 920 DER (14) 144/2
28 December 1858
Heron Court

I am afraid we shall have a great deal of trouble with the Principalities[135] — I have telegraphed to our different ministers to say that if Servia shows a determined wish to have Prince Milosh[136] instead [of] Prince Alexander[137] we should probably advise the Porte to put a good face on the matter & take him — If the Austrians meddle they will make a civil war. The Porte has proposed to put off the elections in Moldavia & Wallachia on the score of illegality for 22 days but it has no right by the constitution to do so — I think the interpretations of the treaty[138] required on several points had much better be given by a meeting of the PP[139] at Paris who made it, than second hand at Constantinople – The conference w^d have more prestige with the Principalities than the RR[140] in Turkey – but Buol & the Porte are against it & if the latter is so I do not believe we c^d call it legally.

Apponyi is here & very anxious about Italy – I told him that Hubner[141] at Paris was so disliked that he was useless to his Gov^t. & Apponyi agreed & said every body [sic] wished a change but Buol's temper will not let him do it.

P.S.

Apponyi asked me what we should do if France[,] Russia & Sardinia made war on Austria — I said that in a purely Italian war the object of wh was carried out by Italians he must never look for help from an English Govt although we should not assist the Italians to break the Treaties of 1815. but [sic] that our attitude & subsequent action in the event of a war of aggression upon Austria by France & Russia must depend upon the circumstances of the case & whether provocation had been given to justify it – That public opinion in England w^d be

---

[135] With regard to the elections in the Danubian Principalities, Moldavia and Wallachia, as Malmesbury went on to explain.

[136] Milosh Obrenović (1780–1860), Prince of Serbia, 1817–1839 and December 1858–1860.

[137] Alexander Karageorgević (1806–1885), Prince of Serbia, 1843–December 1858.

[138] The convention signed at Paris, 19 August 1858, by Walewski and the ambassadors of the other great powers, with those of Sardinia and Turkey, attempting to resolve the future status of the Danubian Principalities and their relationship with Turkey.

[139] The signatories of the convention of 19 August 1858.

[140] The great powers' representatives in Constantinople.

[141] Josef Alexander, Baron (from 1888, Count) Hübner (1811–1892), Austrian ambassador to France.

strongly for Italian independence, but that it would be equally strong against any wanton aggression of France or Russia, so Austria must take care to be forbearing & always in the right.

140

Derby to Malmesbury, MP 9M73/20/46
30 December 1858
Knowsley

I am glad to see by a telegram from Loftus* of the 28$\underline{\text{th}}$ that Austria is better inclined, and is giving better advice to the Porte than we expected – that she gives up Alexander, and advises the Porte not to quarrel with the Milosch family; and if the Porte has the good sense to swallow the leek without making wry faces, all may go well; but if she takes the high line, asserts her right of independent action, and does not accept Milosch, the consequent complications may be very serious.[142] I see Russia is ready to acquiesce in Milosch. Has she been doing more?

You gave quite the right answer to Apponyi about Italy; but I do not much like his language as you report it to me. I should have thought that the state of Austrian finance would have been a sufficient reason for taking every step to avoid rupture with France; but they seem at best as anxious to take offence as France seems careless of giving it. Still I do not think we shall have an Italian war, and I feel very confident that Russia will not be over anxious to engage in new hostilities, especially when she can hope for no advantage. [. . .]

141

Malmesbury to Derby, DP 920 DER (14) 144/2
1 January 1859

The Queen has just told me of the marriage between Prince Napoleon[143] & the eldest daughter of the King of Sardinia,[144]

---

[142] See above, **139**.

[143] Napoleon Jerome Charles Paul Bonaparte (1822–1891), cousin of Napoleon III, second son of Jerome Bonaparte (the former King of Westphalia); known as 'Plon-Plon'.

[144] Clotilde of Savoy (1843–1911).

announced by the Emperor — It proves a complete alliance between
France[,] Russia & Sardinia —[145]

142

Malmesbury to Derby, DP 920 DER (14) 144/2
2 January 1859
Windsor

[. . .] I hope you will approve of my reply to the French note
respecting the Austrian interference at Belgrade[146] — My time is passed
in smoothing down the quarrels between Buol & Walewski[.]

143

Malmesbury to Disraeli, Dep. Hughenden, 99/2, fos 43–44
Monday [3 January 1859][147]

I found yr note in passing thro' from Windsor to Heron Court —
The Servian news is very good – things taking a legal course —
The eventuality feared of Austrian intervention at Belgrade will not
occur —
I do not see & have never seen the slightest danger of anything but
a war of notes & this has disappeared —
There is a difference as to whether the Conference at Paris or the
Ambassadors in Turkey sh[d] settle disputed points in the constitution
of the Principalities[148] – I am for the former —

[145]This was the first phase of the Franco-Piedmontese plan to provoke a war with Austria,
by which Cavour sought the aggrandisement of Piedmont. Napoleon hoped to satisfy Italian
nationalist demands, increase French territory and influence, and deliver the *coup de grâce* to
what remained of the Vienna settlement. At Plombières in July 1858, Cavour and Napoleon
had agreed that, if Piedmont could provoke a war in which they then defeated Austria,
Piedmont would gain Lombardy and Venetia, while France would receive Savoy and Nice.
As an earnest of their intent, the marital bargain was also agreed. The Russians played no
direct part in this, but their benevolent neutrality was separately ensured in March. See
below, **175**.
[146]Buol had announced that Austria, if requested, would provide assistance to the Turkish
pasha at the fortress of Belgrade in repelling a Serbian attack. Malmesbury conveyed British
displeasure to Apponyi and wrote to Cowley on 1 January, supporting Walewski's protest to
Austria. He also instructed Bulwer to urge the Porte not to permit an appeal for Austrian
assistance. TNA, FO 146/815.
[147]This is clearly a response to Disraeli's letter of 2 January, in which he mentioned 'bad'
accounts he had received from Paris, and asked to see Malmesbury 'as soon as possible,
particularly about Servia'. *BDL*, VII, no. 3269.
[148]The Danubian Principalities of Moldavia and Wallachia.

I go at 2 PM. & you will find me here but it is not worth a walk[149] –
I return Monday — [. . .]

144

Derby to Malmesbury, MP 9M73/20/47
4 January 1859
Knowsley

I quite approve of your despatch in reference to Buol's unnecessary
announcement of what Austria would do in the event of a demand
being made from Belgrade for succour[150] – but France and Austria
both seem so much inclined to fly at each other's throats, that it will
not be very easy to keep matters quiet. Russia fortunately, does not
seem inclined to brouiller les affaires.[151] I do not like the marriage you
announce.[152] It looks very anxious for Austria; and Lombardy seems
very unquiet. [. . .]

145

Malmesbury to Derby, DP 920 DER (14) 144/2
4 January 1859
Heron Court

The despatch from Bloomfield wh I send you is of such importance
that I cannot answer it until I have your opinion & the Queen[']s[153] —
I do not believe the crisis so near as most people who are frightened
by foolish speeches of Napoleon[']s, whose hatred of Buol & his envoy
Hubner is unbounded.[154] But the danger is that should disturbances
take place in the Legations Austria will interfere & Napoleon will
make this a casus belli. Cavour* is ready to join him, & <u>until now</u>

---

[149] Given the description of Disraeli in Malmesbury's letter to Derby on 4 January (see
below, **145**), and Disraeli's reference to Malmesbury 'whom I cd. only catch on his way to
Heron Court' in a letter to Derby, also on 4 January (*BDL*, VII, no. 3272), it seems that the
two men did meet at some point on 3 January.

[150] See above, **142**.

[151] 'confuse matters'.

[152] In letter **141**.

[153] Bloomfield's despatch, dated 20 December and received on 3 January, conveyed an
enquiry from the Prussian Prince Regent as to Britain's course if war broke out between
France and Austria.

[154] In an incident that had been widely reported, Napoleon had deliberately snubbed the
Austrian ambassador at a New Year gathering in Paris.

Russia had agreed not to take an active part in the war but to keep so strong a corps of observation on her Austrian frontier as to paralyse one third of the Austrian army. On the other hand the secret telegram from Loftus stating that Alexander* has invited the Austrian Emperor to meet him looks as if he wished to prevent a smash in Italy — Subservient to yr judgement my opinion is that we should reply to Prussia what I did to Apponyi, & to keep ourselves perfectly at liberty to act or remain neuter[,] stating that France & Austria could, if they chose to work together, improve the condition of central Italy & that they ought to be urged to do so, we England & Prussia being Protestant nations not taking any active part, w^h w^d do more harm than good, but supporting any plan which would give the Roman states a better Gov^t even if a remodelling of the territorial arrangements of the Papal dominions were desirable. So far, being the contracting Powers of the treaties of 1815 we would approve of an infringement of those treaties, but no farther, & should not be prepared to sanction any change of the present territorial distribution of Europe.— Then to press Prussia to urge upon Buol the extreme importance of keeping <u>in the right</u> —[155] This last piece of useless folly about Belgrade is incredible, tho I hope nothing will come of it but his having been snubbed by France —

I send you a letter I got yesterday when I was in London from Disraeli by w^h you will judge of his nervous system[156] — He wanted to send for <u>you</u> but he went away more tranquil.

146

Derby to Malmesbury, MP 9M73/20/48
5 January 1859
Knowsley

I cannot but entertain the hope that Schlienitz's[157] inexperience has led him to exaggerate the magnitude and imminence of the danger. The language used by the Emperor to Hübner was quite enough to put the alarmists on the qui vive, and lead to all sorts of unfounded reports.[158] Nevertheless, it is impossible to deny that there has been

---

[155] On 7 January, a secret despatch was drafted along the lines Malmesbury outlined. No copy has been found among Foreign Office papers, although a copy was sent to Cowley (see below, **146**). The draft remains in the Royal Archive, and is helpfully reproduced in Kenneth Bourne, *The Foreign Policy of Victorian England, 1830–1902* (Oxford, 1970), pp. 336–339.

[156] See above, **143**.

[157] Alexander, Freiherr (Count, 1879) von Schlienitz (1807–1885), Prussian foreign minister, 1858–1861; he had only been in the job two months.

[158] See above, **145**.

something ominous of late in the proceedings of our 'August Ally', and the contemplated alliance (matrimonial) with Piedmont looks threatening. If Sardinia is fool enough to throw herself bodily into the arms of France, it will be the old fable of the Horse, the Stag, and the Man:[159] but there is no saying what ambition, and hatred of Austria may lead her to do. Meantime, affairs in Lombardy look critical; and though the despatch which you send me today from Consul James[160] expresses no apprehension of an immediate rising, he speaks very strongly not only of an uneasy feeling, but of its being fomented by French, Sardinian, and Russian emissaries. The worst is that with France longing to pick a quarrel, and Sardinia too much inclined to be made a catspaw of, Austria, or rather Buol, is only too likely to give them a fair pretext, and he is too dogged, and too little adroit, to get well out of a difficulty when he has made one. I think your proposed answer and advice to Prussia quite the right one. I would add that the best check upon France is the cordiality of feeling, and unity of purpose, between Prussia and Austria. She will not like to risk a quarrel on light grounds with united Germany. If Austria, by any imprudence, leads to war in Italy, our position would be a very embarrassing one – for public sympathy in this country would be on the side of France, or rather of Italy, and this country would never raise a finger in support of Austrian rule over Lombardy. Of course you have put Cowley in possession of Bloomfield's secret despatch, and begged him to keep his eyes and ears open.[161]

I am sorry for the state of Disraeli's nerves. I do not exactly see what influence, for good or for evil, my being in Town three days sooner or later could have upon the affairs of Servia – you know however how soon he is up and down again. I have been able to give his friend Lucas,[162] (who boasts that he put us into office) a distributorship of stamps; with which both he and D[israeli]. are well pleased.

[. . .] I shall be in Town on Monday.

---

[159] One of Aesop's fables, in which the horse (in this case, Sardinia) obtained the man's (French) help in ejecting the stag (Austria) from his meadow, only to find that he had enslaved himself to the man.

[160] George Payne Rainsford James, consul-general for the Austrian Coasts of the Adriatic Sea (i.e. Venice) since 24 July 1858.

[161] Malmesbury wrote to Cowley on 7 January, promising to send on Bloomfield's despatch. He also sent Cowley a copy of his secret reply to the Prussians. Cowley MSS, TNA, FO 519/196, fo. 695.

[162] Samuel Lucas (1818–1868), editor of The Press, 1853–1854. Appointed Derby stamp distributor, 1858.

147

Malmesbury to Derby, DP 920 DER (14) 144/2
6 January [1859]
Heron Court

[. . .] I think everything is quieting [*sic*] down again – Thiers[163] had assured Peel[164] that the want of horses in the French army was a sure proof that Napoleon did not meditate a campaign <u>this year</u> – & you will see that Claremont confirms his opinion but he is preparing material on a vast scale — [. . .]

P.S.

You will see by these letters that Cowley is altogether French & that like all men he imbibes the complexion of the Court at w^h he resides. Walewski has written a despatch to Pelissier w^h he has sent me to read regretting that we do not go the whole hog with him, & he ends very absurdly by saying that Austria's <u>intention</u> to interfere at Belgrade is of itself a breach of the treaty – I wonder whether he takes the same view as regards his own Emperor & his own wife! I have replied merely to acknowledge the perusal permitted & saying I w^d keep my remarks on the contents till I had the pleasure of seeing Pelissier next week —

148

Derby to Malmesbury, MP 9M73/20/49
6 January 1859
Knowsley

Disraeli writes to me in such excessive agitation,[165] that I have told him that if I can possibly make my arrangements, I will anticipate my return to Town, and will go up on Saturday evening, in which case I would see him after Church on Sunday. I do not urge upon you, if you

---

[163]Adolphe Marie Joseph Louis Thiers (1797–1877), French foreign minister, 1836–1840; became first President of the Third Republic, 1871–1873, after long years in opposition during the Second Empire.

[164]General Jonathan Peel (1799–1879), a younger brother of the late Prime Minister, Sir Robert Peel; Secretary of State for War, 1858–1859 and 1866–1867; Major-General 1854–December 1859; Lieutenant-General, 1859–1863; formerly Surveyor-General of the Ordnance under his brother, 1841–1846.

[165]Disraeli had written to Derby on 4 January, complaining that the leading British ministers were 'all scattered' despite the 'critical' state of affairs. He criticized Malmesbury's absence from the Foreign Office, and alleged that Cowley's letters were 'deceptive'. Disraeli's proposed solution was that 'a calm & decisive carriage would oblige Austria to consent to the evacuation of the Roman states, & that would conclude the business'. *BDL*, VII, no. 3272.

think it unnecessary, that you should be there as soon; though if you are it would be convenient that I should see you, either with him, or as soon after as possible. I hope however that you will not delay your return beyond Monday, and that you will let me see you on that day. Even if I only come up on Monday, I shall be in S^t. James's Square by 5PM, or soon after. Matters abroad are critical, there is no doubt; and we have plenty to occupy our attention at home. I do not know from what reason, but it is evident to me that Disraeli greatly mistrusts Cowley, and that he has some secret informant in Paris, on whom he places far greater reliance.[166] Do you know who this is?

149

Malmesbury to Derby, DP 920 DER (14) 144/2
7 January [1859][167]
Heron Court

My house will not be ready & the cleaners out of it till tomorrow night & the servants want one day to clean the dirt of the cleaners — This wd not prevent my coming up to an hotel if I could do any good or desirable harm, but I cannot see any cause for agitation w^h only breeds more alarm. There is actually so little at the F.O today that Hammond writes to say he will not send the daily messenger, a thing w^h has never happened to me in the two years of our official connexion! Disraeli never reads a word of my papers w^h go round, & knows nothing but what the Jews at Paris & London tell him — Undoubtedly any moment may bring forth a revolution in the Papal States w^h Buol might try in his bad humour to repress without concert with France, but I do not believe the Emperor is ready for such a business as a double campaign with Austria. Both Claremont & Thiers tell us he has no horses to move his troops — If however he does mean war I can do nothing more than what I have done, w^h is to urge Buol to be prudent, to tell Napoleon that he risks his crown, & Sardinia that she is humbugged by him. To press on Prussia to be neutral if the war does break out, & to support the above advice & warnings to the various parties — I will call on you at 5 P.M. on Monday.

---

[166]Disraeli's informant was Ralph Earle, his private secretary, who had been sent by him on a secret mission to Napoleon. Malmesbury, like Derby, knew nothing of this. See M&B, IV, pp. 216–220; Geoffrey Hicks, *Peace, War and Party Politics: the Conservatives and Europe, 1846–59* (Manchester, 2007), pp. 217–219.

[167]Malmesbury wrote '1858', but this was clearly an error made as the year turned.

150

Derby to Malmesbury, MP 9M73/450/6
8 January 1859
Knowsley

I send you an extract, a tolerably long one, from a letter which I have received this morning from Disraeli,[168] and one which the same post has brought me from Sir C. Wood.* I think you ought to see both of them, but I will thank you to let me have them back. Disraeli's viewing of the working of the Emperor's mind is, I believe, substantially correct. I doubt if he is equally right in supposing the state of the French army to be such that he could not, at a very short notice, enter upon a campaign in Italy; and especially on account of the defective condition of his artillery. In cavalry, he is doubtless short-handed, but an Italian campaign, in aid of a popular insurrection, would go far to supply this description of matériel. D. may be right in supposing that he will not risk a war which he believes to be in contravention of public opinion in England. But who shall say that if Lombardy should rise, and Piedmont support her, such a war, even if France took part in it, would not meet with much popular sympathy here? I think you have, as Disraeli allows, fully impressed upon Apponyi that in such a case Austria must not look for assistance from us. I am sure we should not be supported by the country in offering it. The cause would be most unpopular, and there would be always found some more or less valid pretext on the part of France for an interference, even in direct opposition to the treaties of 1815. I can hardly think D. is correct in his belief that Austria is encouraged, in high places,[169] to expect a different result; and I am sure he greatly underrates the stubbornness of Buol's nature, if he expects that any apprehension whatever will induce him to initiate a 'conciliatory' proposition for a revival of the

[168]The letter, written on 7 January, criticized Malmesbury's 'incipient reserve & jealousy' on foreign policy, and alleged that the Foreign Secretary was 'very imperfectly acquainted' with the situation in France. Disraeli suggested that Napoleon had been 'brooding over Italy' ever since the Orsini affair, but thought that 'the French army is not in a condition to move with effect'. He revealed that Napoleon was 'meditating a great rhetorical coup', by which he would make an overture to Britain in his speech to Chambers. This news had been obtained from Earle, though the 'great rhetorical coup' ultimately came to nothing. This time, Disraeli's proposal was to impress upon Austria that Britain would remain neutral in any war, because then Austria would be 'conciliatory' and agree to consider the condition of central and southern Italy in a European conference. It made no mention of his previous suggestion about evacuation of the Papal States. Derby proved to be a more accurate prophet of Austrian behaviour. *BDL*, VII, no. 3275. For Derby's reply to Disraeli, see M&B, IV, p. 224.
[169]The Court.

conferences of Paris, to take into consideration the state of central and southern Italy. I am convinced he and his Emperor would prefer being dispossessed by force of their Milanese possessions, to making (I believe even to accepting) such a proposition. Disraeli leaves me in doubt as to the 'second' point which he considers as urgent in point of time;[170] but I agree with him, and I think you will do so also, that it is high time we were all assembled, and I hope to see you in town on Monday afternoon. You will judge better than I can what reliance is to be placed on the information furnished by Wood. He seems to have no doubt that it comes from Mazzini[171] himself; but I own I find it difficult to reconcile the nature of the scheme said to be agreed upon with his apparent approval; for it tends directly to augment the influence and power, not only of Sardinia, but, personally, of Victor Emmanuel, whom he hates, and believes to be the greatest obstacle to the regeneration of Italy. Perhaps he calculates that the result of such an attempt would be to subvert the constitutional government of Sardinia, and substitute a north Italian republic. But he must greatly misjudge L. Napoleon, if he thinks that such a project would find favour in his eyes – unless it were such a 'republic' as we have had in the Ionian Islands – under the 'protection' of France.

151

Malmesbury to Derby, DP 920 DER (14) 144/2
15 January 1859

The Prince[172] has just sent me this box & inclosure –[173] It confirms Cowley[']s report[174] w^h crossed it on its way to Windsor, & looks like business – but by the date (the 11th) I am still in hopes that the damper the Emperor got at the Bourse on the 3 following days & is still feeling,

---

[170] Disraeli had said that there were 'two things, at this conjuncture, most urgent'. He only outlined one (stressing that Britain would remain neutral in a war). *BDL*, VII, no. 3275.

[171] Giuseppe Mazzini (1805–1872), Italian patriot and republican.

[172] Albert.

[173] The Prince Consort had received a report detailing a meeting between Napoleon and the Belgian Prince de Chimay, in which the emperor had suggested that Albert, his brother (the Duke of Saxe-Coburg), and the Prince of Prussia were getting up a German league against France. He had also threatened the Belgians by saying that the very existence of Belgium was dependent upon the intimacy of their alliance with France. It appeared that the Belgians had been less than robust in defending their neutrality. Theodore Martin, *The Life of the Prince Consort*, IV (London, 1879), pp. 354–355.

[174] On 12 January, Cowley had written a letter to Malmesbury describing the meeting between Chimay and Napoleon, about which Prince Albert had been informed separately. MP 9M73/8/11.

may choke him — I only wish he may command in Italy & Pelissier on the Rhine – I fear McMahon* will be the man, a very accomplished & gallant Irishman — 'Our Uncle'^{175} is a sad burden upon us – If attacked we must defend him & his cowardly army, but from what I understand of the P. of Chimay's^{176} despatch it is not impossible that in a row he may go over to the French – However it w^d not suit us to see them in the Scheldt & in Antwerp — A greater public iniquity never was committed than that of the Whigs who left our Navy in the state shewn by the papers we discussed today. — [. . .]

152

Derby to Malmesbury, MP 9M73/450/7
[17 January 1859]^{177}

[. . .] I am more than ever glad that you sent Cowley's letter to the Prince.^{178} It is well that he should see that when Crowned Heads (or quasi-Crowned ones) take upon themselves to meddle in la haute politique,^{179} they cannot do so with impunity, and that they may create complications which they cannot easily resolve. 'Our Uncle' is beat in playing too fine a pawn; and he must be made to feel that he is not the dependant of France but that he is the occupier of a petty throne, whose neutrality is guaranteed only so long as it is real and actual; and that while he may depend on us (and I hope you will urge this language on Prussia also) for the support we are bound to give him in the event of his being attacked, he must not expect to run at the same time with the hare and the hound. If he thinks fit to put himself under the protection of France, he must take all the consequences of that protection; on the other hand, if by such intrigues he gives just cause of offence to France, he must not expect us to drag him out of the mire. What you have said to Austria, you must say to Belgium, 'keep in the right, and appeal to treaties'.^{180} I think the events of the last few days have given the Emperor a lesson he will not forget; and notwithstanding the telegram today of the movements (slow from want of money) of that madman the King of Sardinia, I have better hopes than I had a few days ago of the preservation of peace. But I

^{175}King Leopold of Belgium, uncle to both the Queen and the Prince Consort.

^{176}A senior Belgian prince, used as an emissary by King Leopold.

^{177}Undated, but the date is recorded in Derby's out-book, DP 920 DER (14) 187/1.

^{178}See above, **151**.

^{179}'high politics'; generally used in a diplomatic context.

^{180}On 18 March, the Prince Consort wrote a letter to Leopold to that effect. Martin, *Prince Consort*, IV, pp. 356–358.

think the neutrality of Belgium is a point on which it would be well to come to an understanding with Prussia, Austria, <u>and Russia</u>; and that we should not conceal from France our determination to abide by the terms of treaties. But for this, Belgium must go honestly with us, or must be left to her fate.

153

Malmesbury to Derby, DP 920 DER (14) 144/2
27 January [1859]

The precis of Buol[']s wishes is here inclosed as sent me by Apponyi – It appears to me that we have said to France & Sardinia exactly what he recommends.

He mistakes our suggestion as to the Pope's territory – What we said was that if France & Austria thought fit to entertain that question after a concert in [*sic*] the affairs of central Italy, we as parties to the Treaty of Vienna w^d consider it, but not take the initiation. —

You will see in the Post[181] a categorical statement every word of w^h in reference to present & past is a lie – & the phrase in my letter to Cowley is quoted, thereby entirely verifying the truth of my information respecting the Emperor[']s orders to write me down when he saw M^r. Borthwick[182] — It may do us much harm if not contradicted.

I wish you joy of our Cabinet yesterday.

154

Derby to Malmesbury, MP 9M73/20/50
27 January [1859]

I return Buol's and Apponyi's letters. We have said <u>in substance</u> what B[uol]. wishes; but as usual, he wishes us to put it in the least

---

[181] The *Morning Post* of 27 January 1859 had quoted Malmesbury's suggestion to Cowley, in a letter of 7 December 1858, that Austria's position in Italy might be compared to that of Britain in India and Ireland. The *Post* alleged that 'Lord Malmesbury is for committing this country to an alliance with the German powers, for the maintenance of German rule in Italy.' Malmesbury had for some time been convinced that the *Post* was in the pay of the French government. See *Memoirs*, I, p. 362 and II, pp. 151–152. When his *Memoirs* were published in 1884, his allegation to that effect caused a public row with the editor of the *Post*.

[182] Sir Algernon Borthwick (1830–1908), created Baron Glenesk in 1895; editor of the *Morning Post*.

conciliatory form – and I do not think L. N. would like to be told, after his assurances that if Austria confines herself to her own territories, he will not interfere (though I don't believe him) that 'we should not see him enter on an aggressive war['], with an 'avis indifférent'.[183] Such an expression would commit us far more than is prudent or safe. [. . .]

155

Derby to Malmesbury, MP 9M73/450/8
6 February [1859]
St James's Square

These are subjects on which it would be very much better that princes, at all events in constitutional countries, should leave to the responsible advisers of the Crown, and not make them matters of private irresponsible correspondence.[184] The question you have marked is one for Prussia alone – and which we are not called upon to answer. It is a mere question of her losing 'carte' in Germany by apparent indifference, in a case in which Austria should be successful without her aid – What have we to do with that? I hope however there will after all be no war – at least not now — Cowley's telegram is most satisfactory[185] – but we must not abate our naval preparations.

[183] 'with indifference'; more literally, 'with an indifferent opinion'.
[184] The Prince Regent of Prussia, reflecting wider nervousness in Berlin, had written to the Prince Consort, asking what Albert saw Prussia's situation being if 'England and Russia should remain neutral, and Austria be victorious against the Franco-Italian alliance'. Martin, *Prince Consort*, IV, pp. 379–382.
[185] There had been a favourable reception in France for Derby's speech at the opening of Parliament.

156

Malmesbury to Derby, DP 920 DER (14) 144/2
21 February [1859]

I return you Disraeli[']s letter[186] & when I have seen Cowley will send you back the other papers — Disraeli, as usual, has neglected to read a word of what has passed between the F.O.[,] Germany & France or he w^d know that we & Prussia understand each other perfectly on the Italian questions but without any binding agreement. Any thing like the 'demonstration['] he speaks of is in my opinion to be positively avoided – It w^d drive Napoleon mad & bring us at once into the row —

[P.S.] I feel as sure as one has a right to feel on such subjects that the Emperor of Russia has no intention of going to war now or hereafter if he can help it – that it is entirely against his nature & that his whole mind is bent on internal improvements – His armies are reduced to the lowest scale —

157

Malmesbury to Disraeli, Dep. Hughenden 99/2, fos 100–101[187]
[Undated][188]

The policy of insisting & threatening is Palmerstonian & w^d commit us to one side or the other — From the moment we show a bias to one side our influence is gone – because they are now bidding for our friendship — We never can I hope be induced to join a protectorate of Italy — We have enough of the protectorate of Belgium

---

[186] Disraeli's latest salvo in his campaign for a more vigorous foreign policy was a letter written on 20 February, in which he suggested that the real danger 'to Germany' was 'not from France, but Russia'. He proposed a joint diplomatic initiative with Prussia, which would advocate reform in Italy, ensure a Franco-Austrian evacuation of the Papal States, nullify Austrian influence holding back Italian reform, and, in the event of 'European complications', pursue 'a joint course of action, to guard the equilibrium of Europe against any dangers'. This could, he suggested, be 'a significant demonstration'. *BDL*, VII, no. 3294. The first three points already constituted part of Britain's diplomatic position; Malmesbury clearly thought the last was provocative enough to be dangerous. He was right about Russian intentions.

[187] This letter is reproduced in M&B, IV, pp. 228–229.

[188] It is impossible to date this letter precisely, although it clearly comes from the early part of the Italian crisis, prior to the war itself, and on the occasion of a demand by Disraeli for more robust action. It could have been written at any point during the early part of 1859, but it is certainly plausible that it dates from late February, given the diplomatic configuration at that time. It is significant for its statement of Malmesbury's principles in foreign policy.

who will probably be invaded by one of its protectors, & now of the Principalities[189] whose protectors are all pulling different ways — England always acts de bonne foi[190] in these cases & therefore has the disadvantage of being like a respectable clergyman cotrustee with 5 horsedealers.

158

Malmesbury to Derby, DP 920 DER (14) 144/2
23 February [1859][191]

Cowley will be much obliged to you to lend him the draft of the paper you meant to send to the Queen. – He says it will be of great use to him as a memorandum on the subjects on w^h he will have to treat.[192] He lives at 3 Upper Belgrave S^t. & goes to Vienna tomorrow morning.

159

Malmesbury to Derby, DP 920 DER (14) 144/2
3 March [1859]

This account leaves little hope of preventing the fixed resolve of the unprincipled men who threaten Europe with war, but with this knowledge we must be awkward if we do not put them completely in the wrong—[193]

---

[189]The Danubian Principalities of Moldavia and Wallachia.
[190]'honestly' or 'sincerely'.
[191]Date appended; filed with letters from 1858, but, given the context, clearly written in 1859.
[192]Cowley was about to leave on a peace mission to Vienna, which was upstaged by the Russian offer of a European conference on Italy.
[193]It is unclear precisely to what this refers; no enclosure remains.

160

Malmesbury's unpublished diary, MP 9M73/79

18 March 1859

Telegram from Cowley proposing from Emperor Congress – Emperor apparently wishing to retreat — Pelissier called later making official demand to this effect — Russian proposal originally – Prussia agrees — Saw Apponyi about it & telegraphed to Loftus —

161

Malmesbury to Derby, DP 920 DER (14) 144/2
19 March [1859]

I will come to you in $\frac{1}{2}$ an hour when you have read these important papers —

Can we consent to excluding Sardinia from any share in the discussion? There are reasons to justify it —

Should I make Austria pledge herself by a Note not to attack Sardinia if we ask her to disarm – & agree to Cowley's proposal?

Is not a Congress too solemn a proceeding & w^d not a Conference at some neutral capital be better to consider how the Italian question cd be settled.

162

Note in Derby's handwriting, MP 9M73/20/62
19 March 1859

Will Austria consent to Congress or Conference (the latter preferably) on Italian questions, including substitute for Treaties of 1847, conditionally upon France calling on Sardinia to disarm, under guarantee for five years by England & France against invasion of Sardinia by Austria, so long as Sardinia confines herself to her own territory?[194]

---

[194]This and **163** were evidently Derby's suggestions for a resolution of the diplomatic crisis, which Malmesbury proposed the following day. See below, **164**.

163

Note in Derby's handwriting, MP 9M73/20/63
19 March 1859

Will France consent to call on Sardinia to disarm, she being
guaranteed for five years by England and France, against invasion
by Austria, so long as Sardinia confines herself to her own territory
– conditionally upon Austria consenting to Congress or Conference
(the latter preferably) on other Italian questions, including substitute
for Treaties of 1847?

164

Malmesbury's unpublished diary, MP 9M73/79

20 March 1859

Saw Brunnow who knew nothing but agreed in our view of restricting
Congress to Italian subjects & not touching treaties of 1815. — Saw
Apponyi who agreed that it w^d be better to leave out all Italian states
& refer our plans of reform &c to them rather than admit Sardinia
— Wrote to Cowley to urge his obtaining disarmament of Austria &
Sardinia on condition that France & England guaranteed Sardinia for
5 years — [. . .]

21 March 1859

[. . .] France hesitates about guarantee to Sardinia[.]

24 March 1859

[. . .] Berlin & Petersburgh [*sic*] accede to my proposal to admit the
Italian states to be heard but not sit by their table at Congress — [. . .]

165

Malmesbury to Derby, DP 920 DER (14) 144/2
25 March [1859]

[. . .] If the Emperors, either Austrian or French[,] refuse my
proposal of admitting the Italian states by delegates in the same
manner as Belgium & Holland at the Congress of London, it will
be evident that neither of them want a compromise.

What Cowley says of the attendance of Cabinet Ministers is true in the abstract, but if I go to the Conference it will be because the Queen must be represented in the same manner as the other Courts, & I sh^d not decide any doubtful or new points without reference to you, but if Cowley does not go, (as he hints) & I do not go, I really do not know what two men to send —[195] I am in hopes that as Russia accepts all our 4 points[196] & all our conditions, she will prevent an abandonment of the Congress — It is now evident that the French Emperor is no longer the same man in mind or body that he was formerly —[197]

166

Malmesbury's unpublished diary, MP 9M73/79

27 March 1859

Brunnow came – Invited him to join in inducing Sardinia & Austria to disarm we & France giving guarantee to former — Austria very recalcitrant — [...]

1 April 1859

[...] Cabinet at 12 – Resolved not to resign but dissolve as soon as parliamentary business permitted – Only Estcourt[198] & Stanley for immediate resignation — Ld. Derby went to the Queen who was very anxious we should go on & at once gave him leave to dissolve Parl[iamen].^t [...]

[195] According to Malmesbury's *Memoirs*, II, p. 162, Derby was 'annoyed at my having to go to the Conference'.

[196] The four points were those Malmesbury had proposed that Cowley should use as the basis for a settlement when he had visited Vienna in February: withdrawal of Franco-Austrian forces from the Papal Sates; reform of the Papal States; a declaration of peaceful intentions; and the revision or annulment of Austria's treaties with Italian states.

[197] Malmesbury knew the emperor well; his friendship with Napoleon III dated back to their early adulthood in the 1820s. Malmesbury felt that Napoleon was scheming with Cavour because, ever since the Orsini affair, he had been haunted by fears of assassination by Italian terrorists. See, e.g., *Memoirs*, II, p. 148.

[198] Thomas Henry Sutton Sotheron Estcourt (1801–1876), President of the Poor Law Board, 1858–March 1859; Home Secretary, March–June 1859.

14 April 1859

Fresh proofs of the insincerity of France — [. . .][199]

16 April 1859

New French proposal to invite Sardinia to disarm on condition all the Italians were admitted as principals to the Congress — Apponyi came with a despatch stating that Austria meant to submit ultimatum to Sardinia to disarm — He thought it meant war – I gave him my opinion that it must be made with a declaration that Austria was ready to disarm also — [. . .]

17 April 1859

Agreed with Bernstorff to demand Sardinia to [*sic*] agree to principle of general disarmament — [. . .]

167

Malmesbury to Disraeli, Dep. Hughenden 99/2, fo. 66
[18 April 1859][200]

The present state of things is this[:]

————————

Austria & France have agreed to the principle of a general disarmament —

They have not agreed as to whether it shall be effected before the Congress or shall be arranged at it —

[199] Disappointingly, he gives no examples, but his *Memoirs*, II, p. 170, record that, on 12 April, Napoleon had refused to ask Sardinia to disarm, thus making the French offer to do so 'perfectly useless'; on 15 April, Malmesbury noted that Napoleon made a 'ridiculous counter-proposition' that Austria disarm if Britain and France guaranteed that Sardinia would not attack.

[200] Undated. Archivist's note: '?April 1859'. This advice, like that in **168**, was clearly given to Disraeli in preparation for his Commons statement on 18 April, in which he explained precisely this situation, though it must have predated the advice in **168**, by which time Sardinia's initial reply had been received. *Parl. Deb.*, CLIII, cols 1869–1871. On 19 April, this was superseded by the news that Sardinia had agreed to preliminary and simultaneous disarmament: that is, before the proposed Congress. This was too late to stop the Austrian ultimatum demanding Sardinia's disarmament.

HMG. prefer the Austrian view wh is the former – Sardinia has not answered but is considering the subject & the Chevalier d'Azeglio[201] is come on a special mission in reference to it —

168

Malmesbury to Disraeli, Dep. Hughenden, 99/2, fos 68–69
[18 April 1859][202]

The Sardinian answer has arrived vide Fitzgerald[']s telegram.[203] We must say therefore that Sardinia has not consented to the disarmament in consequence of not being admitted to Congress & this makes it the more necessary that you should make it clear before that she was excluded by opinion of all the 5 Powers both France and Russia maintaining it & that we urged her admittance & that of other states as in Congress of London on Belgium in 1832 —

169

Malmesbury to Disraeli, Dep. Hughenden 99/2, fos 86–87
[20 April 1859][204]

The summons was made at 5-30 yesterday at Turin[205] – No answer given yet — The demand included disarmament of volunteers. I cannot help thinking that Austria will profess to be satisfied with Sardinia[']s answer if it is what we advised & that she will fall back upon a mediation of England between her and France to w^h I have agreed provided 'all three disarm previously or all three remain in exact status quo as regards military movements.'

I do not think a Cabinet can be of any use whatever happens – the Congress is at an end — We have nothing to do but either to mediate as above or be spectators of the battle —

---

[201]Massimo Taparelli, marchese d'Azeglio (1798–1866), Cavour's predecessor as Prime Minister of Piedmont-Sardinia, 1849–1852. His nephew was Sardinian minister in London.
[202]Undated. Archivist's note: '?April 1859'. For dating see above, **167**.
[203]See above, **167**.
[204]Undated but, given Malmesbury's receipt on 20 April of the news of Buol's summons on the night of 19/20, and the fact that a Cabinet *was* later held on 20 April, it seems likeliest that this was written on the morning of 20 April.
[205]The Austrian ultimatum to Piedmont. See above, **167**.

170

Malmesbury's unpublished diary, MP 9M73/79

21 April 1859[206]

News arrives that Austria rejects our proposal and summons Sardinia to disarm in 3 days. [. . .] Protest strongly ag[ain]st Austria [. . .]

171

Malmesbury to Disraeli, Dep. Hughenden, 99/2, fo. 98
[22 April 1859][207]

The French & we have advised Cavour to reply 'that he has already agreed to a general disarmament to be arranged by Comm[issione]r^s in London.' Buol had not heard of this when he sent the summons. Hudson goes back tonight — The French cannot be in line under 6 weeks — I think it may still be stopped.

[PS] A strong protest is gone to Vienna[.]

172

Derby to Malmesbury, MP 9M73/20/51
26 April 1859
St James's Square

Hammond has been here with a letter from the Admiralty to the effect that Fanshawe[208] is very unwilling to detach a Line of Battle ship for Genoa, and wishes to substitute Terrible for Orion. As the former is a very large vessel, and as her only object is protection of British life and property, I have authorised this substitution. I have also written to Pakington on the state of our naval preparations, and as to the amount of force which we could raise in two or three months, and how long it would take us to have the means of competing (le cas échéant)[209] with a French & Russian fleet <u>combined</u>. Such a necessity I hope is not imminent; but in the present state of affairs, and notwithstanding

---

[206] Despite the date, Malmesbury has compressed the events of two days into this entry.
[207] Undated, but Hudson was leaving on the evening of 22 April.
[208] Vice-Admiral Sir Arthur Fanshawe, Commander-in-Chief in the Mediterranean.
[209] 'if need be'.

Gortchakoff's* assurances to Crampton,[210] we ought to be prepared for all emergencies.

The refusal of France to hear of our renewed mediation puts an end to all chance of arresting the progress of war. [...]

I was <u>very</u> well received last night[211] – the country is all for peace – almost à tout prix – and Austria's intolerable stupidity has completely turned the scale against her.

173

Malmesbury to Derby, DP 920 DER (14) 144/2
27 April 1859

Both France & Austria were offered our mediation on the 25th – Austria having in fact <u>originated</u> the idea on the 23rd. So far then she is in the right – & France is now using arrogant language & hints at a Congress on <u>wider bases</u> than our 4 points. Those 4 points however comprise all desirable reforms political & social in Italy, & if the base is to be wider it can only be [?interpreted][212] by a breach of the treaties of 1815 —

I have therefore said we will have nothing more to do with a Congress – at w^h France w^d be unbearable & w^h wd lead us into a quarrel with her —

The people of England will end by seeing that there is not a pin to choose between the merits of the antagonists —

Gortchakoff[']s assertion respecting the Treaty is so solemn as far as regards us that I really believe it only concerns Germany. It may however have something to do with Turkey.— Your speech will be very popular & was excellent – Apponyi did not like your word 'criminal' but I told him that according to Talleyrand a political <u>crime</u> is less bad than a <u>fault</u>.[213]

---

[210] About Russian treaty commitments. On 3 March, France and Russia had agreed a secret treaty by which Russia promised 'benevolent neutrality' in the event of a Franco-Austrian war.

[211] In his Mansion House speech, Derby had described Austrian policy as 'criminal'.

[212] The word in question is almost completely illegible.

[213] Malmesbury's consolatory comment ('c'est pire qu'un crime, c'est une faute') is generally misattributed to the French statesman Talleyrand, and was either made by Antoine Boulay de la Meurthe or Joseph Fouché. Whatever its origin, it can have been of little comfort to Apponyi.

174

Malmesbury to Derby, DP 920 DER (14) 144/2
28 April [1859]

This telegram has just arrived [. . .][214]
I am against accepting the suggestion because with Russia it will end
in nothing but a gain of time for the French who Malaret[215] owned were
not nearly ready — Besides this, Russia has taken such a decidedly
French line that she is not a neutral Power. — On the other hand it
may be said hereafter that we have not tried every chance if we decline
— [. . .]

175

Malmesbury's unpublished diary, MP 9M73/79

28 April 1859

Return to London – Great panic at belief of Russian & French treaties
offensive & defensive [. . .]

3 May 1859

[. . .] Cabinet on Proclamation of Neutrality[216] and increasing navy —

6 May 1859

[. . .] Cabinet on Proclamation of Neutrality, and building 18 gun
vessels – Disraeli said there was a deficit of 6 000 000£ [. . .]

---

[214]Not found. The 'suggestion' is unclear, but may relate to another proposal for Russian
mediation.

[215]Baron de Malaret, First Secretary at the French Embassy in London.

[216]Austria declared war against Piedmont on 29 April; France came to Piedmont's aid on
3 May. British neutrality was officially proclaimed on 13 May.

176

Derby to Disraeli, DP 186/2/108–109
8 May 1859

Your secret communication, just received, is too important to be answered hastily. I will ponder it well over before tomorrow. Elgin[217] had occurred to me; but the difficulty, supposing him willing to accept, would be his being in the H[ouse] of Lords, while you want strength in the Commons – otherwise the Col[onial]. Office would have suited him better than the For[eign]. Office.[218] I should, I confess, be very sorry to see any change made in that Department at the present moment. It is of great importance to have a man there who has at his fingers' ends the whole thread of the complicated negotiations in which we have been engaged – & whatever may be Elgin's ability, he has been for nearly two years wholly out of the way of European politics. I should much deprecate such a change, though he would be useful in the Government, & his accession would facilitate that of Gladstone, if he is a desirable acquisition. Recollect however his extreme opinions on Italian affairs, which would be very embarrassing just now.

177

Malmesbury's unpublished diary, MP 9M73/79

9 May 1859

[...] Malaret called to apologise for Persigny's app[ointmen]^t.[219] — I was very cold to him —

---

[217]James Bruce (1811–1863), eighth Earl of Elgin and twelfth Earl of Kincardine, Britain's High Commissioner and Plenipotentiary in China and the Far East, who had negotiated the Treaty of Tientsin in June 1858. He was due back in London later in May 1859. He went on to accept ministerial office from Palmerston.

[218]Earlier the same day, Disraeli had proposed obtaining 'some additional weight & character' to strengthen the Cabinet, and suggested that Lord Elgin would be a useful acquisition. Disraeli proposed that Elgin should be Foreign Secretary. *BDL*, VII, no. 3345.

[219]Pélissier had been recalled, to be replaced by Persigny, who had resigned in a huff the previous year. It was interpreted as a deliberate snub to Derby's government, whose cold relations with Persigny were well known.

178

Malmesbury to Derby, DP 920 DER (14) 144/2
11 May [1859]

I send you an important letter from Mr Craven[220] tho not requiring immediate action — I begin to think that the course events will take is a retreat of the Austrians on their old line of the Mincio & that we sh^d be ready when that happens to stop the war if possible by inducing them to take some <u>large</u> measure as to Italy – w^h Napoleon w^d be either obliged to consent to, or declare himself for their total expulsion — The danger is from Germany w^h I fear will break upon France before that moment arrives, & produce an inextinguishable conflagration — If they do not, we might press both upon France & Austria with a high tone when the critical phase w^h I foresee should arrive. —

The young king of Naples'[221] game is to restore the suspended constitution when he succeeds to the throne, & perhaps to send an army to assist his countrymen – but that is the last move — It w^d certainly stave off the French domination & the Muratists[222] —

179

Malmesbury's unpublished diary, MP 9M73/79

12 May 1859

Ld Clarendon called – long conversation about Parties – said L^d J Russell and Palmerston men[223] w^d join – agreed cordially that it w^d be a great benefit if moderate Whigs and Derbyites w^d join – there was little difference, if any, between them – abused Palmerston[']s speech at Tiverton[224] — [. . .]

---

[220]Presumably Augustus Craven, who had been attached to the British Legation at Naples until diplomatic relations were suspended in October 1856. His letter has not been found.

[221]Francis II (1836–1894), King of Naples, 1859–1861.

[222]Napoleon I's marshal, Murat, had ruled as King of Naples, and his son remained a pretender to the Neapolitan throne.

[223]Almost illegible: 'men' is plausible in terms of handwriting and context.

[224]Palmerston's speech on re-election at Tiverton, 29 April 1859. See *The Times*, 2 May 1859.

18 May 1859

[. . .] Persigny very low – declaring before God the Emperor never meant war — [. . .]

20 May 1859

[. . .] Queen very jealous of asking Russia to assist to avert the war.[225] She & Prince evidently anxious not to stop the war but to let Germany go at the French — [. . .]

28 May 1859

[. . .] Dined at Palace – Princess Royal[226] there very anxious for the help of England – Queen touched the second string — [. . .]

29 May 1859

Bernstorff called – asked & I assured him we sh[d] be ready to act with Prussia to stop the war if we saw a chance. [. . .]

180

Derby to Disraeli, Dep. Hughenden 57/2, fo. 11
2 June 1859
St James's Square

I send you the Queen's letter respecting the speech.[227] I should be obliged to you to return it to me as soon as you can, with any remarks you may have to make – as I ought to write to H.M. in the course of the morning. My own impression is to accept her amendment on the subject of the navy, but strongly to urge upon her the reconsideration of the other paragraph. We must avoid any thing which throws a doubt upon our neutrality.

[225] St Petersburg had proposed a joint Anglo-Russian effort to localize and 'arrest' the war, but this was strenuously resisted by the Court. See, e.g., H. Hearder, 'Queen Victoria and foreign policy: royal intervention in the Italian Question, 1859–60', in K. Bourne and D.C. Watt (eds), *Studies in International History* (London, 1967), pp. 176–177.

[226] Princess Victoria, the Queen's eldest daughter, by that stage married to Prince Frederick of Prussia, but still known as the Princess Royal in Britain.

[227] The speech due to be given by the Queen to the new Parliament. The Queen, strongly pro-Austrian in her views, wanted a more ambiguous description of British neutrality than that proposed by the Government. Derby successfully resisted her. See *LQV*, first series, III, pp. 335–340; *BDL*, VII, no. 3359.

181

Malmesbury to Disraeli, Dep. Hughenden 99/2, fo. 78
2 June 1859

The papers[228] will not be printed till Saturday night as our printer has been ill & he must be a confidential man. They have gone thro' 3 careful weedings by Fitzgerald and me & I do not think you will find any delenda[229] but you shall have a copy as soon as possible.

182

Malmesbury's unpublished diary, MP 9M73/79

6 June 1859

[. . .] Queen very anxious about Austrian defeat at Magenta.[230]

183

Malmesbury to Disraeli, Dep. Hughenden 99/2, fo. 80
7 June [1859]

In the event of an <u>adverse</u> division how are the Italian papers to be presented at all? We cannot do so after we have tendered our resignation – My successor will then publish the <u>originals</u> unrevised & very likely our <u>intended</u> proofs side by side —

---

[228] The parliamentary papers on Italian affairs.
[229] 'things to be erased or blotted out'.
[230] MacMahon had led the Franco-Piedmontese forces to victory at Magenta on 4 June.

184

Malmesbury to Disraeli, Dep. Hughenden 99/2, fo. 102
[?8/9 June 1859][231]

Can you not present the papers before you adjourn after the division? You are however the best judge – I will send you a dummy down to the House & distribute when you tell me.

185

Malmesbury's unpublished diary, MP 9M73/79

18 June 1859

Went with my colleagues to Windsor to give up the seals[232] — Queen said 'I am very sorry to part with you' – she spoke of the state of Europe &c with great anxiety. She doubted evidently the power of the new Govt to hold – Hoped we w^d support the navy – lamented loss of Clarendon – who refused to join.— Saw Ld J. Russell in the evening to explain foreign affairs. Gathered from him that strict neutrality w^d be kept – but that Gladstone the new Ch[ancellor]. of the Ex[cheque]^r. meant to reduce the navy wh he did not approve.

[231] This letter deals with the vexed issue of the Italian papers, and seems to follow the previous letters. Malmesbury had prepared the parliamentary papers on the Italian crisis for presentation to the House of Commons. This had been done partly in the hope that it would disprove Liberal allegations that the Conservatives were pro-Austrian, which might in turn help the Government win the imminent vote on the Address, on which its fate was hanging. The decision as to when and if these papers were presented was Disraeli's, as Leader of the House of Commons. Given that Malmesbury's previous letter on the subject, **183**, was written on 7 June, and the division was expected to take place on 10 June, either 8 or 9 June seems plausible. Malmesbury remained convinced that Disraeli's decision not to lay the Italian papers before Parliament helped the Government lose the crucial division early on 11 June 1859. *Memoirs*, I, p. 41; II, pp. 188–189.

[232] The Government was defeated in the division on the Address in the early hours of 11 June, by 323 votes to 310. It resigned immediately.

CHAPTER 3
THE THIRD DERBY AND FIRST
DISRAELI GOVERNMENTS,
JUNE 1866–DECEMBER 1868

186

Malmesbury to Derby, DP 920 DER (14) 144/2B
20 April 1866
Stratford Place

I have for some time intended to write to you on a subject w^h the possible political crisis now impending[1] renders more urgent — It relates to the state of my health w^h w^d make it impossible for me to take my old office w^h is not only a very laborious & responsible one, but unlike others never allows of repose at any hour of the day — My nervous system is not what it was, & suffers at once from overexertion of mind —

[. . .][2] You have always been so truly generous & indulgent to me in all our political relations, & I am so entirely devoted to yr wishes, that nothing but necessity w^d make me anticipate yr arrangements, but if you have to make them beforehand, it appears to me right that I sh^d say how far you can depend upon me. — If I took the Foreign Office I know I sh^d be obliged to resign it soon after, & a change of offices is always damaging to an Administration.[3]

In myself I should be quite content to support you in a private capacity if you were again Prime Minister, but I am ready to make myself useful in any office w^h has not the <u>unceasing</u> work & anxiety of the Foreign Dep[artmen]^t.

---

[1]The crisis was over the Liberals' reform bill, the opposition to which (on both sides of the House) was threatening the stability of Russell's government.

[2]The editorial ellipsis covers an illegible Latin quotation.

[3]Malmesbury noted in his unpublished diary: 'I had another reason for this determination[,] namely the hostile feeling of Disraeli who has always coveted & asked for that Dept'. He feared that, with his old deputy Seymour Fitzgerald out of Parliament, he would have been 'left entirely at the mercy of [. . .] Disraeli who was always too lazy or too sulky to go into foreign affairs & then blamed me for not keeping him informed'. MP, 9M73/79.

187

Derby to Malmesbury, DP 920 DER (14) 190/2, fos 87–90[4]
22 April 1866

Whatever may be my regret at the decision which you have come to as announced in your letter of Friday, I cannot say that it has taken me by surprise, or that I think your objections, with your frequent attacks of ill health, to take an office involving such incessant and anxious labour as the F.O. are unreasonable. Your withdrawal will no doubt increase the difficulty of my position, if I should be called on again to attempt the task of forming a government; and though I should still hope to have the advantage of your services in some less hard-worked department, I confess that I do not, in the present state of parties, see my way to acceptance of office. I know that the disappointment of our friends, should I be called on, and decline, will be very great; but I cannot, especially in the present unsettled state of affairs both at home and abroad, again undertake the duty without at least a reasonable prospect of an assured majority; and even if we should succeed in carrying L[d] Grosvenor's[5] amendment, of which there is a fair prospect, the men who would vote with us on that question are so diametrically opposed to us on others of no less importance, that even if they had leaders with whom it would be more easy to confer than with those apparently at their head, I do not see how we could come to such an understanding as would enable us to carry on a government together; and of the ordinary supporters of the present administration, who will reluctantly go with them on this occasion, I cannot look to any one who would have the courage to break off from their party to support a government of which Disraeli & I should be the leaders. The prospect however of my being <u>sent for</u>, with whatever result, is sufficiently near to make it necessary to consider all possible courses; & I should be very glad to have an opportunity of talking the matter over with you, if you could call here at almost any hour tomorrow or Tuesday – [. . .]

---

[4]This letter was reproduced in *Memoirs*, II, pp. 351–352. The text here is that of the copy retained in Derby's papers; the original has not been found among Malmesbury's papers.

[5]Hugh Lupus Grosvenor (1825–1899), third Marquess and first Duke of Westminster; MP for Chester, 1847–1869 (known as Earl Grosvenor); one of the leading 'Adullamite' opponents of the Reform Bill. He had proposed a resolution opposing its second reading.

188

Derby to Stanley, DP 920 DER (15) 12/3/7/1
24 April 1866[6]
St James's Square

I shall not be back in Town till the question is on the eve of decision. I do not think the result is likely to be my being called on again to form an Administration; and that I should be able to do so is less likely still. There is however a possibility, for which it is desirable to be prepared: and what I wish you to consider, is, whether in that contingency, should I find it desirable to offer you the Foreign Office, you would be willing to undertake it? I have not forgotten that some time ago I expressed myself as thinking that it was not one which would suit you, or which you would wish to accept; but subsequent consideration has materially changed my views, and the letter I showed you from Malmesbury renders a change indispensable. Disraeli is very strongly opposed to the Pr[ime]. Minister & the Foreign Secretary being both in the House of Lords; and he, I know, would not be unwilling to take it himself; but to this there are many and valid objections: and in the H[ouse]. of Commons I know of no one except yourself to whom I should like to entrust it. Moreover, with a view to your future prospects, it would place you in a much more prominent position than the Indian Sec[r][etary].ship, which takes a man more or less out of the general course of European politics. I don't want an answer to this – nor do I make any definite offer. I must be guided by a variety of circumstances which I cannot foresee; but I wish you to think the matter well over, before the case arises in which it is necessary to <u>act</u>.

189

Stanley to Derby, DP 920 DER (14) 105/7
27 April 1866
St James's Square

I should be sorry to see you (or myself either) a minister on sufferance; and I do not see how with the present H[ouse]. of

---

[6]A typographical error in *DDCP*, p. 248, dates the entry describing this letter to 24 March, but the original diary confirms 24 April as the correct date. The point is material: the offer to Stanley was only made once Malmesbury's letter had been received and acknowledged.

C[ommons]. we can be anything else. I think this will be your feeling also.

I do not hold as strongly as Disraeli does the theory that a Foreign Sec. must be in the H[ouse]. of C[ommons]. The contrary has been the case during the greater part of the last 25 years, (v[ide]. mem[orandum]. enclosed):[7] under Liberal as well as Conservative administrations: and I never heard objections taken on that ground, though I have heard complaints, not wholly unreasonable, of the two great departments of expenditure (War and Admiralty) being represented in our House by under secretaries.

Between ourselves, I conceive that D.'s theory on that subject had a merely personal origin. Our friend Malmesbury never succeeded in obtaining public confidence: he did not do himself justice in debate, and justice was not done him.[8] I can understand that D. should have desired a change of persons: and it was obviously expedient to suggest for such a change a general rather than a personal reason. This difficulty is now removed.

In the event of your determining to undertake the government, is Lord Cowley, as Foreign Secretary impossible? The Queen, I am nearly sure, would suggest that arrangement. Clarendon is his personal friend, you would support him in debate, he ought to understand foreign affairs, he is fairly respected, and too little known here to have enemies.

I am in your hands, but the place in question is that of all others for which I judge myself least fit.[9] Nor do I think, if it can be avoided with honour, that you ought to hold office without a majority. But that question will keep.

[7] Stanley's accompanying memorandum listed the foreign secretaries since 1841 (excluding the brief tenures of Granville and Russell in 1852 and 1853 respectively). It concluded: 'The office has therefore been held. [sic] In the Lords, about 16 years. In the Commons, about 9 years. Out of these 25 years, Liberals have held office nearly 23.'

[8] If Stanley's suspicions were correct about Disraeli's feelings, the latter were warmly reciprocated by Malmesbury. See above, **186**.

[9] The Government having been defeated on 18 June, Stanley noted on 21 June, in the interim before the announcement of Russell's resignation, that he had 'reluctantly' assented to take the Foreign Office. *DDCP*, p. 253. At the Queen's request, on 28 June, Derby went through the motions of offering the post to Clarendon, but – as Derby expected – he refused.

190

Stanley to Disraeli, Dep. Hughenden, 111/3, fo. 89
4 July [?1866][10]

Stirling won't do.[11] In the debates of 1858 he made a violent personal attack on the Emperor. For any other place he would be very fit, if he would accept it: but not for F.O. — I have told Ld D[erby]. this.

191

Derby to Stanley, DP 920 DER (15) 12/3/7/3
[9 July 1866][12]

Of course I will attend to the F.O. business in the H[ouse]. of L[ords]. but I should like M[almesbury][13] to be kept au courant as he suggests.
With regard to the 'note identique', if it is right to protest ag[ain]st. the right of Prussia to dissolve the Confed[eratio]n. I think we may, and ought to join in it, as we have a Minister accredited to it.[14]

192

Derby to Stanley, DP 920 DER (15) 12/3/7/5
11 July 1866
Downing Street

[...] You will see that the news from Paris today is most important.[15] As far as one can judge the Emperor's intentions are very friendly

---

[10]Year with question mark appended by archivist, but the date is not contentious.

[11]As parliamentary under-secretary at the Foreign Office. Sir William Stirling Maxwell (1818–1878), Conservative MP for Perthshire, 1852–1868 and 1874–1878; friend of Disraeli; succeeded as ninth Baronet Maxwell, 1865. He made a hostile speech on the theme of the will of Napoleon I, 12 February 1858. See *Parl. Deb.*, CXLVIII, cols 1269–1273. Disraeli was clearly keen to get an ally in the job, and also suggested Ralph Earle. The appointment was one of the more difficult ones, and in the end the post went to E.C. Egerton. See Derby's diary entries for 2 and 3 July, *DDCP*, pp. 256, 257.

[12]Date in another hand.

[13]Derby only wrote 'M', but the reference could be to no other.

[14]The Austro-Prussian War had broken out in June. On 12 June Austria had broken off relations with Prussia, and carried a motion for federal mobilization against Prussia in the German Diet. The same day, Prussia had declared the German Confederation at an end. Italy had gone to war as Prussia's ally.

[15]On 10 July, telegrams from the embassy in Paris had sent word that the French fleet was ordered to the Adriatic, that French generals had been sent to headquarters, and that Napoleon intended to enforce an armistice. On 11 July, however, the news was received that

towards us, and we must not intimate any jealousy of his proceedings.[16]
I think he has got into a scrape.

193

Stanley to Disraeli, Dep. Hughenden, 111/3, fo. 93
12 July [1866]
Foreign Office

I send you Cowley's private letters. Also drafts of mine to him.

The Emp[eror]. has got into hot water. He jumped at the position which the Austrian offer of Venice gave him, and forgot the difficulties in his way.[17] These are great, & increasing. Words will not stop Prussia: and he is not ready to go to war.

We are well out of it.

The language I hold is that while generally favoring [*sic*] peace, we maintain an attitude of reserve, and do not pledge ourselves to any specific proposals.

I think the Prussians will begin again, and reach Vienna. Farther I don't see.

194

Disraeli to Stanley, DP 920 DER (15) 12/3/8/8
[12 July 1866][18]
11 Downing Street

What a crisis![19]

All you have done turns out quite right —

I go to my election tomorrow, but congratulate you on being again an M.P.

Napoleon had backed off, and the order to the generals had been countermanded. Prussia had made it clear that it would grant no armistice without preliminary peace terms. TNA, FO 27/1626.

[16]The Austrians had been beaten at Sadowa/Königgrätz on 3 July, and it seemed as if France might intervene militarily. On 4 July Napoleon declared unilaterally that Austria had ceded Venetia to France (in advance of its being united with Italy), and that France would mediate, but on 10 July he decided to pursue negotiations with Prussia. See above, **191**.

[17]In the wake of defeat and the French declaration that they would mediate, the Austrians had ceded Venetia to France (from whence it would pass to Italy), as a preliminary to a final settlement of the situation in northern Italy. See above, **192**.

[18]Date in another hand. Also a note: 'Observations on Lord Cowley's letters.'

[19]The reference is to the continental war and French machinations.

195

Stanley to Disraeli, Dep. Hughenden, 111/3, fo. 97
19 July [1866]

Nothing new. Austrians seem determined to try another battle. Venetian reinforcements coming up rapidly. I think they will lose Vienna.

196

Stanley to Derby, DP 920 DER (14) 105/7
26 July [1866]
Foreign Office

Brunnow was here on Tuesday, and is coming again tomorrow: his object to ascertain what course England will take, in the event of being called upon to go into a Congress.[20] I told him I thought it would be premature to discuss that question until we were invited by the belligerent parties, which had not as yet happened, and possibly might not happen: he dwelt at length on the inconvenience of England & Russia being shut out from a European settlement, and was especially anxious that I should consult you on the subject. I am bound therefore to let you know his wish: but I think it would be wiser to reserve our decision until we know by whom, and under what circumstances, we are to be invited to confer.

197

Derby to Stanley, DP 920 DER (15) 12/3/7/7
[30 July 1866][21]
St James's Square

I enclose you a letter which I found on my return from the H[ouse]. of L[ords]. this evening.[22] I think the Queen is right, that 'it would hardly be becoming if no interest was expressed by the English

---

[20] As Stanley rightly suspected, discussion on this question would have been premature, as Prussia had no need or desire to call a European Congress, and a preliminary peace was concluded the same day.
[21] Date in another hand.
[22] Not found.

Government in the fate' of the K[ing]. of Hanover.[23] I do not think that it would be in the least degree inconsistent with the system of absolute neutrality which we have adopted, & I think wisely, that you should send something like the enclosed to Loftus. We <u>may</u> receive a <u>snub</u>. I don't think we shall; but an absolute indifference as to a case which nearly touches our own Royal Family will hardly be consistent with our international position, and, if known, will not be well looked on by the country.

[Enclosed:]

Suggested[24]

I have to instruct you to call upon Mr. Bismarck, & represent to him that neither H.M. nor H.M.'s Gov[t]. can view without very painful feelings, the absolute ruin of a Sovereign so nearly connected as is the K[ing]. of Hanover with H.M. & whose dominions were the birthplace of H.M's family. While therefore H.M's Gov[t]. disclaim any title to interfere with those rights which the K[ing]. of Prussia has acquired by successful war, they desire earnestly to urge upon H.M, in relation to the Kingdom of Hanover, such a moderate and generous exercise of those rights as may tend to enhance the triumph of his Arms, and give additional strength to those friendly feelings which it is the desire of H.M's Gov[t]. to see subsisting between H.M. & the K[ing]. of Prussia.

---

[23]The King of Hanover, Georg V (1819–1878), was the Queen's cousin. This was the beginning of a long series of exchanges about the financial settlement relating to the king's estates, in which Britain had a residual interest, given that the title Elector of Hanover had been held by the British monarch between 1714 and 1837, and that Georg was a British prince by birth. As a result of Prussia's victory over Austria, Hanover had been absorbed into the new North German Confederation. The matter dragged on for more than a year until, in September 1867, King Georg and the Prussians agreed on an amount of capital on which the king could live, if the North German Confederation received Hanoverian state funds that he had sent to Britain. Stanley noted in his diary on 1 October 1867 that 'the arrangement as to the K. of Hanover's fortune is at last made, and the treaty signed: a good end of a matter which though not important has been troublesome'. *DDCP*, p. 319.

[24]This enclosure is a proposed despatch to the British ambassador at Berlin. A communication in exactly this form has not been found in either of the relevant series of drafts and despatches, TNA, FO 64 and FO 244.

198

Stanley to Derby, DP 920 DER (14) 105/7
8 August 1866
Foreign Office

I feel bound to send this to you, as I told Apponyi I would take till tomorrow to consult you as to the answer.[25] But I have not the slightest doubt as to what the answer ought to be. We ought simply to decline.

There is no reason to think that Italy would accept our advice if offered in the sense proposed.[26] Indeed we know to the contrary.

Nor do I believe Austria sincere in making the proposition. She is massing forces in the Tyrol with a view to another battle.

Both nations are in the same position. Both have been beaten, and both want a victory to restore their military prestige.

Either Napoleon has blundered in his diplomacy, or he is playing a double game, and trying to revive the quarrel: in which he is likely enough to succeed.

I called on you, but you were out. Disraeli concurs in the above.

199

Stanley to Derby, DP 920 DER (15) 12/3/7/9
8 August [1866]

I do not think we can act at this stage.[27]

The French government does not ask us to help them. It is only the opinion of the French ambassador at Vienna. If the Emperor wants us to join he will ask us. To interfere unasked is to risk a rebuff, and probably do more harm than good. S

[Derby's response noted on reverse:

I concur with L^d. S. Moreover if the application were made and acceded to, there would be no security, if M^r. Elliot's despatches are to be entirely trusted, that Italy would not continue the war single-handed. I think it might be hinted to M^r. E. not to give to the Ital.

[25] Apponyi had suggested British diplomatic intervention. Derby was of the same opinion as his son (see below, **199**), and, on 9 August, Stanley met with Apponyi and 'gave him an answer to his question of yesterday: in the negative'. *DDCP*, p. 264.

[26] Neither Stanley's diary nor his letters to Bloomfield in Vienna state precisely what the proposal was. However, given this letter and **199**, below, it seems that Austria had suggested, following an idea floated by the French representative in Vienna, that Britain convey to Italy an Austrian offer for a preliminary peace.

[27] See above, **198**.

Gov^t. reason to expect support from us. He seems to me to have given rather too much encouragement in this sense.]

200

Stanley to Derby, DP 920 DER (14) 105/7
16 August 1866
Foreign Office

It would never do to recall Odo Russell.* It would be a bad move, even if we meant to fight the Pope's battles, which we cannot and ought not. I don't expect that the present Pope will consent to any changes, but he cannot last long, and terms may be made with his successor. I do not believe the Italians are hostile to the Papacy, or that they grudge him his sovereign dignity: what they want is the territory, and that in one way or another they are sure to get. Many of them would be content to leave him Rome, or a part of it, (this was About's[28] plan): but they will never be in a mood to treat the question calmly, until the French occupation is at an end. It is the foreigner they object to. I fear the Emperor will find it hard to give way on this point, after his other defeats – Mexico[29] and Germany. But we shall see when the time comes. Russell is coming away on leave for the next month or six weeks. [. . .]

201

Disraeli to Stanley, DP 920 DER (15) 12/3/8/10[30]
17 August 1866
Grosvenor Gate

I have read Cowley's letters with much interest.

Bloomfield's, both handwriting & matter, are those of a greengrocer: Loftus sh^d. be the foreign editor of the Morning Herald: Morier, as ambassador,[31] is 'high life below stairs'[.]

Elliot a partisan — [. . .]

---

[28]Edmond François Valentin About (1828–1885), French journalist and author of a pamphlet about the Roman question.

[29]The French had installed the Emperor Maximilian in Mexico, but in the face of Mexican republicanism and American opposition they had been forced to withdraw their occupying forces early in 1866. Maximilian himself would be executed by the victorious republicans in 1867.

[30]This letter is reproduced in full in M&B, IV, p. 468.

[31]Robert Burnet David Morier (1826–1893) was not an ambassador, but chargé d'affaires at Frankfurt.

202

Stanley to Disraeli, Dep. Hughenden, 111/3, fos 105–106
22 August 1866
Foreign Office

Cowley is not in haste to get away, and will probably stay till the end of the year. The selection of his successor is therefore not urgent.[32]
[. . .]
All going on peaceably: in Italy the feeling is cooling down fast, and I think the great European question is in a fair way to being settled.
The Greeks are doing all they can to stir up a civil war in Crete, and seem likely to succeed.[33] But they will not command much sympathy: Greece itself is in such a state that no change could be for the worse.
[. . .]

203

Stanley to Disraeli, Dep. Hughenden, 111/3, fo. 107
23 August 1866
Foreign Office

I fear I must trouble you to read the enclosed papers. You will see by them what Musurus proposes. It cannot in any case be done without the sanction of an Act of Parl[iamen]t, and I can see no reason why it should be done at all. The Turkish security is bad enough at best: why go out of our way to weaken the hold we have upon that government?[34]
I fear this Candian[35] business will grow into a war. The Greeks in Greece are encouraging the movement, and though all but bankrupt, are said to be trying to provide arms.

---

[32]Much discussion followed, in this letter and in other correspondence, as to who should be the successor to Cowley, before the choice fell on Lyons, then at Constantinople.

[33]In Crete, still part of the Ottoman Empire, local leaders (encouraged by the Greeks) were demanding union with Greece. A revolt against Turkish rule had begun on 14 May, with a demand for lower taxes and legal reforms. On 3 August, the Cretans had informed Britain, France, and Russia that they would have to defend themselves by force. Small-scale fighting had begun by the end of August.

[34]Disraeli agreed. See below, **204**.

[35]Cretan.

204

Disraeli to Stanley, DP 920 DER (15) 12/3/8/12
26 August [1866]
Hughenden

The proposition of the Turkish government seems to me inadmissible.

It is a good rule never to change a security: but to change an unlimited security, for a limited one, could never be justified. The proposal is to transform an imperial Turkish security into an Egyptian one —

The Ho: of Commons, wh: originally looked with great disfavor [*sic*] on the Turkish loan, would never countenance this modification of the security for an unpopular advance.

205

Derby to Stanley, DP 920 DER (15) 12/3/7/16
6 September 1866
Knowsley

[. . .] Cowley's account of the new foreign minister,[36] confirmed as it is by Fane,* does not hold out a pleasant prospect; but it will not have escaped you that Cowley says the only man he had got on well with was <u>Lyons</u>.[37]

206

Stanley to Disraeli, Dep. Hughenden, 111/3, fos 111–112
6 September 1866
Foreign Office

[. . .] Nothing urgent in my department: Brunnow is doing what he can to make the Cretan affair a European question, but I am acting, or rather postponing action, with the utmost caution, as I have good hope that the Turks may be able to settle the matter by a display of force, with little or no fighting.[38] [. . .]

---

[36] Moustier, the new French foreign minister, who had been appointed on 1 September, though La Valette was acting foreign minister until Moustier's return. See below, **209**.

[37] Lyons was one of the leading candidates to succeed Cowley. See above, **202**.

[38] In early September, the Cretan rebels had declared union with Greece and the abolition of Turkish rule; the Russian consuls in Crete had been encouraging the revolt against Turkish rule.

207

Stanley to Derby, DP 920 DER (14) 105/7
10 September 1866
Foreign Office

[. . .] The Greeks, with their accustomed mendacity, have put about a report that we, the British government, had been advising the cession of Crete to Greece! Erskine* telegraphs to me to contradict this, which I have done in the plainest terms.

All this diplomatic disturbance inclines me to think that the Cretans are now aware they have no choice in the way of armed resistance, and that they are trying to bring about foreign intervention before the movement collapses of itself. If I am right, our policy of delay is justified: and in any event it can do no harm. [. . .]

208

Stanley to Derby, DP 920 DER (14) 105/7
19 September 1866
Foreign Office

[. . .] The Turkish victory in Crete does not appear decisive,[39] but I hope it may be enough to stave off the eastern question for the moment. The sick man is very sick, and if handing over Crete to Greece would avert a general collapse, it might be the best thing for all parties: but the Porte can hardly give way on one point without provoking a general rising among the Christian populations.

I believe Brunnow to be sincere when he says his government does not desire to precipitate events in the east. Russia has enough on hand at present. Disordered finance – railroads to the Black Sea not yet made – serfs hardly settled down as free peasants – Poland still deeply discontented – are the real reasons which induce the Russian government to wish things may go on as they are for a while. [. . .]

---

[39] Turkey had made some advances, but not enough, and fierce fighting continued.

209

Stanley to Derby, DP 920 DER (14) 105/7
22 September 1866
Foreign Office

[. . .] You will see from the despatches of this morning that Moustier*
is more of a Turk than we supposed.[40] Now that the Cretan war has
fairly begun, I think the less we commit ourselves the better, until time
and failure shows [sic] that the Turks cannot regain effectual & quiet
possession of the island. If they win, there is nothing to be done except
to preach moderation &c as before: if they lose, and the war drags on,
we shall have to interfere: but not yet.

210

Derby to Stanley, DP 920 DER (15) 12/3/7/21
23 September 1866
Balmoral

[. . .] I have sent to the Queen Howard de Walden's despatch &
private letter. I should think the case of Belgium serious, if it were
not for the more than antagonism which subsists between France &
Prussia; but I do not think the former has any hostile intentions; and
would not be sorry to appear as the protector of Belgium if the latter
should attack her, especially if such a quarrel (as soon as she is ready to
fight) should give her a pretext for obtaining the Rhenish provinces.[41]

I do not attach much importance (at present) to the Cretan
question – nor, I confess, have I much sympathy with these eastern
Christians. [. . .] I do not think their condition would be improved
by being handed over, like the Ionian Islands, to the constitutional
(?)[42] monarchy of Greece. But their success would be the beginning
of the end; for an immediate flame would be kindled throughout
all the Greek population, and the 'Eastern question' be precipitated,
while no power is prepared with a solution of it. I hope therefore
that the insurrection will be promptly and effectually put down,

---

[40]Moustier had made it clear that the Cretan rebels could expect no support from France.
Stanley noted on 1 November that he 'professes warm sympathy with England, and desire
to act in concert with us, especially on eastern affairs'. *DDCP*, p. 270.

[41]The Queen had received a letter from an alarmed King of the Belgians, written on 10
September, in which he discussed Bismarck's machinations and the possible offer of Belgium
to France. *LQV*, second series, I, pp. 367–368.

[42]Derby's question mark.

whatever influence the protecting powers may afterwards exercise towards mitigating Turkish ferocity. [. . .]

211

Stanley to Derby, DP 920 DER (14) 105/7
24 September 1866
Foreign Office

[. . .] The Cretan business grows more and more serious:[43] but Lavallette* [*sic*] will do nothing, being only at his post provisionally, and Moustier seems Turkishly inclined.[44] The telegrams are not very trustworthy, but it cannot be doubted that the Turks have been beaten.[45] [. . .]

212

Stanley to Derby, DP 920 DER (14) 105/7
6 October 1866
Foreign Office

[. . .] I hear that the Austrians are going to bring over Beust* from Saxony to manage their affairs. They want a man, and he wants power, so both will be suited. Both Apponyi & Bloomfield give a lamentable description of the finances and general position of the Empire.

I have nothing in today.

213

Stanley to Derby, DP 920 DER (14) 105/7
11 October 1866
Foreign Office

Brunnow has been here a long while, discussing Cretan affairs chiefly: I shall make into a draft the substance of what he said, and therefore only send you these papers which he wished that you should see. Please return them.

---

[43]The fighting had spread, and by October there would be conflict across the island.
[44]See above, **209**.
[45]The Turks had not been comprehensively beaten, though at Vrises the Cretans had defeated Egyptian forces.

214

Derby to Stanley, DP 920 DER (15) 12/3/7/31
12 October 1866
Knowsley

I return, without delay, the papers confidentially left with you by Brünnow. Your conversation with him may have thrown some additional light upon their meaning; but as I read them the dominant idea seems to be the impossibility of a really good understanding between Russia and France, and a desire to come to one with us, to the exclusion of the latter power. You will not, I am sure, fall into this trap. It is very probably true that the mutual jealousies of France and Russia are much against their united action; it is so much the more our interest and duty to keep on such terms with both as to prevent separate action on the part of either; and, to do justice to France, she seems well disposed to fall in with this view. Russia professes to have no arrière penseé[46] with regard to the Turkish empire; but Prince Gortchacow lays down as a 'condition de rigueur' as to its continued existence the establishment of peace with its Christian subjects, based on the satisfaction of their 'aspirations légitimes['].
Now there is no question that so far as Crete is concerned the Christian 'aspirations' are, and are admitted to be, the subversion of the Ottoman sovereignty; and although the last paragraph only suggests a pressure on the Turks 'de ne pas abuser de leur victoire',[47] the whole tenor of the despatch is to encourage, and to induce us to encourage with them, this 'aspiration'. When the insurrection shall have been put down, there is no reason why the three courts should not interpose, even by a note identique in the cause of humanity, and especially if the Egyptian troops have been guilty of the barbarities which are hardly denied; but to concur with one of the great powers in attempting any ulterior object would be alike contrary to our duty and our interests. I shall be anxious to see your draft recording your conversation with Brünnow, or I may say your conversations, for I see by your note to your Mother that you were to have another today.

---

[46]'hidden motive'.
[47]'not to take advantage of their victory'.

215

Stanley to Derby, DP 920 DER (14) 105/7
18 October 1866
Foreign Office

I send, separate, a paper which the P[rince]. of W[ales].* wished you should see. It is part of a letter from the K[ing]. of Greece.[48] The P. talked to me chiefly about the Cretan affair: he is very anti-Turk, but I think I made him understand the position, and that it is not expedient, if we can help it, to bring the whole eastern question on our heads. [. . .]

216

Stanley to Derby, DP 920 DER (14) 105/7
19 October 1866
Foreign Office

[. . .] Since I began this letter Brunnow has been here (as usual) and hinted, or rather told me in plain terms, that the Emperor would be much gratified at having the Garter! Why an Emperor should care to have the Garter I don't understand: but that is his business, and if it pleases him I should think you will have no objection. It seems that he has decorated, as they call it, some of our princes. B. told me the details, but I fear I have forgotten them. If he considers the thing a compliment, it would be a good way of marking the complete reconciliation which has taken place since the war of 1854–6. Please answer as to this.[49]

217

Derby to Stanley, DP 920 DER (15) 12/3/7/36
20 October 1866
Knowsley

If the Emperor of Russia would take it as a compliment to have the Garter, I can see no reason for not giving it to him, but rather the

---

[48] Stanley noted on 1 November that he suspected the Prince to be encouraging the King of Greece in supporting the Cretan rebels. *DDCP*, p. 271.
[49] See below, **217** and **218**.

reverse. So if you think fit to recommend it to the Queen, you may say that you do so with my concurrence.[50] [. . .]

218

Derby to Stanley, DP 920 DER (15) 12/3/7/37
26 October 1866
Knowsley

I return Genl. Grey's* letter,[51] which I received just in time to answer one from the P. of Wales, who suggested that such a proposition should be made to the Queen. H.M.'s reasons are tolerably plausible; but I have no doubt you are right as to the real motive. It is unlucky that Brünnow should have <u>asked</u> for the Garter. [. . .]

219

Derby to Stanley, DP 920 DER (15) 12/3/7/39
8 November 1866
St James's Square

I quite approve of your proposed draft to Odo Russell. I think it would be useful if you were to circulate it in the Cabinet. They like to know what is done or said, even if they are not consulted about it.

220

Stanley to Derby, DP 920 DER (14) 105/7
9 November 1866
Foreign Office

I send a draft of instructions which I propose to send to Odo Russell. He knows my wishes already, and as far as he is concerned I have no

---

[50] Stanley's note appended: '<u>Ans[were]</u>d. Am writing to the Queen.' He duly wrote to her on 22 October. See *LQV*, second series, I, pp. 369–370.

[51] On 23 October, Grey conveyed the Queen's refusal, on the dubious grounds that she never gave the Garter to foreign rulers unless they visited her, were near relatives, or 'unless there was some special reason for deviating from the ordinary practice'. *LQV*, second series, I, p. 370. In his diary on 1 November 1866, Stanley suggested that the real reason was a reluctance to concede any authority to the Prince of Wales, who would have bestowed the honour while visiting Russia for the Tsarevitch's wedding. *DDCP*, p. 271. Eventually, Alexander was awarded the Garter on 14 August 1867, the same day as the Austrian emperor.

fear of any want of caution: but it may hereafter be convenient to have defined beforehand our position.

The French desire only that we should not meddle. The Italians don't ask our interference. In this country there is less feeling than there was on the question, though what sympathy there is is, no doubt Italian and anti-papal.

221

Stanley to Derby, DP 920 DER (14) 105/7
11 December 1866
Foreign Office

[. . .] — I shall send you in a day or two a couple of drafts on Servian affairs, which I hope you will concur in. France and Austria have already expressed similar opinions.

The Greek government is doing all it can (happily that is not much) to bring about a war.

I have nothing today of importance.

222

Disraeli to Stanley, DP 920 DER (15) 12/3/8/19
12 December 1866
Grosvenor Gate

What do you hear from Paris?
I have your accounts.
I shall be at that paradise, D[owning].S[treet]. N°. 11, early this morning.[52]

223

Derby to Stanley, DP 920 DER (15) 12/3/7/48
13 December 1866
Knowsley

[. . .] I returned your Servian despatches yesterday.[53] Hammond said it was wished they should go out by today's mail. I concur in the view

---

[52] In his diary for the same date, Stanley recorded that Disraeli had come to see him, saying that 'he had received from one of the Rothschild family alarming news as to the state of France. It was thought that people were getting tired of the empire.' *DDCP*, p. 279.

[53] The Serbs were continuing to press, as they had been doing for some years, for the Turkish garrisons in Serbia to be removed.

which they take; but I cannot say I think the suggestion contained in that which I received and return today is likely to be acceptable to either party. [. . .]

224

Stanley to Derby, DP 920 DER (14) 105/7
14 December 1866
Foreign Office

[. . .] I lay very little stress on the alternative proposition as to Belgrade. Hammond seemed to think it might be useful as avoiding the name [*sic*] of a total surrender of the fortress. But the main point is that the Turks should cease to hold it: and that we have advised. It is their best chance for continuing to exist, but I fear they will be obstinate.[54] [. . .]

225

Derby to Stanley, DP 920 DER (15) 12/3/7/50
21 December 1866
Knowsley

Look at a minute I have made on a despatch of Erskine's returned to Hammond today — We are really carrying to an extreme our forbearance towards that wretched little Kingdom of Greece, whose utter incapacity of government at home is only equalled by its activity for mischief abroad.[55]

226

Stanley to Derby, DP 920 DER (14) 105/7
22 December 1866
Foreign Office

I will send the Greek despatches which you have noted to the law officers for report: but I hardly see what is to be done. Armed interference in the present state of eastern affairs would even if

[54]In fact, on 3 March 1867, Turkey agreed to evacuate the Serbian fortresses, and the principality was all but independent thereafter.

[55]On 27 December 1866, Stanley noted that 'unluckily our minister, Erskine, allows his philhellene sympathies to be much too manifest, thereby stirring up unfounded hopes among the Greek population'. *DDCP*, p. 281.

justifiable be exceedingly impolitic: it would be regarded not as a mere matter of police but as a demonstration in favour of Turkey.

I have as low an opinion of the Greeks as you: nevertheless Turkey is all but exhausted, we shall inevitably have the eastern question on our hands in a year or two, (perhaps in a few months) and I do not want England to be always on the losing side. I don't mean that we should take part against the Turks, but only that we should avoid doing anything that looks like giving them direct assistance. Remember that nothing can be done to remedy such a state of feeling as exists throughout Greece, short of an occupation by an armed force.

I write in great haste.

227

Derby to Stanley, DP 920 DER (15) 12/3/7/51
[?26 December 1866][56]
Knowsley

Bismarck* surpasses himself in the audacity of his avowals of bad faith, and of having designedly thrown dust in the eyes of France!

228

Disraeli to Stanley, DP 920 DER (15) 12/3/8/21[57]
30 December 1866
Grosvenor Gate

I have just heard, from a first-rate quarter, that, at the last Cab: Council at the Thuilleries [sic], a proposition, from Bismarck, suggesting an arrangement, by wh: the southern states of Germany should blend with Prussia, & that France sh^d take possession of Belgium, was absolutely brought forward, & favored [sic] by several of the ministers: principally by Lavalette. It was opposed by the Min[istr]^y. for F[oreign].Aff[air]^s:

Can this be true? And if so, or if there be any foundation for it – what are Bismarck's relations with us? Have you heard anything from our goosey gander at Berlin,[58] a pretty instrument to cope with the Prussian minister! And Mr Fane – what does he say?

---

[56]Date, with attendant question mark, in another hand.
[57]This letter is reproduced in M&B, IV, p. 469, though without the last two sentences. For Stanley's subsequent enquiries and private views, see below, **229**.
[58]Loftus.

And what shall we say?

The Emperor is like a gambler, who has lost half his fortune, & restless to recover: likely to make a coup, wh: may be fatally final for himself.

I doubt, whether this country w^d. see any further glaring case of public violence & treachery with composure — Reaction is the law of all human affairs: & the re-action from non-intervention must, sooner or later, set in — I wd. rather, however, try to prevent mischief – i.e. as long as we can.

I go to Q[uarter]-Sess[ions]: tomorrow morning, & in the evening to Hughenden, where I shall remain till the 8th.

Write to me there, if you have anything to say= and what about Crete?

229

Stanley to Disraeli, Dep. Hughenden, 111/3, fo. 142
31 December 1866
Foreign Office

In Napoleon's position, which though not quite as bad as your friends described it, is unsatisfactory enough, there is no saying what he may or may not do. But nothing that is known here encourages the supposition that there is any understanding between him and Bismark [*sic*].

That Bismark [*sic*] offered him Belgium during the war is certain: and it is equally certain that he rejected the proposal with some warmth, probably thinking it a trap.

The feeling in southern Germany, though divided, points in general to union with Prussia: that is, to close alliance offensive and defensive. There is a report that secret treaties to that effect have been entered into by Baden and Wurtemburg: which seems likely enough, but is not certain. But this alliance is directed expressly against France, and is certainly not made with her consent, if it is made at all.

I will try and find out what is passing.[59] At present I can hardly believe in a deliberate proposal to annex Belgium, though like many other wild ideas, it may have passed through the Emperor's brain.

The Cretan question is likely to give trouble. Up to this point we are perfectly uncommitted and free to act, if we act at all, as events

[59] Stanley noted in his diary on 31 December that he had asked Fane to investigate, 'but I have told him at the same time I do not believe a word of it'. *DDCP*, p. 282. In fact, such an arrangement had been discussed earlier in 1866, but had come to nothing, and in 1870 the draft treaty to that effect was used by Bismarck to discredit Napoleon.

may lead us. Moustier has got a plan of some sort which he will communicate shortly.[60] I do not know its purport.

230

Stanley to Disraeli, Dep. Hughenden, 111/3, fo. 146
2 January 1867
Foreign Office

All good wishes for the new year!

I wrote the substance of your French report[61] to Fane, who has answered, but knows nothing to confirm it, and evidently disbelieves. I think it a canard, but it is always well to attend to such warnings.[62]
[...]

231

Stanley to Derby, DP 920 DER (14) 105/8
4 January 1867
Foreign Office

[...] You will see what Fane says about the Emperor's growing indolence and irresolution. The same story reaches me from other quarters. La Tour* mildly hints that Moustier seldom sends him any instructions. I don't know that we have cause to regret that state of things.

Beust seems inclined to have a finger in the eastern fire. One would imagine that an Austrian premier had enough to do at home.

La Tour is coming this afternoon, but too late, probably, to allow of my letting you know what he says. [...]

[60] Eventually, on 25 January 1867, Stanley recorded a volte-face by Moustier, 'saying that nothing can now be done with Crete except to let it be annexed to Greece'. *DDCP*, p. 286.

[61] See above, **228**.

[62] M&B, IV, p. 469, misrepresent this reply by suggesting that Stanley treated the suggestion of a 'threat to Belgium' as a canard, rather than the particular rumour to which he referred. Stanley was correct in his supposition that there was no specific agreement. His concern about the general threat to Belgium is clear from both this letter and others.

232

Stanley to Disraeli, Dep. Hughenden, 111/3, fo. 156
'M. 27' [27 March 1867][63]
Foreign Office

Luxemburg is farther advanced than we thought.[64] An intercepted telegram states that the demand for it is about to be made.[65] Bentinck[66] knows nothing. Bernstorff, who knows a good deal, looks alarmed, and talks of the danger of a war. I meant to have told you this verbally but hear you are not at your office. [. . .]

233

Stanley to Disraeli, Dep. Hughenden, 111/3, fo. 158
3 April 1867 '2.40 P.M.'
Foreign Office

The enclosed has just come in. I don't see how war can now be avoided.[67]

[63]Given the content, the month cannot be May.

[64]In 1866, propelled by domestic opinion, Napoleon sought compensation for the territorial expansion of Prussia. The Grand Duchy of Luxembourg was held by the King of Holland, but its fortress was manned by a Prussian garrison as part of the defensive arrangements of the German Confederation. Given that the Confederation had been dissolved after the Austro-Prussian War, the situation was anomalous and Luxembourg was an obvious target for French ambitions. Franco-Prussian negotiations on the subject achieved nothing, and Bismarck confounded Napoleon's attempt to buy Luxembourg from Holland. See also letters **233–246**, below.

[65]Stanley recorded in his diary that day that he had received an intercepted telegram suggesting that France would shortly reclaim 'the occupation of the fort and country of Luxemburg'. *DDCP*, p. 296.

[66]William Charles Philip Otho, Baron Bentinck, seventh Count of Waldeck-Limburg, the Dutch minister in London.

[67]In the enclosure, fo. 160, it was reported that Napoleon had told the Prussians that the possession of Luxembourg 'involved the question of his own existence'. Stanley noted this down in his diary that day. *DDCP*, p. 298.

234

Disraeli to Stanley, DP 920 DER (15) 12/3/8/26
'Wednesday' [3 April 1867][68]
Grosvenor Gate

Rothschilds[69] have received information that the Emperor has definitely informed Bismarck, that the arrangement between himself & King of Holland is concluded, & that he shall act at once on it.[70] What have you heard?

235

Stanley to Disraeli, Dep. Hughenden, 111/3, fo. 162
3 April [1867][71]

The Dutch government are willing to sell, if they can get the consent of Prussia. Bismarck says positively that the feeling of Germany makes it impossible for him to give way. Bernstorff has been here this morning. He expects war – and asks whether we will join![72]
If the Emperor moves, it will be war. At least I think so.

236

Stanley to Disraeli, Dep. Hughenden, 111/3, fo. 164
4 April [1867] '2.30.'
Foreign Office

Bernstorff has been with me this morning, and says the K[ing]. of Holland has given way, withdrawn from his offer, and the Luxemburg question is at an end. What dish [*sic*] for the Emperor to eat! I am not bound to secrecy, and shall make the thing public in answer to any question that may be asked. I think there can be no doubt of the truth

---

[68] Date in another hand.

[69] Disraeli had close contacts with the Rothschild family, principally the banker Lionel de Rothschild, whose European links provided a useful flow of continental intelligence. See below, **254–257.**

[70] In other words, that France would buy Luxembourg from the King of Holland. This failed when Bismarck objected. See below, **238, 240.**

[71] An archivist has appended in pencil '?1867', but it is clearly a response to letter **234.**

[72] In his diary entry for 3 April, Stanley recorded Bernstorff's request, 'which of course I declined in the plainest terms'. *DDCP*, p. 298.

of his story: it is an official telegram: but I have telegraphed to Cowley for confirmation.

237

Derby to Stanley, DP 920 DER (15) 12/3/7/58
'Wednesday' [17 April 1867][73]
Roehampton

I send you the enclosed, which please return, by the Queen's command. I see by Telegram that the K[ing]. of the Belgians will not hear of the proposed solution – in which I cannot but think he is ill-advised.

[Enclosed:]

General Grey to Derby
16 April 1867
Windsor Castle

The Queen desires me to send you, very confidentially, for your information and that of Lord Stanley, the enclosed copy of a letter from the Queen of Prussia.

You will doubtless have seen what the Queen has written to Lord Stanley on the subject of Luxemburg, and are aware of HM's anxiety, while we carefully avoid being mixed up in the quarrel between France and Prussia, that we should exert our utmost influence at both Courts to prevent a rupture by assisting, as far as we are able, in finding a mode of settlement honourable to both Parties. Her Majesty is strongly inclined to the opinion, which Lord Cowley seemed to entertain, that the neutralisation of Luxemburg would afford the best chance of effecting this object; but she fears that such an arrangement could hardly be depended upon, if the Grand Duchy were to remain in the possession of the King of Holland, whose necessities would probably soon drive him to make his private Bargain with France. H.M. cannot therefore but think that the most satisfactory settlement of the question would be, the transfer of Luxemburg to Belgium, whose own safety and independence would require the maintenance of the state of neutrality which, in that case, would naturally be extended to the Grand Duchy.

---

[73] Date in another hand.

It might be well worth while for Belgium to pay the money required for an acquisition of so much importance to her safety.

P.S. Since I wrote the abr,·e the Queen has sent down a telegram from Vienna, dated yesterday, in which Lord Bloomfield says that Baron Beust has made the same suggestion and that it has been well received at Berlin.

238

Stanley to Derby, DP 920 DER (14) 105/8
17 April 1867
Foreign Office

I return Grey's letter and its enclosure. We are in the dark altogether. Nothing can be more positive than the language of Bismarck in the despatch read to me on Monday, the substance of which you have seen. He says that on no condition whatever will Prussia consent to evacuate the fortress. If Beust has not deceived himself, Bismarck's language to him has been exactly in an opposite sense. Which is one to believe? Till the point of Prussia's willingness to go out of Luxemburg is settled, it is premature to consider how the fortress is to be disposed of. This is what I have been telling Apponyi within the last half hour, and what I shall tell La Tour if he comes.

I don't think, in any event[,] the K[ing]. of the Belgians will consent to an exchange of territory: in which case there remains only the simple solution of leaving things as they are, and the territory and fortress in the hands of the K[ing]. of Holland, minus the German garrison.

239

Disraeli to Stanley, DP 920 DER (15) 12/3/8/27
17 April 1867
Grosvenor Gate

I like Beust's scheme: it wd. satisfy everybody, if, as appears, Prussia sanctions – let me have a line to Hughenden, where I am now going, if you think there is anything in it.

Your approval, perhaps, wd. help.

240

Stanley to Disraeli, Dep. Hughenden, 111/3, fo. 166
17 April [1867]
Foreign Office

I like Beust's scheme too: but you and I are close in our taste. Bismarck declared to me, through Bernstorff, on Monday, that on no condition whatever would Prussia consent to give up her right of garrison: and the K[ing]. of the Belgians on the other hand affirms that nothing shall induce him to consent to the proposed exchange. This does not look like a settlement. I shall hear more in a day or two. [. . .]

241

Disraeli to Stanley, DP 920 DER (15) 12/3/8/28[74]
[22 April 1867][75]
Windsor Castle

My visit here has tumbled me into the midst of the Luxembourg [*sic*] business; & I have had all the despatches, & all the private letters of all the cousins, submitted to me= & you know all the rest.

I assured our Royal Mistress, & most sincerely, that she was quite under a mistake in supposing, that you wd. not act if necessary, & that, I knew, you had well considered all the eventualities about Belgium; that you w[d]. never act with[ou]t determination & constancy; & that anything you did, or said, w[d]. have double the effect of the old stagers[76] with their mechanical interference; sometimes bluster & sometimes blundering.

I told her Majesty also, that we were not really a half Governmen[t]. until the division of last Friday,[77] & that a hint from you c[d]., & w[d], do more now, than reams of despatches a month ago.

I think she understood all this: & I think I did good.

---

[74]Reproduced in M&B, IV, pp. 470–471.
[75]Disraeli had recorded 'Easter Monday 1867' at the top of the letter. Someone has noted '22 April 1867', which it was.
[76]Presumably, *inter alia*, Palmerston and Russell.
[77]The vote at the beginning of the committee stage of clause 3 of the Reform Bill; not, strictly speaking, the previous Friday, but 12 April. The vote had been on Gladstone's amendment about compound householders, proposing to reject the personal payment principle. Disraeli's victory was a critical moment in the process, and put the Government and the bill on a surer foundation.

I pointed out also, that, so far as matters went, the question of Belgium was not really on the tapis.[78] This, after reflection, she agreed to = but still thought that, in confidential conversation, our people might let it be known at Berlin & Paris, that the violation of Belgian neutrality sh[d]. not pass with impunity.

At present it seems the pressure sh[d]. rather be put upon Berlin, than on the ancient capital of Julian the Apostate.[79]

Two things seem to me clear: that France is not prepared, & that Bismark [sic] lies to everyone – His explanations prove his perfidy.

I think, myself, as old Brunnow says, 'it is time for a little re-action', & that we might begin to dictate a little to Europe – Gladstonism is at a discount.

It[']s very lucky, however, we didn't take off any taxes: & that by paying off some debt, we shall be able to borrow any amount at a very moderate price. That is to say, in case we want it. Nevertheless, as nothing happens wh: one expects, I begin to believe you will turn out a regular Chatham.[80] [. . .]

242

Stanley to Disraeli, Dep. Hughenden, 111/3, fo. 168
23 April [1867]
Foreign Office

Thanks for your letter. It is satisfactory to see that even the dulness [sic] of a Windsor visit has not affected your spirits.

H.M. has written to the K[ing]. of Prussia in the strongest terms that can be used deprecating war and advising him to give way. The Belgian influence has helped to bring about this interference: Leopold thinks that if a war were to break out, it would very probably end in France getting Belgium and Prussia Holland.

I am ready to go as far as may be necessary in support of Belgium, short of giving an absolute pledge to fight for its independence. Suppose we gave such a pledge, that France and Prussia came to an understanding, Russia and Austria standing aloof, where should we be? But I say nothing in an opposite sense, lest we should lose our influence.

---

[78]'under consideration' or 'under discussion'.

[79]Paris. Flavius Claudius Julianus, Emperor Julian (c.332–363), fought a series of campaigns in Gaul and was first declared emperor by the soldiers at Lutetia (Parisii) in February 360.

[80]William Pitt, first Earl of Chatham ('Pitt the Elder') (1708–1778), secretary of state and leading minister in the Devonshire and Newcastle coalitions during the Seven Years' War; Prime Minister, 1766–1768. Disraeli evidently liked the allusion, repeating it in letter **255**.

The neutralisation of Luxemburg is the one indispensable condition of peace. If that can be obtained from Prussia, arrangements of detail may be easily made.

Bismarck has chosen this time of all times to go off into the country. He returns tomorrow, when Loftus will see him.

The French say they can put 400,000 men into the field. Our reports give them from 300,000 to 350,000. Excitement at Paris very great. [...]

243

Stanley to Derby, DP 920 DER (14) 105/8
'7.P.M.' [29 April 1867][81]
Foreign Office

I send one line to say that La Tour, Bernstorff, Brunnow, Azeglio, and Apponyi, all of whom I have seen today, look on the Luxemburg affair as settled. I had forgotten Van de Weyer, who holds the same language. I hope it is so – but I don't feel as if the fish were quite landed yet. Still on their joint authority I have held out more hopes to the House than I should otherwise have done.[82]

Italy wants to be in the conference,[83] which as we know how it is to end, will be a cheap civility. I told Azeglio my personal opinion was favorable [*sic*], but I could give no pledge.

The House is evidently pleased, and the whole affair will have done us good.

I hope your head is getting right again. I have been incessantly at work since 9.30. but am pretty clear now.

---

[81] The dating of this letter is straightforward. Italy made its request on 29 April, on which date in his diary Stanley noted receiving Azeglio, and used almost exactly the same words as in this letter (*DDCP*, p. 305). Given that Stanley also answered a parliamentary question about Luxembourg that day (see below), the date is clear.

[82] Stanley reassured the Commons: 'Although it is too early to speak with absolute confidence on the matter, yet I have every reason to hope, and even to believe, that this question of Luxembourg [...] is in a fair way to be speedily and amicably arranged.' *Parl. Deb.*, CLXXXVI, col. 1705.

[83] The conference to discuss the Luxembourg question, to which Stanley had formally agreed on 28 April, and which would be held in London, 7–11 May 1867.

244

Derby to Stanley, DP 920 DER (15) 12/3/7/60
[3 May 1867][84]

I think the course suggested by Hammond quite the right one. For the reason assigned in his letters to Cowley, I should have thought that Belgium should <u>not</u> take part in the Conference – but it is not very material. The despatch explanatory of the telegram will not reach Petersburg till after the Conference has met.

245

Derby to Stanley, DP 920 DER (15) 12/3/7/61
Sunday night [5 May 1867][85]
St James's Square

Let me see you, if not at breakfast tomorrow, as early as you can after.[86]

Bernstorff was with me today, and I think the settlement of the European question now hangs on the course we are prepared to take. If the 'European guarantee' can be accepted in the sense in which Prussia is willing to accept it, I do not see that it need interpose an insuperable obstacle to a settlement.

246

Derby to Stanley, DP 920 DER (15) 12/3/7/63
13 May 1867
St James's Square

[. . .] I thought it as well to <u>volunteer</u> a statement to the H[ouse]. of L[ords]. as to the signature and purport of the treaty[.]

---

[84]Date in another hand.
[85]Date in another hand.
[86]That day, the news had been received that Prussia insisted upon a European guarantee of the neutralization of Luxembourg. *DDCP*, p. 307.

247

Note by Hammond, DP 920 DER (15) 12/3/7/63[87]
14 May 1867

As the conference has not entered on the Turkish question and was never intended to do so, there seems no occasion to deal with the matters raised in Lord Denbigh's[88] papers, which from a cursory inspection seem to partake very much of the character of those which at various former times have been put forth in different quarters.[89]

I am not afraid for Turkey so long as England holds aloof from any joint interference in its internal affairs, which we have no right to exercise, which is uncalled for, and which is only invoked by Russia in order to ensure the destruction of the Turkish empire.

248

Stanley to Cowley, Cowley MSS, TNA, FO 519/182, fo. 321
29 May 1867
Foreign Office

I have thought a great deal about the Luxemburg papers, and consulted Hammond: and I cannot avoid the conclusion that we must publish. In the first place, both Lord Derby and I have promised the papers. In the next, we have entered into certain national engagements, and Parliament has a right to know from us why we did so. But the passages to which you objected have been wholly or partly struck out. [. . .]

---

[87] Stanley's note appended: 'Lord Derby has sent me these papers to look at. I do not think, nor does he, that they are of much importance. S'

[88] Rudolph William Basil Feilding, eighth Earl of Denbigh (1823–1892).

[89] The enclosures have not been found; they presumably included proposals by Denbigh about the reform and/or security of the Ottoman Empire.

249

Disraeli to Stanley, DP 920 DER (15) 12/3/8/29
10 June 1867
11 Downing Street

What do you hear from Paris?
I hear rather strange things.
I shall be at D[owning]. S[treet]. all day from 2 o'[clo]ck: I could
see you at four o'[clo]ck: [...][90]

250

Stanley to Cowley, Cowley MSS, TNA, FO 519/182, fo. 335
15 June 1867
Foreign Office

[...] We had Luxemburg brought on last night, in a thin House:
the result entirely satisfactory: the guarantee went down more easily
than I had ventured to expect or even to hope. [...]

251

Derby to Stanley, DP 920 DER (15) 12/3/7/69
[16 June 1867][91]
St James's Square

[...] I congratulate you on your triumph of Friday —[92]

252

Derby to Stanley, DP 920 DER (15) 12/3/7/73
[27 June 1867][93]

[...] Can you send me a copy of your last despatch to Loftus,
remarking on the cases of collective guarantee on which Prussia has

---

[90]Stanley duly called on Disraeli on 11 June. The news, from Rothschild, was 'vague, but
alarming intelligence of intrigues now going on at Paris'. Stanley 'could not make much of
what he said, but promised to watch and make all necessary enquiries'. *DDCP*, p. 311.
[91]Date in another hand.
[92]Stanley's speech of 14 June. See above, **250**.
[93]Date in another hand.

not thought herself called upon to act? I sh^d. like to see it before tomorrow.

253

Stanley to Disraeli, Dep. Hughenden, 111/3, fo. 213
'9.A.M. Wed.' [?June 1867][94]
St James's Square

[. . .] D[']Azeglio wants to see me today – I have fixed him for 3 — He will press for intervention – I am against this – what do you say?

254

Stanley to Disraeli, Dep. Hughenden, 111/3, fo. 176
30 August 1867
Knowsley

A letter from Fane, which I enclose, tells all the little that is known to me of what has passed at Saltzburg [*sic*].[95] The Emperor's speeches, and the tone of the French press, are reassuring on the whole: the press of Berlin on the other hand is using the most offensive language, defying the French [:] 'We know you would fight us if you dared, but you dare not.' Whether this is only stupidity, or a premeditated purpose of forcing on a quarrel, the result is the same. What do the Rothschilds say?[96] [. . .]

255

Disraeli to Stanley, DP 920 DER (15) 12/3/8/31[97]
1 September 1867
Hughenden

I return Fane's letter with many thanks —
I have heard nothing from the R[othschild]s – I observe, they never write, & only speak, indeed, on these matters in a corner, & a whisper.

---

[94]Archivist's note: '?Nov. 1867'. There is no internal or contextual evidence to suggest that this letter was written in November. There are other possibilities. On 1 June (though not a Wednesday), Stanley recorded in his diary a meeting with Azeglio, who urged joint Anglo-Italian intervention in the near east. It is possible that this letter dates from that period.

[95]There were signs of a French rapprochement with Austria. Franz Josef and Napoleon had met at Salzburg earlier that month, where they had, rather inconclusively, discussed a 'policy of resistance' to Prussia and Russia.

[96]See below, **255**, **256**, **257**.

[97]This letter is reproduced in M&B, V, pp. 83–84, but without the first line or, in a telling omission, the last sentence.

To form a judgment [*sic*] of the present state of affairs, one must be greatly guided by our knowledge of the personal character of the chief actors.

The Emperor will never act alone; Bismarck wants quiet; & Beust, tho' vain, is shrewd & prudent.

Gorthc^{ff}. [*sic*] is the only man, who could, & wo^{d}, act with the Emperor, in order to gain his own ends, on wh: he is much set, but if the Emperor combines with him, he will so alarm, & agonise, Austria, that she will throw herself into the arms of Prussia, in order than an united Germany may save her from the destruction of all her Danubian dreams. I think affairs will trail on, at least for a time, & the longer the time, the stronger will be y^{r} position. In such a balanced state of circumstances, you will be master. I expect you to become the greatest foreign minister since Chatham.

256

Disraeli to Stanley, DP 920 DER (15) 12/3/8/32
5 September 1867
Hughenden

I took y^{r} hint & wrote to R[othschild].[98] & not receiving an answer, rather regretted it; but, this morning, the enclosed came —[99]

There is not much in it, but he is a man, who never dresses up a tale, & always understates. It is as well, too, that you sh^{d}. have the power of comparing accounts & impressions from quarters of equal, & first-rate, authenticity. I shall, therefore, encourage him. [. . .]

257

Stanley to Disraeli, Dep. Hughenden, 111/3, fos 178–179
9 September 1867
Foreign Office

I return Rothschild's letter, with many thanks. My intelligence is not positive as to what passed at Saltzburg [*sic*],[100] but all peaceable as far as it goes.

---

[98] Baron Lionel Nathan de Rothschild (1808–1879), banker and formerly Liberal MP for the City of London.
[99] Disraeli enclosed a letter from Rothschild of 3 September 1867.
[100] See above, **254**.

[...] — I found the great lady[101] in good spirits [,] living out of doors in all weathers: not a word said of home affairs, not much of any business: I don't see that she has at present any political idea, except the old one of supporting Prussia against France, which is not practical, and quite harmless.

La Valette holds language as regards Crete &c entirely opposed to that of Moustier, and it looks as though the French policy was going round again. What fellows they are, not knowing their own minds for six months together. [...]

258

Stanley to Disraeli, Dep. Hughenden, 111/3, fos 182–183
17 September 1867
Foreign Office

[...] All quiet in Europe. Bismarck gives up the Prussian F.O. but retains the chief direction of affairs. I fancy the change is only on grounds of health. I have been long expecting to hear of Moustier's retirement, but he seems to have got a new lease. [...]

259

Stanley to Disraeli, Dep. Hughenden, 111/3, fo. 185
23 September 1867
Foreign Office

[...] Bismarck's circular[102] has produced a bad effect in France. It was quite unnecessary, and somewhat offensive.

Another Garibaldian row seems likely: but I think the Italian government will stop him.[103]

---

[101] The Queen. Stanley had been at Balmoral from 31 August to 7 September. For a record of his visit, see *DDCP*, pp. 316–317.

[102] On 7 September 1867, in the wake of Napoleon's meeting with Franz Josef of Austria at Salzburg in August, Bismarck had issued an open circular to Prussian diplomatic representatives, in which he had welcomed the 'formal denial' by the French and Austrians 'of all projects of intervention in the internal affairs of Germany', but had included a veiled threat that any 'foreign combinations' would 'legitimately excite' the sentiments of the German people. *The Times*, 20 September 1867.

[103] Garibaldi was set on a new military adventure, leading a revolutionary force in an attempt to depose the Pope and gain Rome. In the short term, Stanley was right: Garibaldi was arrested on 23 September, but he escaped on 17 October and the Italian government refused to re-arrest him.

260

Stanley to Derby, DP 920 DER (14) 105/8
9 October 1867
Foreign Office

[...] Nothing very definite is known as to the state of the Roman business. I incline to think that the revolutionary parties have not made much way. The flight of the Pope, or the occupation of Rome by Italian troops, would at this moment be a very serious addition to the other perplexities of the Emperor.

261

Disraeli to Stanley, DP 920 DER (15) 12/3/8/38[104]
14 October 1867
Grosvenor Gate

I thought it wise to reconnoitre, & called on our friend yesterday.[105]

He said the Emperor was no longer master of the position, & repeated this rather significantly.

In time, I extracted from him, that they had information from Paris, that there was a second treaty bet[wee]^n. Prussia & Italy.

I rather expressed doubts about this, & hinted that it seemed inconsistent with what had reached us, that there was an understanding bet[wee]^n. France & Italy, that the Emperor sh^d give notice of his course &c.

He was up to all this, & showed me, or rather read, a telegram, I sh^d. think of yesterday, in precisely the same words as you expressed, so I inferred the same person had given the news to Fane & his correspondent. Probably Nigra[106] himself.

The information of the secret treaty[107] had arrived subsequently, & he stuck to it, & evidently believed it.

I give no opinion, but as I c^d. not see you today till late, & might interfere with your railroad, I thought it best to write this.

---

[104]This letter is reproduced in M&B, V, p. 84, without the sentence beginning 'I give no opinion' or the last sentence.

[105]Baron Lionel de Rothschild.

[106]The Italian representative in Paris.

[107]Stanley could find nothing out about a treaty between Prussia and Italy. See his diary entry for 19 October 1867, *DDCP*, p. 320. Given the events of the previous year, rumours as to Prussian intentions were rife; this seems to have been another of them.

The Berlin ministry have consulted another member of the family about ironclads. They are going to expend $\frac{1}{2}$ mill: sterling immediately thereon. & told him they thought of having the order executed in America, as, in case of war with France, the ships would not be allowed to defend it if they were constructed in England.

He told me a good many other things, that may wait, as I am very busy this morning — [. . .]

262

Stanley to Disraeli, Dep. Hughenden, 111/3, fo. 194
14 October [1867][108]
Foreign Office

Many thanks for your information. I am disposed to believe it: so far at least as to assume that there is an understanding, even if no actual treaty has been concluded. [. . .]

263

Disraeli to Stanley, DP 920 DER (15) 12/3/8/40
[16 October 1867][109]

I had not seen it – They don't send me the telegrams now.[110] It[']s very grave. I will be with you at F.O. at $\frac{1}{2}$ past two [. . .]

264

Stanley to Derby, DP 920 DER (14) 105/8
30 October 1867
Foreign Office

No fresh telegrams from Italy up to this date (4.P.M.)[.] Baude[111] and Azeglio both suppose that things are going on quietly. The French

[108] An archivist has added a question mark, but the letter is clearly a response to **261**.
[109] Dated by another hand, and a note appended: 'France & Italy'.
[110] In his diary that day, Stanley recorded a meeting with Disraeli about 'the Roman trouble', to which the telegrams clearly referred. To deal with Garibaldi's offensive and defend the Pope's temporalities, it was looking likely that Napoleon would order French troops back to Rome, from where they had withdrawn in December 1866. *DDCP*, p. 319.
[111] La Tour's deputy at the French Embassy, Baron Baude. On 1 November 1866, Stanley had recorded that Baude was 'a great ultramontane in his ideas, and curiously unguarded in language. In fact he talks as if he were an English politician in opposition'. *DDCP*, p. 269.

must by this time be at Rome.[112] Moustier's circular suggests, in effect, a conference of the Great Powers to settle the position of the Pope: I do not myself see how such a conference can be got together. Without a previous understanding it would be a mere debating-club, and what chance is there of such an understanding being come to? I shall however try and ascertain what the Prussians mean to say in answer to this invitation. – The Queen is anxious that we should not be mixed up in the business, and in that I agree with her: but she is more fidgety on the subject than is necessary.

265

Disraeli to Stanley, DP 920 DER (15) 12/3/8/45
31 December 1867
Grosvenor Gate

I have just come up from Quart[er]: Sess[ions]: but find here strange accounts from Paris.[113] I will try to see you in the course of the day: about three o'[clo]ck: in [*sic*] my way to D[owning].S[treet].: if you are there engaged, we might meet for ten minutes later.

266

Stanley to Disraeli, Dep. Hughenden, 112/1, fos 1–2
16 January 1868
Knowsley

I enclose copy of a note from Lyons, by which you will see that it is doubtful whether the Danubian loan guarantee[114] will be called for. The secret I suspect to be, that a French company have got the money, which they would like to lend to the commissioners[115]

---

[112]On 26 October, French troops had arrived to defend the Pope. Garibaldi's troops were defeated by them at Mentana on 3 November.

[113]It is not clear what these 'strange accounts' were; Stanley made no note of them in his diary.

[114]Funds were being sought by the European Commission of the Danube, established by Article 16 of the Treaty of Paris (30 March 1856) to oversee works to clear the mouth of the River Danube. Stanley helped secure British funding and successfully led efforts to secure a European guarantee for a loan. The resultant Danube Works Loan Act was passed in the summer of 1868.

[115]The members of the European Commission of the Danube; representatives of all the signatories of the 1856 Treaty of Paris sat on the Commission. Britain's representative was Sir John Stokes (1825–1902).

on usurious terms, knowing the security to be good: but of course the commission will not close with the offer if a guarantee can be had enabling them to get what they want more cheaply. Bismarck is personally favorable [*sic*] to the guarantee, but says he must consult his colleagues. [. . .]

On 19 February 1868, on the grounds of ill-health, Derby informed Disraeli that he proposed to resign. A letter to the Queen followed on 21 February. On 25 February, after a delay occasioned by the Queen ignoring Derby's requests about peerages, Disraeli went to Osborne to kiss hands and accept the premiership. The Cabinet was left almost completely unchanged, with Stanley remaining as Foreign Secretary.

267

Stanley to Disraeli, Dep. Hughenden, 112/1, fo. 15
21 February [1868]

As you are now <u>de facto</u> Premier, I send on my semi-official letters to you, as I have been in the habit of doing to Lord Derby. Please forward them when read, to the Queen. I enclose a label.

268

Disraeli to Stanley, DP 920 DER (15) 12/3/8/55[116]
23 April 1868
Grosvenor Gate

This appears to me important.[117]
Charles[118] is virtually Bismarck.[119]
A few days ago, B was all fury against France, & declared that France was resolved on war &c. but on Monday the R[othschild]s wrote to Berlin, that they understood England was so satisfied with Prussia, so convinced, that she really wished peace &c, that England would take no step, at the instance of France, wh: would imply doubt of Prussia &c.

---

[116]This letter is reproduced in M&B, V, p. 85.
[117]Note in another hand: 'Reduction of Prussian Army'.
[118]Stanley added 'Rothschild'.
[119]Stanley added: 'They see one another daily'.

This is the answer[120] – I can't help thinking, that you have another grand opportunity of securing the peace of Europe & establishing your fame —[121]

I will call as I go by.

269

Stanley to Disraeli, Dep. Hughenden, 112/1, fo. 28
24 April 1868
Foreign Office

I have seen Bernstorff. He knows nothing of intended reductions. I told him the substance of your telegram, not naming the authority, but saying it was good. He promised to enquire and let me know. He says that the language held at Berlin is that they are satisfied, generally, with French assurances.

270

Disraeli to Stanley, DP 920 DER (15) 12/3/8/60[122]
24 April 1868
10 Downing Street

Bernstorff never knows anything. I am sure there is something on the tapis,[123] & I want you to have the credit of it. Vide Reuters tels– in Times of today 'Berlin Ap: 23' rumor [sic] on the Bourse &c.[124]

---

[120] Encloses a copy of a telegram from Berlin, dated 23 April, from Charles Rothschild to Baron Lionel de Rothschild, London: 'Tell your friend that from the 1st of May army reduction here has been decided upon, and will be continued on a larger scale if same system is adopted elsewhere. Details by post.'

[121] When Disraeli called on Stanley that day, as the latter recorded in his diary, he had conceived a scheme by which Britain would suggest to France that Prussian disarmament was Britain's doing. Britain would, by this means, obtain a pledge of disarmament from France, too. Stanley was sceptical: 'I doubt the feasibility of this combination, ingenious as it is.' DDCP, p. 332.

[122] This letter is reproduced in M&B, V, p. 85.

[123] 'under consideration' or 'under discussion'.

[124] It was reported from Berlin, in news dated 23 April, that: 'A rumour was current on the Bourse to-day that France, Prussia, and Austria had agreed to effect a reduction of their military forces by means of furloughs.' The Times, 24 April 1868. Disraeli's letter was the latest attempt to persuade Stanley of the virtues of a British intervention to encourage disarmament. See above, 268.

What I sh^d do w^d be to telegraph to Loftus, & bring things to a point, & then act.

I feel sure it will be done without you, if you don't look sharp.

[P.S.] You risk nothing and may gain everything[.]

271

Disraeli to Stanley, DP 920 DER (15) 12/3/8/61[125]
[25 April 1868][126]
10 Downing Street

I feel persuaded it[']s all true —
They have a letter this morning in detail, explaining the telegram, & enforcing it. The writer, fresh from Bismarck himself, does not speak as if doubt were possible: gives all the details of the military reductions to commence on 1st May, & the larger ones, wh: will be immediately set afoot, if France responds. How can you explain all this?

What of Loftus?

272

Stanley to Disraeli, Dep. Hughenden, 112/1, fo. 30[127]
'Sat[urday]. 6.P.M' [25 April 1868][128]

The telegram confirms your friend's expectations. I spoke to La Tour in anticipation of it, 'supposing the news were true, what would you do?' His answer was discouraging. He says (and indeed the tel. confirms him in that respect) that Prussian reductions mean nothing. 'What security do they give, when it is admitted that the men can be brought back in a week's time, if not in 24 hours'? I am compelled to own there is some force in the reply. Still, with the facts actually before us, we may press them a little.

---

[125] This letter is reproduced in M&B, V, p. 85.
[126] Date in another hand.
[127] This letter is reproduced in M&B, V, p. 86.
[128] Archivist's note, with question mark as to date. Given **271**, Saturday 25 April seems likely. That was certainly Buckle's assumption.

273

Disraeli to Stanley, DP 920 DER (15) 12/3/8/70
12 September 1868[129]

Just received enclosed.[130] What think you of it? You know, Colonel Feilding[131] was our manager of secret matters during the Fenian affair, & was sent by us to Paris? He is supposed to have first-rate information, having a genius that way, & knowing every one who has. [. . .]

274

Stanley to Disraeli, Dep. Hughenden, 112/1, fo. 46
12 September 1868
Foreign Office

Supposing things were as your friend imagines, what can we do? There is no dispute, no cause of war apparent.

If the French want to pick a quarrel they can manage it: any excuse will serve. But as yet we have not the slightest reason to suppose that such is their intention. Lyons believes in peace, while admitting that if war were intended the language would still be equally pacific.

I see no possibility of useful action. Can't call tomorrow, but we shall meet at Windsor. Thanks for the news.

275

Disraeli to Stanley, DP 920 DER (15) 12/3/8/72
21 September 1868
Balmoral

[. . .] Last night, a little before midnight, a telegram from Julius Reuter[132] disturbed us with the Spanish insurrection – shall I say revolution? Something from you today will perhaps tell us that. [. . .][133]

---

[129]Note in another hand: 'Letter from Col Feilding as to supposed warlike intentions of French Govt.'

[130]A letter from Feilding, dated 11 September, is enclosed.

[131]Lieutenant-Colonel William Henry Adelbert Feilding (1836–1895), fifth son of the seventh Earl of Denbigh; created general, 1893; investigated Fenianism and headed up the short-lived Home Office intelligence bureau established in the wake of a Fenian bomb being exploded in Clerkenwell in December 1867.

[132](Paul) Julius de Reuter (1816–1899), founder of the news agency bearing his name.

[133]Forces in rebellion against Queen Isabella had mustered at Cadiz on 18 and 19 September, and over the subsequent days much of the country declared for the rebels.

276

Stanley to Disraeli, Dep. Hughenden, 112/1, fos 65–66
25 September 1868
Foreign Office

I return the Belgian letter. What I have always told the Belgian government on the question of a commercial union is that if it should be proposed to them they have the clearest right to refuse, and that then, if any attempt should be made to use pressure to induce them to reconsider their decision, it will be time for them to appeal to us in defence of their right of free action.

What they want is, that we should interfere to prevent any overture of the kind being made, so as to save them from incurring the responsibility of a refusal.

I do not think this request reasonable. It would, if granted, place us in a false and invidious position as regards France, and it would give a plausible handle to French politicians to represent Belgium as willing to come into the scheme, and prevented only by English jealousy.

I have explained my view on this point again and again, but the state of panic in which all Belgian politicians habitually live on the subject of French designs makes it difficult for them to listen to reason.

277

Stanley to Disraeli, Dep. Hughenden, 112/1, fos 73–74
26 September 1868
Foreign Office

I leave town for three days, Northcote* taking my place, and Egerton[134] attending at the office. There is nothing urgent, and I shall take a cypher, and my secretary, so as to be in constant communication with this place. [. . .]

If Moustier can be trusted, the panic has blown over (v[ide]. the despatches received today): I always thought it was the work of journalists and speculators on the Bourse. — The Spanish minister here knows nothing of what is doing in his country, but does not deny that the affair is very serious.

I have explained to Lyons, for Moustier's benefit, that the ships sent to Spain are only for the protection of British interests. The French as yet have sent none. I do not imagine the Queen is in any personal danger: the insurgents would be only too glad to see her safe over the

---

[134]Edward Christopher Egerton, parliamentary under-secretary at the Foreign Office, 1866–1868.

border. It is [in] no way clear to me that if they succeed, they will be able to agree as to her successor. Union with Portugal would seem the best way out of the difficulty, but I suppose it is too rational a thing to be popular in either country. – I think you will admire the ingenuity of the Emperor's last reason for not removing his troops from the papal territory. He tells the Italians, 'If I did, people would say it was because I was going to war, and wanted them elsewhere.'

278

Stanley to Disraeli, Dep. Hughenden, 112/1, fo. 79
1 October 1868
Foreign Office

I return Grey's letter.[135] There is nothing to be done upon it just now, but the question may and probably will become serious. The Belgian government, backed by our Queen, desires to turn the European guarantee which now exists into what will be <u>de facto</u> an exclusive British protectorate.

Results – the loss of all the military advantage which our insular position gives us, and the creation of a second Hanover.

279

Stanley to Disraeli, Dep. Hughenden, 112/1, fo. 83
14 October 1868
Foreign Office

Do you see any reason for delaying the recognition of the <u>de facto</u> government of Spain? We may get something out of them in the way of improved commercial relations, and it is clear now that there will be no general reaction, such as might put Isabella back again on the throne.[136]

Of course we should not, like the Americans, say anything in the way of congratulation: simple recognition is all that can be required. There are some inconveniences in keeping this question long open. What do you think?

[135] Not found. Presumably another manifestation of the epistolary campaign conducted by the Belgian monarchy.
[136] See above, **275, 277**. On 28 September, the rebels had defeated the loyalists at Alcolea. Isabella fled on 29 September, and the leading rebel general, Serrano, entered Madrid on 3 October. He then formed a provisional government.

280

Disraeli to Stanley, DP 920 DER (15) 12/3/8/77
15 October 1868
Eridge Castle[137]

I cannot doubt, that we sh^d. at once recognise the Government, apparently established, at Madrid; though without phrase.[138]

281

Stanley to Derby, DP 920 DER (14) 105/9
30 November 1868
St James's Square

The question of immediate or deferred resignation was discussed by the Cabinet on Saturday, very fully, very calmly, and with the result that an unanimous decision was arrived at, in favor [sic] of the former course.[139] I placed your letter in Disraeli's hands, and he communicated the substance of it to our colleagues: I need not say that your expressed opinion carried the weight which it always does, but we believed that the bad effect which you fear on the minds of the party would be sufficiently counteracted by the publication of a letter from Disraeli explaining the cause of our retirement: and I must say, that as far as my limited observation goes, I am led to believe that our friends will be better pleased to see us in opposition than in the disagreeable situation of a ministry about to be forcibly expelled from power. I have already explained the reasons which weighed with us, but there is one which I omitted; the state of foreign affairs. It is possible that at almost any moment trouble may break out in Roumania, involving the whole eastern question: [. . .] As a provisional minister, I could hardly commit the country to a decided course of action in the east – and the question whether such action will or will not be necessary may arise at any moment – and thus England will be paralysed at what may be a very critical juncture. [. . .]

[137] The Sussex home of the Marquess of Abergavenny.
[138] Presumably, Disraeli meant 'without expressing any view' – favourable or unfavourable – as to the events in Spain.
[139] The Liberals had won the election and the Cabinet had agreed to resign immediately, rather than wait for Parliament to meet. They surrendered the seals of office on 9 December 1868.

CHAPTER 4

THE SECOND DISRAELI GOVERNMENT, FEBRUARY 1874–MARCH 1878

282

Disraeli to 15th Earl of Derby, DP 920 DER (15) 16/2/1
17 May 1874
10 Downing Street

L[yons]'s meagre & frigid letter,[1] enclosed, is another instance of the infelicitous judgment [*sic*] of our diplomatists[.]

It may almost rank with Cowley[']s letter to Malmesbury about the Hubner outrage.[2]

Pray, may I ask you, did you receive any telegram of the fall of the French Ministry? I did not: had I not been dining, en famille, with Lionel Rothschild I sh^d. have known nothing. His telegram arrived while we were at dinner. This sh^d be looked after.[3]

283

Disraeli to Derby, DP 920 DER (15) 16/2/1
19 May 1874
10 Downing Street

I must call your attention more particularly, & more formally, than I did on Sunday, to the affair of the Paris telegram.[4]

---

[1] About the fall of the MacMahon government in France.

[2] The letter discussing an incident on New Year's Day 1859, when Napoleon III had deliberately snubbed the Austrian ambassador to France, Count Joseph Alexander Hübner, which was the first clear warning of impending Franco-Austrian conflict. It had been the occasion for an alarmed foray into foreign policy by Disraeli. See above, **145**.

[3] Derby may have chosen to ignore this letter until he received that of 19 May; his diary makes no record of it until the second letter was received.

[4] Derby thought Disraeli's 'language shows an irritability quite unusual with him'. *DD*, 19 May 1874, p. 173. Thereafter, however, the Prime Minister regularly complained about the dilatoriness of the Foreign Office.

I pointed out to you, then, that no official information, respecting the division in the French chamber, had reached me, altho', on Saturday, during dinner, I had become acquainted with the fact.

If a telegram had been received in D[owning].S[treet]. on Saturday afternoon, there was great negligence in not furnishing it to me: if it had not, the service of the Queen is most inefficiently & injuriously conducted. [. . .]

284

Derby to Disraeli, Dep. Hughenden 112/2, fo. 59
19 May 1874
Foreign Office

I have been enquiring into the matter to which your note refers: I don't apprehend Lord Lyons is to blame, but there was somewhere great neglect in not sending you the telegram as soon as it arrived. I shall know more presently; but I suspect the fault has not been at Paris.

285

Disraeli to Derby, DP 920 DER (15) 16/2/1
20 May 1874
2 Whitehall Gardens

I have received an answer from Tenterden.*

His reason, that the tel:, when it arrived, was not sent to us, is not a bad reason, tho', strictly, not an adequate one.[5]

It is, that everybody knew the event, & that the news was stale.

This proves, that those in fault are at Paris.

With a priority on the lines, why was the telegram to Her Majesty's Government hours after those received by private individuals?

[5]Derby was mystified by Disraeli's persistence with this, 'for the event was one on which no action could be taken, and whether the news reached us at 10 p.m. on Sat or next morning at breakfast could be of no practical importance to anybody'. *DD*, 20 May 1874, p. 173.

286

Derby to Disraeli, Dep. Hughenden 112/2, fo. 61
20 May 1874

As you appear to attach some importance to the delay of the
telegram on Saturday, I will ascertain exactly

(1) When the event took place.
(2) When it was telegraphed from the embassy.
(3) When the telegram arrived.

I am not sure that we have a priority over the French lines for our
messages. At any rate the French government has precedence for its
own messages over ours.

287

Disraeli to Derby, DP 920 DER (15) 16/2/1
12 January 1875
Whitehall

It is a capital despatch; comprehensive and complete; & will please
the country.[6] You did well to have a recital of the past. In these days,
one must write, or speak, as if people had no memory. [. . .]
What about Spain?
It is unfortunate, we have such a man as Layard* there.[7] Tho' of
unquestionable talents, he is prejudiced & passionate, and always – I
will not say misleads – but certainly misinforms, us. I am told he was
the same with our predecessors, & entirely misled Granville & C°. as
to the Italian king.
He was as wrong about him, as he has always been about Serrano.[8]
I wish you c^d. get rid of him.

---

[6]It is uncertain what this despatch was about, though it is possible it was the Brussels
conference on the usages of war. That and Spain were the only matters of foreign policy
discussed at Cabinet that day.

[7]Derby agreed: 'Layard is wanting in tact and diplomatic smoothness: indeed diplomacy
is the last profession he should have chosen.' *DD*, 22 February 1875, p. 197. Disraeli changed
his mind later, when Layard was his tool in the undermining of Derby's policy.

[8]Francisco Serrano Domínguez, Duke de la Torre (1813–1885), Spanish statesman;
sometime acting regent, acting president, president, prime minister, and chairman of the
executive.

288

Derby to Disraeli, Dep. Hughenden 112/4, fos 13–14
12 January 1875
Foreign Office

I hear the most alarming reports of financial demands likely to be made by army & navy – whether in Cabinet today, or later, you know better than I.[9]

It seems to me that we are in a strong position to repel such attacks. We have next to no available surplus.

To borrow in time of peace is on the face of it absurd.

To impose new taxes would discredit us doubly.

First, because it is a reproach on our want of foresight, if we take off taxation in 1874 and put it on again in 1875. Next, because the late Cabinet made large reductions during their tenure of power; they may fairly claim half the credit for last year's budget, as they prepared the surplus: and the contrast will be rather too marked, if we begin spending and taxing as soon as we get a chance.

Europe is at peace: no present cause of quarrel exists.

The division of France and Germany makes it extremely improbable that either state will quarrel with us. As a matter of fact, both court our alliance.

It is not for me to say how largely augmented estimates will be received by the H[ouse]. of Commons: but that body must be greatly altered if they are popular, even on our own side.

Can we not tell these people that there is hardly anything for them this year but that 1876–7 may possibly be more productive?

Remember the D. of Northumberland and the house-tax in 1852.

289

Derby to Disraeli, Dep. Hughenden 112/4, fo. 26
25 February 1875
Foreign Office

The enclosed tells its own story.[10] I do not think the matter to which it refers is serious. It is part of Bismarck's policy – or an effect of his

[9]Derby passed this note to Disraeli 'before the Cabinet began'. According to Derby's diary, he, Salisbury, and Cairns, with Disraeli's support, led the successful case against increased expenditure. *DD*, 12 January 1875, p. 189.

[10]The enclosure does not remain, but evidently discussed Bismarck's aggressive treatment of Belgium. The German Chancellor, engaged in his *Kulturkampf* campaign against domestic 'ultramontanism', was using alleged support by Belgian clergy for his opponents in Germany as a pretext for putting pressure on the Belgian government. It followed an incident in which

temper – to keep questions of this sort open, and stir them from time to time. And it is Belgian nature to live in fear of some neighbor [*sic*], and to be constantly appealing to England for protection. When we were in last you remember how every six weeks there was a fresh rumour of French invasion. Now, the danger is thought to lie in the direction of Germany.

290

Derby to Disraeli, Dep. Hughenden 112/4, fo. 50
2 May [1875]

The enclosed is worth your reading. I believe the alarm is over now, but nobody will answer for next year."

291

Disraeli to Derby, DP 920 DER (15) 16/2/1[12]
6 May 1875
2 Whitehall Gardens

I had an audience yesterday:[13] she was very gracious, &, speaking entirely on foreign affairs, I thought very sagacious & intelligent. [. . .]

My own impression is that we sh^{d}. construct some concerted movement to preserve the peace of Europe, like Pam did when he baffled France & expelled the Egyptians from Syria.[14]

---

a Belgian, Alexandre Duchesne, asked a senior French cleric to pay him to assassinate Bismarck. The dispute added to tension between France and Germany, the latter ever suspicious of French designs on Belgium, and formed part of the backdrop to the 'War-in-Sight' crisis. See below, **290**.

[11] The reference is to the 'War-in-Sight' crisis. Bismarck's aggressiveness had increased tension between Germany and France, and France suspected it was the prelude to a general war. The issue reached a crisis point with the publication in *Die Post*, on 19 April, of an officially inspired article headed 'Ist der Krieg in Sicht?' Peace was secured by 11 May. At a meeting in Berlin between the Kaiser and the Tsar, Odo Russell made it clear to Bismarck that Britain would support Russian attempts to prevent war.

[12] This letter is reproduced in M&B, V, p. 422.

[13] With the Queen.

[14] Despite Disraeli's grand aspirations, Russia was already warning Bismarck not to move against France, which proved sufficient to stop Germany. The Prime Minister nevertheless had the satisfaction of being able to ride on Russia's coat-tails. His reference was to Britain's intervention in the eastern crisis of 1839–1841, when Palmerston had co-operated with Russia to stop the Egyptians, under Mehmet Ali, defeating the Turks and precipitating the collapse of the Ottoman Empire. As part of the settlement, Mehmet Ali lost control of

There might be an alliance between Russia & ourself for this special purpose; & other powers, as Austria, & perhaps Italy, might be invited to accede. [. . .]

292

Disraeli to Derby, DP 920 DER (15) 16/2/1[15]
18 May 1875
Hughenden

Your policy seems to [be] very popular, & very successful – I congratulate you heartily. It is encouraging. We must not be afraid of saying 'Bo[o] to a goose'.[16]

But we must get our forces in trim. We shall be able to do that next year. The revenue is coming in well. [. . .]

293

Derby to Disraeli, Dep. Hughenden 112/2, fo. 202[17]
[Undated][18]

I should be more impressed by these papers if I could remember a time when the C[ommander]. in Chief[19] had not been seriously alarmed at the state of our armaments.

No doubt the continent is arming; but with Germany & France watching one another, both are more likely to be civil to us than if they were on good terms.

It is a question, too, how long these enormous armaments will be endured by the masses who are compelled to serve. [. . .]

Syria, which he had conquered. Orleanist France, which saw Mehmet Ali as its protégé, was outraged at Palmerston's intervention in concert with autocratic Russia. Historians have regarded it as one of his diplomatic triumphs, reversing the Russian advantage achieved in the Treaty of Unkiar Skelessi, which Russia had forced on a weakened Turkey in 1833.

[15] This letter is reproduced in M&B, V, p. 423.

[16] Disraeli's reference was to the success of British policy over 'War in Sight'. See above, **290** and **291**.

[17] A larger part of this letter, with two further, short paragraphs, is reproduced in M&B, V, p. 426.

[18] Archivist's note: '?June 1875'. Buckle agreed, though there seems no particular reason for assuming it was written then, other than its proximity to the 'War-in-Sight' crisis.

[19] The post still held by George, Duke of Cambridge.

294

Derby to Disraeli, Dep. Hughenden 112/4, fos 54–55
22 August 1875
Fairhill, Tonbridge

You will have seen Elliot's telegram of the 20th on the Herzegovina affair.[20] And you will observe by it that all the Great Powers have agreed to send consuls to inform the insurgents that they are to expect no support &c and advise them to lay down their arms. The Porte accepts their proposal, and asks England to join.

Whether the Turks are well advised in accepting this kind of mediation may be a question: but they have accepted it: and that being so, and the Grand Vizier asking us not to stand aloof, I conceive that we have practically no option. I propose therefore at once to signify our willingness to join. If the apparent friendliness shown by the other Powers is sincere, there is no harm done, and some good: if otherwise, we shall be of more use in checking mischief by taking part than we could be if we declined to act.

I shall go on at once with the affair, unless you telegraph to stop me. I will be in London on Tuesday, and shall defer acting till then, to give time for your answer.

295

Disraeli to Derby, DP 920 DER (15) 16/2/1[21]
24 August 1875
Weston Park, Shifnal

There is no alternative after telegram of the 20th. But I don[']t like it —[22]

---

[20] A revolt against local misgovernment broke out in Herzegovina in early July 1875; by the end of August the whole of Bosnia was involved. On 19 August, Turkey had agreed to a Russian proposal for mediation by consuls representing the great powers. The British ambassador, Sir Henry Elliot (see above, **127**), had indicated British support for the consular mission, as his telegram explained.

[21] Telegram. A note on the reverse: 'Herzegovina Assents reluctantly to joint mediation.'

[22] See above, **294**. Count Gyula Andrássy, the Austro-Hungarian foreign minister, had brought pressure to bear at the Porte, through a joint representation from his own ambassador and those of Russia and Germany. The Porte had urged Britain to act with the other powers in making it clear to the insurgents that they could expect no outside aid. Disraeli reluctantly consented to do so.

296

Derby to Disraeli, Dep. Hughenden 112/4, fo. 56
4 September 1875
Fairhill, Tonbridge

[. . .] — I have not written to you about Turkish affairs, for your sources of information are the same as mine. What strikes me most strongly in connection with them is the very small progress which the insurgents seem to have made, though for all practical purposes unopposed.

Andrassy* is either quite undecided, or playing a double game. The Russians appear to be rather disposed to keep things quiet. I have no belief in the success of the consular mediation.[23]

297

Malmesbury's unpublished diary, MP 9M73/79
24 November 1875

Cabinet suddenly called to consider a tel. from Egypt.[24] Khedive asks 4 millions for his shares. Agree to give it. Rothchild [*sic*][25] finds the money & holds the shares at 5^{prct}. 1 million down – 3 in Jan[uar]^{y} & Feb[ruar]^{y} – Telegraph to Stanton[26] to close. Then a pressing demand

---

[23]Derby was wise. The consular mission that was supposed to mediate between the insurgents and the Turks arrived in Mostar in mid-September. The rebels refused to meet its representatives or to accept Turkish promises. By the end of the month the mission had failed.

[24]This Cabinet meeting made the decision to purchase the reversion of the Khedive's shares in the Suez Canal Company. In early October 1875, the Ottoman Empire announced its bankruptcy, undermining the Egyptian ability to borrow money. On 15 November 1875, Frederick Greenwood, the editor of the *Pall Mall Gazette*, had warned Derby that the Khedive was thinking of selling to France the reversion of his 176,602 canal shares, equivalent to a 44% interest in the Company. When Greenwood called at the Foreign Office on 16 November, he found that a British bid for the shares was 'as good as settled'. Derby raised the question in Cabinet on 17 November and it was agreed in principle that the Government would seek to obtain the shares. The Khedive formally offered them for £4 million on 23 November. After the meeting on 24 November, Rothschilds the bankers provided the money in the absence of Parliament. For Derby's account of the meeting, see *DD*, p. 256. He recorded that 'all attended, except J. Manners', though Gathorne Hardy, too, was absent (*DGH*, p. 254).

[25]Lionel Nathan de Rothschild. See above, **257**.

[26]General Edward Stanton, consul-general in Egypt.

from Hunt* for 12 gunboats for China – Refused in an offhand manner. I tried for six but not one member seems to care for the state of the navy & Derby tho' F[oreign]. Sec[retary] less than any one[27] – It is inconceivable unless they <u>disbelieve</u> the statements of the Admiralty. We are 10 ships <u>short</u> of our peace establish[men][t] & the Cabinet will only give 2 gunboats & 6 sloops – therefore the deficit will increase yearly in effective men of war. Some day we must rue this policy, & at the same meeting we borrow £4 000 000 to hold less than half the shares of the French Suez Canal Co – desirable in itself but not to be compared in importance to having ships to guard our commerce & support our foreign policy!

298

Disraeli to Derby, DP 920 DER (15) 16/2/1
26 November 1875
2 Whitehall Gardens

[. . .] I have just come from Windsor: the great lady, in a state of utmost excitement, & unbridled delight, about the Suez-purchase. She kept saying 'it is a blow to Bismarck'. That was evidently her Sovereign impression. I suppose, she referred to Bismarck's insolent declarations, that England had ceased to be a political power. [. . .]

299

Derby to Disraeli, Dep. Hughenden 112/2, fo. 238
26 November 1875

[. . .] As far as I can make out, the Suez business is likely to be popular. First impressions are everywhere in its favor [sic]. [. . .]

---

[27]Buckle (M&B, V, p. 442) accused Derby of being against the Suez shares purchase, but there is no evidence to support the accusation. Neither Malmesbury's account, nor Derby's diary, nor Carnarvon's, lists any objection to the purchase. In his diary entry for 24 November, Derby noted that 'there was no difference of opinion among us'. *DD*, p. 256. Indeed, it was he who first brought the issue to Cabinet.

300

Derby to Disraeli, Dep. Hughenden 112/2, fo. 242
30 November 1875
Windsor Castle

[. . .] — When I wrote to you that 'Harcourt said his friends were a little sore' I meant the French Harcourt,* not the English.[28] However, he is mollified. I have allowed him to publish a report, which I have seen and in some particulars amended, of a conversation which he had with me, and of another reported by Gavard.[29] Decazes* will read these to the Assembly, or lay them before the Assembly in some form, by way of showing that nothing against French interests is intended. [. . .]

301

Derby to Disraeli, Dep. Hughenden 112/2, fos 249–250
2 December 1875
Foreign Office

The Chancellor[30] and Northcote have been with me about this telegram of Stanton's, and we are all agreed that it would not be desirable to bid against the French.[31] It would be a bad bargain: at least a very speculative one: it would look as if we wanted exclusive possession of the canal which is just what we have always disclaimed: and it would excite the French government and people, who at present seem disposed to take the matter calmly.

If we don't buy, we can hardly object to their buying, after our own performance in that line: no territorial rights being involved in the proposed sale. Moreover, it is not certain that a second purchase by us would be as popular as the first.

---

[28] The French ambassador, rather than the Liberal politician, Sir William Harcourt. Derby was concerned that the public desire for an active British policy might create difficulties overseas, especially if it later turned into a 'war-cry'. *DD*, 29 November 1875, p. 257. His desire to dampen down public opinion and mollify France would irritate some of his colleagues and the Queen. See below, **303**.

[29] Charles Gavard, the French chargé d'affaires in London. The conversation with Harcourt was on 27 November; that with Gavard on 20 November.

[30] The Lord Chancellor, Lord Cairns.

[31] The Khedive was offering, for £2 million, to sell his right to 15% on all Suez profits over 5%, 'a very shadowy kind of property'. *DD*, p. 257. He said the French were prepared to offer the money; Derby was sceptical. This second offer was rejected; it has been confused by some with Derby's *support* for the initial purchase. On 24 December, Derby advised the Khedive not to sell his rights to France and the Khedive backed down.

This is our view, but we shall wait to hear from you.

If you agree, we must tell Stanton that we are not prepared to buy, and that we make no objection to the sale, provided no territorial rights are conveyed by it.

302

Disraeli to Derby, DP 920 DER (15) 16/2/1[32]
3 December 1875

I am clearly of opinion that we ought not to act. My principal reason is that, having asked for a mission, he has no right to enter into any new financial arrangements. Corry* will call on you to-morrow afternoon with my views.

303

Derby to Disraeli, Dep. Hughenden 112/2, fo. 261
3 December 1875
F.O.

[. . .] I don't altogether go with Carnarvon* about the canal,[33] and have told him so: but it is useless now to discuss the point, since what I said to Gavard & Harcourt is in the Times.[34] Remember that France is not all the world, and that there is a wide difference between the attitude of objecting to monopoly in other hands, and claiming monopoly for yourself. And what we want is security for free passage through Egypt under all circumstances: not Egypt itself.

304

Disraeli to Derby, DP 920 DER (15) 16/2/1
18 December 1875
2 Whitehall Gardens

I congratulate you on all yr triumphs.

---

[32] 'Decypher [sic] telegram from M[r]. Disraeli'. No address. Note on reverse: 'Suez Canal As to Khedive's power to sell his right to 15% profits.'

[33] Carnarvon had expressed alarm at Derby's public offer to the French of an international commission to manage the Canal. Disraeli had written to Derby from Longleat on 2 December on other matters, noting that he had received a letter from Carnarvon, 'the vein of wh: in my mind is correct'. Derby firmly deflected both men's objections.

[34] His exchanges were reported in letters written by Gavard and Harcourt to Decazes, and published in The Times on 3 December.

I need not trouble you with a line on the matter on wh: I wished to see you. Lady Derby* knows all about it & will tell you. I hope it will blow over quietly – but it is amazing.[35]

305

Derby to Disraeli, Dep. Hughenden 112/2, fo. 265
20 December 1875
Knowsley

My lady has told me the story of 'Alfred's secret' getting out.[36] You may like to know from myself that I never mentioned it to anybody. But I fancy he himself has not been discreet, and probably if the public knows anything it is through some of his private friends.

After all, the public will care very little how he gets the money, provided that Parliament is not asked for it. — The only thing I don't understand is Schouvaloff* saying that he got the story from a minister. He must be a reckless kind of talker, for a diplomatist.

306

Derby to Disraeli, Dep. Hughenden 112/4, fos 60–63
7 January 1876
Knowsley

By this time you have the Austrian note[37] in your hand: printed.

Beust is here, having asked himself, to explain it: he has not however added much to what appears on the face of the document.

My impression is that the reforms proposed are moderate and reasonable enough in the main. [. . .] — I gather that France will undoubtedly join in the move, and Italy also: and I do not think that we can hold aloof. If we decline to join, what follows? The Porte will refuse, and then we are responsible for the failure of what is at least a

---

[35] Presumably the royal embarrassment referred to in Derby's letter of 20 December, **305**.

[36] Alfred, Duke of Edinburgh (1844–1900), the Queen's second son, who had run up huge debts. Two days later, Derby recorded a letter from Disraeli, who had 'been reproached by the Queen' for letting the secret out. *DD*, p. 259.

[37] The Andrássy Note of 30 December 1875, which embodied proposals from Austria-Hungary, Russia, and Germany asking the Turks to provide guarantees to implement the reforms to which they had agreed in August. Derby received the Note at Knowsley on 4 January: 'The long-expected Austrian note is come: I read it rapidly, and with satisfaction, for in tone and general purport it appears moderate, and I can see nothing in it dangerous to Turkish power'. *DD*, 4 January 1876, p. 265.

promising attempt at conciliation: or the Porte will accept, and then we stand in the foolish position of being more Turkish than the Turks. Either way, we are isolated in Europe: and not backed by opinion at home.

[. . .] If we join, we ought to insist on the form being as little unpleasant to the Porte as it can be made: about which I do not suppose there will be much difficulty; and also on some sort of pledge being given by the Austrian & Russian governments that they will use their utmost exertions to induce the insurgents to lay down their arms. It is still possible that they may fail, and that the war may go on; but in that event we are no worse off than if the attempt at pacification had not been made. If, contrary to advice, the Porte ignores the suggestions addressed to it, our hands are free: we cannot take the responsibility of results arising from a policy which we have deprecated.

I should be glad to know your views, even in the briefest outline. It is too late to stand on the dignity and independence of the Sultan: a sovereign who can neither keep the peace at home nor pay his debts must expect to submit to some disagreeable consequences.

We may be dupes, but I think both Austria & Russia desire peace. Mutual jealousy, and fear of the establishment of an independent Sclave [*sic*] state, make it reasonable & natural that they should wish to see the status quo maintained. Whether the old fabric is not too rotten to bear patching, is another question: but a question we cannot answer till we have tried.

307

Derby to Marquis of Salisbury, SP, fo. 40
9 January 1876
Knowsley

I have read more than once your able letter.[38] I am waiting for a communication from Disraeli, and as yet the Cabinet is not in any degree committed on the Austrian proposals.

To stand aloof absolutely is to my mind out of the question. France & Italy will support Andrassy, therefore we should stand close, and with what result? The Porte, encouraged by our abstention, might resist: in which case we should be responsible for the failure of the whole

[38] Derby had received a letter from Salisbury on 8 January, 'the purport of it that we ought to accept the Austrian reforms in the lump, but take care not to engage ourselves in such a manner as to be drawn into further proceedings which may be contemplated by the three Emperors'. Derby agreed with Salisbury's conclusions, if not all his assumptions regarding the other powers. *DD*, p. 266.

scheme, and the continuance of the war. If [on] the other hand he[39] gave way against our advice, our position would be simply ludicrous. Nor should we be supported at home, for however little hopeful may be the prospect of a pacification, we have nothing better to suggest, and could only advise the parties to fight it out. But while thinking that a rejection of the Austrian scheme is not our interest, I agree with you that there is no need of being identified with it. All we have to do is to consider whether we can honestly tell the Sultan that he will on the whole lose more by rejecting than by accepting the advice offered by the three powers. As to the question of what will happen in the event of the insurgents rejecting all schemes of conciliation, I do not see that he can discuss it in the present state of affairs. Austria can do much to check the movement by merely closing the frontier: and Russia by warning Servia & Montenegro that they must not take part. If there is any part of your letter from which I dissent, it is that in which you seem to assume that a military occupation of the disturbed districts is contemplated. It may be: but various reasons lead me to a different conclusion. The jealousy between Austria & Russia is strong and marked: it is only kept in check by the fear which both feel of the formation of an independent Sclave [sic] state. The Magyars, who are too powerful to be quarrelled with, detest the notion of an increase of the Austrian Sclaves [sic]: and Andrassy is a Magyar, imbued with their feelings. It is rather dread and perplexity than ambition which seems to be the predominant motive at work in Vienna. – I could explain all this fully in conversation, but it is a long story to write. – I agree, generally, in the purport of your advice: and more especially as to our having nothing to do with the suppression of the insurrection by force. That is not our business in any case. But the insurrection is mainly fed from beyond the frontier: and if that external support were cut off, I believe even those wretched Turks could deal with it. [. . .]

308

Disraeli to Derby, DP 920 DER (15) 16/2/2[40]
9 January 1876
Hughenden

Three considerations first strike me.

Firstly. Is Austria justified in sending a note advising measures which the Porte has, generally speaking, announced, with the exception of

---

[39] The Sultan.
[40] Via telegram. Reproduced in M&B, VI, pp. 18–19.

one or two points which are extremely vague, and which, so far as they are intelligible, would appear to be erroneous in principle and pernicious in practice?

Secondly. This would seem an act of imbecility or of treachery. It may begin in one and end in the other. In all probability it will have no effect upon existing circumstances; then Austria and Russia, who probably contemplate an ulterior policy or should do so, will turn around upon the other Powers and say 'The advice you gave has been rejected, you are bound to see that it is carried into effect.'

Thirdly. Whether in the advice which we are asked to give Turkey, we are not committing ourselves to principles which are, or which may be soon, matters of controversy in our own country: for instance, the apportionment of local taxation to local purposes and the right of the peasantry to the soil.

These are three suggestions which occur to me, which should make us hesitate, but there are others. I write by post.

309

Disraeli to Derby, DP 920 DER (15) 16/2/2[41]
9 January 1876

[. . .] I cannot resist from expressing to you, by letter as well, my strong conviction, that we should pause before assenting to the Austrian proposal.

You know how great is my confidence in your judgement, &, therefore, you can better appreciate the hesitation wh: I feel in differing from the course wh: you recommend.

I think it will land us in a false position, & it would be preferable to appear isolated, wh: I usually deprecate, than, for the sake of a simulated union, wh: will not last many months, embarrass ourselves, when independent action may be necessary.

In declining to identify ourselves, as requested, with the Note, is it necessary to appear as Turkish, or more Turkish, than the Turks? Could we not devise a course wh: might avoid that? [. . .][42]

[41]Reproduced in M&B, VI, p. 19.
[42]Italy and France agreed to support the Andrássy Note in early January. The *Daily Telegraph* (4 January) and *The Times* (19 January) urged Britain to follow suit. The Cabinet agreed to support the Note on 18 January. The Turks accepted it on 13 February and the results were communicated to the Bosnian insurgents, who were granted a general amnesty on 22 February.

310

Disraeli to Derby, DP 920 DER (15) 16/2/2[43]
19 April 1876
Hughenden

[. . .] I say nothing about Turkish affairs.[44] You are a younger man, than yr friend & correspondent, & will have eno' to do for the rest of yr life in these matters.

311

Disraeli to Derby, DP 920 DER (15) 16/2/2[45]
20 April 1876
Hughenden

[. . .] Altho' I am not very surprised at the position of Turkish affairs, I confess there is something cynical about Gortchakow's treatment, wh: I think is not exactly respectful to us, after his representations.[46] But with no Russian ambassador here, & a mere Polonius at St Petersburg,[47] it is difficult to ascertain with precision the situation.

The illimitable trust, wh: all the great powers have in Andrassy while, apparently, they do everything to counteract his efforts, would be amusing were it not so dangerous. [. . .][48]

[43]Reproduced in M&B, VI, pp. 22–23.

[44]Although there was an armistice in the fighting between the Turks and the insurgents from 1 to 12 April 1876, it broke down because the demands of the latter were deemed 'inadmissible'. Fighting resumed in the region. On 1 April the Ottoman Empire defaulted on payments to its bondholders. On 18 April *The Times* pronounced the Andrássy Note dead: 'a memorial of good intentions'.

[45]Reproduced in M&B, VI, p. 23.

[46]Possibly a reference to Gorchakov's reversion to acting first with the *Dreikaiserbund*, as would be the case with the Berlin Memorandum, despite the Anglo-Russian co-operation over 'War in Sight' in 1875.

[47]Loftus. Polonius was Ophelia's father, regarded by Hamlet (Act 2, scene ii) as a 'tedious old fool'; Disraeli's view of Loftus might be similarly summarized.

[48]On 26 April, *The Times* reported that the Austrians, Germans, and Russians were thinking of submitting more drastic proposals to the Porte, but that disagreement between St Petersburg and Vienna was holding up any new diplomatic initiative.

312

Derby to Disraeli, Dep. Hughenden 112/3, fo. 44
27 April 1876

I presume we have a Cabinet on Saturday: if so, I shall be present.[49] You know why it has been impossible for me to call upon you: but as far as F.O. is concerned, there is not much to discuss. Egypt I think is settling itself: and as to the great question of the east, there is nothing any way urgent. Matters here come to a dead lock [*sic*], and it is clearly for the Powers which initiated the policy of the Andrassy note to suggest a new way out of the difficulty. [. . .]

313

Disraeli to Derby, DP 920 DER (15) 16/2/2
15 May 1876
2 Whitehall Gardens

I must, I am sorry to say, again complain of the want of order & discipline in your office.

The Queen sent to me twice on Saturday, to enquire, whether there was news from Berlin, & wrote to me on her point of departure, requesting, that I wd. forward the expected information immediately.

I did not go to the German embassy on Saturday, but I have since heard that the communication made to the excluded ambassadors was generally known there.[50]

Nothing had reached me, & on Sunday morning, when the messenger went to Windsor, I had to inform the Queen, that Her Majy[s] Gov[t]. knew nothing.

At one o'[clo]ck: I received Odo Russell[']s tel:, wh: left Berlin at 5 o'[clo]ck: on Saturday, & wh: ought to have been here before you left town!

I went instantly to the 'resident clerk' for an explanation, & with an enquiry (to have in writing) at what hour the Berlin tel: reached him.

[49]The Cabinet met on Saturday 29 April, principally on the Merchant Shipping Bill. Given the death of Derby's mother on 26 April, doubt about his attendance might have arisen. *DD*, p. 292; *DGH*, p. 271.

[50]On 6 May 1876 the German and French consuls in Salonika were murdered in a Turkish mosque by a mob; an immediate demand for satisfaction was presented to the Porte, which promised redress. On 11 May, Gorchakov, Bismarck, and Andrássy met in Berlin to draw up a set of demands calling for fresh guarantees from the Sultan. The Berlin Memorandum was drawn up on 12 May, and its contents were made known to Odo Russell the following day. The 'excluded ambassadors' were, therefore, those of Britain, France, and Italy.

The 'resident clerk' was not in residence!

I believe yr office is very badly managed – the clerks attend there later, than any other public office, witht. the excuse of being worked at night as they were by Palm[n]. It is only a default at a most critical moment like the present, that the negligence becomes insufferable – & so one complains.

I say nothing here of the contents of the tel:, respecting wh: we can confer when you like.

[PS] The Queen complains, that she never receives tels: direct: only in a bag when they are stale.

314

Derby to Disraeli, Dep. Hughenden 112/3, fos 48–49
16 May 1876
Foreign Office

I don't know whether you will care to look at the enclosed papers – the result of your letter to me of yesterday.[51]

It seems that the German telegram did not arrive till late at night. Probably the German authorities took care that their own messages should have a good start.

You might have received it the first thing on Sunday morning: and to that extent there has been negligence. I do not suppose you would have wished to be called up for it in the night.

Some loss of time must occur in the case of long telegrams. This one would probably take an hour and a half to decypher [*sic*].

I do not think the resident clerk can be blamed for being out for a couple of hours. The same man is on duty for a week and close confinement to the office would be impracticable.

I will consult with Tenterden about the Queen's telegrams.

[51]Appended in another hand at the bottom of the letter: 'This relates to the "Berlin Proposals", of which Count Munster told me Sat[urda][y] night but wh: had not yet reached Mr D. when I called on Sunday at 12.'

315

Note by Disraeli, DP 920 DER (15) 16/2/2[52]
16 May 1876

Mr Disraeli fears that we are being drawn step by step into participating in a scheme which must end very soon in the disintegration of Turkey.

Though we may not be able to resist the decision of the three military empires, he does not think we ought to sanction or approve their proposals.

It is almost a mockery for them to talk of a desire that the powers should act in concert and then exclude France, Italy, and England from their deliberations, and ask us by telegraph to say yes or no to propositions which we have never heard discussed.

Moreover it is asking us to sanction them in putting a knife to the throat of Turkey, whether we like it or not. [. . .][53]

316

Disraeli to Derby, DP 920 DER (15) 16/2/2
[17 May 1876][54]
2 Whitehall Gardens

I have just returned from Windsor, & am very unwell.

Odo Russell, in his tel: to day [sic], talks of 'most serious consequences' from the course we are contemplating.

Would it not be as well to enquire of him by tel: what he means by that phrase?

---

[52]Reproduced in full in M&B, VI, pp. 24–26. This note was drafted by Disraeli to be read to the Cabinet on 16 May 1876 (see DD, p. 297). The paper was written in another hand (Corry's?) and was clearly passed to Derby for filing, given that it remains in his papers.

[53]The Berlin Memorandum asked the Sultan for fresh guarantees for the protection of Christians in the Ottoman Empire. Its final clause suggested that, if a proposed armistice failed to bring peace, it would become necessary for the powers 'to supplement their diplomatic action by [. . .] efficacious measures'. According to Derby, Disraeli 'seemed to care very little about the plan itself, whether good or bad, but wished me to profess indignation at our not having been consulted earlier'. DD, 15 May 1876, p. 296. Derby objected to the Memorandum, in conversations with the Austrian, Russian, and German ambassadors, on 15 May. The Cabinet agreed to reject it on 16 May.

[54]Date in another hand.

317

Derby to Disraeli, Dep. Hughenden 112/4, fo. 70
17 May [1876][55]
Foreign Office

On every account I am very sorry for your being unwell. I am puzzled by O[do].R[ussell].'s telegram: having just seen Macdonell [*sic*],[56] who tells me that he (O.R.) is quite aware of the impracticable nature of the scheme, & expected us to withhold our assent. I have telegraphed to him today that he may announce our refusal confidentially to Bismarck: and Münster* will telegraph also.

I will ask as you suggest what are the dangers that R. apprehends; but it is too late to draw back, nor do we wish it.

318

Disraeli to Derby, DP 920 DER (15) 16/2/2
18 May 1876
2 Whitehall Gardens

Nothing can be better;[57] it touches all the points.

The proposal to support an armistice, with[ou]t. any reference to the other propositions, is absurd – They always argue, as if the armistice depended merely on the assent of the Turks. They always evade the reciprocity due from the insurgents.

I don't think much of Odo's reply to the 'serious consequences' tel: Whatever is done now, the consequences will probably be serious.[58]

I think you will find, that public opinion will ratify your policy.[59]

[55] Year appended by another hand, which has also noted 'Berlin proposals' at the top of the letter.
[56] Hugh Guion MacDonell, secretary and periodically acting chargé d'affaires at the Berlin embassy, January 1875–May 1878.
[57] Than the wording of Derby's reply, presumably.
[58] Russell had urged Derby to reconsider his intention to reject the Memorandum and warned of serious consequences if Britain did reject it.
[59] The press, at least, approved of the government's policy. *The Times* (23 May) thought rejection was 'in accordance with a foreign policy which has been practised by each party in succession' – non-intervention. *The Globe, The Standard*, the *Pall Mall Gazette*, and the *Daily Telegraph* followed suit.

319

Disraeli to Derby, DP 920 DER (15) 16/2/2
20 May 1876
2 Whitehall Gardens

[...] Don't you think we ought to ascertain the exact naval force of for[eign]: powers in the Mediterranean, & consider about strengthening our own? [...][60]

320

Derby to Disraeli, Dep. Hughenden 112/4, fo. 75
24 May 1876
Foreign Office

We telegraphed yesterday, at the request of the Admiralty, to know the strength of the Turkish fleet: asking various details.

Here is the answer: just come. Do we require further information? If so, can you tell me more exactly what it is? I failed to gather this morning what were the further details required.[61]

321

Derby to Disraeli, Dep. Hughenden 112/4, fo. 83
27 May [?1876]
Foreign Office

You have seen the long Vienna telegrams. Our resident clerk was up till 5.A.M. this morning deciphering, and began again at 8. So we are not always lazy![62]

---

[60]As early as 9 May, Elliot had urged Vice-Admiral Drummond to send ships to Besika Bay because of the danger of unrest in Constantinople; on 22 May, the Cabinet agreed to strengthen the fleet in Turkish waters.

[61]The extent to which the British fleet should be strengthened had been the subject of a debate in Cabinet, in which the Prime Minister and the Foreign Secretary had disagreed. *DD*, 24 May 1876, p. 298. This letter hints at Derby's frustration with Disraeli's Eastern preoccupations. The Prime Minister replied on 25 May that they should await the results of a conference between Elliot and Admiral Phipps Hornby 'before troubling them further'. M&B, VI, p. 29.

[62]A reference to previous exchanges about FO dilatoriness (see **313**, above, and note); but Disraeli's complaints continued. See below, **335**.

322

Disraeli to Derby, DP 920 DER (15) 16/2/2[63]
28 May 1876
10 Downing Street

[...] The Turkish Fleet is at present in everybody's mind: a prize the possession of wh: may influence the fate of nations. [...]

The danger from the Dardanelles is of another kind. The treaty of 1841 must not be violated.[64] That should be a cardinal principle with us. But if violated, there is but little compensation to be found in the consciousness, that we have made a protest. What if secret instructions were given to our admiral, that, if any of the naval forces assembled propose to violate the treaty of 1841, he sh^d. warn them, that it must be on their responsibility, & that he is instructed to maintain that treaty by force? [...]

323

Disraeli to Derby, DP 920 DER (15) 16/2/2
28 May 1876
2 Whitehall Gardens

It reaches me from a high quarter, that yesterday it was all but settled, that a proposal sh^d be made to us for a congress: the proposal really coming from the three powers – but, – to spare their pride as much as possible, – to originate with France.[65] Not [that], as I am told, either Germany or Austria have any pride they care to be spared, Gortch[ako]^{ff}. having a monopoly, in this instance, of that quality. The wires bet[wee]n. Paris & Ems had little rest yesterday. It was understood, that the proposal was to be made to us immediately.

If the Berlin Memorandum be not presented to the Porte, & a congress proposed in its stead, I think our diplomatic triumph w^d. be complete= but the withdrawal sh^d. be a condition precedent of any assent on our part. I have myself no fear of a congress, tho' I doubt it doing much.

[63]Reproduced in M&B, VI, p. 29.

[64]The Convention of London of 13 July 1841, negotiated by Palmerston and signed by Austria, Britain, France, Prussia, Russia, and Turkey. This closed the Straits of the Dardanelles and the Bosphorus to non-Turkish warships when the Ottoman Empire was not at war.

[65]Derby already knew this: see *DD*, 27 May 1876, p. 299.

324

Derby to Disraeli, Dep. Hughenden 112/4, fos 91–92
28 May 1876
Keston

A draft has gone or is going to you, founded on a conversation between Harcourt and me of yesterday's date: in which he made overtures in the sense you mention, saying that in Decazes's opinion a congress was the only expedient to get us all out of the mess. I had no doubt in my mind but that this was a Russian proposal.

No immediate answer was expected or asked for: and I should not have given one without consulting the Cabinet.

I have no objection to a congress or conference in principle, but unless we go into it with a fairly clear idea of what we want, it will only add to the muddle.

The rest when we meet.

325

Disraeli to Derby, DP 920 DER (15) 16/2/2
29 May 1876
2 Whitehall Gardens

I do not like Lord Odo's letter, or anything, so far as I can gather, he has done — He was not, originally, justified in offering his personal opinion, that our Gov^t would accept the Russian note – an unheard-of step![66] And the worst of it is, it indicates such a want of ability – He does not even seem now to comprehend the situation. I have myself no doubt, that, if we are stiff, we shall gain all our points, because no one is really adverse to them, except Russia —

I have no fear of a congress, but I entirely agree with you, that before we enter it, our scheme sh^d. be matured. I am myself inclined to stipulate, that it should be founded on status quo= but that a liberal interpretation shd be placed on that phrase, so that we may create other vassal states.

I think it would be better not to increase the territories of Montenegro or Servia. I fancy all the powers, ex[cep]^t Russia, w^d. agree with us in this= & if secured, the defeat of Russian designs would be complete.

---

[66]It appears that Russell gave an initial indication in Berlin that he expected Britain to assent to the Memorandum; certainly, he was in favour of such a course. See above, **318**.

326

Derby to Disraeli, Dep. Hughenden 112/4, fo. 93
29 May 1876
Foreign Office

I should quite agree with you about Odo Russell, if I felt sure that he had expressed himself in the sense of the views ascribed to him. But I doubt it. Russians are not scrupulous, and Gortschakoff may probably enough have told the French ambassador & others that he had ascertained that we were ready to join, on the mere speculation that such a statement would be useful. It is possible that Russell may have allowed his personal opinion to be guessed at, but without more proof I cannot believe that he has gone further. — I will think well over what you say as to the basis of a conference.

327

Disraeli to Derby, DP 920 DER (15) 16/2/2[67]
31 May 1876
2 Whitehall Gardens

Elliot tells us nothing as to who brought all this about.[68] It is always one man who does these things – It ought to have been Elliot himself, but that, I fear, is not the case.[69]

What will happen? Until we know, we can scarcely shape our course. If the Turks were to establish 'a constitution', they would go up in the market of Europe, wh: is always liberal= perhaps get a new loan.

But pray think of our last conversation as to possible congress – I feel convinced it is the only practical solution in the long run – conference or congress on the basis of status quo; admitting creation of new vassal states but siné quâ non [sic], no increase of the territory of any existing vassal state. If Bismarck agrees to this, the affair is finished, & for a generation.

---

[67] **326** and **327** are reproduced in M&B, VI, p. 30, as one letter, but they appear to be two separate letters, perhaps sent in the same envelope. The latter is unaddressed, unsigned, and undated.

[68] The news had arrived of the deposition of Abdul Aziz (1830–1876), Ottoman sultan since 1861.

[69] Disraeli seemed to believe that Elliot should have inspired the *coup*; for Disraeli, Elliot's negligence in palace conspiracy was merely one note on a long charge-sheet.

328

Disraeli to Derby, DP 920 DER (15) 16/2/2
[31 May 1876][70]

I am very anxious about Besika Bay & its contents.

Instructions as I intimated mean, you say, war. That depends entirely on the men instructed[.] With a competent ambassador & admiral, it sh^d. mean peace not war.

The ambassador & adm[ira]^l: under existing circumstances, must be in confidential communication with the other envoys and commanders, & it is their principal duty to make these colleagues aware of contingencies.

Instructions may lead to war, but non-instructions may bring about catastrophes.[71] Witness Navarino![72] The circumstances were very similar & the British admiral was left entirely with[ou]^t instructions.

329

Derby to Disraeli, Dep. Hughenden 112/4, fo. 97
4 June 1876

I return the letter with many thanks.[73] It is curious & interesting. All that reaches me, from whatever quarter (and I have heard comments from many quarters) tends in the same direction. Our refusal of the Berlin note is a success both at home & abroad.[74]

[70] See note above, **327**.

[71] Derby thought this fear was absurd, given the existence of the telegraph, but at the Cabinet of 1 June he agreed 'that we shall tell the Powers that strict orders have been given to our fleet to do nothing that can ever be misconstrued as a violation of treaties, and that we hope and expect that similar instructions have been issued by them'. He regarded this as 'needless, but it is also harmless'. *DD*, p. 300.

[72] The Battle of Navarino, 20 October 1827, in which the British, French, and Russian fleets had destroyed the Turkish fleet; there had been confusion about Admiral Codrington's instructions and he was widely felt to have exceeded them, leaving Turkey dangerously exposed to Russia. 'I reminded him', Derby noted, 'that in the days of Navarino there were no telegraphs.' *DD*, 1 June 1876, p. 300.

[73] Not found.

[74] On 9 June the powers withdrew the Berlin Memorandum. *The Times* (10 June) and most of the other journals concurred in seeing this as a diplomatic success for the Government.

330

Disraeli to Derby, DP 920 DER (15) 16/2/2[75]
24 June 1876
2 Whitehall Gardens

I met Schou: last night at dinner, & he got me in a corner before he went to Beust's ball.[76]

He was full of matter: clear, for him calm, & not at all clarety[77] — This is the upshot, wh: I thought you ought to know.

The affairs must be settled: there must be a thoro' good understanding between Eng: & Russia. The despatch was one of confiance & bon vouloir[78] – This he repeated often: at last, he asked me whether I did not think it so? Obliged to speak, I said I w^d. not doubt it, but he must admit, that with all its confiance &^{c}, it suggested, or proposed, a great deal.

Really, he replied, not more, than, we believe, you wish & is for your interest — But if you disapprove, propose yourselves & we will follow you —

Now this is the important part —

England is under a false impression about autonomy:[79] we [the Russians] don[']t propose, or wish, a military or political autonomy; only an administrative one. The sultan may have his troops, his fortresses, his political affairs, provided the people may manage their own affairs.

As for Montenegro, it has got about, that Russia is intriguing for a port under the pretence of increasing the territory of Montenegro. No such thing, we renounce the idea, Montenegro need have no port, only a little garden to grow cabbages and potatoes.[80] We do not care for Servia as we do for Montenegro, but what Servia wants is not much, & I believe the Sultan has more than once been on the point of granting what they wish — [. . .]

---

[75]Reproduced in M&B, VI, pp. 34–35.

[76]This meeting was one in a series of exchanges, formal and informal, between the great powers as they manoeuvred in the period immediately before Serbia and Montenegro went to war with the Turks.

[77]In other words, he was sober. Presumably, the claret in question was either the wine he consumed or the colour of his cheeks thereafter; possibly both.

[78]'good will'.

[79]For Bosnia-Herzegovina, a Russian proposition.

[80]There is a useful account of this meeting in R.W. Seton-Watson, *Disraeli, Gladstone and the Eastern Question: a study in diplomacy and party politics* (London, 1962), p. 43. Shuvalov was making his point about Montenegro in response to Disraeli dismissing suggestions that Britain wished to annex Egypt.

331

Disraeli to Derby, DP 920 DER (15) 16/2/2[81]
28 June 1876[82]
2 Whitehall Gardens

If war takes place between Turkey & Servia, & the Porte is victorious, & seeks the legitimate consequences of victory, as, for example, the restoration of Belgrade, it sh^d. at once be distinctly signified to Russia, that if Russia interfere under these circumstances, the position of affairs will be considered by England as most grave.

Servia will not move, unless she is confident, that Russia will step in, in case of Servia being worsted, & so save her from the consequences of her headstrong audacity.

At present, it[']s heads I win, tails you lose.

If this declaration, on our part, is simultaneously accompanied by a determined effort to detach Montenegro from Servia, war will not take place – but this decided course ought to be taken today. Even hours are precious.

332

Derby to Disraeli, Dep. Hughenden 112/4, fo. 123
28 June [1876]
Foreign Office

Can you see me about one o'clock (sooner, if you like) about the Russian proposal?[83] Circumstances have changed since we talked about it last. Andrassy objects strongly to Bosnian autonomy. — The Montenegrin part of the business is done as far as we are concerned. — Servia seems hopeless. It is a new world since last week. I am to see the Russian at 3.[84]

---

[81] Reproduced in M&B, VI, p. 36.

[82] With a flurry of letters on 28 June, the precise chronological order is difficult to establish, but, given the lack of either a clear reply to this letter from Derby or any comment by Disraeli on the points made by Derby in his letters, it seems likely that this letter was written in the morning and the matter dealt with when the two men met. As usual, Derby took little notice of Disraeli's sabre-rattling.

[83] Gorchakov had proposed granting more territory for Montenegro and Serbia, and autonomy for Bosnia-Herzegovina. The Russians were also very keen for Britain to make joint representations with the other powers at the Porte, but Britain made it clear that this would not happen. On 9 July, the Queen (after advice from the Cabinet) formally responded to a Russian proposal for such a joint approach, as conveyed by a letter from the Tsar on 4 July. *LQV*, series two, II, pp. 468–470.

[84] On 30 June the Serbs declared war, followed by Montenegro on 1 July.

333

Derby to Disraeli, Dep. Hughenden 112/4, fo. 121
[?28] June 1876[85]
Foreign Office

I am making a note of my conversation with Schou. which you shall have as soon as it is written out fair.[86]

He pressed very hard on the question of autonomy – gave up the notion of asking anything for Servia at present – did not know much of what was doing there &c[.] He has been misrepresenting us both in a wild manner, as I learn from Harcourt.

334

Derby to Disraeli, Dep. Hughenden 112/4, fos 125–126
28 June 1876
Foreign Office

All other considerations apart, I suspect the Russian proposal is too late. The Servians seem bent on fighting. I have the answer to Schouvaloff in hand, and hope to have it ready today.

Andrassy is strongly against all suggestions of autonomy, saying that the two parties in Bosnia will do nothing if left alone, but cut at one another's throats. I am afraid he is not far wrong. Beust read me his telegram, which I copied, a little abridged, and you will have it in the shape of a draft.

Our debate on Monday[87] & Hammond being so much more Turkish than the government, make L[or]d Granville's position difficult. He felt it, and was very obviously annoyed.

---

[85] The letter is dated 27 June, but Derby's diary records the meetings with Shuvalov and Harcourt as being held on 28 June. *DD*, p. 305.

[86] According to Derby, he had told Shuvalov that, of the three points made by Gorchakov's last despatch (see above, **332**), Britain agreed with Russia on the question of Montenegro, on which the Turks ought to be conciliatory, but thought it was too late as Serbia had 'evidently decided on war'. DD, 28 June 1876, p. 305.

[87] Monday 26 June 1876. *Parl. Deb.*, CCXXX, cols 395–418. For Derby's contribution, see cols 411–417.

[88] Francis Napier, tenth Lord Napier of Merchistoun and first Baron Ettrick (1819–1898), who had briefly acted as Indian Viceroy in 1872.

335

Disraeli to Derby, DP 920 DER (15) 16/2/2[89]
14 July 1876
2 Whitehall Gardens

I must again complain of the management of your office, & request your personal attention to it.

It is impossible to represent F.O. in the House of Commons, in these critical times, with[ou]t. sufficient information. What I receive is neither ample, nor accurate.

After I had made the declarations,[90] wh: I did on y^r authority respecting the Bulgarian 'atrocities', I find a despatch from our consul at Rustchuk, received, if I remember right, on the 28th June, & which reached me a fortnight afterwards, wh: if it do [*sic*] not confirm them as facts, refers to them as rumors [*sic*], wh: are probable, & refers to them in some detail.

Last night Mr Baxter[91] gave notice of a question to be put on Monday to me. =whether the Bulgarian outrages, referred to in the Daily News, were not regularly communicated, at the time, by our consul at Adrianople, & whe[the]^r. our ambassador at Const[antinople]: had not consequently remonstrated with the Turkish Gov^t?

This was pretty well giving me the lie in the H[ouse]: of Commons, &, under ordinary circumstances, I shd. have at once risen, & not waited for moving for the reply. But I have no confidence what[eve]^r. in y^r office, & I was obliged to submit in silence to the indignity, & for aught I know, Monday may increase the pain of my position.

---

[89] This letter is reproduced in M&B, VI, pp. 44–45, but, as was Buckle's general practice, without Derby's reply. This is one of many examples of skilful omission by Disraeli's biographers.

[90] On the 'Bulgarian Horrors', the massacre of Bulgarians by Turkish Bashi-Bazouks, the first news of which had reached London via the *Daily News* on 23 June. Disraeli was clearly embarrassed by his own mishandling of the question. The fault lay with him, however, not the Foreign Office. In the House of Commons on 10 July he had denied the scale of the atrocities on the grounds that 'oriental' people 'seldom, I believe, resort to torture, but generally terminate their connection with culprits in a more expeditious manner'. This provoked laughter among MPs. *Parl. Deb.,* CCXXX, col. 1182.

[91] William Edward Baxter (1825–1890), Liberal MP for Montrose, formerly a junior minister.

336

Derby to Disraeli, Dep. Hughenden 112/4, fos 127–128
14 July 1876
Foreign Office

I communicated your letter of yesterday[92] to Tenterden, from whom I understand you had the information on which your answer was given; and he tells me that he has explained to you verbally the circumstances. I do not see that you have anything to retract or even to modify in your answer. The despatch which you did not see, as well as I remember did not bear on the particular subject on which you were questioned. I am not disposed to defend the office where they have been negligent, but where papers must pass through various hands (mine, Tenterden's, Bourke's*, and afterwards the Queen's and those of our colleagues) I don't see how it is possible to guard against the chance of a paper which you want at very short notice being out of the hands of the department. I have often asked for papers to refer to and been told that they were in circulation – and this must happen, unless every despatch of importance here [is] to be copied and only the copy sent round.

There is later intelligence since come in, which will supply material for your answer on Monday.[93]

337

Disraeli to 6th Duke of Richmond,* Goodwood MS 865[94]
24 July 1876[95]
10 Downing Street

Some little time ago, when we had extricated ourselves from our difficulties, & the government was not less popular & strong, than at present, I was obliged to inform the Queen, that it would not be possible for me to carry on Her Majesty's affairs after the present session.

---

[92] This clearly refers to the Prime Minister's letter of the same date.

[93] A note at the foot of the letter adds: 'I enclose a mem. sent me by Tenterden.'

[94] Reproduced in M&B, V, pp. 491–492, along with Richmond's reply of 26 July, pp. 492–493.

[95] Intriguingly, this letter is dated the day *before* the letter Disraeli wrote to Derby, his 'faithful companion', but the date may be an error; Richmond's letter to Cairns of 27 July (see below) suggests that the duke received it on 26 July, the same day on which Derby recorded receiving his own copy. *DD*, 26 July 1876, p. 313. Whether error or no, had Derby demurred, the simultaneous (or perhaps prior) despatch of letters to others would have marshalled support for Disraeli to negate any objection.

Altho', being well acquainted with the Queen's sensitiveness, or perhaps I ought to say constitutional convictions, on the subject, I did not presume to recommend my successor, I ventured to observe, that, if Her Majesty wished to retain Her present Cabinet, I thought there would be no difficulty in keeping them together under an individual, whose fitness would be generally admitted by themselves & the country.

Her Majesty did not seem to believe in this, or to approve of my communication, & wrote to me from Scotland to propose, that I should continue in my present post, & go to the House of Lords, which, she was graciously pleased to say, she had always contemplated since my illness at Balmoral two years ago.

As I have no heir, I was unwilling, in the decline of life, to commence a new career in a House of Parliament of which I had no experience, & where I should be looked upon as an intruder, & I requested Her Majesty's permission to adhere to my original feeling & to make some confidential enquiries on the subject.

I found, to my great surprise, that the Queen had judged the situation more accurately than myself, & that my secession might lead to serious consequences.

Altho' my continuing in the House of Commons for another session would shorten my remaining life, I was prepared to make such a sacrifice, if, at the end of the year, I could have found the difficulties, occasioned by my withdrawal, removed: but I see no prospect of that. The identical difficulties would reappear.

Under these circumstances, I have had to reconsider the Queen's proposal, & to bring myself to contemplate, as an act of duty to Her Majesty & my colleagues, the possibility of my going to the upper house as a minister, a condition which I had never foreseen. I invite you as a colleague, whom I greatly value, & with whose parliamentary position such a step on my part would necessarily, in some degree, interfere, to speak to me frankly on this subject: clearly understanding, that my only motive now is the maintenance of the ministry & the party, & to secure these, I am ready still to try to serve them, or cheerfully altogether to disappear.

338

Disraeli to Derby, DP 920 DER (15) 16/2/2
25 July 1876
10 Downing Street

Altho' I have not spoken to you before on the subject of this letter, it has not been from reserve, but because I was aware, that, thro' the medium of our dearest friend,[96] we were not altogether uninformed of what was passing thro' each others' mind on the matter.

Some little time ago, when we had extricated ourselves from our difficulties, & the government was not less popular & strong, than at present, I was obliged to inform the Queen, that it w^d not be possible for me to carry on Her Majesty's affairs after the present session.

Altho', being acquainted with the Queen's sensitiveness, or perhaps I ought to say, constitutional convictions, on the subject, I did not presume to recommend my successor, I ventured to observe, that, if Her Majesty wished to retain Her present Cabinet, I thought there would be no difficulty in keeping them together under an individual, whose fitness would be generally admitted by themselves & the country.

Her Majesty did not receive this communication very graciously, nor did she generally approve of my communication, & she wrote to me from Scotland to propose, that I sh^d. continue in my present position, & go to the House of Lords, which she was pleased to say, that she had always, since my illness at Balmoral two years ago, contemplated.

As I have no heir, I was unwilling, in the decline of life, to commence a new career in a House of Parliament of which I had no experience, & where, in an official position, I might be looked upon as an intruder, & I requested Her Majesty's permission to adhere to my original feeling, & to make some confidential enquiries on the subject.

I found, I may say to my great surprise, that the Queen had judged the situation more accurately than myself, & that my secession might lead to serious consequences.

Altho' my continuing in the Commons, for another session, would shorten my remaining life, I was prepared to make such a sacrifice, if, at the end of the year, I could have found the difficulties, occasioned by my withdrawal, removed: but I see no prospect of that. The identical difficulties would re-appear.

Under these circumstances, I have had to reconsider the Queen's proposal, & to bring myself to contemplate, as an act of duty, the possibility of my going to the upper house as a minister; a condition which I had never foreseen.

I invite you, not only as my principal colleague, & whom I wished to be my successor, but as a very old friend, & the faithful

---

[96]Lady Derby.

companion of all my public fortunes, to speak to me frankly on this subject: distinctly bearing in mind, that I have, now, no other object but the maintenance of the ministry & the welfare of the party = & that, to secure these results, I am prepared, either to endeavour still to serve them, or altogether cheerfully to disappear.

339

Duke of Richmond to Earl Cairns, Cairns Papers, PRO 30/51/3, fos 101–102
27 July 1876
Goodwood

[...] I recd a box from the Prime Minister yesterday, detailing his views as to the House of Lords &c and asking me what I felt about [it]. I answered in the terms we had agreed on and said no one would welcome him more sincerely or cordially than I should, and that I considered it not only the best but the only arrangement that I considered was at all practicable and likely to keep all parties together. I hope he will be satisfied with my answer. I wrote it in a hurry. I intended it to be very cordial.

[...] I had a long talk last night with Lady Bradford but did not mention Disraeli[']s letter: she seems to know everything down to the most minute details of every thing that passes.[97] She actually knew that I had written to the P.M. to complain of Hardwicke[']s[98] non attendance. He also told her we had a stormy Cabinet on Monday, which I do not admit was the case.[99]

[97] Lady Bradford was one of Disraeli's closest confidantes; as this letter suggests, neither she nor he was very discreet with gossip about Cabinet. It is interesting to compare this letter with those of late 1877 and early 1878, in which the Derbys were identified as the likely sources of Cabinet leaks. In fact, the Cabinet had been leaking from the very top for some time.

[98] Charles Philip Yorke (1836–1897), fifth Earl of Hardwicke; son of the Cabinet minister of 1852 and 1858–1859 of the same name. Known as 'Champagne Charlie', he held a Court appointment as Master of the Buckhounds.

[99] On 25 July, Disraeli told Lady Bradford, 'We had a stormy Cabinet yesterday'. See Marquis of Zetland (ed.), *The Letters of Disraeli to Lady Bradford and Lady Chesterfield*, 2 vols (London, 1929), II, p. 58. The Cabinet evidently had a different view. Derby made no note of any debate (*DD*, p. 312) and nor did Hardy in his diary (*DGH*, p. 284).

340

Disraeli to Derby, DP 920 DER (15) 16/2/2
2 August 1876
2 Whitehall Gardens

I don't think we ought to let France & Germany bully the poor Turks with ultimatums about the Salonika compensation.[100]

Surely we have influence eno' with F. and G. to gain a little reasonable time; particularly as their governments expressed themselves satisfied to Sir H. Elliott.

Ought we not to send a tel. to Paris & Berlin?

341

Disraeli to Derby, DP 920 DER (15) 16/2/2[101]
7 August 1876
House of Commons

We have had a very damaging debate on Bulgarian atrocities,[102] & it is lucky for us, in this respect, that the session is dying.

Had it not been for an adroit and ingenious speech by Bourke, who much distinguished himself, the consequences might have been rather serious.

But two grave results are now evident:

> 1. That Elliot has shown a lamentable want of energy & deficiency of information:[103] &
>
> 2nd. That our own F.O. is liable to the same imputations.

The F.O. misled me in the first replies wh: I gave on their voucher, & had I seen that despatch of Consul Reade,[104] which never reached

---

[100] For the murder of the French and German consuls on 6 May.

[101] Reproduced in M&B, VI, p. 46.

[102] See *Parl. Deb.*, CCXXXI, cols 721–746.

[103] Disraeli blamed Sir Henry Elliot for taking too long to send an official report.

[104] Richard Reade, British consul for the Ottoman *vilayet* of the Danube since 16 July 1874; resided at Rustchuk (variously spelt by contemporaries), now the Bulgarian city of Ruse. Reade served in the British delegation to the Constantinople Conference in December 1876. He was appointed consul for the Ionian Islands in 1879.

me, I w^d. never have made those answers, &, what is more, sh^d have pressed it on you to follow up Reade's revelations.[105]

I write this now, because Hartington[106] wants more papers, & wants them before Prorogation, that he may have more damaging debates.

It is a very awkward business, &, I feel, a great exposure of our diplomatic system abroad & at home.

342

Derby to Disraeli, Dep. Hughenden 112/4, fo. 147
21 August 1876
Fairhill, Tunbridge

[...] The Servian government does not seem to know its own mind as to war or peace. But we have done all that under the circumstances can be attempted. Pressure put on the Prince[107] would only be misconstrued.

I am to see Beust & Schouvaloff tomorrow.

343

Derby to Disraeli, Dep. Hughenden 112/4, fo. 149
25 August 1876
Fairhill, Tunbridge

You will have seen White's[108] telegram. The Servians ask for mediation. I have sent off in reply the two telegrams of which I enclose copy. There was no time to lose, and I know the view you take: therefore I acted at once.

---

[105] Disraeli, still convinced that the press reports of atrocities were exaggerations, had made another gaffe in the House of Commons on 31 July, referring to the accounts as 'coffee house babble'. *Parl. Deb.*, vol. CCXXXI, col. 203.

[106] Spencer Compton Cavendish, Marquess of Hartington (1833–1908), eighth Duke of Devonshire from 1891; Liberal leader in the House of Commons.

[107] Milan Obrenović (1854–1901), ruled as Prince Milan IV (1868–1882) and King Milan I (1882–1889).

[108] Sir William Arthur White (1824–1891), British consul-general in Serbia, 1875–1878; thereafter in Bucharest.

344

Disraeli to Derby, DP 920 DER (15) 16/2/2
26 August 1876
Hughenden

I received your tels: last night, by messenger, of which I quite approve.

I fear from Elliot's letter, just read, that the position at Constantinople is too strained for his nerve.

I cannot believe in the 15 000 Russian soldiers & all that. If true, the Turks have licked the Russians.

I hope you will be able to arrange affairs with[ou]t. a conference. That is a sort of thing at which 'the old coxcomb'[109] plays a great part, & invents questions for solution, wh: need not be solved.

345

Gathorne Hardy* to Cairns, Cairns Papers, PRO 30/51/7, fo. 43
29 August 1876
Hemsted

I do not know whether you get intelligence of foreign affairs. The Eastern matter is so serious that I did not like to remain in total darkness & wrote to Derby for some information.[110] I send you his note to read. The stir about the atrocities is I think real and is penetrating deep. My impression is that in any negotiations they must be recognised and a repetition if possible provided against. Derby is I fear not enough alive to this[111] but I hope our chief who generally tries the public pulse will not be unmindful of it on this occasion. Horrible as war is at its best[,] the accounts of what took place exceed[,] as they become more authentic[,] what was first reported. I write to

[109] Gorchakov.
[110] Hardy had asked for information about the massacres and Britain's response. He recorded receipt of Derby's reply in his diary on 29 August, and noted that the terms of any international mediation 'ought to be such as the Powers will have a claim to compel adherence to and protection for the Christians should in some way be *secured*'. *DGH*, p. 288.
[111] On 10 August, Hardy had recorded his concern that Derby 'does not seem to be aware of the feeling existing in & out of Parliament'. *DGH*, p. 287. R.A. Cross, on the other hand, told Mary Derby on 7 September that the agitation would 'show the country what he [Derby] can do', while leading members of the Opposition, such as John Bright and Lord Granville, were openly supportive of the Foreign Secretary, as a means of contrasting Derby's approach with Disraeli's.

you because I know that you generally are more consulted on foreign affairs than others of the Cabinet. [. . .][112]

346

Derby to Disraeli, Dep. Hughenden 112/4, fos 151–153
31 August 1876
Fairhill, Tunbridge

I have been thinking seriously over what you say of Sir H. Elliot; but with only, so far, a negative result.[113]

I am clear that to remove him at the present moment would be unwise.

First, it would look too [much] like making him a scapegoat, which is always a shabby & unsatisfactory expedient: and those who now ask for his recall would be the first to say we were throwing on him the blame of our own acts or omissions.

Next, it is ill to change your instrument at a crisis: as President Lincoln told the American public, – it is not the moment to 'swop horses when you are crossing the ford.'

No new man could at once know as much of what is required as Elliot must do: however superior in ability:– and the most important work is that which will have to be done in the next few weeks. Again, he is trusted and liked by the Turks: and a sudden removal of him, if employed by the enemy to convey the notion of a change of policy, would lessen our influence just when we are in a position to use it to the most advantage.

Peace made, he might not be unwilling to retire, and the same objections would not apply. The one essential thing now is to make a peace, and for my part I am prepared to put any necessary amount of pressure on the Porte. In fact it is in the interest of the Turks, for continued war means Russian intervention, and their destruction. We could not save them, or even try it, as English feeling

---

[112]This is one of the few references that we have to Cairns being in any sort of 'inner Cabinet', and might be noted in view of Salisbury's later comments about his influence. See Memorandum by Arthur Balfour, 8 May 1880, in Robin Harcourt-Williams (ed.), *Salisbury–Balfour Correspondence: letters exchanged between the third Marquess of Salisbury and his nephew Arthur James Balfour 1869–1892* (Hertfordshire Record Society, 1988), p. 43.

[113]Disraeli had written to Derby on 15 August proposing either Elliot's dismissal or the appointment of an 'extraordinary envoy', on the grounds of Elliot's ill-health, to carry out the meaningful duties of ambassador instead. M&B, VI, p. 49. See also *DD*, 30 August 1876, p. 322. As usual, Buckle did not reproduce Derby's reply. Given his response, Disraeli agreed, and Elliot was retained at Constantinople until February 1877. *DD*, 3 September 1876, p. 323. See also below, **349**.

is now. You will see by my telegrams that I have made that clear at Constantinople.

It looks as if all the world, with possibly the exception of Austria, wished for an early settlement: but the more mechanical difficulty of getting the assent of six governments to every proposition causes delay.

I shall be in town tomorrow, and no doubt shall see most of the ambassadors or their substitutes.

347

Derby to Disraeli, Dep. Hughenden 112/4, fo. 155[114]
1 September 1876

I propose to send the following telegram to Sir H. Elliot. Let me know if you concur. Time is of great importance.[115]

'As Austrian Government objects to collective action, and as time presses, I have to instruct you to propose at once to the Turkish Gov^t. an armistice of not less than a month's duration, with a view to the immediate discussion of terms of peace. The armistice should include all combatants. You will inform your colleagues of these instructions and ask for their support.[']'[116]

348

Disraeli to Derby, DP 920 DER (15) 16/2/2
1 September 1876
Hughenden

I concur, for I think you ought to be supported in every thing at this moment. But with so long a term, I think some of the principal preliminaries sh^d., if possible, have accompanied it. But, probably, that's not possible.

The great thing is to bind Russia to something — [. . .]

---

[114]A telegram, recorded in another hand.

[115]The Prince of Montenegro had proposed an armistice; Britain would act as mediator. *DD*, 30 August 1876, p. 322.

[116]Both Serbia and Montenegro, having suffered heavy defeats, had accepted Derby's offer of mediation. The Porte, on the verge of victory, hesitated, but eventually agreed to a ceasefire on 15 September.

349

Disraeli to Derby, DP 920 DER (15) 16/2/2
2 September 1876
Hughenden

What you say about removing Elliot, at this moment, is quite unanswerable, but when I brought the matter before you, the application of Prince Milan had not been made.

Elliot's stupidity has brought us near to a great peril. If he had acted with promptitude – or even kept himself, & us, informed, these 'atrocities' might have been checked much earlier. As it is, he has brought us into the position, most unjustly, of being thought to connive at them. — And yet Tenterden will maintain he has not committed a single fault! He has nearly destroyed a strong and popular government.

But in a scrape, we sh^d. turn it into 'commodities' as Falstaff says, or something like it.[117] These 'atrocities' will permit us to dictate to the Porte, & they must be told, that, unless they follow our counsels, they must be prepared for autonomy in Bulgaria, & other things. [. . .]

350

Disraeli to Salisbury, SP, fos 149–151[118]
3 September 1876
Hughenden

[. . .] Affairs are most critical. Had it not been for those unhappy 'atrocities,' we should have settled a peace very honorable [*sic*] to England, & satisfactory to Europe.

Now, we are obliged to work from a new point of departure, & dictate to Turkey, who has forfeited all sympathy. If these efforts fail, Russia & Austria will march their armies into the Balkan [*sic*] in the spring, either simultaneously & with an understanding, or the one following the example of the other from jealousy & fear.

All this must lead to partition. I think we ought to get the lead in our own hands & anticipate all this. But I won't go on, & perhaps mislead you by my imperfect expressions. Derby is behaving with energy, & I hope will be up to the mark – It will not be from want of bottle holding. It is the most difficult business I have ever had to touch.

[117] The reference is to *Henry IV Part 2*, Act 1, scene ii, where Falstaff talks of turning 'diseases to commodity'.
[118] Reproduced, without the section 'If these efforts [. . .] imperfect expressions', in M&B, VI, pp. 51–52.

351

Disraeli to Derby, DP 920 DER (15) 16/2/2[119]
4 September 1876
Hughenden

I have been thinking much about the present state of affairs, & our new point of departure: wise & inevitable, & wise because inevitable. But it is difficult to conceal from ourselves, that it is a course, which will probably bring about a result very different from that originally contemplated.

I cannot help doubting whether any arrangement, tho' I have confidence in your skill & your fortune, a quality as important as skill, is now practicable. I fear affairs will linger on till the spring, when Russia & Austria will march their armies into the Balkan [*sic*], either simultaneously, & with a certain understanding, or one following the other's example from jealousy and fear.

As Count Andrassy observed to Sir Andrew Buchanan,[120] 'There is no alternative between the notes of this year, & the solution of the Eastern Question.'

I think, the probability is, that it will be the 'solution of the Eastern question', &, if so, it is wise, that we sh^d. take the lead in it – Our chance of success will be greater, because, from us it will be unexpected.

If old Brunnow were here, the work, so far as Russia is concerned, might be shorter than with others. Perhaps Schouvaloff may be equally handy, but, certainly, Palmerston with Brunnow managed in 1840 the solution of the Eastern Question, in the other direction, and admirably.

Whatever the jealousies of Austria & Russia, they would prefer a division of the Balkan spoil under the friendly offices of England to war, between themselves, certainly, &, probably, with others: Constantinople, with an adequate district, should be neutralised, & made a free port, in the custody, & under the guardianship, of England, as the Ionian Isles were.

I fancy there would be no difficulty in the enlargement of Greece. Nature indicates, & policy would not oppose, it. [. . .][121]

I write this on the assumption, that the present attempt at peace will fail. God grant it may not! But if it do, I humbly think we cannot act too powerfully & too promptly. Decision & energy will render

---

[119]Reproduced in full in M&B, VI, pp. 52–53.

[120]Sir Andrew Buchanan (1807–1882), ambassador at Vienna until February 1878: 'safe and sensible, but at no time has he been very efficient'. *DD*, 24 August 1875, p. 239. Disraeli thought him 'a hopeless mediocrity'. M&B, VI, p. 49.

[121]Disraeli went on to speculate at length about German policy.

the work practicable; hesitation & timidity will involve us in infinite difficulty & peril, in the whirlpool of wh: we should disappear.

352

Derby to Disraeli, Dep. Hughenden 112/4, fos 159–160
5 September 1876
Fairhill, Tunbridge

I return Northcote's letter.[122] It seems to me that we are acting in the sense that he recommends. I can't write officially about the 'atrocities' till Baring's report arrives,[123] but shall then lose no time. I agree as to the necessity of making some stipulations for the better government of the disturbed provinces – including Bulgaria. But the first step is the armistice. If you have seen my telegrams, you will, I think, be of opinion that I could scarcely have impressed on the Porte the necessity of making peace in more decided language. I have warned the Turks in plain terms that as matters stand we could not now protect them from a Russian attack. What more is it possible to say? Your letter raises much wider questions, and I must think it well over before giving any answer. If once we raise the question of partition, the risk of war is great, for the Powers will all want something, and the division of the spoil is not likely to be made in an amicable manner. — For my own part, I do not believe any territorial advantage on the frontier would reconcile Russia to seeing Constantinople in the hands of a Great Power, friendly or not. But all this I reserve for further & fuller consideration.

353

Disraeli to Derby, DP 920 DER (15) 16/2/2[124]
6 September 1876
Hughenden

I got your box this morning —
I sent you Northcote's letter, because he has an ingenious mind, with popular sympathies, but timid, unwisely timid – which timidity

---

[122]Northcote had written to Disraeli on 2 September, with suggestions about punishments for the atrocities and concessions on autonomy.

[123]Walter Baring, second secretary at the Constantinople embassy since 1873, had been ordered to carry out an investigation into the atrocities, which he duly did from 19 July to 20 August. He estimated that some 12,000 Bulgarians were massacred, as opposed to the much larger figures mentioned in the press. The official Turkish estimate, on the other hand, was just 1,830.

[124]Reproduced in M&B, VI, pp. 53–54, but without the first line or the section after 'Bulgarian Bogy'.

always is, tho' caution has many charms.[125] What I wish to impress upon you, at this moment, as regards home, is not to act, as if you were under the control of popular opinion.[126] If so, you may do what they like, but they won't respect you for doing it.

After all, all this tumult is on a false assumption, that we have been, or are, upholding Turkey – all the Turks may be in the Propontis, so far as I am concerned, & the first thing, after we had declined the Berlin mem[orandum]:, that you did, was to tell Musurus so.

If the thing goes well & we get what we want, all this row will subside, & be forgotten before our first Cab[inet]. Council, & we shall get the credit of the arrangement, but if an arrangement takes place, & it is supposed that we have acted under the pressure of this Hudibrastic[127] crew of high ritualists, dissenting ministers & 'the great Liberal Party', we shall be contemptible.

Now, what is going on? [. . .] I fear there must be a congress, tho' I hate it & I am quite confident we c^d. have managed without it, had it not been for this Bulgarian Bogy.

I fancy the report of the joint Mus[lim]: & Xtian[128] Commission at Phil[ippopol]:^{i}[129] is well founded. It agrees with the reports of the Belg[ian]: Cons[ul]-Gen[era]l. &, what is better, it agrees with the probability of human nature — But Baring is, probably, such an intense ass, that he will not dare to speak the truth.

It is fearful to think we had Elliot – but his entourage seems worse.

354

Derby to Disraeli, Dep. Hughenden 112/4, fos 161–162
7 September 1876
Fairhill, Tunbridge

I have your letter: many thanks. I am not more discomposed than you by the Bulgarian agitation; which as far as it is sincere, is directed against the Turks rather than against the Cabinet; though naturally it

---

[125]Northcote was one of the Cabinet ministers unhappy with the Government's public response to the atrocities. Referring to the 'unfortunate levity of our chief', he complained to Carnarvon, on 4 September, of the government's 'insanely' allowing 'the idea to get abroad that we are indifferent to the cruelties which have been committed'.
[126]In his diary, Derby wrote that Disraeli's plea 'was hardly necessary, since I agree with him'. *DD*, 7 September 1876, p. 324.
[127]In the manner of *Hudibras*, the seventeenth-century mock-heroic poem by Samuel Butler; suggestive of the ridiculous.
[128]i.e. 'Christian'.
[129]Philippopoli/Philippopolis; modern-day Plovdiv in Bulgaria.

is utilised by the enemy. It is only so far serious, that being known to all Europe, and probably exaggerated by foreign journals, it weakens our hands. I have thought it only fair to warn the Porte of our position in that respect, and it was in the interest of our policy to do so: but peace, if we get it, will stop all the noise. I have not yet read with close attention the 'verbosa et grandis epistola' that has come from Hawarden.[130] From what I have seen, it appears to resolve itself into a demand for autonomy for Bulgaria: a small result for so large a document. [...]

355

Lord John Manners* to Disraeli, Dep. Hughenden 106/3, fos 92–93
7 September 1876
St Marys Tower, Birnam

[...] To turn to graver matters – the country, under skilful management,[131] has gone stark staring mad, and there is little or no use in endeavouring to stem the tide of foolish talk. I don't think however that it will last much longer.

The chief danger to my mind is the possible effect at S^t. Petersburg. Derby's declaration to Elliot of August 29th that if Russia attacked Turkey we should not interfere having unluckily got wind Russia may be tempted to act upon it, and the circumstances and end of a war so commenced no one can predicate. My own belief is that Turkey, left to her own resources, would make a much better fight of it than most people here anticipate, and I conclude with her maritime supremacy in the Black Sea she would not, as we did, spare Odessa. But what a prospect! I hope you will not, in deference to this outcry, withdraw the fleet from Besika Bay. [...]

356

Disraeli to Derby, DP 920 DER (15) 16/2/2[132]
8 September 1876
Hughenden

[...] Gladstone has had the impudence to send me his pamphlet, tho' he accuses me of several crimes. The document is passionate &

---

[130] Gladstone's pamphlet, 'Bulgarian Horrors and the Question of the East' – which contained his famous, if misinterpreted, phrase on removing the Turk from Europe 'bag and baggage' – had been published on 6 September. The Latin tag (loosely translated), referring to the 'wordy and dignified' letters of antiquity, or perhaps to papal epistles, poked fun at Gladstone's pretensions.

[131] Principally Gladstone's.

[132] Reproduced in M&B, VI, p. 60.

not strong; vindictive & ill-written – that of course. Indeed, in that respect, of all the Bulgarian horrors perhaps the greatest. [. . .]

357

Sir Stafford Northcote to R.A. Cross,* Cross Papers, BL Add. MS 51265, fos 112–113
8 September 1876
Balmoral

[. . .] I forget whether I told you that I am likely to have to address the Cons. W.M. at Edinburgh before I go south.[133] I must say something about the Eastern question then; and I shall be rather glad of the opportunity.[134] I don't think Gladstone's pamphlet will do us much harm. It is a powerful bit of rhetoric; but its conclusions are very weak and inconclusive. I expect that we shall see a subsidence in the agitation before very long. What I am anxious about is the obstinate resistance which the Turks seem likely to make to an armistice, and the effect which their refusal may have upon Russia. Derby has sent very strongly worded telegrams to impress moderation upon them; but the result is still doubtful. [. . .]

358

Derby to Disraeli, Dep. Hughenden 112/4, fos 173–174
12 September 1876
Fairhill, Tunbridge

My deputations went off well.[135] There were two of them. The first respectable and sensible; the second a gathering of idiots who talked about doing away with war, abolishing standing armies, and all that sort of thing. To these last I said nothing beyond what civility required: the others I answered at length: [. . .][136]

---

[133]Northcote was due to speak at the Edinburgh Conservative Working Men's Association on 16 September.
[134]Disraeli was *not* glad that Northcote would be speaking. His instructions, in a letter of 11 September, are reproduced in M&B, VI, pp. 61–62. Northcote was warned to give no indication that the Government was altering its policy in response to public opinion. He duly stated that it would be 'an unwise hasty policy [. . .] to drive the Turk out of Europe'.
[135]From the London Trades Unionists and the Working Men's Peace Association.
[136]Derby told the first that 'there are a great many people in England who fancy that Lord Beaconsfield is the Sultan and I am the Grand Vizier'. *The Times*, 12 September 1876.

359

Derby to Disraeli, Dep. Hughenden 112/4, fo. 175
13 September 1876
Foreign Office

I have just parted with Odo Russell. He goes tomorrow to his post. He says Bismarck has no plan about this eastern question – wishes for peace – but otherwise does not care how it is settled.

Bismarck's chief anxiety is to keep Austria & Russia on the terms that best suit his views – not hostile, nor yet intimate. He, Bismarck, is especially desirous of keeping Andrassy where he is, thinking him a friend to Germany.

I asked Odo to do all he could to find out what danger there really is of Russian intervention. He does not consider it great. [. . .]

360

Salisbury to Earl of Carnarvon, Carnarvon Papers, BL Add. MS
60758, fos 180–181
13 September 1876
Chalet Cecil, Puys

[. . .] For the present, I think Derby's speech is as much as can be said. I gather that at Constantinople we are still pressing for an armistice. If we fail, I presume Russia will act: & an entire change of scene will take place. If we succeed, there will of course be a conference: & the instructions given for the conference will [be] of primary importance. Elliot is evidently very much disposed to make everything pleasant to [*sic*] the Turk. No advantage to England can result from such a policy now: & their alliance & friendship is a reproach to us. The Turk[']s teeth must be drawn: even if he be allowed to live. [. . .]

361

Hardy to Cairns, Cairns Papers, PRO 30/51/7, fos 99–101
14 September 1876
Hemsted

[. . .] Derby's speech[137] is calm & clear but cold and too much addressed to the reasonable world only.[138] At the same time it proves

---

[137] His speech of 11 September.
[138] 'I doubt', noted Hardy, 'if Derby's cold water will quench the fire wh. however may burn itself out.' *DGH*, 14 September 1876, p. 290.

non complicity in fact by dates and otherwise and he was right not to answer the violent men like Freeman who impute wilful connivance.[139] I hope his histories are more impartial than his letters[,] which are specimens of malignant calumny[,] particularly against Beaconsfield & Derby[,] such as one seldom has seen. I wish the Cabinet were more fully informed of what is going on [...] What he [Gladstone] calls 'easy' is a task which might baffle the highest order of politician for it requires the cordial concurrence of six Powers – three at least of w[h.] have or think they have conflicting interests. I suppose Northcote will speak 'by authority' on Saturday[140] – & I hope may do some good but he cannot aid diplomatic negotiation[.] Indeed Russia as it seems to me never occupied such a position for mischief as she does now. If she decides upon open action public feeling (I won't call it opinion) would tie our hands. The present indignation[,] well founded as it is[,] of the mass would furnish the factions with means of obstruction to all useful diplomatic action — It is clear that Russia has no sincere desire for peace and I question whether Austria wants it yet. Has Derby any scheme in his mind for there is no inkling of it in his speech or in the blue books. [...]

362

Cairns to Hardy, Cranbrook Papers, HA43: T501/262
16 September 1876
Millden Brechin, N.B.

[...] I am very glad to hear your views about the East, & I entirely share your anxiety & uneasiness about it. As to knowing what are D[erby]'s views & intentions, I fear there is little to know. All seems to me to be negative, like his speech, wh was good as far as it went, but sadly deficient in sentiment or suggestion. [...] But what are we doing, or going to do? I have said to Northcote, & Carnarvon [...] & I am saying to B[eaconsfield]. today, that if we are to take any distinct step, I think the Cabinet shd meet, however inconvenient it wd be. [...]

My idea is that we (with the other powers) shd force Turkey to a reasonable peace with all the existing combatants, & then have a conference, at wh the powers who now guarantee Turkey might guarantee a system of autonomous provinces. But all this needs talking over.

---

[139] The historian E.A. Freeman (1823–1892) was one of Derby's harshest critics during the atrocities agitation. See *DD*, pp. 314, 320.

[140] In his speech at Edinburgh on 16 September. See his letter to Cross of 8 September, above, **357**.

363

Disraeli to Derby, DP 920 DER (15) 16/2/2
21 September 1876
Hughenden

[. . .] I am convinced myself, that Russia, at the present moment, w^d be glad to wind up affairs, & apparently with us. I think you will succeed in yr undertaking, & gain glory.

Cairns, in the wilds of Scotland, harks about calling the Cabinet together, & suggests 'a distinct' policy – wh. as far as I can judge consists of every thing wh: the other powers w^d. not assent to = but all is to be done by a conference, creating & guaranteeing autonomous, but tributary states! A few more Servias!

We must do without a conference now that Gortch[akov]: has given that up; no one can want it.

Let nothing shake you[141] — The more I think & see, the more sure is my conviction, that this outcry is all froth, except where it is faction.

[. . .] Yesterday was the largest dinner of the kind ever known in this county = all the notables of both sides. I was forced to speak[142] – & every mention of your name was received with rapturous cheering. [. . .]

364

Cairns to Disraeli, Dep. Hughenden 91/3, fo. 75
21 September 1876
Millden Brechin, N.B.

[. . .] I am most anxious to see your reference to eastern affairs at the meeting at Wycombe last night. I cannot help feeling that D[erby]. is wrong in not letting the Cabinet know what proposals he is making or supporting for adjusting the difficulties betw[ee]^n. the Porte & Servia, & the other provinces. It may result in some dissent in the Cabinet on the subject, which will be most unfortunate. The F.O. send me papers, & ask me questions about extradition & other rubbish, but, on this all important subject, they send nothing but telegrams a fortnight old.

[141]'Letter from Disraeli [. . .] urging me (needlessly) not to make any concession to the popular cry.' *DD*, 22 September 1876, p. 328. The next day, too, Disraeli wrote, telling Derby: 'You can't be too firm.' See M&B, VI, p. 68.
[142]See account, below, **365**.

365

Cairns to Richmond, Goodwood MS 868, B37
23 September 1876
Millden Brechin, N.B.

[...] The Bucks election is a narrow squeak.[143] We sh^d have had 1000 maj[orit]^y. However it is safe now, & we may hope that next time there will be no Bulgaria.

I wish Disr[ael]^i.'s speech has [*sic*] not been so defiant of public opinion.[144] The F.O. papers, wh came to me yesterday (& to you also, no doubt: I wrote strongly, & said we ought to know what was going on:) shew that D[erby]. has made propositions which I think are good, & w^d. be generally approved of: but I can't see why he & our chief don't put a little more sentiment, & sympathy with public feeling, into their speeches. [...]

366

Disraeli to Cairns, Cairns Papers, PRO 30/51/1, fos 141–145
23 September 1876

I can't help feeling that you are misconceiving the course wh: L[or]^d Derby is taking. There is no use in calling the Cabinet together, for there is nothing to consult them about. He is acting on the lines wh: the Cabinet approved when we separated, & has not got beyond them. He has availed himself of an opportunity of a successful mediation, wh: was not easy; & he has obtained a virtual armistice wh: was still more difficult. He has proposed to the five powers that (roughly speaking, recurring in the cases of Servia & Montenegro to the status quo.) they sh^d. agree to establish administrative autonomy in Herz[egovina]: & Bosnia after signing preliminaries of peace, & also consider what guarantees for fair government can be devised for Bulgaria. If he succeeds in this, & can get the preliminaries signed, there will no doubt be questions to consider for the Cabinet.

---

[143]The by-election had been called in the wake of Disraeli's elevation to the Lords. T.F. Fremantle, the Conservative candidate, received 2,725 votes, while R.C.G. Carington, the Liberal, had 2,539. This majority of 186 contrasted with Disraeli's total of 2,999 in 1874, as opposed to the nearest Liberal (also elected, as Buckinghamshire was a three-member seat), who only received 1,720 votes.

[144]In an eve-of-poll speech at Aylesbury on 20 September, Disraeli had declared that 'a great portion of the people of this country' had 'arrived at a conclusion' that, 'if carried into effect, would alike be injurious to the permanent and important interests of England, and fatal to any chance of preserving the peace of Europe'.

But he has not yet succeeded in doing this, tho' he has shown an energy & fertility of resource, & fixity of purpose, in the matter for wh: I never previously gave him credit.

One great point is, Russia has assented to these proposals, but Austria demurs even to administrative autonomy tho the last accounts from Vienna are more favorable [*sic*].

Germany will not decide till Russia & Austria are d'accord.

I think that Derby will succeed, & that in a few days, these preliminaries may be submitted to the Porte – but I am not at all clear, that we may not find great difficulties in that quarter. Derby however, of late, has been successful in controlling the Porte. Nevertheless I understand a real resistance is to be expected.

As for the plans you suggested for consideration in one of your letters; autonomous & tributary states, & a conference, or Congress, to settle affairs generally:– every power is opposed to political autonomy. Servia has not proved a very encouraging example, having never paid her tribute, & then made war on her Suzerain.

Russia was once for a conference, the only power; but P[rince] Gort[chak]^{ov}: has now quite relinquished the idea as unnecessary. He says this in accepting Derby's preliminaries.

In fact it comes to this, if the English people insist upon the resolutions being carried into effect, we must make war on Turkey with that object with[ou]t. allies, & then the Grand Signor will appeal to the Russians to enter his dominion to protect him. [. . .]

367

Derby to Disraeli, Dep. Hughenden 112/4, fo. 185
26 September 1876
Foreign Office

I return Salisbury's letter with thanks. His plan is large and new: it amounts to a new constitution for the Turkish empire. — I hardly think we could get it adopted, or that if adopted it would work.[145] But it deserves consideration[.]

---

[145] In his letter to Disraeli of 23 September, Salisbury had claimed that 'the traditional Palmerstonian policy is at an end' and had advocated, among other ideas, an official 'Protector of Christians'. The letter is reproduced in M&B, VI, pp. 70–71. Derby noted: 'I keep copy of the proposal, though not believing that it will work.' *DD*, 25 September 1876, p. 329. On 26 September, Disraeli wrote to Salisbury, politely acknowledging the proposal but commending Derby's policy. M&B, VI, pp. 71–72.

368

Derby to Disraeli, Dep. Hughenden 112/4, fo. 187
27 September 1876
Foreign Office

I telegraphed to you about the meeting.[146] It was chiefly composed of Liberals, though the Lord Mayor[147] & Hubbard[148] were there. The feeling against Turkey very strong. Evident disappointment was felt that I could not support Gladstone's plan of complete autonomy.[149] They were civil enough on the whole, but could not refrain from interrupting and expressing dissent. I have stuck to our colours pretty steadily, and I think said nothing that can be twisted so as to make mischief. But I will have no more deputations! They don't help one to negociate. The numbers were about 150, as far as could be judged.

369

Disraeli to Derby, DP 920 DER (15) 16/2/2[150]
29 September 1876
Hughenden

[...] I had written you a long letter yesterday congratulating you on yʳ speech – wh: was perfect; and wh: induced the 'Times' to throw over both Lowe[151] & Gladstone specifically, showing, after all, we were exactly in the right.

But the Serv[ian]: tel: upset me.[152] I don't see my way. If Austria step in to put an end to the conspiracy, the same reason that prevents

---

[146]With a deputation from the City. For an account, see *The Times*, 28 September 1876.

[147]Sir William James Richmond Cotton (1822–1902), Lord Mayor of London, 1875–1876; businessman and Conservative MP for the City of London, 1874–1885; a critic of Disraeli's policy in the East.

[148]John Gellibrand Hubbard (1805–1889), first Baron Addington from 1887, merchant and fiscal reformer; Conservative MP for the City of London.

[149]The same day, Derby's diary recorded: 'The general feeling seemed to be that if nothing else would accomplish the object, we ought to go to war to drive the Turks out of Europe.' *DD*, p. 330.

[150]This is the second half of the letter. Both halves are reproduced in almost complete form in M&B, VI, pp. 74–75. The first half deals with a royal intervention of no broader significance.

[151]Robert Lowe (1811–1892), later Viscount Sherbrooke; Liberal MP; formerly Chancellor of the Exchequer and Home Secretary under Gladstone.

[152]Serbia resumed hostilities on 27 September. A telegram announcing this intelligence appeared in *The Times* on 29 September, dated the previous day.

Russia interfering herself, will force her to oppose Austria. There is war, & a long one. [...]

I don't think we ought to join in the war, but I think with an understanding with the Porte, we sh^d. occupy Const[antinop]^l[e]. as a 'material guarantee.'

Everybody will be wanting something: even Italy.

It is now or never with Bismarck, if he really wants peace.

370

Disraeli to Derby, DP 920 DER (15) 16/2/2^{153}
30 September 1876
Hughenden

[...] You are in great favor [*sic*],^{154} which pleases and amuses me.

Keep up y^r spirits – You have shown some of the highest qualities of public life, & I believe the great mass of the nation believe in you.

We may yet confound their politics.

371

Derby to Disraeli, Dep. Hughenden 112/4, fo. 200^{155}
1 October 1876
Keston

A thousand thanks for your cordial note. One really wants encouragement just now. I sometimes feel like the juryman who complained of having been sitting along with eleven of the most obstinate men he ever met. [...]

372

Derby to Disraeli, Dep. Hughenden 112/4, fos 208–209
6 October 1876
Foreign Office

[...] I am to see Schou. today and will find out whether he can or will tell anything.^{156}

---

^{153}A longer version of this letter appears in M&B, VI, p. 76.

^{154}With the Queen; a rare honour for Derby.

^{155}Reproduced in M&B, VI, p. 76.

^{156}Loftus had sent reports that Russia, 'with the consent of Austria', would occupy Bulgaria with 150,000 men. The rumours coincided with a marked change in Russia's official attitude

I am disposed to think that the intelligence has been purposely allowed to get out, in order to frighten Loftus and us: and that the object is to drive us into sending up our fleet to bully the Porte as being a lesser evil than the threatened occupation.

I cannot think that after having agreed on a joint course of action, the Emp. would suddenly take a step of this kind. It would be a declaration to all Europe that he meditates a war of aggression – which is not in his character or ideas, for which we know Russia is not prepared, and which if it were intended would probably be disguised under some more plausible pretext. [. . .]

373

Derby to Disraeli, Dep. Hughenden 112/4, fos 210–211
10 October 1876
Foreign Office

[. . .] Matters at home are looking better – see the Times of today on Gladstone – but I do not like the look of them abroad.[157] The Russians now seem to wish to exclude from the conference any representative of the Porte; which is hardly an admissible proposal; and the Austrians, though they agree to a conference in principle, evidently do so with reluctance, and are disposed to make as much as they can of all possible objections of detail.

Bismarck is still silent and impenetrable. France & Italy are with us sincerely enough, but can do little. The Sultan is prepared to go as far as he can to meet our wishes: he has however immense difficulties, and after all it is not certain that we can help him.

374

Derby to Disraeli, Dep. Hughenden 112/4, fos 212–213
11 October 1876
Foreign Office

I don't like the notion of a special mission to Livadia.[158] First – we don't know how long the Emperor is to stay there, and it might very probably come too late for any useful purpose.

in favour of Serbia, most notably the partial mobilization ordered by Gorchakov on 22 September. Unsurprisingly, Shuvalov denied all knowledge of the news. *DD*, 6 October 1876, p. 332.

[157] 'Since the Russians have shown their hand, public feeling has changed in a singular way.' *DD*, 10 October 1876, p. 332.

[158] The Queen wanted to send a special mission to Russia. Livadia was Alexander II's Black Sea retreat, a hotbed of pan-Slav intrigue.

Next – I doubt if the Emperor wants to receive an English diplomatist — Schou., whatever else he may be, is on the side of peace, and not likely to make mischief. Then there is a certain awkwardness in communicating with the Russian government through three channels at once. You cannot be sure that the same communications will arrive in exactly the same form.

And lastly, I dislike the idea of seeming to make Russia the supreme arbiter of European peace or war. It may be that Russia is so – but is it for us to give prominence to the fact? Does not the sending out of a special mission to the Czar look a little like placing him in a position of superiority? He would not think of sending a special ambassador here!

As to Loftus & his telegram. I think there are really military preparations making in Russia & perhaps on a large scale: but I have no doubt that care is taken to make the most of them in his eyes, so as to impress him with the absolute necessity of peace.[159]

375

Disraeli to Derby, DP 920 DER (15) 16/2/2
12 October 1876
Hughenden

I must congratulate you on the good news, & can hardly believe, that any conditions have been made, which will not be granted, or relinquished.

In that case, we have six months to breathe in, & much may be done in 6 mo[nth]s.

By that time, England will have quite recovered her nerves, & an English Minister, backed by the nation, can do a great deal. That will be your condition[,] I believe, & you will deserve it.

Posterity will do justice to that unprincipled maniac Gladstone – extraordinary mixture of envy, vindictiveness, hypocrisy, & superstition: & with one commanding characteristic: whether Prime Minister or Leader of [the] Opposition, whether preaching, praying, speechifying or scribbling – never a gentleman!

---

[159] A postscript adds: 'The news of today is good.' Turkey had agreed to an armistice of five to six months.

376

Derby to Disraeli, Dep. Hughenden 112/4, fo. 214
13 October 1876
Foreign Office

Thanks for your letter. Gladstone is wilder than ever. What can his last letter mean? Does it refer to the Rothschilds and the Bucks election?[160]

We are not yet out of our troubles. Russia will do all that is possible in the way of making difficulties about the armistice. This is plain from the reports that reach us from all quarters. Schou. says he has telegraphed urging an acceptance, but he admitted that the first impression at Livadia was unfavorable [sic]. What is gained is that the Russians must now show their hand; if they reject, or encourage others to reject, this armistice, they mean war, and all Europe will see it. [. . .]

377

Derby to Disraeli, Dep. Hughenden 112/4, fo. 217
14 October 1876
Foreign Office

[. . .] You will see what is passing. Russia dislikes the armistice which she asked for in the expectation of a refusal, and will break off if a pretext can be found. Schou. is I think sincere in his wish for peace, and professes to be doing all he can.[161] Italy is also making difficulties: Germany gives a cold and reserved support – but it is support.

I am not sanguine, but the chances vary from day to day.

Carnarvon has had Liddon staying with him at Highclere for some time – so I am told. Considering that Liddon has attacked us more acrimoniously than any one [sic], I think our colleague might have postponed his hospitalities.[162] But he has not shown any sign of dissent from our policy so far.

---

[160] 'Gladstone has written a strange letter, which nobody understands: in it he deplores the influence of "Judaic sympathies", not confined to professing Jews, on the eastern question.' *DD*, 13 October 1876, p. 333.

[161] Shuvalov had, on his own initiative, signalled his agreement for a ceasefire of 'not less than a month', and was happy to accept the six-month armistice. But on 11 October Gorchakov angrily telegraphed in favour of a shorter armistice, giving Russia the flexibility to begin war if it wished.

[162] H.P. Liddon (1829–1890), the high church canon of St Paul's, one of the first to write vivid accounts of impaled Bulgarians; a supporter of the Greek Christians and critic of the Government's policy. This remark later grew into Salisbury's claim to Carnarvon, in February 1877, that Derby had in fact tried to stop Liddon going to Highclere. Exchanges between Derby, Disraeli, and Salisbury about the irritation caused by Carnarvon, who in November was prepared to tolerate a Russian occupation of Turkish territory to protect

378

Manners to Disraeli, Dep. Hughenden 106/3, fos 102–103
14 October 1876

[. . .] The question which the Cabinet, perhaps wisely, declined to discuss t'other day, viz what should be done if Russia invades Turkey?, seems to require prompt attention.

The extreme cleverness of the last Turkish move must apparently unmask the real intentions of Russia, and if they are war, it will be war without delay.

There will then be no time to consider with our co-signatories what steps should be taken to guard the neutrality of Roumania, or any other of the peaceful provisions of 1856: and I see nothing for it but what you hinted at in Cabinet, the friendly occupation of Constantinople.[163]

But I noticed with alarm that the most energetic spirits were inclined to pummel not the strong aggressor, but the weak victim; and unless the assumed misconduct of Russia changes their views you may encounter serious difficulties in that quarter. [. . .]

379

Manners to Disraeli, Dep. Hughenden 106/3, fos 104–105
15 October 1876
Balmoral

[. . .] She[164] received the news of the Russian refusal[165] with sorrow and some anger, but without any appearance of dismay, and expressed her opinion in favour of meeting it, and it's [*sic*] possible results boldly and, to use her own words, 'without flinching'. I am convinced that any resolute policy her ministers may think fit to recommend will meet with her assent and approbation.

Orthodox Christians, can be found in M&B, VI, pp. 94–96. See also *DD*, 18 November 1876, pp. 344–345.

[163] According to Derby, Disraeli had suggested occupying Constantinople, as a 'material guarantee', in the Cabinet of 4 October. *DD*, 4 October, p. 331.

[164] The Queen.

[165] Of the Turkish armistice proposal. The duration of the proposed armistice was the nub of the problem: Russia considered it too long a period.

The whole feeling here is strongly anti-Russian, and the Princess Alice[166] last night told me that it is so among the younger men in Germany: they wish to break the ties which bind the 2 empires so closely together. Is Bismarck biding his time to take advantage of this feeling, and pay off Gortshakoff for his conduct last year? [...][167]

380

Derby to Disraeli, Dep. Hughenden 112/4, fos 218–219
16 October 1876
Foreign Office

I have today received the Russian refusal of a five or six months' armistice. The reasons given for it are on the face of them mere pretexts[.] Schou. (I believe) has really exerted himself against this decision, and he told my lady this evening that a week ago he should have said confidently that his Emperor wished for nothing but peace, but now he did not know what to think of it. This is pretty strong coming from an ambassador.

It is clear that I can make no new proposal. It is equally so that the six months' armistice will not do – Italy sides with Russia, France wavers and advises compromise, Austria hesitates, Germany is silent.[168] We had a German approval, as we understood it; but as nothing was said about the armistice being too long, (a point not then raised by any one [sic]) Bismarck has not pledged himself on the present question. I shall send for Münster tomorrow, and try and get from him what Bismarck really wants. If his professions are sincere, now is the time.

But I suspect he would like a war between England and Russia, crippling two Powers neither of which he loves. [...]

---

[166] Alice Maud Mary (1843–1878), the Queen's third child, who had married Prince Louis of Hesse in 1862 and who, ironically, was the mother of the future Tsarina of Russia.

[167] Bismarck's dislike of Gorchakov dated back to the late 1840s and was well known in Europe's chancelleries. The reference to the previous year's 'conduct' was to the 'War-in-Sight' crisis.

[168] In early October both Russia and Austria had asked Bismarck whether Germany would remain neutral in the event of an Austro-Russian war. Bismarck, realizing that an answer either way would spell the end of the *Dreikaiserbund*, remained silent.

381

Disraeli to Salisbury, SP, fos 161–163[169]
17 October 1876
Hughenden

[. . .] Elliot was successful in his last move[170] but the state of affairs, throughout Europe, & Asia too, is highly unsatisfactory – Russia is mischievous, but 'willing to wound & yet afraid to strike'[.]

If she continues to hesitate, she may give time to infuse some energy into public affairs. I believe the old Emperor of Germany is the great stumbling block to haute politique;[171] clinging, as he does, to family traditions —

My own feeling is, & I request your opinion upon it, is that it w^d. be desirable to make a treaty with Germany to maintain the status quo – not an alliance, offensive & defensive, as Brunow [*sic*] proposed to Derby père [*sic*], in 1852,[172] & wh. was wisely & promptly refused: but the maintenance of the status quo. It would make us easy about Constantinople, & w^d. lay the bugbear of Bismarck, wh: is an eventual Anglo-French alliance, that may make him restore the two captured provinces.[173] [. . .]

382

Disraeli to Derby, DP 920 DER (15) 16/2/2[174]
17 October 1876
Hughenden

Nothing can be more unsatisfactory, than the whole state of Europe – & Asia too – in a great degree. [. . .]

What if we could negotiate a treaty with Germany to maintain the present status quo generally? Not an alliance offensive & defensive, as Brunnow offered to yr father in 1852 – & wh: was wisely & promptly declined; but a treaty for the maintenance of the status quo. This wd. make us easy about Constantinople, & relieve Bismarck of his real

---

[169] The first (and less significant) half of this letter appears in M&B, VI, p. 94, but without the section reproduced here. The section in M&B immediately precedes the material here.

[170] It is unclear precisely what Disraeli meant here, though it seems likely that it was Elliot's part in persuading the Turks to put forward their offer of an armistice a few days before. See **374** and **375**, above.

[171] 'high politics'; generally used in a diplomatic context.

[172] This is one of the few extant references to the Russian alliance offer made to the fourteenth Earl of Derby in 1852. See above, **13**.

[173] Alsace and Lorraine.

[174] The full text of this letter appears in M&B, VI, p. 81.

bugbear, the eventual alliance of England & France, & the loss of his two captured provinces. [. . .] it wd. settle everything for our lives, & immortalize yourself.

383

Disraeli to Derby, DP 920 DER (15) 16/2/2
21 October 1876
10 Downing Street

[. . .] I conclude the invasion of Turkey, & conquest of Constantinople, may be rapid.[175]

If so, our determination as to our ultimate course cannot be too soon decided on. Constantinople occupied by the Russians, while the British fleet was in Besica [*sic*] Bay, would be the most humiliating event, that has occurred to England, since the surrenders of Whitelocke & Burgoyne & Cornwallis, but infinitely in its consequences more important & disastrous.[176]

384

Disraeli to Derby, DP 920 DER (15) 16/2/2
22 October 1876
10 Downing Street

I am anxious about the state of affairs.[177]

There seems to me no doubt, that after the passage of the Pruth, the Russians may reach Constantinople in sixty days; at the most sixty four[.] [. . .]

Any movement on our part, whether we fortify the peninsula by lake Durkos, or the Chersonese & the Dardanelles, would be sixteen days too late, if delayed till the Russians cross the Balkan [*sic*].

But what alarms me, is that Turkey, feeling she is utterly deserted, may make some mad compact with Russia, opening the Straits, & giving to her complete control over the Asiatic shore.

---

[175]Disraeli was anxious after receipt of intelligence from Colonel F.A. Wellesley, British military attaché in St Petersburg.

[176]Disraeli at this time believed that Constantinople was 'the key of India'. See Memorandum by Lord Barrington, 23 October 1876, M&B, VI, p. 84.

[177]'In afternoon I had from Disraeli a letter which made me uneasy as it indicated greater alarm [. . .] than anything in our correspondence seems to warrant.' *DD*, 22 October 1876, p. 336.

As for compensation to England by having Egypt & Crete – this is moonshine. If Constantinople is Russian, they w^d. only be an expensive encumbrance. —

Has it been represented to Turkey, that our last move was not intended as a desertion of her, but rather an assertion of her policy? This is necessary to save her from throwing herself into the fatal embrace of Ignatieff.* [. . .]

385

Derby to Disraeli, Dep. Hughenden 112/4, fos 226–227
22 October 1876
Foreign Office

I will be in town early tomorrow. I bear in mind all you say, and your opinion always has the greatest weight with me. But my impression is that the Russians are by no means in the state of readiness which you assume, and that a dash at Constantinople is not their object. However I will not dispute that with you. But are you not taking for granted that their march will be practically unopposed? and is this likely? I do not think that immediate war is expected by any diplomatist – not that they are infallible. If it were intended, why press for six weeks armistice? The Porte might utterly baffle them by an acceptance.

386

Derby to Ward Hunt, Dep. Hughenden 112/4, fos 228–229
24 October 1876
Foreign Office

The step of ordering a British fleet to pass the Dardanelles (the consent of the Porte not having been asked) is not one to be taken offhand, nor without the fullest consideration.[178] — I cannot sanction the order which has been suggested to you as matters now stand. If a Russian vessel went through – which I do not consider as probable – there would be plenty of time to send the order by telegraph. But I repeat that I do not expect the contingency to occur, since the passage would be resisted, and as we know, the Russians have no fleet to match that of Turkey.

[178]Disraeli had asked Ward Hunt to order the fleet up to Constantinople in the event of a Russian ship going through the Bosphorus. According to Derby, 'Hunt naturally demurs, and says he must have the authority of the F.O [. . .] I cannot quite believe that Disraeli would have directed this to be done, without consulting me.' DD, 24 October 1876, p. 337.

387

Derby to Disraeli, Dep. Hughenden 112/4, fo. 243
29 October 1876
Foreign Office

I hear from the War Office privately[179] that a requisition has been made for 80 'guns of position' – 'in consequence of certain engineer officers being sent to Constantinople.' May I ask what this means? We have never sanctioned the sending out of guns to Constantinople. I am told farther that they cannot be supplied without the whole affair becoming public. — I do not think steps of this kind ought to be taken – with the result of creating a panic throughout Europe – unless after full consideration & discussion.[180]

388

Derby to Disraeli, Dep. Hughenden 113/1, fos 7–8
7 November 1876
Foreign Office

As we have the Queen's approval of Salisbury, there is no object in keeping his mission a secret any longer.[181] As to its having got out, I can only say it did not do so through me. There is not a hint of it in any of the papers. [. . .]

Of Bismarck I can tell you nothing certain: but my belief is that his support meant, that he would have been ready to stir us up to a quarrel with Russia, not much caring which side won: and that he is disgusted at the prospect of England and Russia coming to an understanding. His only object is to prevent any two Powers coming to an understanding if he can help it. [. . .]

[179] From Lord Eustace Cecil, Surveyor-General of the Ordnance. *DD*, 29 October 1876, p. 338.
[180] Disraeli assured Derby, the next day, that 'he knew nothing about the matter of the guns'. *DD* 30 October 1876, p. 339. Hardy, 'a good deal annoyed', noted in his diary that he had merely sent an enquiry, and that Cecil had written 'needlessly' to Derby. *DGH*, p. 195.
[181] A conference of the powers at Constantinople had been mooted since October, and was formally proposed by Britain in November. Disraeli and Derby agreed that Salisbury should be their representative. On 3 November, he formally agreed to 'take my part in the comedy with all solemnity'. Salisbury departed for the conference on 20 November 1876, and *en route* conducted what Disraeli called 'a serviceable reconnaissance' of Paris, Berlin, Vienna, and Rome.

389

Disraeli to Salisbury, SP, fos 171–173[182]
10 November 1876
Sandringham

[. . .] You must remember we suffer from a feeble & formal diplomacy,[183] & there has been little real interchange of thought between the English government, & foreign powers. I agree with the Prince,[184] & I think it highly desirable, that at this moment our communications with the powers sh^d. be lifted out of the slough of despond, they have so long grovelled in. [. . .]

Consider this matter for yourself, & whatever you decide on I will support – only don't concede your own convictions on the subject to Tenterdenism, wh: is a dusty affair, & not suited to the times & things we have to grapple with. [. . .]

390

Derby to Disraeli, Dep. Hughenden 113/1, fo. 17
18 November 1876
Foreign Office

I send you at once a very important communication which I have received from Beust. Please send it on to Salisbury.

[Enclosed:]

The Austrian ambassador has been with me, and says he is authorised to assure me confidentially —

(1) That Austria is under no engagements to Russia
(2) That Austria will not adopt a policy of neutrality under all circumstances but will protect her own interests if she thinks them menaced by any act of Russia —

I expressed satisfaction.[185]

---

[182]This letter is reproduced in full in Cecil, II, p. 95.

[183]A criticism of Lord Tenterden and his minions, rather than Derby.

[184]The Prince of Wales, who had suggested a diplomatic tour of the kind on which Salisbury embarked prior to Constantinople. This letter was written to persuade Salisbury to undertake it.

[185]Beust was speaking the truth, as far as he was aware, but only because Andrássy had not told him about the secret agreement he had reached with Russia at Reichstadt in July 1876. There, and at a series of subsequent meetings, Alexander II and Franz Josef effectively agreed to Austria's non-intervention in the event of a Russo-Turkish war. The

391

Derby to Salisbury, SP, fos 52–53
28 November 1876

I add one line to my former letters to say that I have received your deeply interesting letter from Berlin.[186] It confirms and emphasises what we knew, or thought we knew before, as to the ideas and policy of Bismarck. I am inclined to think that he has talked to you sincerely, with the only exception that he publicly wishes for a war more than he has thought fit to acknowledge.

Russia crippled (as, whoever wins,[187] Russia would be for some time) puts an end to the danger which he most fears, that of a Russo-French coalition.[188] The question is, not whether Germany will help us; that we know is out of the question: but whether Germany will interfere actively to prevent Austria from helping us, if so disposed. I wish with some anxiety to know how you have found Andrassy inclined. He does not trust Beust – a feeling wh. is reciprocated – and he does not open out much to old Buchanan, wh. is not surprising. Therefore you will be able to tell me more of his real views than I have yet learnt from anybody. [...]

Two dangers occur to me as specially to be guarded against. One, that we shall be marking plans for 'Bulgaria' without having defined what Bulgaria is. The Russians, left alone, wd bring it to the suburbs of Constantinople. The other is to get us pledged to support something wh. they know can only be enforced by war & then call on us to join in the war which they have brought on. [...]

question of whether an understanding existed between Russia and Austria became one of the most important disagreements between Derby and Disraeli. Disraeli refused to believe in the existence of any Austro-Russian deal, thus believing Austria to be more of a free agent than it was. Derby, on the other hand, increasingly believed in the possibility of an Austro-Russian agreement, not least because Shuvalov repeatedly told him about it.

[186]The letter in question, that of 23 November, is reproduced in Cecil, II, pp. 96–98.

[187]A Russo-Turkish war.

[188]As the British ambassador in Berlin, Lord Odo Russell, had reported to Derby on 3 June 1876: 'Bismarck has never liked England and Russia to become intimate because he fears that the Anglo-Russian sympathies of France might lead to an "entente a 3"'.

392

Disraeli to Salisbury, SP, fo. 183[189]
29 November 1876
10 Downing Street

[...] It is a most critical moment in European politics. If Russia is not checked, the Holy Alliance will be revived in aggravated form & force. Germany will have Holland, & France, Belgium, & England will be in a position I trust I shall never live to witness. [...]

393

Derby to Salisbury, SP, fo. 54
7 December 1876
Foreign Office

I have your interesting letters from Vienna & Rome.[190] You don't seem to have made much out of Andrassy, and I am not surprised. Your description of him as a man pulled different ways by conflicting forces, and not sure of what he shall be able to do, tallies precisely with my observation during the last twelve months. He has been so vacillating & undecided as to create a suspicion of his sincerity: but I do not think he means to deceive, he only does not know his own mind. Add to this a considerable share of indolence, and a strong disposition to let things take their course, and you have the man. I doubt his being as closely connected with Bismarck as you suppose. — I have been very careful in speaking to Beust, and in fact have told him nothing. [...]

Salisbury and the Constantinople Conference

Salisbury had left Britain on 20 November, proceeding via Paris, Berlin, Vienna, and Rome, and thence to Brindisi, where he sailed for Constantinople on 2 December,

---

[189]The much longer letter from which this extract is taken is also reproduced in M&B, VI, pp. 103–106.
[190]Letters of 25 November and 30 November, respectively; reproduced in Cecil, II, pp. 98–99 and 106–107.

arriving on 5 December. On 11 December, after a series of bilateral meetings between Ignatiev and Salisbury, the representatives of the powers gathered in a preliminary conference that met for six sessions and concluded on 19 December. The full Constantinople Conference, with the Turks finally included, began on 23 December, meeting on 28 and 30 December 1876 and 1, 4, 8, 11, and 15 January 1877. The Turks were not prepared to accept the powers' proposals and the conference concluded at its last meeting on 20 January 1877. The great powers withdrew their ambassadors. Salisbury left on 22 January, although Elliot negated the effect somewhat by delaying his own departure.

394

Disraeli to Derby, DP 920 DER (15) 16/2/3
15 January 1877
2 Whitehall Gardens

[...] I have ascertained by an accident,[191] that there is 'no understanding' bet[wee]^n. the 3 Imp[erial]: Courts, & that Schou: lied, & intentionally lied —[192]

But what are we to say of Odo Russell!

Careless & false – perhaps both – I never was more disappointed in a man.

395

Derby to Disraeli, Dep. Hughenden 113/1, fo. 66
15 January 1877
Fairhill, Tunbridge

[...] I agree with you entirely about O Russell. He is quite at sea; knows little, & gets that wrong.

I have no certainty about the union of the three emperors: it is affirmed at Berlin & Petersburgh, and denied at Vienna; on the whole the denial seems most likely to be right. [...]

---

[191] He had heard from the Rothschilds.

[192] Derby was unsurprised by this news, as his diary recorded on 16 January (*DD*, p. 367). He knew Shuvalov's methods, and had previously warned Salisbury 'not to give credit to anything that Ignatieff may say he has heard from Schou as to my views, since he is sure to put something into my mouth that I never said'. *DD*, 12 December 1876, p. 351.

396

Salisbury to Carnarvon, Carnarvon Papers, BL Add. MS 60759, fos 20–21[193]
19 January 1877
Constantinople

[. . .] The telegraph will have informed you that we have failed to make any impression on the obstinacy of the Turk. The terms have been reduced to the lowest possible point, consistent with the preservation of any guarantee: & therefore their refusal must be interpreted as a disposal to escape from European tutelage altogether.

On the whole, I think that a belief in Russia[']s weakness has been the most potent encouragement to resistance; & next to that a belief (encouraged by many persons & writers & by sundry circumstances) that I do not really represent the Government of England. [. . .]

397

Disraeli to Derby, DP 920 DER (15) 16/2/3
30 January 1877
2 Whitehall Gardens

I don't quite reconcile this fidgetiness of Bismarck with the 'intimate understanding' of which we hear so much.[194]

It does not seem to exist among the ministers; & as for the sovereigns, Germany must die tomorrow, Russia may, & Austria is a nincompoop.

398

Derby to Hardy, Cranbrook Papers, BL Add. MS 62537, fo. 74
3 February 1877
Foreign Office

[. . .] I do not like these plans of occupation, 'compensation', and mixing ourselves up needlessly in the affair.[195]

---

[193]This letter is reproduced in the same form (without ellipses marked) in Cecil, II, p. 123.

[194]Odo Russell had written with details of an interview with Bismarck, in which the Chancellor asked, among other things, whether Britain would remain neutral in a Franco-German war.

[195]There was much discussion as to what would happen in the event of the Russo-Turkish war now widely anticipated.

If we tell the Russians that Constantinople is not to be touched, it will not be. You had better consult the Premier on the whole question.[196]

399

Disraeli to Derby, DP 920 DER (15) 16/2/3
5 February 1877
2 Whitehall Gardens

What about a Cabinet?
There are points that ought to be settled as to the statements to be made in both Houses, wh: sh^d. be identical & consistent.
And yet it is awkward to consult on these with[ou]^t. Sarum[197] —

400

Derby to Disraeli, Dep. Hughenden 112/3, fo. 142
5 February 1877
Foreign Office

I think on the whole you had better let it alone. Absolute unity of opinion will not be possible if many speak: but the opening is not likely to lead to very long debate; and for the rest we have time.[198]

401

Disraeli to Derby, DP 920 DER (15) 16/2/3[199]
9 February 1877
10 Downing Street

[. . .] The position of affairs is most critical, & requires decision —[200]
I believe that, at no moment, was Russia more anxious for peace, than the present. She is perfectly conscious of the intrigues of Bismarck to involve her in a struggle, wh:, whatever the ultimate result, must be materially disastrous to her – but she must have a golden bridge – The Moscow speech, & the host on the Pruth, render this necessary.

---

[196] Of the disposition of British forces.
[197] Salisbury.
[198] Parliament opened on 8 February. The Cabinet had already discussed the Queen's Speech on 31 January and 2 February.
[199] Full letter reproduced in M&B, VI, pp. 126–127.
[200] On 4 February, Gorchakov had issued a circular critical of Turkey but announcing Russia's intention to consult the other powers. In early March it was announced that Ignatiev would tour European capitals for this purpose.

If war begins, I think it will end in partition. I cannot learn, that Turkey has any adequate resources: no money; not many men. In that case we must have a decided course, & seize, at the fitting time, what is necessary for the security of our Empire — No one will resist us, either at the time, or afterwards.

But can war be avoided? Only by a reply to Gortchakow[']s note, or a negotiation with Russia thro' the ambassador here, wh: will construct the golden bridge.[201]

[...] He who gains time, gains everything. By that period, France will be armed. [...]

I don't fancy the country will stand laisser faire, but they will back us, I believe, in whatever we do, provided we are doing.

[P.S.] You can <u>talk</u> to me about all this.[202]

402

Mary Derby to Salisbury, SP, fo. 36
10 February 1877
23 St James's Square

C^t. Shouvaloff came yest[erda]^y. to urge strongly that there sh^d. be no delay in answering the circular. He said he had kept – or tried to keep, his Emp[ero]^r. & Gov^t quiet for the last five days on the ground that the Gov^t. here was entirely occupied with the opening of Parl^t. But this w^d. not last forever, & he hoped L^d D[erby] w^d. see the importance of time now.

I promised to push with my small efforts in the same direction & have done so, but I know not with what success. [...]

403

Derby to Northcote, IP, BL Add. MS 50022, fos 131–132
26 February 1877
Foreign Office

[...] — I have never thought Cobden[203] an oracle either on foreign or home affairs. He believed three things with all his heart – That the repeal of the corn laws would break the power of the landed

---

[201] Disraeli then made a series of proposals as to desirable Turkish concessions in its internal government.
[202] 'I did not answer, as we are sure to meet almost daily.' *DD*, 9 February 1877, p. 376.
[203] Richard Cobden (1804–1865), manufacturer and radical politician.

aristocracy. That the example of England would bring about free trade all over the world. That great wars would never be made again, being incompatible with the ideas of an industrial age. In all three points he has been wrong. The landowners are stronger than before – Europe is showing more protectionist tendencies than 20 years ago, and America itself following suit – and all the world is armed to the teeth. [...]

404

Derby to Disraeli, Dep. Hughenden 113/1, fo. 80
1 March 1877
Foreign Office

Here is a draft answer to the Russian circular.[204] [...] — We cannot be too cautious. By saying too little, we risk breaking off the negociation, and causing war: but on the other hand Russia will be anxious to put on our words the construction that we agree to coercion[205] under certain circumstances, the opposition here will take up the cry, and we shall look foolish if we have not a sufficient answer. [...]

405

Disraeli to Derby, DP 920 DER (15) 16/2/3
3 March 1877
10 Downing Street

With reference to my rough note of yesterday,[206] I entirely agree with you, that we must have no controversial matter in our answer to Gort[chakov]. — Yet it may be considered, whether we sh^d. not assume, in our reply, our own view of the raison d'etre [sic] of our proceedings, equally as he does of his own —

But I don't wish in the least to insist on this, but wd. rather leave everything to you in whom I have complete confidence.

---

[204] 'It is short, & avoids controversy as far as possible.' *DD*, 1 March 1877, p. 380. For details of the circular, see **401**, above.
[205] Of Turkey.
[206] Disraeli had sent some general criticisms the previous day.

406

Carnarvon to Salisbury, SP, fo. 290
16 March 1877

Do you notice in one of the telegrams circulated this evening that
HMG: are said to have proposed their modifications of the
Protocol[207] & that Bismarck urges their acceptance at S[t]. Petersburgh
[*sic*]? What does this mean? Are we to be convened tomorrow merely
to register an accepted conclusion? This was not the understanding
of the Cabinet.

407

Salisbury to Carnarvon, Carnarvon Papers, BL Add. MS 60759, fo.
24
24 March 1877
Hatfield

I trust the close of the scene is not appropriate. Lest it should be,
read Norfolk[']s advice to Buckingham – first scene of Henry VIII.[208]
I cannot find out that any one [*sic*] knew what was coming.[209]

[207]Ignatiev was the bearer of a protocol for the Porte, which Russia was proposing should
be signed by the other powers. Derby had first heard of it when Ignatiev reached Berlin.
On 13 March, the Cabinet had agreed to accept the protocol in principle and, on the basis
of that discussion, Derby had indeed suggested amendments to Shuvalov on 15 March. At
the Cabinet on 17 March, at Salisbury's prompting, Derby agreed to one amendment in
the British position. *DD*, pp. 382–383.
    [208] I advise you, –
    And take it from a heart that wishes towards you
    Honour and plenteous safety, – that you read
    The cardinal's malice and his potency
    Together; to consider further, that
    What his high hatred would effect wants not
    A minister in his power. You know his nature,
    That he's revengeful; and I know his sword
    Hath a sharp edge: it's long, and, 'tmay be said,
    It reaches far; and where 'twill not extend,
    Thither he darts it.

The 'Cardinal' in question was, of course, Disraeli.
    [209]The Cabinet had met on 23 March to confirm their stance: they would not agree to
Russia's latest version of its proposals without Russian disarmament. Disraeli made a thinly
veiled attack on Salisbury and Carnarvon, the principal dissenters, in order to force them
into line.

408

Carnarvon to Salisbury, SP, fo. 294
25 March 1877
Windsor Castle[210]

The case is a very serious one – and my impression is that we may be on the edge of a crisis. The ground has been completely undermined here and all the more skilfully that the Queen whilst entirely imbued with Disraeli's ideas & prepared to support him & aware that there is strong difference of opinion and eager to overcome it has not yet been led up to the last point of <u>requiring our resignations</u>. In order not to startle her too much this last measure has been kept back: but the train is all laid and it now only needs the spark to fire it. I do not feel sure that before the Easter holidays are over we shall not have the explosion. [...]

409

Salisbury to Carnarvon, Carnarvon Papers, BL Add. MS 60759, fos 25–28[211]
26 March 1877
India Office

Your letter 'donne à penser.'[212] But I find a difficulty in believing that B[eaconsfield]. contemplates any course so violent as you suggest. I admit that, if he means war with Russia, it is his interest to get rid of us now rather than when the crisis comes. But he can only get rid of us in one of two ways. He must dismiss us: or he must pick a quarrel & provoke us to resign. The first supposition hardly seems to me possible. No Minister has dismissed a colleague in the Cabinet since Pitt dismissed Thurlow: & then the provocation was considerable, because Thurlow spoke & voted against Government bills in the House of Lords.[213] Being an act of so unexampled a kind[,] some cause must be shown – to the Queen, the colleagues, Parliament. But no cause could be even pretended except our prospective unwillingness to go to war with Russia. Assuming – which is a vast assumption – that

---

[210]Carnarvon noted that this letter was finished at Highclere.

[211]This letter was reproduced, with minor changes, in Cecil, II, pp. 138–139.

[212]'makes one think'.

[213]Salisbury was not quite correct. In effect, Russell had dismissed Palmerston in 1851, although there were differing accounts of the episode; but Russell's provocation was also considerable.

such a motive would seem sufficient to the Queen & the colleagues – how would it look in Parliament? Why the statement of it would blow up the whole plot. Whatever change may come when they see blood, the people are in no humour for war at present. The avowal that the Prime Minister had broken up his Cabinet in order to be ready for war would create a terrible outburst of peace – atrocity – & commercial feeling, which might well bring him to the ground. Perhaps he might not give this reason. But he must give some reason – & a cogent one for such a step. However, if he did not give this explanation we should; & that he knows full well. The other plan is to pick a quarrel. But it takes two to make a quarrel: & the opportunities for doing so in our case are not frequent. Nor, though he has courage enough, is he coldblooded enough to maintain the resolution to pick a quarrel over any considerable space of time.

We must be cautious till the crisis comes. There will be no need to interfere very conspicuously in foreign affairs for the present. We are rolling down the incline now: war (between Russia and Turkey[)] seems to me inevitable.

I feel certain that none of our colleagues, except the two,[214] have any notion of any peculiar difficulty or tension. [. . .]

410

Carnarvon to Northcote, IP, BL Add. MS 50022, fos 209–211
30 March 1877
Highclere Castle

I cannot forbear calling your attention – if indeed it has escaped you – to the official article in last night's Pall Mall in which it is said that the resolution to sign the Protocol is due to causes operating within and without the Cabinet.[215] This is in fact an advertisement of our differences of opinion and since I have had anything to do with politics I cannot remember a precedent. For weeks past the Pall Mall has been ostentatiously the F.O. organ: and of course amongst all who are in any way behind the scenes it is known to be inspired. Such a statement therefore as this is a very serious one: nor do I see how a Cabinet can long hold together if one member of it allows a newspaper to announce that a particular line of policy has been forced upon him by colleagues who take a different view of the question – For

---

[214]Presumably Disraeli and Derby.
[215]After a series of exchanges, Shuvalov and Derby had agreed the draft protocol on 29 March and the Russians accepted that it would be 'null & void' if 'peace & disarmament did not follow'. *DD*, 29 March 1877, p. 386.

this is really what it all comes to – and to anyone who has followed the course which has recently been taken by the Pall Mall there can be no doubt as to its' [*sic*] meaning. We have discussed all these questions so often & so unreservedly that I do not hesitate to write this, and to say how anxious I feel as to the future of the Gov^t. — The extraordinary address which Disraeli made us on the disturbers of the unanimity of our Cabinet and which was obviously directed against Salisbury & myself, the things which I know to have been said out of the Cabinet on the same theme – Derby's intemperate conduct even in the ordinary relations of daily life[216] – and now this new method of advertising our differences in the newspapers – all this seems to me to be full of danger & if it were to be carried much further w^d. threaten our existence.

I do not know that there is any thing to be done. I sincerely deplore it all – I am not responsible for its' [*sic*] present or its' [*sic*] future effects – but I feel it wrong to with-hold from you both as an old friend & as the leader of the party in the House of Commons my own great anxiety as to the course along which we are now drifting.

It is not creditable to us personally and it may lead us as a Gov^t. into very great difficulties & mistakes.

411

Montagu Corry to Disraeli, Dep. Hughenden 69/1, fos 86–89
15 April 1877
St James' Club, Piccadilly

I have just had some conversation with Comte Schouvaloff, of which I make a note.

He considers that no possible 'moyen' remains, and that the declaration of war between Russia & Turkey within a few days is inevitable. [. . .]

Our further efforts, he thinks, should, now, be directed towards making the war 'une courte affaire'.

---

[216]This is one of the very few references before late 1877 to anything unusual about Derby's private life, and its meaning is unclear. It seems to proceed from Carnarvon's pique. His feelings were reciprocated by Derby, who noted of Carnarvon that 'in his personal relations he is vain, touchy, and egotistical: defects which were always visible in his character, and which power and responsibility have brought into prominence'. *DD*, 17 January 1878, p. 485.

He proposes, so soon as war is declared, to go to St Petersburg, and hopes to return charged with a proposition which England will not only accept, but endeavour to forward.

He begs that, meanwhile, nothing shall be done by England likely to disturb the friendly understanding between herself and Russia.

He hopes to be able to fix, with the agreement of the two countries a limit – say north of the Balkan [*sic*] – beyond which the victorious Russian army shall not advance.

He proposes that, so soon as that limit is reached, peace shall be concluded, on these bases:– that Bulgaria shall become an autonomous province, – a dependency of, and paying tribute to, the Porte. — That Serbia shall remain as she is. — That Bosnia [. . .] shall be ceded to Austria, together with a 'petit bout'[217] of Herzegovina. — That there shall be a rectification of the frontier of Herzegovina. — That Russia shall again have restored to her the triangle at the mouth of the Danube, which she had to give up in 1856. [. . .]

[. . .] I observed that the Germans in 1870, were forced as it were to march on to Paris, and that the logical and natural 'but'[218] of Russia must be the capital city of Turkey, – to my mind.

He replied 'no', – but gave no reasons for his assertion: – adding that England would be foolish to endeavour to protect Constantinople, – first, because she had no sufficient army to defend it, and, secondly, because all her object would be attained by holding the Dardanelles. But, he added, I might rest assured that Russia had no designs on Constantinople; and that, even should his proposition come to nothing, the Sultan should be left there, with an ample zone of territory, round Constantinople, to preserve his dignity.

I asked what would happen if Austria were to occupy Servia as well as Bosnia? That, he answered, he knew would not be permitted by Germany.

I then asked what achievements he proposed for the army in the Caucasus? He replied, that Russia would, there, look for an increase of territory: but, really, he knew nothing about those parts! True, he had been told by Count Münster that there was a port in the Black Sea, called 'Batoum', which ought to belong to Russia: – but, really, he knew nothing about it! [. . .][219] But it really did not matter to England what occurred in those unknown regions!

I answered that it seemed to me that the interests of this country might be almost more touched by what took place in eastern, than in western, Turkey.

[217] 'little piece'.
[218] 'aim'.
[219] Shuvalov's French exclamations are then recounted.

He shrugged his shoulders, and remarked what dreadful things these complications were! And so we parted!

412

Northcote to Disraeli, Dep. Hughenden 107/1, fos 69–70
21 April 1877
Downing Street

I fear that I may not have made my views clear at the Cabinet, and therefore venture to trouble you with a line to state them.[220]

1. I think that we cannot combine a policy of avowed neutrality with any such step as the occupation of Gallipoli. Yet at the opening of the war we shall be obliged to profess neutrality; and if we wait to occupy Gallipoli till the war has taken such a turn as to prove to all the world, or at all events to all England, that English interests render such a step really necessary, we may run the risk of waiting till it is too late.

2. That there is much danger in our taking a separate line of our own, which may either encourage other powers to join in a scramble, of which they will say we are setting the example, or may lead them to combine with Russia in bringing about a settlement exclusive of ourselves, in which our especial interests in Asia will be very cavalierly treated.

3. That the best chance of at once securing fair play for ourselves, and of bringing pressure to bear upon Russia to make her localise the war lies in concerted action between ourselves and other powers, – some if not all; and that we ought to make an attempt in that direction.

If the other powers could represent to Russia that she must not cross the Balkans, nor extend her territory either in Europe or Asia without their consent, we should have a standing ground from which to act if she showed signs of transgressing these limits; and we should probably keep her within them.

---

[220]The Cabinet had met to consider what to do if war broke out in the east. Disraeli 'pressed strongly for action', which Derby was sure entailed a British 'occupation of the Dardanelles'. There was pressure from the Queen to act. According to Derby, Manners wanted to defend Constantinople, while Cairns thought that action would have to be taken, and Salisbury and Carnarvon opposed helping Turkey. Derby, supported by Hardy, thought that any British occupation of Turkish territory was dangerous, and proposed consultation with the other powers. No decision was taken. *DD*, 21 April 1877, pp. 391–392.

I feel very anxious that we should not drift on in this matter without a policy, and that we should not commit England to any course which she is not strong enough to preserve to the end.[221]

I will only add that I feel how important it is that we should be united — But we shall run great risk of disunion if we do not take full counsel together before anything is done or decided on which commits us to a line of policy which cannot be changed without discredit.

[PS] I also strongly urge the consideration whether we ought not to be prepared to take bodily possession of the Suez Canal in order to keep it open. This I suppose we might do without any breach of neutrality.

413

Derby to Count Shuvalov, Confidential Print, FO 881/3171
6 May 1877

[. . .] Her Majesty's Government do not propose again to enter on the question of the justice or necessity of the present war;[222] they have already expressed their views with regard to it, and further discussion would be unavailing. They have accepted the obligation which a state of war imposed upon them, and have lost no time in issuing a Proclamation of Neutrality. They, from the first, warned the Porte that it must not look to them for assistance, and they are determined to carry impartially into effect the policy thus announced, so long as Turkish interests alone are involved.

At the same time they think it right that there should be no misunderstanding as to their position and intentions. Should the war now in progress unfortunately spread, interests may be imperilled which they are equally bound and determined to defend, and it is

---

[221] In his draft of the same date, IP, BL Add. MS 50018, fo. 22, Northcote had been blunter:

[. . .] There are two or three postulates which I should begin by laying down.

1.   We ought not to allow the matter simply to drift. We ought to have a policy.
2.   We ought not to commit England to a course which she cannot pursue to its end.
3.   We ought not to jeopardise greater interests which we might protect for the sake of making a demonstration in support of lesser interests which we probably shall after all not be able to protect. [. . .]

[222] Russia declared war on Turkey on 24 April 1877.

desirable that they should make it clear [. . .] what the most prominent of those interests are.

Foremost among them is the necessity of keeping open, uninjured and uninterrupted, the communication between Europe and the East by the Suez Canal. An attempt to blockade or otherwise to interfere with the Canal or its approaches would be regarded by them as a menace to India, and as a grave injury to the commerce of the world. On both these grounds any such step [. . .] would be inconsistent with the maintenance by them of an attitude of passive neutrality.

The mercantile and financial interests of European nations are also so largely involved in Egypt that an attack on that country, or its occupation, even temporary [. . .] could scarcely be regarded with unconcern by the neutral Powers, certainly not by England.

The vast importance of Constantinople, whether in a military, a political, or a commercial point of view, is too well understood to require explanation. It is, therefore, scarcely necessary to point out that Her Majesty's Government are not prepared to witness with indifference the passing into other hands than those of its present possessors, of a capital holding so peculiar and commanding a position.

The existing arrangements made under European sanction which regulate the navigation of the Bosphorus and Dardanelles appear to them wise and salutary, and there would be, in their judgement, serious objections to their alteration in any material particular. [. . .][223]

414

Disraeli to Derby, DP 920 DER (15) 16/2/3
9 May 1877
2 Whitehall Gardens

[. . .] There is great anxiety about Austria in certain quarters, & I have been asked, whe[the]ʳ you have had an overture made to you from that quarter on wh: some of our friends rely as a solution of difficulties — [. . .]

---

[223]The contents of this letter were agreed in Cabinet on 2 May.

415

Derby to Disraeli, Dep. Hughenden 112/3, fo. 159
[?9] May [1877][224]
Foreign Office

I will call tomorrow early – on my way to the office. Enclosed is a minute of conversation with Beust. He has told me nothing!

416

Derby to Northcote, IP, BL Add. MS 50022, fo. 140
16 May 1877
Foreign Office

We only differ (if we differ) as to wording.[225] You cannot speak of unconditional & absolute neutrality when you are saying that under certain conditions you will have to make war. The two statements are mutually contradictory. But – as you well know – I agree entirely with you & Cross as to the line to be taken & the language to be held.

417

Derby to Northcote, IP, BL Add. MS 50022, fos 142–143
19 May 1877
Fairhill, Tonbridge

Lyons is perfectly safe, & you can tell him anything. He may, as you say, do something through the Austrian ambassador at Paris: but I doubt the Austrians being able or willing to move. They will say, and probably with truth, that they do not think Constantinople threatened: that they have assurances to that effect: & so forth.

What I expect Russia to stipulate for, if an early peace should be made is

(1) Batoum – & a slice of territory inland; how much we cannot even conjecture.
(2) Freedom of the Dardanelles.

---

[224]Derby himself wrote 'May 11 (?)', but his diary records, first, a meeting with Beust on 9 May ('I made a note of what he said for the cabinet'), and then, on 10 May, a meeting with Disraeli. Beust discussed Austria's response to Russian advances, but 'was vague, & he declared that he had no instructions'. *DD*, p. 399.
[225]There had been much discussion in Cabinet that day as to Britain's response to the war and communicating with Austria as to a possible joint position. See, e.g., *DD*, p. 401.

(3) Bulgaria autonomic and tributary.
(4) Part of the Turkish fleet by way of compensation.

But it is impossible to judge with any certainty what the demands will be. The Turks seem full of fight, and may give more trouble than we expect.

You will find the French too busy with their own affairs to care about those of their neighbours. Never did man so wantonly create a difficulty for himself as MacMahon. He is stupid, & honest; and it is the nature of such men in high authority to fall into the hands of others who are neither stupid nor honest.

418

Derby to Disraeli, Dep. Hughenden 113/1, fos 131–132
20 May 1877
Fairhill, Tunbridge

[. . .] Between ourselves, I expect nothing from the Austrian move.[226] Austria has interests involved, but they are not ours. In some respects they are opposite to ours. Austria cares very much for what is done on the Danube, & nothing at all for what is done in Asia. She will therefore press the Russians to go on in Asia, and only make a demonstration in Europe: which is not what we wish.

Constantinople is equally important to both countries, but I have never thought, & do not think, either that Constantinople is really threatened, or that Austrian statesmen will suppose it to be so.

419

Disraeli to Derby, DP 920 DER (15) 16/2/3[227]
22 May 1877
Hughenden

I think affairs look very bad for us, & that some other body will yet fall before the Ottoman Empire tumbles.[228] [. . .] The tactics of the Opposition are clear: they were laid down by Harcourt[229] in the

---

[226] A Cabinet of 16 May 1877 had agreed to ask Vienna what joint steps Austria might take with Britain to prevent a Russian occupation of Constantinople. See above, **416**.
[227] Reproduced in M&B, VI, p. 140.
[228] '(i.e. the cabinet)', *DD*, 23 May 1877, p. 402.
[229] Sir William Harcourt (1827–1904), Liberal MP and one of the leaders of the party in the Commons during Gladstone's 'retirement' of the later 1870s.

debate — He distinctly laid the ground for an appeal to the people against the Ministry, whose want of foresight & courage will have compelled us to acquiesce either in a ruinous war, or a humiliating peace. Having successfully acted on a nervous & divided Cabinet, & prevented anything being done, they will now turn round & say 'This is the way you protect British interests!' They will probably turn us out in this Parliament, or they will force us to a dissolution under the influence of a disastrous defeat abroad.[230]

When do you expect the answer from Austria? I never thought anything w^d. come of it, but there is a strong party in the Cabinet wh: does, and w^d. agree to nothing till it was tried. I think you ought to press, & press hard for a reply. Every moment is now golden. Austria never acts, only writes despatches. [. . .]

A government can only die once: it is better to die with glory, than vanish in an ignominious end. The country w^d. still rally round British interests: in three months time, Brit[ish]: interests will be in the mud.

I have written this with difficulty, for my hand has relapsed.

420

Carnarvon to Salisbury, SP, fos 304–305[231]
23 May 1877
Melbury, Dorchester

Montgelas* is here and I have had a good deal of conversation with him as to the last note to Beust proposing cooperation to Austria for the defence of Constantinople. The clear understanding of the Cabinet was, as I apprehended it, that Derby s[houl]^d in conversation supplement his note by intimating our readiness to undertake for Austria the transport of her troops to Gallipoli or Constantinople and even further to indicate our readiness to give what Disraeli called a buono-mano.[232]

Derby however seems to have remained absolutely silent and to have said nothing on either of these points. His conversation was confined apparently to the merest generalities of cooperation in it's [sic] vaguest sense – and thus the offer, wanting in all

---

[230] On 14 May, Gladstone had moved a resolution criticizing the Government; it was defeated by 354 to 223 votes.
[231] Two brief sentences from this letter are reproduced in Cecil, II, p. 141.
[232] An Italian term for a gratuity in addition to the regular price.

'practical point' as Montgelas termed it, will probably fail of real acceptance.

It is really despairing: for it shows that whatever may be the decision in the Cabinet it is always liable to be upset afterwards. As to the 'buono-mano', I never thought much of this: I do not believe in subsidies or like them: but the transport was essential – and anyhow it was an understanding.

Pray let me know what you think.[233]

421

Cairns to Disraeli, Dep. Hughenden 91/3, fos 138–139
24 May 1877
Lindisfarne, Bournemouth

[...] I agree with every word you say of our position. I feel it to be deeply critical. We have defined British interests, & said we would protect them: & we are not taking any <u>real</u> step for their protection. It is quite apparent that Russia is trying to bridge over the few weeks which will make her safe against any action of our's [*sic*]. She will then be, potentially, mistress of Constant[inopl]ᶜ., & will arrange the passage of the Straits as she & Germany please, & will snap her fingers at us. Then the opposition will turn on us, – & our own friends will join them – & no mercy will be shewn, or allowance made, on the score of the difficulties in our way in the House of Commons. They will say you had a majority of 130, & might have done whatever was necessary.

It would, in my opinion, be infinitely better for the Cabinet to determine on a strong & (as I think) a wise step; the occupation of Gall[ipol]ⁱ.; & if we are thwarted in taking the step, to lay down the emblems of a power which we are not allowed to use. Were it not that I detest the appearance of a selfish disloyalty to the colleagues of my whole public life, this is the course which, as an individual, I shᵈ. be disposed to pursue.

What is to be done? Should there be a Cabinet, & a fresh, & perhaps final, review of the situation? Every day is of importance. [...]

---

[233]Salisbury replied on 27 May. See below, **425**.

422

Derby to Disraeli, Dep. Hughenden 113/1, fo. 133
24 May 1877
Knowsley

I am very sorry for your renewed attack of the enemy[234] – knowing
from home recollections what an infliction it is – and not less so that
you take a desponding view of the situation. You have been so often
right when others were wrong that I hardly like to express dissent: but
I am quite sure that in the middle class at least the feeling is so strong
against a war that you would lose more support by asking money for
an expedition than you could gain by the seizure of an important
military position. [. . .]

423

Disraeli to Derby, DP 920 DER (15) 16/2/3[235]
25 May 1877
Hughenden

The same messenger, who brings me your letter, brings me a box
from the L[or]^d Chan[cello]^r.[236] It is a very distressing one, as he does
not see affairs in the light you do [. . .][237]

I must say that all this expresses very much my own views, & indeed
I often ask myself, if you had resolved to do nothing, why not have
accepted Bismarck[']s offer?

Nothing can justify isolation on the part of England but a
determination to act.

The L[or]^d. Chancellor wants the Cabinet to be called together
& to review the situation again, preliminarily to a final decision. I
suppose it will break up. [. . .]

[234] Gout. The fourteenth Earl of Derby had suffered from the complaint for decades.
[235] Reproduced in M&B, VI, p. 141.
[236] Cairns.
[237] Disraeli quoted large section of Cairns's letter of 24 May, reproduced above,
421.

424

Derby to Disraeli, Dep. Hughenden 113/1, fo. 125[238]
[?26 May 1877][239]
Foreign Office

I will do as you like, but I do not see what there is to discuss in the present state of affairs. And I doubt as to the wisdom of 'talking over' things when no action is possible. Men only work each other up into a state of agitation, and are then ready to rush into anything rash to relieve it.[240]

Why does not Cairns tell us the points which he wants considered?[241]

425

Salisbury to Carnarvon, Carnarvon Papers, BL Add. MS 60759, fos 38–39
27 May 1877
Hatfield

It is, as you say, quite despairing. It seems to me we must give up all hope of any positive action on the foreign policy[.] We may prevent evil: but we can do no more. The result will be an emasculate, purposeless vacillation, which will be very discreditable: but perhaps it is what suits the nation best.[242]

I shall be in town before the end of the week & hope to see you before you go north. Balmoral is becoming a serious nuisance.

---

[238]Reproduced in M&B, VI, pp. 141–142.

[239]The archivist's note on this letters suggests '?17 May 1877', but it is not clear why. It seems clear that, as Buckle suggested (M&B, VI, p. 141), it was a reply to Disraeli's letter of 25 May, of which Derby noted receipt on 26 May (*DD*, p. 403).

[240]In other words, presumably, to send a British expedition to the Dardanelles, as Disraeli wanted.

[241]Derby was under no illusions about who really wanted to have matters 'considered', noting on 26 May that the letter from which Disraeli quoted 'in effect repeats and reflects his own ideas'. *DD*, p. 403.

[242]Despite these comments, Salisbury and Carnarvon were by now increasingly acting with Derby against Disraeli. The Foreign Secretary first noted in his diary on 21 April that it would 'be singular if the course of events puts me on the side of Salisbury & Co. against Disraeli. Hitherto I have always tried to keep the balance.' *DD*, p. 392.

426

Disraeli to Derby, DP 920 DER (15) 16/2/3
29 May 1877
Hughenden

[. . .] I return Odo[243] & Loftus' letters. That of the latter would justify
the immediate assembling of the Cabinet.

427

Derby to Disraeli, Dep. Hughenden 113/1, fo. 139
30 May 1877
Fairhill, Tunbridge

I don't think much of Don Pomposo's[244] alarm: if he had had a
grain of sense he would have seen long ago what the Russians were
after, instead of telling us that they thought of nothing except peace &
philanthropy. Now he has been taken by surprise, he has gone sharp
round, and exaggerates his new opinions as all converts do. Still –
what he says may have force, though he says it. [. . .]

428

Disraeli to Layard, LP, BL Add. MS 39136, fos 31–36[245]
6 June 1877
2 Whitehall Gardens

I find, at the last moment & on a busy day, I have the opportunity of
communicating with you by a trusty hand — Understand, this is not
an official communication, but one strictly personal, & of the utmost
confidence.

The campaign has hitherto realised my anticipations= disastrous in
Asia, on the Danube, doubtful, but big with menacing consequences.

Are there no means, notwithstanding the paralysing neutrality in
vogue, which might lend, if effected, to maintain generally the status
quo, &, at the same time, place England in a commanding position
when the conditions of peace are discussed?

Is it impossible for the Porte to invite the presence of our fleet at
Constantinople, & for us to accede to the invitation, still asserting our

---

[243] Odo Russell.
[244] Loftus.
[245] Marked 'secret'. Reproduced in M&B, VI, pp. 142–143.

neutrality, on the ground, that we are taking a material guarantee for the observance of existing treaties?

A maritime movement of that kind could not be hazarded without securing our communications; otherwise, the Russians might be at the Dardanelles before they occupy Constantinople, & our fleet might be caught in a trap.

The material guarantee, therefore, should also consist of a military occupation of the Peninsula of Gallipoli by England. Twenty thousand men would secure this. We sho[ul]^d engage to evacuate this position on the termination of the war.

If such a proposal came from the Porte, I would recommend its adoption by the Cabinet, but the proposal must come from Constantinople.

I wish you would consider these matters, & communicate with me in entire confidence. Time is of inestimable value, as I sh[oul]^d think the preparation & despatch of the military portion of the expedition might require ten weeks. It could hardly be delayed later than the passage of the Danube by the Russians, & it would be most appropriate, if that event were the occasion of the appeal to us of the Porte.

[P.S] I cannot refrain from mentioning my sense of the skill & energy with which Yr Excellency is conducting the Queen's business at your Court.[246]

429

Disraeli to Derby, DP 920 DER (15) 16/2/3
11 June 1877
2 Whitehall Gardens

I return you Layard's letter[247] — He certainly ought to be encouraged in his efforts to prepare the Sultan to treat for peace, but the Russians are intent on not making peace until they are at Constantinople, & all Schouvaloff[']s intrigues and secret memoranda are to that end.

They cannot reach Constantinople if England takes an efficient step – & that they know. They will promise anything now, so as they can secure our 'neutrality', & no English expedition to the Dardanelles.

If we were to consent to their proposals, they w^d. offer, in due time, not to cross the Balkan [*sic*] according to their engagement, but they

---

[246] A contrast with his earlier judgement: 'Tho' of unquestionable talents, he is prejudiced & passionate, and always [. . .] misinforms us' (to Derby, 12 January 1875; see above, **287**).
[247] It is unclear precisely which letter.

will take steps to ensure the refusal of their terms by the Turks, & then the crossing will be a 'necessity'[.]

P.S. [...] The 'Times' is now a Russian journal, & Delane[248] calls daily for his instructions[249] — [...]

I saw Odo yesterday – not satisfactory. He is not English eno' for our ambassador. His mind & culture are entirely continental.

430

Manners to Disraeli, Dep. Hughenden 106/3, fos 154–155
12 June 1877

The Queen sent for me this afternoon, and told me to read the enclosed 'distressing' letter from Derby.[250]

I have never seen her more moved.

She reads it as contradicting the views of herself and her government, and as accepting whatever terms Russia chooses to ask for. 'They must get another sovereign than me to agree to them'!

She wishes you to return Derby's letter when you have read it.

At her request I place it in a sealed envelope. [...]

I cannot understand that blind belief in Turkey's warlike incapacity – nor the complacency with which Derby appears to view the Russian occupation of Constantinople, and acquisition of Batoum and territory.

What has happened between the last Cabinet & yesterday?

431

Disraeli to Salisbury, SP, fos 246–247[251]
14 June 1877
2 Whitehall Gardens

Derby saw Beust yesterday; the conference was long, &, so far as I can understand, D. faithfully made the proposition, as to active alliance, wh: the Cabinet sanctioned. D. pressed for a reply with[ou]ᵗ.

---

[248]John Thadeus Delane (1817–1879), editor of *The Times*, whose physical deterioration meant that control over his newspaper was by that stage largely nominal; he retired in 1877.
[249]From Shuvalov.
[250]The letter in question, of 11 June, is reproduced in *LQV*, series two, II, pp. 541–542. In it, Derby stressed the desirability of Britain remaining out of the war, that public opinion was against British involvement, and that 'even unsatisfactory conditions of peace will be better for Turkey than none'.
[251]Reproduced in M&B, VI, pp. 144–145.

delay, & said it was, if possible, most desirable it sh^d. be laid before Cab[inet]: on Saturday next[.] I think it best, therefore, to have no Cab[inet]. till that time, & I will fix it at three o'[clo]ck, so that we may have the morning for the chance of the arrival of the Austrian answer.

Beust promised to telegraph instantly.

It is but ingenuous to tell you, that the Queen is 'greatly distressed' about the very wavering language of L^d. Salisbury, wh: will encourage Russia & the Russian party. This with a reply from Ld Derby, which 'fills her with despair,' 'greatly moves' her. 'Another Sov[ereig]^n. must be got to carry out Ld Derby's policy.'

432

Derby to Disraeli, Dep. Hughenden 113/1, fo. 145
14 June 1877
Foreign Office

Nothing in the nature of sanction or approval has been given by us to the Russian proposition. — Absolutely nothing. — We merely communicated the fact of its having been made – and asked what was thought about it at Vienna. Nor should we have done this but for Schou.'s assurance that it had been sent confidentially to Andrassy. [. . .]²⁵²

433

Disraeli to Derby, DP 920 DER (15) 16/2/3
14 June 1877
2 Whitehall Gardens

It is my conviction, that nothing of their plans, as to peace, had been communicated by Russia to Andrassy.

You must not believe a word that Schou: says on this subject – It is all part of a system of ceaseless mendacity, to convince us, that Austria is bound hand & foot to them.

---

[252] Shuvalov first told Derby of Russia's bases for peace on 8 June. They were amended on 14 June to include the demand that the whole of Bulgaria become a vassal state. Shuvalov insisted to Derby that not only was Andrássy aware of the peace terms, but that Russia and Austria had a 'complete understanding on all points: which is absolutely incompatible with the language held by Andrássy. One of the two is lying: possibly both.' *DD*, 11 June 1877, p. 408.

The mischief is, that Andrassy, apparently approving of the terms, & under the impression that they are favored [*sic*] by us, will speak in that spirit to the Emperor, &, so, will be disinclined to break to his master the English proposals to Austria.

434

Disraeli to Derby, DP 920 DER (15) 16/2/3[253]
17 June 1877
2 Whitehall Gardens

I hope you will support me at this juncture. It is necessary, that I sh^d. take this issue to decide the existence of the present Cabinet. It is quite evident to me, that L^d. Salisbury wishes the Russians to enter, & indefinitely occupy, Constantinople, acting, as he has done throughout, under the influence & counsel of Lyddon —[254]

It is the conference over again, in wh: unquestionably, he much compromised us, tho' both you, & myself, then, treated him with generous magnanimity; wh: however was thrown away on his sacerdotal convictions.

The ministry will not be weakened by his secession, &, I think, I can supply his place, & if necessary, that of others, in a manner wh: w^d. commend itself to the country at this exigency.

But your course, on this occasion, is not that of an ordinary colleague — My heart is as much concerned in it as my intelligence, & I wish not to conceal, how grievous would be to me the blow, that severed our long connection & faithful friendship.

My colleagues are bound to no particular course by the vote I am suggesting. I sh^d. be sorry to take any future step, wh:, after mature reflection, did not meet with your particular sanction, & their general approval — All I want now is, to reassure the country, that is alarmed & perplexed; to show, that we are in a state not of puzzled inertness, but of preparedness for action; – so to assist negotiations, wh: will be constantly cropping up & place ourselves in a position, if there be eventually a crash, to assume a tone, wh: will be respected. [. . .]

---

[253] Reproduced in M&B, VI, pp. 145–146.
[254] According to Derby, Salisbury had declared in Cabinet on 16 June that 'Russia at Constantinople would do us no harm'. *DD*, p. 410.

435

Derby to Disraeli, Dep. Hughenden 113/1, fo. 149
17 June 1877
Foreign Office

I will write, or, (better,) speak to you tomorrow on the whole question. Enough for the present to say that as far as you and I are concerned, I do not think we shall have any difficulty in agreeing, at least in the present stage of the affair. It seems to me that the vital question is not yet raised: and I hardly anticipate a disruption until it is raised. No doubt Salisbury's language was anxious, but he did not absolutely declare himself against preparation.[255] I need not add that a political separation between us two would be as painful to me as it could possibly be to you.

436

Layard to Disraeli, Dep. Hughenden 70/2, fos 116–117[256]
18 June 1877

[...] We are now informed by Russia of the terms she is willing to accept before reaching the Balkans. It cannot be disguised that they amount to the dismemberment of Turkey in Europe with all its consequences to England & to the balance of power. [...] Should Russia cross the Balkans she may & probably will demand the greater part of Armenia and the freedom of the Straits, thus virtually commanding our alternative routes to India. The gravity of the situation cannot be exaggerated. The news from Asia looks a little more favourable, & the Russians still hesitate to attempt to cross the Danube, but if we are to rely upon our military authorities the Turks must yield in the end. [...] It appears to me of the utmost urgence [*sic*] and importance that something should be done without loss of time to form proper defences on Gallipoli peninsula, and we ought to occupy it as a material guarantee as soon as the Russians cross the Danube. I think that I could get the Sultan to ask me to do so, but until I know that H.M.G. have determined upon the occupation it would not be safe to hint at the subject. The result of such occupation as regards Germany, Austria and Italy and perhaps France must not be lost sight of. In my judgement the occupation of Gallipoli is of far more importance at present than bringing the fleet up to Constantinople. The latter

---

[255] Of a military expedition.
[256] Copy of deciphered telegram.

could be done at any moment, and if we determined upon occupying Gallipoli the fleet should be stationed at Besika Bay. Gallipoli can be taken by a dash, Constantinople could not. If you will instruct me to get the Sultan to appeal to us to occupy Gallipoli as soon as the Russians cross the Danube I will ascertain what can be done. But you must remember that my position here is a most difficult one, with much to ask and nothing to give, & what has passed has given the Porte great suspicion and distrust of us. There are no doubt means at our disposal if we chose to resort to them of checking Russia, of maintaining the status quo, & of placing England in a commanding position, but to avail ourselves of them we must abandon our position of unconditional neutrality.

437

Layard to Disraeli, Dep. Hughenden 70/2, fos 126–127[257]
10 July 1877

If anything is to be done to save the Turkish Empire, and our own interests in Europe and the East, no time should be lost. [. . .] It appears to me that the time is come for Her Majesty's Government to decide upon the course to be taken, and that I should receive definite instructions upon the subject. [. . .]

Admiral Hornby*, who is here, informs me that the fleet could do something for the defence of the Gallipoli lines, if the matter were very urgent. [. . .]

438

Layard to Disraeli, Dep. Hughenden 70/2, fo. 128[258]
10 July 1877

The Russians may soon cross the Balkans and advance upon Adrianople. If Her Majesty's Government have decided upon occupying the Gallipoli Peninsula, not a moment should be lost in getting the Sultan to consent to our doing so. The very fact of our being there, even if marines and sailors were to be landed, provisionally, from the fleet, would raise the Turks from their present state of depression, and encourage them to resist in Bulgaria, and, at the same time, perhaps, make it more easy to obtain for them moderate

---

[257] Deciphered telegram in Corry's handwriting.
[258] Copy of deciphered telegram, 'read July 11'.

terms of peace, especially now that they have been so successful in Asia. Admiral Hornby agrees entirely with me.

439

Disraeli to Richmond, Goodwood MS 865
12 July 1877
Whitehall Gardens

I wish to know what force we have of the marines in the present Medit[erranean]: squadron, &, also, whether we could re-inforce the existing force thro' the ships about to join Hornby.

440

Manners to Disraeli, Dep. Hughenden 106/3, fos 158–159
12 July 1877

At the Ball last night I had an opportunity of putting some questions to Admiral Commerell.[259] [. . .]

The result is as follows —

In his opinion

The Fleet at Constantinople would be able to render valuable fighting assistance to the defence of the city.

If thought necessary a body of 5000 blue jackets and marines could be sent ashore forming a highly disciplined and most effective force of artillerists who could by themselves maintain a defensive position for a considerable time —

But important as would be the material assistance so rendered by the ships, and by that detached force, he estimates far higher the moral effect which would be produced by the presence of the fleet at Constantinople; and lastly

Although of course he would prefer that the Gallipoli lines should be in our, or in friendly hands, he derided the idea of the fleet being seriously impeded in it's [sic] movements by them even if they were held by the Russians. [. . .]

---

[259] Sir John Edmund Commerell (1829–1901), from 1877, second-in-command of the Mediterranean fleet; a close friend of Admiral Phipps Hornby. See above, **437**.

441

Derby to Disraeli, Dep. Hughenden 113/1, fos 169–170
14 July 1877

In reference to our conversation after the Cabinet, I think it right to say, in writing, so that there may be no mistake about it, that any one proposing to have seen notes of mine, or to have been made acquainted with their contents – such notes referring to current political affairs – is either saying what he must know not to be true, or has been hoaxed by somebody else.

The notes which I generally take at Cabinets have never been seen except by Lady Derby or by my secretary.[260]* They have been kept merely for purposes of convenient reference, those of old date have been from time to time destroyed, and all will be. — I have always understood it to be an unwritten rule of administrative practice, that no permanent record should remain of what passes in Cabinet. But to temporary memoranda kept, while they exist, for personal use, I know of no objection.

442

Disraeli to Salisbury, SP, fos 248–249
18 July 1877
2 Whitehall Gardens

[...] The more I reflect about the Med[iterranean]: garrisons, the more I am convinced, that sending out some troops to Malta is desirable. It w^d. have a great effect on the continent, & like every warlike move of England, lead to peace.[261] [...]

443

Manners to Disraeli, Dep. Hughenden 106/3, fos 162–163
22 July 1877
Hemsted Park, Staplehurst

With a heavy heart, but with no misgiving as to the necessity of the course I am taking I am compelled by the decision at which the

[260]Thomas Henry Sanderson. This defence would, of course, come back to haunt Derby.
[261]This was a questionable assumption, given the way in which tensions had escalated with fleet movements prior to the Crimean War.

Cabinet arrived yesterday[262] to place my resignation in your hands, and to ask you to request Her Majesty to be pleased to accept it at such time and in such manner as shall seem to you least inconvenient to Her service, and least hurtful to the Government.

I need say nothing of the reasons which force me to this step, nor of the pain it occasions me.

You well understand both.

I had confidently hoped to remain by your side, and to render you what little assistance it was in my power to render to the close of your administration; but it was not to be.

444

Disraeli to Derby, DP 920 DER (15) 16/2/3
23 July 1877
2 Whitehall Gardens

[. . .] A defensive treaty with Austria for a term of years, say seven or ten, might yet put all right, & even the emperor might accept it. Austria is terribly afraid of the Italian navy, from which we sh^d. protect her, & she is not a power, like Germany, who would convert her defensive, into an offensive, alliance.

445

Disraeli to Manners[263]
24 July 1877
2 Whitehall Gardens

Your letter is a great blow to me, and most unexpected. I really don't exactly understand what decision of the Cabinet you refer to.[264]

I must beg you, at all events, to keep your resignation secret, until I can communicate it to the Queen personally, as a written announcement would lead to much excitement. Her Majesty, of all my colleagues, most depended on your supporting me, and now, when, for the first time, her Cabinet has unanimously and heartily agreed to declare war against Russia, if she evinces the slightest intention to

---

[262]The Cabinet had not really made a decision, but Manners had been unable to persuade his colleagues that Russia's 'approach' to Constantinople should be a *casus belli*. *DD*, 21 July 1877, pp. 422–423.

[263]Taken from M&B, VI, p. 156. It has not been possible to view the original.

[264]Disraeli's puzzlement was understandable; the Cabinet had not made any clear decision.

fortify, or remain in, Constantinople (if she ever get there), the Queen will be greatly distressed and surprised at your determination.

I most earnestly request, therefore, that all may be suspended until I see Her Majesty, which I will try to effect on Saturday next.

446

Manners to Disraeli, Dep. Hughenden 106/3, fos 164–166
24 July 1877

I have not said a word to anybody on the subject of my communication to you, and will refrain from doing so until I hear from you again.[265]

The decision of the Cabinet which forces me to leave it is that which allows Russia to occupy Constantinople and Gallipoli —

I am not aware of any unanimous decision to go to war with her afterwards, nor do I believe that any such intention, if it exists now, would or could be carried into effect then.

The occupation by Russia of Constantinople and Gallipoli is, in my judgment, the destruction of Turkey, and the establishment of Russian supremacy in the East, and I cannot support a policy which produces such results. [. . .]

I leave it entirely to you to settle the time and mode of making this known to the Queen, and my colleagues, and will attend, or not attend the next Cabinet as you think best.

Nothing can ever alter the feelings I entertain towards you, and I shall slip back into private life with only an encreased [*sic*] admiration of your great qualities and character; but I cannot consent to bear a part in what I believe to be a policy fatal to English interests in the East. [. . .]

447

Disraeli to Layard, LP, BL Add. MS 39136, fo. 66[266]
29 July 1877
Osborne

The telegram sent you yesterday from the Cabinet opens a prospect of recurring to the wise and ancient policy of England. The British fleet in the Turkish waters with the consent of the Sultan may be the first step in the virtual preservation of his Empire. I much depend on your energy and skill in both [of] which I have the utmost confidence.

---

[265] Disraeli managed to persuade him not to resign.
[266] This seems to be the record of a telegram received by Layard.

448

Queen Victoria to Disraeli, Dep. Hughenden 80/3, fo. 18[267]
5 August 1877
Osborne House

I hope you will see Colonel Wellesley* at once and warn him about Lord Derby's views[.] Let me have a notion of what his mission is as soon as possible. Would like to see him before he returns. Merely assurances must not be accepted.[268]

449

Disraeli to Layard, LP, BL Add. MS 39136, fos 72–75[269]
6 August 1877

Many thanks for your letter. I regret the suspicions in the mind of the Sultan as regards our intentions — I admit they are reasonable but they are not true – at least, so far as I am concerned; being resolved to maintain, if possible, 'the integrity & independence' of the Ottoman Empire — The Turks have proved their independence, for without allies they have gallantly, &, I think, successfully, defended their country, & I still hope to see, at the conclusion of the war, the Porte a recognised power, & no despicable one, in Europe.

If there is 'a second campaign', I have the greatest hopes this country will interfere, & pronounce its veto against a war of extermination, & the dark designs of a secret partition, from wh: the spirit of the 19th Century recoils — As we have the command of the sea, why sh[d] not a British corps d'armée (viâ [sic] Batoum) march into Armenia, & even occupy Tiflis?

We might send another to Varna, & act on the Russian flank —

But all this requires time. The Turks gain victories, but don't follow them up. After Plevna, they sh[d] have driven the Russians across the Danube, destroyed the bridge, & taken the Emperor prisoner — Wellesley tells me, that might have been done—

The thing is – to secure another campaign, or rather the necessity for one, for if Russia is told by England, that 'another campaign' will

---

[267]'Decypher [sic] telegram'.
[268]In a scheme which appealed to both the Queen and Disraeli, Wellesley was to be sent on a secret mission to the Tsar. For his instructions, see below, **451**.
[269]Marked 'secret' and, in a significant omission, *not* published in M&B.

be a casus belli, she may be inclined to make what P. Gortchakow calls 'une pavé boiteuse'.[270]

The danger is, if the Russians rally, again successfully advance, & reach Adrianople this autumn.

What then is to be done? With her suspicions of England, Turkey would be ruined — That is why I sh^d like to see our fleet in her immediate waters, & Gallipoli in our possession as a material guarantee, & with her full sanction. We sh^d then be able to save Turkey — [...]

450

Northcote to Corry, Dep. Hughenden 107/1, fos 115–116
15 August 1877
Pynes, Exeter

[...] We are always discussing[271] some 'minor premiss' without being agreed upon the major, and so are continually arriving at absurd conclusions. [...] Each of us, when a particular step is proposed, considers how it will agree with his main view, or how it can be made to do so. The proposal is modified accordingly, and modified so often that at last it suits nobody; and then some unmeaning step is decided on; after which it is taken in a manner which was not exactly what any one expected; and lastly it is explained according to every man's separate theory.

How we have got on so far without getting into a worse scrape is a marvel to me. [...]

451

Wellesley to Corry, Dep. Hughenden 80/3, fo. 57
17 August 1877
London

My dear Monty – please forgive my sending you such a rough copy.

[Enclosed:][272]

The subject of the correspondence and conversations which have passed between the Queen, Lord Beaconsfield and Col. Wellesley to be considered secret and on no account to be mentioned at the Foreign Office.

---

[270]Translating Disraeli's rendering of a second-hand Franco-Russian colloquialism is not straightforward, but presumably a 'misstep' of some kind.
[271]In Cabinet.
[272]Reproduced with minor changes in M&B, VI, pp. 174–175.

Col. Wellesley is the bearer of an answer from Her Majesty's Government which he will communicate officially to the Emperor. Although Col. Wellesley has no orders from Lord Beaconsfield to make any further statement to His Majesty, it is thought advisable in the interests of Russia as well as of England that the Emperor be informed with regard to the future attitude of this country under certain contingencies.

His Lordship has therefore communicated to Col. Wellesley his views and intentions, which coincide entirely with those of the Queen, and which it is left to Col. Wellesley's discretion to make known to the Emperor, should a favorable [sic] opportunity present itself.

The policy of the Government is as follows:

The Queen and H.M. G^t. have a sincere desire to see the speedy re-establishment of peace on terms honorable [sic] to Russia and would be glad to contribute to such a result; should however the war be prolonged and a second campaign undertaken, the neutrality of England could not be maintained and she would take her part as a belligerent.

In bringing the above facts to the knowledge of the Emperor it is most important that Col. Wellesley should disabuse His Majesty's mind of certain misconceptions which could only lead to a false appreciation of the actual state of affairs.

It has been stated that there are dissensions in the Cabinet which would prevent active intervention on the part of England.

This is entirely false. The Cabinet is led by one mind and has the entire support of the Sovereign.

There exists perfect harmony of opinion between the Queen and Lord Beaconsfield respecting the foreign policy of the country. The Government is as strong as ever, and possesses the confidence of the people[,] which is proved by the present tranquil attitude of the public, who are convinced that the interests of England are safe in their hands.

It must not be thought that the policy of Lord Beaconsfield is one of hostility to Russia, and it might fairly be asked who has proved himself the greatest friend to Russia, Prince Bismarck or Lord Beaconsfield, the Chancellor who has done all in his power to urge Russia to undertake this disastrous war, or the Prime Minister who has endeavoured to save her from it?

It is commonly supposed in Russia that the mind of the English public is poisoned against Russia by Lord Beaconsfield and that His Lordship is responsible for the present relations which exist between the two countries[.]

Col. Wellesley is in a position to deny these statements, and to show that on the contrary it is Lord Beaconsfield who has recently discouraged discussions in Parliament with a view to avoiding the possibility of leading Turkey to believe that sooner or later England may be on her side, a belief which would no doubt have been created had the Government been compelled to make a distinct statement with regard to their future policy.

A private letter from Lord Beaconsfield to the Queen[,] which Her Majesty shewed Col. Wellesley[,] proved that Lord Beaconsfield has checked parliamentary discussion as well as anti-Russian public meetings with the object of avoiding all encouragement to Turkey.

However much Lord Beaconsfield may desire peace he is equally determined to uphold the honor [*sic*] and defend the interests of England, and Russia should not indulge in any erroneous impressions as to the weakness or vacillation of the British Gov^t.[,] which, Colonel Wellesley knows, enjoys the support of the Sovereign and the confidence of the nation.

Col. Wellesley should not fail to point out to the Emperor that the influence of the English Gov^t. at Constantinople is not by any means such as His Majesty appears to think, and that as a matter of fact the influence which Mr. Layard can bring to bear on the Porte is far more personal than official.

Col. Wellesley has had the exceptional advantage of two interviews with the Queen as well as frequent conversations with the Prime Minister[,] which has enabled him to obtain the most correct information with regard to the policy of England[,] and he is authorised if necessary to make use of the name of the Queen and that of Lord Beaconsfield in making this confidential communication to the Emperor of Russia.

452

Disraeli to Derby, DP 920 DER (15) 16/2/3
21 August 1877
Hughenden

[. . .] I doubt not the Russians are really in a state approaching to desperation. As for a second campaign, England ought not to permit it.[273] Turkey has shown a vigor [*sic*] & resources, wh: entitle her to rank among the nations, & justify her position of 400 years.

Besides, civilized Europe must shrink from countenancing, even by neutrality, a war of extermination!

---

[273] Although Disraeli was, in fact, encouraging Layard to try and obtain just such a campaign, as his instructions of 6 August had stipulated. See above, **449**.

We must speak very strongly to Servia, & must not acknowledge that a great & multiform power like England cannot strike even an inland mongrel like Servia. [. . .]

In Odo's[274] curious letter there is a remark, wh: shows that the 2 Emperors contemplate, if possible, indirectly assisting Russia, thro' Servia.

This must not be tolerated – & you ought to tell Beust, & Buchanan, that if this sort of thing is encouraged, all our understandings with Austria on all points are tabula rasa.[275] [. . .]

453

Layard to Disraeli, Dep. Hughenden 70/2, fo. 142
29 August 1877
British Embassy, Constantinople

Our influence here is now reestablished beyond what I could possibly have hoped; I must do the best I can to maintain it. The Sultan is convinced that of the European powers, England alone can give him help – if not in money and men, at least in sympathy and moral support – and he looks to us. [. . .] I have made use of this influence that we at present enjoy to get the Porte to take measures to complete the defences of Constantinople and to make various changes in the commanders and positions of the Turkish troops suggested by our military attachés, whose hints have been of very great use to me, and whose advice is now readily, and even eagerly, received by the Turkish War Office and military authorities. [. . .]

454

Disraeli to Derby, DP 920 DER (15) 16/2/3[276]
1 September 1877
Hughenden

I observe you have to go to some meeting in your county. I suppose it will be necessary to say something on public affairs, tho' silence is golden.

Let me impress upon you not to mistake the feeling of this country. It is for peace, but it is, every day, getting more Turkish.

---

[274] Odo Russell.
[275] 'clean slates', presumably to be written anew.
[276] Reproduced in M&B, VI, pp. 177–178.

It is for peace, because it has confidence in our policy: i.e. peace with British interests all safe.

But we know this is a mere delusion; & that, had it not been for our good luck, British interests would not have been safe, the Russians w^d. virtually have been at Constantinople, & H.M.'s Government no where [*sic*].

Opinion is getting more pro-Turkish every day, because the country recognises, that the Turks have the vigor [*sic*] & the resources, & the national spirit, which entitle them to rank, & to remain, among the sovereign powers of the world; & that there is no clear evidence, that a better government than the Ottoman can be established in the regions in question. [. . .]

It is to Russia & to Austria, that we ought to have addressed ourselves, & to have warned those powers, that, if they wish to preserve the neutrality of England, they must be careful in this matter.

The feeling is, that our honor [*sic*] is concerned in the issue, & I cannot say I think the feeling unfounded.

Pardon these rough hints.

455

Disraeli to Richmond, Goodwood MS 865
4 September 1877
Hughenden

[. . .] The Turks go on fighting, & fighting well; yet not quite well eno' to remove all my uneasiness. I am afraid, now & then, of large re-inforcements & the Shipka pass.[277]

I am extremely annoyed to find, that, notwithstanding the positive orders of the Cabinet, renewed to Smith,* the Admiralty has not ordered a single Torpedo boat.

456

Hardy to Cairns, Cairns Papers, PRO 30/51/7, fo. 47
6 September 1877
Balmoral

The Queen notified her wish to me yesterday that I should remain here until Monday next. She will I believe go away on her excursion

---

[277] The Turks, under Osman Pasha, were holding out at Plevna in Bulgaria.

the next day. Cross will probably not be required for about a week. This information will I hope enable you to judge of your own prospects. I told her that you were third on the list. She said she had only asked those who were likely to give her support although Carnarvon was the only one from whom she expected none. After a long interview during w^h. she shewed me Beaconsfield's letter[278] and freely laid open her mind she lent me her reply to him and I may as well give you the effect of it for your guidance. She thinks that for humanity's sake as well as grounds of policy we should do all in our power to prevent a second campaign[,] the first having shewn us that a war of extermination is going on. [She thinks] That the Cabinet should come to a distinct conclusion what it will not allow without intervention and that it should do so at once even if 2 or 3 are opposed or even retire. This would be better than such a disruption at a moment when decision was urgent & necessary. She complains much of Derby's dilatoriness & put a curious question to me whether I thought that in case Lord Lytton's[279] health should fail he would go to India. I answered in the negative & told her how strong Derby was in public opinion especially in the North though perhaps on grounds which w^d not bear examination. She thought that it was justly said that the Gov^t. had done too much or too little but admitted that it was partly her fault as she had pressed constantly that 'something should be done'. I need not go into all she said of Gladstone – Granville &c: Their conduct on the Title[280] rankles and her feeling against them is increased by their Turkish bias. [. . .] I was glad to see that Beaconsfield spoke of his own health as quite re-established by some new system.

457

Northcote to Cross, Cross Papers, BL Add. MS 51265, fo. 134
9 September 1877
Pynes, Exeter

[. . .] I hear that you go to Balmoral next week, and that you will find H.M. much excited about the war news. I hope we shall be calm, for we have a most difficult task before us. I am not sure that the defeat of Russia would not be even more dangerous than her success. If it led

---

[278] Presumably that written by Disraeli on 4 September in which he bemoaned the lack of positive news from Wellesley.

[279] Edward Robert Bulwer Lytton (1831–1891), created Baron Lytton 1873, first Earl Lytton 1880; son of the fourteenth Earl of Derby's Cabinet colleague in 1858, Edward Bulwer Lytton, and nephew of Sir Henry Bulwer; Viceroy of India, 1876–1880.

[280] The Royal Titles Bill, making Victoria Empress of India.

to a break-up of that great Empire it would indeed be a letting out of waters.

It seems to me to be a time at which the neutral nations ought to take free counsel together, and to endeavour to agree on a modus vivendi which they could authoritatively recommend to the belligerents. But I fear there is little chance of our doing anything but 'wait and see'.

458

Disraeli to Derby, DP 920 DER (15) 16/2/3[281]
13 September 1877
Hughenden

I have re-opened y^r box, to [say] that I have received yr letter & entirely approve of yr projected appointments. It will be a great thing to have got rid of Harris[282] & Buchanan – I wish we c^d. get rid of the whole lot. They seem to me to be quite useless. It is difficult to control events, but none of them try to. I think Odo Russell the worst of all.[283] He contents himself with reporting all Bismarck's cynical bravadoes, wh: he evidently listens to in an ecstasy of sycophantic wonder.

Why does not he try to influence Bismarck, as the Prince controls him? Why does not he impress upon Bis., for instance, that if Germany & Austria police Poland, in order that Russia sh^d. add 50,000 men to her legions, England will look upon that as a gross breach of neutrality?

Why does he not confidentially impress upon Bismarck, that Turkey has shown such vigor [sic] & resource that she has established her place among the sovereign powers of Europe, & that if they continue to play their dark game of partition they must come in collision with England, who will not permit the breaking up of the Ottoman Empire.

As for the arrangement, that Russian compensation is to be found in Armenia & so on, an English army, 40,000, men, with the Black Sea & Batoum at our command, c^d. march to Tiflis.

We want no allies. We are not going to fight in Bulgaria. The situation is much the same as when Wellington went to the peninsula, except that a Turk as a soldier is worth 20 Spaniards – What allies had we then?

---

[281] Reproduced in M&B, VI, pp. 178–179.
[282] Sir Edward Harris, Malmesbury's younger brother. See above, **116**. He retired on 19 November 1877.
[283] Derby thought this letter 'a most amusing denunciation of all our diplomatists, especially O. Russell, who just now is his favourite aversion'. *DD*, 14 September 1877, p. 437.

459

Disraeli to Derby, DP 920 DER (15) 16/2/3
16 September 1877
Hughenden

[. . .] If Bismarck does not play fair, we ought to make an example of him. It can be done.

460

Disraeli to Derby, DP 920 DER (15) 16/2/3
17 September 1877
Hughenden

I entirely approve your appointments, & only trust you may soon have the opportunity of making more, as I am quite wearied with the present men, who seem to me to have sunk into being the mere parasites of the courts & ministers with whom they are placed in relation. Our principal ambassadors ought now to be confidentially informing the great powers, that neutrality can only be the occasional policy of England; we have given Russia her fair chance; & she cannot be allowed to enter into a second campaign of a war of extermination, at least on the conditions under wh: she has conducted the present. [. . .]

461

Disraeli to Derby, DP 920 DER (15) 16/2/3[284]
28 September 1877
Hughenden

I have summoned the Cabinet for next Friday.[285]

I wish to place, before it, this proposal[:]

It being of the utmost importance, that there sh^d. not be a second campaign, the only object of wh: w^d. be the seizure of Constantinople, it is proposed, that Her Majesty's ambassadors sh^d. sound the Porte as to the terms of peace it is prepared to offer.

If they include the settlement of Bulgaria on the basis of the Protocol of London & the restoration to Russia of the portion of Bessarabia,

---

[284]Reproduced in M&B, VI, pp. 182–183.
[285]5 October.

forfeited by the Treaty of Paris, it would seem that the honor [sic] of Russia would be sufficiently vindicated.

It is assumed, that the Porte would agree to these, or any other reasonable terms, provided England, if empowered, as mediator, to make them to Russia, & they being rejected by that power, would assure the Porte, that, under such circumstances, we sh^d. depart from our present position of neutrality, & inform Russia, that, if Constantinople be menaced, England would afford material assistance to Turkey to prevent its seizure —

This is a clear and precise policy: it gets us out of all the embarrassing distinctions bet[wee]^n. temporary & permanent occupation, wh: harassed, & nearly humiliated, us last session; &, if rejected by Russia, w^d. put her more in the wrong in the eyes of Europe, while it w^d. place H.M. Government in an honorable [sic], an intelligible, & popular position.

What I sh^d. like most is, that the proposal sh^d. be made by yourself; the natural organ of the government on these high matters, & it will be a source of the highest satisfaction to me, if, on reflection, you will comply with my wishes.[286]

462

Derby to Disraeli, Dep. Hughenden 113/1, fos 205–206[287]
29 September 1877
Knowsley

I am not sorry that you mean to call the Cabinet; both for the sake of the effort out-of-doors, and also because after two months, or nearly that time, it is well to compare notes.

There can be no harm in trying to find out what terms of peace the Turks would accept, when once the campaign of this year is over. I doubt whether they would give any opinion now, as they may still hope for successes that will alter their position[.]

I am not prepared to support the proposal which you suggest, still less to put it forward; but a preliminary discussion will be of use as showing how far, and on what points, there is likely to be agreement among us as to the course which we ought to take.

[286] Derby was unmoved: 'Letter from Ld Beaconsfield [. . .] full of a scheme for intervention which he wants me to propose. It is characteristic of him that he should do this, knowing that the scheme is utterly opposed to my ideas.' DD, 27 September 1877, p. 440.
[287] Reproduced in M&B, VI, p. 183.

463

Disraeli to Richmond, Goodwood MS 865
30 September 1877
Hughenden

[...] A second campaign is greatly to be deprecated, for it wd. not be undertaken by Russia exc[ep]^t. with the determination of seizing Constantinople.

Can the Porte be induced to offer, thro' us, terms to Russia, wh: that power may accept?

I think so. You will have to consider, & decide.

If Russia refuse them, she will put herself more in the wrong in the eyes of Europe, but, at all events, we ought to take up a clear & precise position, & extricate ourselves from all these embarrassments about 'temporary & permanent occupation', wh: hampered us last year, & almost humiliated us. [...]

464

Northcote to Disraeli, Dep. Hughenden 107/1, fos 125–126
1 October 1877
Pynes, Exeter

I am very glad to hear of the proposed Cabinet. It is time that we should consider our position with regard to this war, and the possibility of doing something to put an end to it.[288] Its continuance for another year would, as it seems to me, be not only an outrage on humanity, but might be the cause of serious danger to Europe and to ourselves.

What I am anxious for is, that we should be seen to take a broad view of the questions involved. I do not disguise from myself the desirableness of averting the capture of Constantinople, or the dangers which might be apprehended from its falling, even for a time, into the hands of the Russians. But I think we have other, and larger, interests to look to; and I am anxious that we should not jeopardise them by placing ourselves in a position resembling selfish isolation.

If we are still to limit ourselves to a neutrality, qualified by a regard for the maintenance of our road to India, I don't know that we can do much better than sit still and see the fight out. Russia, if she succeeds in her object, will have exhausted herself so much, and will have such difficult work to do, that it must be many years before she could

---

[288] In Derby's record, at the Cabinet meeting on 5 October, Northcote 'gave a hesitating opinion, neither for nor against'. *DD*, p. 442.

turn even the permanent possession of Constantinople to any such account as to threaten our communications. And on the other hand, assuming that the other Powers do not wish to see her mistress of the Black Sea, she will be in no condition to disregard their notice to quit. The danger, therefore, of her permanently taking possession is much less than it was; and, if we did not think it right to enter into the field before, it is questionable whether (on this ground) we ought to enter it now. You must also consider the danger of our taking up an attitude which might bring Germany into the business in opposition to us. Germany may say, we don't desire to see Russia in possession of Constantinople; if she attempts to take it for her own, we will, in concert with Austria, interfere to prevent her; but we wish to see her vindicate her superiority over Turkey, and we think she ought to be allowed to march to the capital if she can, and to dictate a peace as we did at Paris. Suppose England to step in and to say, we cannot consent to this, may we not give Germany a plausible ground for declaring that we are selfishly impeding the settlement of a great question of general interest, and for encouraging Russia to disregard our opposition? We might in that case find ourselves awkwardly situated.

But I think we should have a really good line open to us if we could induce the Porte to make some such proposals as you indicate; and could then come forward to support them in the face of Europe, as affording the best and perhaps the only means of stopping a war which must entail such ruin and misery on all, and bring so little good to anybody; and I think we might go the length of offering not only our moral support, but of intimating that, in the event of Russia's refusing to desist from her aggression after fair terms had been offered, we would give Turkey our material support likewise. Everything will depend upon how this is done. If we do not carry public opinion with us, we shall make matters much worse. [. . .]

465

Carnarvon to Salisbury, SP, fos 314–315[289]
8 October 1877
Highclere

I conclude that we shall have before very long another – and an important – Cabinet.

---

[289]The last paragraph of this letter is reproduced in Cecil, II, p. 161, without its last sentence.

From my point of view the question of terms is a specious absurdity: but I suppose that some scheme will be put forward. As yet none has been suggested. Disraeli seemed studiously to avoid any statement on the subject: & though Cairns had intimated that there were possible terms none have been brought forward. Have you any idea what he is likely to propose? & have you any notion of any active course in the way of counter proposal that could be with advantage taken? I see none —

I conclude that the interval between our last & our next Cabinet will be employed in an attempt to win over the hesitating element amongst them= and to secure a distinct and overwhelming majority. When that is accomplished, I shall not be surprised if extreme pressure is applied. The influence from Balmoral was curiously manifested on Friday: but you will see that I was not wrong in the summer when I told you that Richmond was morally what he is intellectually. [...]

466

Cairns to Disraeli, Dep. Hughenden, fos 152–153
10 October 1877
Pitlochry

[...] I am very glad we are to meet to consider our position with reference to a second campaign. I am convinced that a policy of inactivity will be fatal to our own interests & to the peace of Europe, & I trust we shall never again be driven, as we were last summer, to deliberate on what our interests required to be done at Constantinople & the Dardanelles, with the consciousness that, whatever might be required, it was too late to do it. It will be too miserable if this war is renewed another year, & I am quite for taking some step, such as you suggest, to prevent it. [...]

467

Disraeli to Layard, LP, BL Add. MS 39136, fos 99–106[290]
11 October 1877
Brighton

I received your letter yesterday, & answer your enquiries at once.

The feeling in favor [*sic*] of Turkey has greatly improved in England, & not slightly in Europe. This is to be attributed, 1st, & mainly, to the

---

[290] Marked 'secret'.

gallantry of the Ottomans, & 2^{ndly}, to the relief felt by the diminished prestige of Russia.

I think the appeal, wh: you suggest, by the Sultan, to the parties to the Treaty of Paris, would still more favourably enlist public feeling on his side: but I question, whether it wd. do more. No power is for peace except England.

England cannot offer to mediate, unless solicited by one of the belligerents. I do not think Russia, in her present position, c^{d}. solicit any one, = certainly not us.

If Turkey invited our good offices, we sh^{d}. be indisposed to interfere, unless there was a fair chance of effecting the common object.

Would this be possible? Turkey to sketch the outline of terms, &, if approved of by England as sufficient and satisfactory, then, to ask England to present them to Russia, & to advise their adoption.

If Russia refused, she would put herself much more in the wrong: &, if the terms were publicly acknowledged by England as just & satisfactory, it would be very difficult for us to adhere to our present neutrality. Opinion at home w^{d}. force us to action. [...]

I mark this letter 'secret', for it expresses, & very roughly, only my own views & thoughts. It is not, therefore, the letter of a minister as much as of an individual, who sympathises with your views & entirely approves of yr conduct in these difficult affairs of the East = but if you find the suggestions I have thrown out feasible, I sh^{d}. be prepared to recommend them to the Cabinet. Of course, before that however, they would be made by you, in due course, to the Secretary of State.

468

Derby to Disraeli, Dep. Hughenden 113/1, fos 211–212
12 October 1877
Knowsley

[...] Beust was so anxious to see me that he asked to come down here, though I told him I should be in town next week. I conclude therefore that he or Andrassy, attach [*sic*] more than usual importance to his communication: of which you have the substance in this draft.[291]

You will probably come to the same conclusion that I do: that Andrassy is only playing with us. His reason for not choosing to interfere just now is absurd: and one does not understand how he can suppose that anybody will be taken in by it.

---

[291] Andrassy declined to mediate between Russia and Turkey.

The deception is useless and silly; for if he had simply told the truth – that Austria cannot afford to quarrel with her two big neighbours, everybody would have known what he meant, and few people would have blamed. To make the game of cross-purposes more complicated, Zichy[292] appears to be holding at Constantinople language quite different from that of Andrassy. — I cannot make it out – possibly because the parties concerned don't know their own minds. You have all the information I possess.

469

Salisbury to Carnarvon, Carnarvon Papers, BL Add. MS 60759, fos 40–43
14 October 1877
Hatfield

My letters were not forwarded to me in Yorkshire – so I only got yours of the 14th when I got back.[293]

At present I do not see very serious danger ahead. Offers of mediation – so long as they contain no pledges of assistance, are – at worst – ridiculous. I think we may be sure that Derby will not allow them to contain any such element.

For anything more than this there is at present no pretext. It would be impossible to say that C[onstantino]ple is in danger now. I trust it will continue impossible till the first week in February. By that time many things may have happened: but in any case, the country will have very much changed, if it desires any increase of taxation in order to help the Turk. My impression from what I have seen is that, though the feeling against Russia is strong, it nowhere rises nearly to income-tax point. When Parliament has once met we shall I trust be safer[.] I do not see any opening for a counterproposition on our part.

The terms D. talked of proposing, in a letter he wrote to me before the Cabinet – are the terms contained in the Protocol. As I pointed out to Hardy who spoke from that text, there are no terms in the Protocol. There is only a recital of intentions couched in the vaguest possible language. Russia must be very much beaten indeed before she will accept any such suggestion.

---

[292] Count Ferenc Zichy, Austrian ambassador at Constantinople. According to Layard, he was actively canvassing the idea of Austrian mediation.
[293] The letter 'of the 14th' not found.

470

Disraeli to Derby, DP 920 DER (15) 16/2/3
15 October 1877
10 Downing Street

Your letters arrived so late yesterday, that my messenger, as well as Lord Tenterden, had departed, & I c^d. not reply to you, as I had intended. [...]
Before Tenterden arrived on Saturday, C[oun]^t. Beust made his appearance & stayed an hour, of which 55 minutes were devoted to himself & his affairs. He said to me everything he had said to you at Knowsley, but I don't think anything else= except, when I rather pressed him about mediation, I don't think he was as firm as I had expected.
Andrassy, if one may speak of a man one does not know, seems to me to be both tortuous & careless, & capable of directing Zichy to make a reconnaissance, which Zichy has perhaps magnified into a greater movement. I don't think we ought to show any eagerness in the matter either at London or Constantinople, but it is as well, that Layard sh^d. not throw cold water on the communications, as they may have a really tentative character, tho' not of immediately practical application. [...]

471

Disraeli to Corry, Dep. Hughenden 69/1, fos 16–18
20 October 1877
Brighton

I have broken to the Faery,[294] that it is very doubtful, whether, in my present state, I can manage to lead the House of Lords, & remembering my sufferings last session, it seems to me impossible. [...]
[...] There is no striking news. I fear our friends the Turks have done their best & the Russians have done their worst. [...]
[...] In my own part, I firmly believe Bismarck is contemplating the partition of France, & if Spain, instead of 15 mill[ion] of population, had 30, wh: w^d. be the average according to her territory, so that she c^d. send 500,000 armed men into the field, I believe Germany, Italy & Spain – & perhaps Belgium let in for a slice, – could do it.

[294]The Queen.

I don't think B[ismarck] wishes to destroy our Empire but he wishes to deprive us of all influence. An Empire with[ou]^t. influence wo[ul]^d not be of long duration.

472

Disraeli to Derby, DP 920 DER (15) 16/2/3
27 October 1877
Brighton

I believe that Bismarck's great, general policy is the partition of France, as the possession of Constantinople is that of Russia [. . .][295]

I don't think Bismarck, which some do, wants to destroy the British empire, & probably would have been glad originally to have worked with us, but what he wants is to destroy our influence, & expel us from the political arena, & I fear he may succeed. Empires without influence do not endure.

473

Northcote to Disraeli, Dep. Hughenden 107/1, fos 129–130
3 November 1877

Though I like your suggestion of yesterday better than the one which we had before us last month, and am willing to agree to it if Derby approves, yet I cannot say I am much in love with it.[296]

I therefore wish to ask you to consider one other suggestion, which seems to me worthy of discussion.

Why should we not address a carefully drawn review of the situation, as it appears to us, to the four other neutral Powers, and invite them to join us in making some kind of appeal to the belligerents?[297] [. . .]

---

[295] Much of this letter reprises the points Disraeli had made to Corry on 20 October, about a meditated partition of France by Germany, Spain, and Italy.

[296] That Britain would promise continued neutrality if Russia pledged not to occupy Constantinople. Northcote, like the rest of the Cabinet, was unaware that, through the Wellesley mission, Disraeli had already told the Tsar that Britain would not remain neutral if there were a second campaign.

[297] In his letter to the Queen of the same date, Disraeli described this suggestion as constituting 'the 5th policy' in the Cabinet. He thought Northcote's views 'utterly futile', and, in the assumption that Bismarck would associate himself with such an appeal, 'they approach silliness'. M&B, VI, p. 194.

I cannot help fearing that a private communication, either to Turkey or to Russia, would lead to misunderstandings and complications; while, being secret, it could not be turned to account in the way of explaining our attitude, either to the people of England, or to other countries. [. . .]

Forgive me for adding a 7th. party to the Cabinet[.][298]

474

Disraeli to Derby, DP 920 DER (15) 16/2/3
19 November 1877
10 Downing Street

The Lord Chancellor called on me on Saturday, & he spoke, not only for himself but for some of his colleagues, about the despatch to the Russian government.

I told him, there was a sort of indirect communication, wh: had reached us, from wh: we gathered, that, in negotiating a peace, a demand w^d. be made with respect to Bulgaria, of wh: we c^d. not approve, & that if our note, respecting Const[antinople]: &^c., were forwarded & pressed at this moment, the Russians might conclude, that we agreed to their Bulgarian proposal.

He agreed with me, under these circumstances, it was best not to send in the note, but he thought it ought to be prepared, & considered by the Cabinet–

The unfortunate fall of Kars will, I fear, revive those agitations in another quarter, wh: I had quieted.[299]

[298]Disraeli had coined a story that there were 'six parties in the Cabinet', which had not included Northcote. Derby recorded one version of the story in his diary: 'The party of war at any price: Hardy, J. Manners, Hicks Beach. The Party who are for declaring war if Russia reaches Constantinople: Cross, Smith and Cairns. The party who are for letting the Russians go to Constantinople but not stay there: Lord Salisbury. The party who are for having a Christian service in St. Sofia: Carnarvon. The party for peace at any price–Lord Derby. The party who are for reconciling all these parties, and standing by our political engagements: The Queen and himself. – In this ingenious summary he has left out Richmond, who may be classed as a follower of the [Lord] Chancellor wherever it pleases the latter to take him: and Northcote, I suppose, as undecided.' *DD*, 21 October 1877, p. 446.

[299]The Queen's. Kars, in the far east of Turkey near the border, faced the Russians' second front.

475

Derby to Disraeli, Dep. Hughenden 113/1, fo. 223
19 November 1877
Foreign Office

I will see what I can do about the draft. — I accept the decision of the Cabinet,[300] and indeed approve of the general policy indicated: but it is a very awkward paper to draw, as matters stand. — I don't believe the Russians would care to go further than Adrianople, where they stopped in 1828, and where they are near enough to overawe the capital without entering it. We shall have to take care that we don't seem to give them more freedom of action than we desire.

476

Manners, Memorandum, Dep. Hughenden 106/3, fos 184–185
26 November 1877

I think the time has come when the Cabinet ought to determine and act upon a definite line of policy in the Turco-Russian question. [. . .]
Russia should be asked to give a positive answer as to the occupation, whether temporary or not, of Constantinople and the Dardanelles; and, pending it's [sic] arrival, preparations should be made for sending a corps d'armée to the East.
If the answer should be unsatisfactory or evasive, or should a Russian force cross the Balkans before it's [sic] receipt, the expedition should be despatched forthwith [. . .]
It is submitted that this would not necessarily constitute, or produce a state of war against Russia; but would be in strict accordance with our conduct when there was an apprehension that Russia intended to force the Suez Canal by her ships of war, in consequence of which we despatched an ironclad to the mouth of the Canal with orders to resist any attack upon it. [. . .]
In my judgment such action would greatly contribute to a pacification; and it is obvious that were peace negociations once entered upon, the presence of an English army and fleet at and

---

[300] Corry's marginal note indicates that this refers to the decision of the Cabinet of 5 November to send 'a fresh communication' to Russia. 'It is so harmless that no one can object: and so useless, that one does not see why he prefers it.' *DD*, 5 November 1877, p. 450.

about Constantinople would enormously strengthen the hands of our diplomatists. [. . .]

477

Cairns to Disraeli, Dep. Hughenden, fos 160–163
30 November 1877
London

Layard's letter to L^d. D[erby]. (1333) as to the consequences of Servia and Greece coming into the war [. . .] is very serious: & so is the information of Sir C. Dickson[301] as to the defenceless state of the country south of the Balkan [*sic*].

In conjunction with these, I have been reading the private note given by Schouv^{ff}. to L^d. D. in June last: & also the conversation between Bismarck & Ld Odo R[ussell]., in the secret despatch of the latter (May 27 last): & I cannot help thinking that any one applying these documents to the present crisis would say not only that an overture for mediation from this country would not be officious, but that it has been invited both by Russia & Germany. Pray read these documents before the Cabinet.

[Enclosed:]

1. The tripartite treaty of 15 April 1856[302] has never been formally cancelled or abrogated.
2. On the other hand various events have occurred since that date in reference to which the provisions of the treaty might have been invoked, & yet none of the Powers parties to the treaty have, so far as we know, called upon the other Powers to put in force its' [*sic*] provision.
3. Whether any of the other signatory powers may hereafter invoke the provisions of the treaty H.M. Gov^t. cannot of course foretell. If an appeal should be made to H.M. Gov^t. founded upon the treaty, it will be the duty of the Gov^t. to consider the appeal with

---

[301] General Sir Collingwood Dickson, additional military attaché at Constantinople from 5 May 1877 to 10 September 1879.

[302] This treaty, signed by Britain, Austria, and France at the end of the Crimean War, guaranteed the 'independence and integrity of the Ottoman Empire', and its second article stipulated that: 'Any infraction of the stipulations of the said treaty will be considered by the Powers signing the present treaty as a *casus belli*.'

reference to the circumstances under which it is made, & the events which have occurred since the date of the treaty.

N.B. I have myself no doubt that the treaty is at an end, & that the specific 'independence & integrity recorded in the Treaty of Paris', which the tripartite treaty guaranteed, no longer exists. There is therefore no danger in the answer assuming this complexion, tho' it may be unnecessary & undesirable to affirm it categorically.[303]

478

Manners to Disraeli, Dep. Hughenden 106/3, fos 186–187
1 December 1877
Balmoral

I have not much to report. H.M is – as you may suppose, displeased with Derby's speech,[304] and not satisfied with Northcote's language while here.

I endeavoured to put the best possible construction on Derby's speech, explaining the character of his interlocutors; but the question naturally arises – what was meant in our declaration – or rather definition of conditional neutrality by the allusion to our interests in the Persian Gulf if – as D's language would seem to imply – the occupation of Armenia by Russia will not be resisted by us?[305]

It is true Trebizond[306] alone was mentioned; but the whole tone was one of indifference to anything that might happen in Armenia. Meanwhile I still put trust in the Turks, and the weather. [...]

[303]The central question for the Cabinet at this point was the nature of what constituted a *casus belli* if the Turks' military situation deteriorated further. The danger of a Russian occupation of Constantinople made the question a pressing one, and Cairns was in favour of offering British mediation. Since he was the Cabinet's senior legal authority, it fell to him to pronounce as to the nature of British treaty engagements. As this enclosure outlines, the status of the 1856 treaty was decidedly ambiguous by 1877.

[304]To a deputation of 28 November, which, Derby noted, 'has naturally disappointed & disgusted the war-party'. *DD*, 29 November 1877, p. 458.

[305]Derby had reiterated the Government's commitment to 'conditional neutrality', and had stated his scepticism about Constantinople being in immediate danger. In his view, the notion that Russian occupation of Turkey's north-east Black Sea coast would threaten the Suez Canal seemed 'somewhat difficult of proof'. See *The Times*, 29 November 1877. Manners drew a series of implications that went far beyond anything Derby had said.

[306]Trébizonde, as it was known to contemporary diplomatists; modern-day Trabzon, on Turkey's Black Sea coast. Not claimed by Russia, even under the terms of San Stefano. The Turkish resistance prevented so dramatic an incursion, as Derby predicted in his address on 28 November.

479

Disraeli to Derby, DP 920 DER (15) 16/2/3[307]
5 December 1877
10 Downing Street

[. . .] I consented to change, yesterday, the form of the note to Russia,[308] wh: the Cabinet had previously agreed to, in compliance with your wishes, wh: I always wish to meet if possible, but I prefer the original proposal. [. . .]

Its tone cannot be too firm & clear — Whatever may be told to you, I believe, that Russia, generally, is more ready for peace, than her journals pretend, but the war party is encouraged by our presumed supineness.

I was sorry to hear you say yesterday, that you were not prepared to make the occupation of Constant[inopl]^e, or rather the menaced occupation of that city, a casus belli. I hope I misunderstood you. I hold, myself, both this event, if impending, as well as the simultaneous opening of the Straits to Russia & then closing to other powers, should decidedly be casus belli for this country, with or without allies – and with regard to this last consideration, we sh^d. remember, that Turkey herself is now a powerful ally. In the Crimean war, she literally had no army. After a fierce campaign, she has still 400,000 men in the field, armed with admirable weapons & her arsenals are well supplied [. . .]^309

480

Wellesley to Disraeli, Dep. Hughenden 80/4, fos 178–181
7 December 1877
Torad[?eric] near Plevna

The Emperor yesterday informed General Werder, my German colleague, that he had received a telegram from Count Schouvaloff to the effect that, at a cabinet council recently held in London on the subject of the Eastern Question, the peace party had been victorious,

---

^307Reproduced in M&B, VI, p. 199.

^308With regard to the conditions of Britain's continuing neutrality, upon which there had been much discussion in Cabinet on 4 December. For two contrasting accounts, see DD, p. 459, and Manners to Queen Victoria, 4 December 1877, M&B, VI, pp. 198–199.

^309'Unsatisfactory in tone', thought Derby on 6 December (DD, p. 460). According to him, the Cabinet of 4 December had agreed not to make a Russian occupation of Constantinople a casus belli, for fear that the ultimatum would be refused, which 'would only lead to unpleasantness'. DD, p. 459.

but that notwithstanding this, it had been decided to address another note to Russia.[310]

It is needless to say that this intelligence was received with the greatest satisfaction, and his majesty is doubtless now convinced that there does exist a difference of opinion among the members of H.M's Government, which will permit him to push his aggressive policy, or rather that of his counsellors, further than would otherwise have been deemed safe.

Whether there be a divergence of opinion among Her Majesty's ministers or no, it is fatal that the Emperor should be induced to believe that it exists, especially at such a critical moment, when all Russians are speculating as to the possible conditions of peace, and loudly proclaiming their views as to what is due to them for the sacrifices they have made. [. . .]

[. . .] Holding the Quadrilateral to the east, the Turks ought to be able to make a formidable stand on the road to Adrianople, and if they had but English officers to command them, the Russians would find an advance to that city as difficult, if not more difficult a matter than the capture of the Plevna position.

War is, no doubt, a great calamity, but if it be true, as most Russians affirm, that a conflict between their country and England is inevitable sooner or later, then surely it would be better to fight Russia now that she is well nigh exhausted, and before our ally, and perhaps the only one, is completely crushed. [. . .]

481

Hardy to Disraeli, Dep. Hughenden 80/4, fo. 189
11 December 1877
Edinburgh

The startling news of the fall of Plevna[311] and our knowledge of the little force which intervenes between that place and Adrianople must make us very anxious. The possession of Plevna secures a fortified road to the Russians and may make the great fortresses of less importance. The time has come when mediation should be pressed & if refused ought we not to call Parliament & ask for increase of force. Events will I fear hurry on & find us as we were.[312]

---

[310]Derby recorded on 8 December his fear that the Cabinet's proceedings were being leaked. *DD*, p. 461.

[311]On 10 December, after a siege lasting almost six months.

[312]On 13 December, Shuvalov was officially informed by Derby of Britain's hope that neither Constantinople nor the Dardanelles would be occupied, since such a step would alarm British public opinion and 'seriously endanger' relations between the two countries.

482

Layard to Disraeli, Dep. Hughenden 70/2, fos 163–167[313]
12 December 1877
British Embassy, Constantinople

The last messenger brought me your letter of the 27 Ult[im]°.[314] I had an opportunity on Monday last to obtain some information which may enable me to answer some of your enquiries. The Minister for Foreign Affairs, upon whom I was calling, shewed me a telegram from Musurus relating his conversation with you on the subject of a loan to Turkey. [...]

[...] He then took up Musurus' idea of making an arrangement with the creditors, and of freeing a part of the guarantees assigned to them, for the purpose of raising a new loan. He seemed to think that by this means, and with the help of H.M. Government, the Porte might get the money it required. I pointed out to him that after Mahmoud Pasha's decree, amounting to a declaration of bankruptcy, and the way in which the bondholders had been treated as regards the guarantees given to them, there was very little hope of the Porte being able to raise a loan without giving [?other] solid guarantees, upon the punctual application of which the utmost reliance could be placed. [...]

[...] My conversation with Server Pasha[315] was strictly private and confidential, and for obvious reasons I made it as general as possible. It was merely an 'exchange of ideas', in diplomatic phraseology. I gathered from what fell from him that, under present circumstances, the Porte would not be likely to listen to any proposal for a cession of territory. The Sultan & the Turkish Ministers still cling to the formula of 'the independence and integrity' of the Empire, and they would think that to give up territory would be to renounce the latter. The subject could only be approached with the greatest caution. Their suspicions of our intentions [...] have been revived by the reports sent to them of Lord Derby's recent speech, and of its effect upon public opinion.[316] [...]

[...] I do not believe that, at the present time, the Porte would be prepared to cede Crete, Cyprus or any other island in the Mediterranean to us. [...]

I quite agree with you in thinking that if the Porte could be enabled to enter upon a second campaign, and we could help her to get

---

[313]Marked 'secret'.
[314]Last month.
[315]The Turkish foreign minister.
[316]See above, **478**.

money to do so, and could combine with it the presence of the English fleet in the Bosphorus, and a British army corps at Gallipoli & Derkos, the result as to after negociations might be great. But in order to accomplish this we ought to abandon at once a hesitating and undefined policy. The Turks do not know what to make of us. We seem to them to blow hot and cold. They think that we take an interest in them, and advise them for their good; but that we will abandon them at once should Russia decline to listen to us, and that we are not even ready to make an effort in support of the most vital English interests. [. . .]

483

Northcote to Salisbury, SP, fo. 123[317]
14 December 1877
11 Downing Street

Your concluding sentence adds much to my uneasiness.[318] I am afraid of the most serious consequences if Derby cannot rouse himself to take a lead and give us a line of his own. He would find a good backing in the Cabinet if he would do this; but we cannot go on without a policy, or with nothing but a non possumus:[319] and a break-up in the present state of affairs may lead to chaos and to war. Shall you be visible [*sic*] at any time tomorrow?

484

Carnarvon to Northcote, IP, BL Add. MS 50022, fos 227–231
15 December 1877
Highclere Castle

Though I fear after the discussion of yesterday in the Cabinet[320] that we have reached a stage when it is vain to attempt to reconcile opinions which have long been so divided and are now so divergent, I do not like the next 24 hours to pass without saying to you that I deplore the division which I now see imminent, that in the general

[317]Phrases from this letter were reproduced in Cecil, II, p. 163.

[318]With respect to the 'concluding sentence', no corresponding letter from Salisbury has been found in Northcote's papers.

[319]A phrase meaning an inability or unpreparedness to act. In Latin, literally, 'we cannot'.

[320]This meeting had resulted in stalemate, with Carnarvon, Salisbury, and Derby resisting their colleagues, who wished to support Disraeli's proposed policy; this was to offer mediation to Russia and Turkey at the same time as asking Parliament to vote an extra £5 million for armaments and to increase British forces.

interests of the country I think it dangerous and that so far as I am concerned I would do much to avert it, provided only that the escape from evil is not purchased at the price of still greater dangers. And I say all this to you not only as an old personal friend but because as leader of the H[ouse]. of Commons you seem to me to have a special responsibility cast upon you.

I need to repeat to you – what you know well – that I do not oppose the proposal for an increase in armaments because I oppose all war and am anxious to maintain peace at any cost: I have both in private and in the Cabinet on former occasions advised very strong measures: I desired that we should consider the occupation of Egypt and should have been presently ready to incur considerable risks in such a case: but any such suggestion, whether proceeding from me or others, has as you know been always put aside because competing with the insane scheme of undertaking the defence of Constantinople; and as a consequence a Turkish alliance. My opposition therefore does not arise from a desire to do nothing or a fear of attempting large things if circumstances require them: but it results from a conviction that in the course which is now proposed to us for adoption there are nine chances of war as against one of peace.

It is idle to deny that what is proposed is a threat to Russia and an encouragement to Turkey: and though it is just possible that Russia who does not desire the continuance of war may accept our armed mediation yet she cannot accept it unless she is guarded against humiliation: and who, that has sat in the Cabinet the last twelve months and knows the temper in which these matters have been discussed, will say that there is any guarantee on this point with a reconstructed government? The chances are at least very unfavourable.

As regards war itself I think it is difficult to exaggerate the folly of it. We s^d. [*sic*] go into it not only with inadequate resources and without allies – perhaps even with serious opposition to expect from Germany & Italy if not Austria – but we should certainly open the door wide to European disturbances of every kind if there are any persons who desire to disturb the peace of the world.

Nor have we the miserable excuse of being able to save & restore even to its' [*sic*] former position the Turkish Empire. It is breaking to pieces past all remedy and we are simply shutting our eyes to facts that are as clear as noon-day. I cannot therefore knowingly be a party to the idea of a war with Russia and a Turkish alliance which finds so much favour in many quarters: and it really seems to me a matter of little importance how we arrive at such a result – whether by plainly & distinctly throwing in our lot with the Turks or whether we adopt some circuitous method of reaching this same end. I believe this to be Derby's view and holding it to be the right one I cannot see any reason for refusing my support to it: but I do not the less deplore the fatal tendency of present events.

If indeed any formula could be devised which would give me a sufficient assurance that the increase of armaments would not be applied in direct support of Turkey and more particularly in the impossible scheme of a defence of Constantinople – thereby involving us actively in the present war – I should be ready at all events to consider whether some increase of our forces might not be made: but here it is that the last discussion in the Cabinet makes me feel how hard it will be to come to a clear understanding.

On re-reading this letter I think it right to say that though I have marked it private I do not desire to interpose any objection to your showing it to anyone, if you think it desirable to do so. I need not say that none of our colleagues have seen it —

485

Salisbury to Northcote, IP, BL Add. MS 50019, fos 53–57[321]
15 December 1877
India Office

I have put down in a separate note the difficulties, which the present proposition combined with Derby's almost certain resignation if they are pressed, raise in my mind.

I quite agree with you that the non possumus is leading to very blank results.[322]

But this remedy is worse than the disease.

An active policy is only possible under one of two conditions – that you shall help the Turks, or coerce them. I have no objection to the latter policy: or to a combination of the two. With the former alone, I cannot be content. But, as you know, neither the Queen nor the Prime Minister will have anything to do with the latter.

[Enclosed:]

It is proposed to summon Parliament in great haste to ask for money wherewith to arm. Before the recess, the money might have been obtained as a measure of precaution, without any full exposition of policy. But money which is so urgently wanted that we cannot

---

[321] This letter and the enclosed memorandum were reproduced, with a series of minor alterations, in Cecil, II, pp. 163–166.
[322] See above, 483.

wait three weeks to have it in the usual session of Parliament, must be wanted for a special purpose. Parliament will insist on knowing what that special purpose is. Your reply, I presume, will be, 'the defence of Constantinople.' But, if you want money so urgently for this purpose, you must, in consistency, use it without delay. You must arm at once: & send your contingent to Constantinople at the earliest possible date. Meanwhile, at the very first moment of the announcement that Parliament is summoned, the Turks will abandon all idea of negotiation, & prepare for a desperate defence. The infernal newspapers, who dog our footsteps, pretending to belong to us, & howling for blood, will from the very first moment place the most belligerent interpretation on the summons of Parliament: & I doubt not, they will know of the vote of money to be asked for. The result will be that the war will go on; the Turkish resistance will be renewed: & the campaign will be raging at the foot of the Balkans, when our troops arrive in Constantinople. Do you imagine that they can remain there in an attitude of 'conditional neutrality' – not helping or encouraging the Turk, not showing any sign of life, until the first Russian shows himself on the slope of the Dyrkos earthworks? Even if the Turks permitted us to come otherwise than as allies – which is very doubtful, such a proceeding, taken at this time, must end in cooperation with the Turks. It will be a Crimean war: only postponed until our allies have been half destroyed.

The proposal of yesterday seems to me therefore to place us on the steep slope which leads to war. Is there any justification in danger to 'British interests'[?] Russia has not yet crossed the Balkans; – the roads are still impassable to artillery, or nearly so; there is a long distance to traverse for commissariat: & winter has but just begun. But the most important consideration of all, is that Austria has pledged herself not to suffer any Russian possession of Constantinople in language so distinct, that unless we are [to] treat her as a Power with whom language has no binding force, she <u>must</u> prevent it.

I hold, therefore, that Constantinople is in no real danger: & that a call to arms, hasty & urgent, may have the effect, & probably succeeds from the wish, of involving us in war to uphold Turkey.

This would be difficult enough to swallow. But to me the matter presents itself in a still more serious light. I shall have to ask myself how, with such a policy laid down, affairs are likely to be conducted in a Cabinet, in which the Queen's[323] and the Prime Minister's wishes are no longer balanced by Derby's well-known aversion for war. His resignation will create, at such a juncture, the utmost consternation. Not only will it unite all sections of the Opposition, & throw into great

[323] The Queen was missed out of the version published by Cecil.

discouragement the non-warlike portion of our own party: but it will divide the nation into two camps – those who are for aiding the Turks, & those who are for leaving them to their fate. The latter will attack furiously, by every weapon which popular agitation or parliamentary forces can furnish: the fight will become intensely bitter: those who are for war will become more warlike, those who are for peace will become more anti-Turkish. In such a melée all half opinions, all nice distinctions will be crushed out. It cannot be doubted, that under pressure of engagements into which they will have slid, & in the heat of the fight with the Opposition, the Cabinet will surrender itself to the war party: & any advocates of peace who may have stayed behind Derby will not be in a pleasant position.

These are the thoughts which were suggested to me by[324] the Cabinet of yesterday – & found expression in the few words I added to my note to you.

I shall be in town early on Monday & will try to see you.

486

Northcote to Salisbury, SP, fo. 127
16 December 1877
Athenaeum

I agree with almost every word of your letter, – though perhaps I could not go with you in your hypothetical willingness to coerce both sides; which however we need not discuss, as it lies outside the range of p.p.[325] [. . .]

487

Salisbury to Northcote, IP, BL Add. MS 50019, fo. 59
16 December 1877
Hatfield

I will try and find you towards midday tomorrow.

The postponement of the summoning of Parliament to the end of the month[326] will take all the sting out of the proposition – or nearly

---

[324] Cecil erroneously has 'in' for 'by'.

[325] The definition of 'p.p.' here is not clear, but the meaning of the sentence is that the scenario was not relevant to the situation as it stood.

[326] The fall of Plevna had accelerated Disraeli's wish to summon Parliament to vote funds for a potential British expedition. In the event, on 17 December the summoning of Parliament was delayed, though not to as late a date as Salisbury or Derby would have preferred.

all: for there will then be no hot haste – & consequently no implied pledges of immediate action[.]

488

Manners to Disraeli, Dep. Hughenden 106/3, fos 188–189
17 December 1877
6 Cumberland Terrace, Regent's Park

I was surprized at Smith's[327] defection on the main point, but was relieved by his saying as we were breaking up that it was far more important for the country that your administration should continue than that his or any individual's view on that question should prevail.

I expect therefore to see him tomorrow ranged on our side.

If you think there would be the slightest use in referring to my tender of resignation last summer[328] in conversation with Derby, or in the Cabinet[,] don't hesitate to do so.

Your's [*sic*] in disgust

489

Corry to Disraeli, Dep. Hughenden 69/1, fos 130–131
17 December 1877
10 Downing Street

Count Schouvaloff informed me last night that, for certain, Germany would decline to mediate, according, he said, to a distinct understanding come to between the Chancellors at Gastein. – that Russia would decline an armistice, her army, now, in Turkey being almost exactly three to the enemy's one – that mediation by England would undoubtedly be refused by Russia – and that he felt confident that Turkey during the winter would herself sue for and conclude peace.

So far as his information went, even now, Russia would be content with the terms which, six months ago, he had stated to Lord Derby.

His general tone was that of entire confidence that England would not interfere, except to offer mediation.

---

[327] Smith had declared at the crucial Cabinet of 17 December that he was against sending an expedition to Constantinople in advance of any Russian designs on the city. Disraeli, according to Derby, 'hinted broadly at his wish to resign' (*DD*, 17 December, p. 465).

[328] See above, **443**.

Count Montgelas is to call upon me before the Cabinet today, with a confidential proposal from Austria to join with England in answering the Porte's circular.[329]

490

Northcote to Disraeli, Dep. Hughenden 107/1, fos 135–136
17 December 1877
11 Downing Street

There was one consideration in my mind which I could not state in Cabinet, but which weighed most heavily with me.

If the adoption of your proposals[330] were followed by Derby's resignation, it is certain that Salisbury and Carnarvon would follow him. This would at once give a colour to the policy, and mark it as being in the opinion of your own Foreign Secretary and others of your colleagues a war policy. And it is obvious that this would give an immense advantage to our opponents. [. . .]

Now as to the policy to be adopted. Is it not possible to come to a compromise, which may prevent a break-up?

The compromise I would suggest is, that we should give up the idea of defending Constantinople, but make all preparations for occupying Gallipoli the moment it is threatened. Smith says we could make preparations quietly which would enable us to land a small force there at three days' notice [. . .]

Could you not propose to Derby to come to an agreement on this basis?

I am strongly impressed with the danger of calling Parliament before we have a policy on which we are united; and I have strong doubts as to whether Derby will ever agree to what we understand by the defence of Constantinople itself.

---

[329] Turkey had asked the other great powers, collectively, for mediation. This request was received by the Foreign Office on 14 December 1877.

[330] This letter followed a stormy Cabinet on 17 December 1877, at which Disraeli had proposed an immediate summons of Parliament, a subsequent vote for increased military spending, and the pursuit of peace negotiations. Northcote's views lay somewhere between Disraeli on the one hand and Derby, Salisbury, and Carnarvon on the other. Northcote's main objection was to the sudden recall of Parliament. The Cabinet meeting resulted in stalemate, and it looked increasingly likely that the government would break up; at the end of the meeting, Disraeli threatened to resign. Northcote, a natural conciliator and the Cabinet's 'go-between', was – as usual – attempting to find an amicable way through the difficulties.

491

Derby to Disraeli, Dep. Hughenden 113/1, fo. 223
17 December [1877]

I will call on you – a little after eleven – and happy indeed I shall be
if we can see our way out of this mess. We all want to keep together:
and no one in the Cabinet will feel as I shall if circumstances separate
me from my old friend and teacher in public life.[331]

492

Northcote to Salisbury, IP, BL Add. MS 50019, fos 61–63
18 December 1877

Will you look at the inclosed and tell me what you think – Cross is
disposed to like the plan.[332]

[Enclosed:]

Would such a policy as this be practicable?
After clearly ascertaining that nothing was to be done by joint
mediation, let England propose to the Porte to act as sole mediator,
sending up the fleet to Constantinople, and stipulating for a position
at Gallipoli to secure it from being caught in a trap?

---

[331] The meeting on 18 December was 'friendly & frank'. Derby noted that Disraeli 'sees
things in a way that is not intelligible to me'. Disraeli also spoke 'of the constant pressure put
upon him by the Queen, who has been in favour of war from the first'. *DD*, 18 December,
pp. 465–466. This meeting preceded a compromise in Cabinet on 18 December, at which
Salisbury shifted his position, after Cairns had visited Hatfield to persuade him. It was
agreed that Parliament would be recalled for 17 January, later than initially proposed, that
some armaments would be increased – with the details to be resolved later – and that Derby
would work on a scheme for mediation in the war, using as his starting-point a suggestion
by Cairns that the Russian peace proposals of June 1877 be its basis. For the last, see below,
493.

[332] The 'plan' to which Northcote referred was his own, contained in the enclosure.
Salisbury noted on the letter 'I think it will furnish a good basis. The [Lord] Chancellor
has a proposition somewhat in the same sense.' It was Cairns's scheme that was the basis
of Cabinet discussion on 18 December, and for Derby's subsequent proposal, for which
Austrian support was to be sought. Derby's draft of a proposal for mediation that might
be presented to Russia was therefore first sent to Austria in a despatch of 19 December.
On 21 December, the Foreign Office learnt from Buchanan in Vienna that the Austrians
had rejected the suggestion, objecting partly on the grounds that the Russian proposals of
June 1877 had not been agreed upon by Austria. That version of the plan was therefore
abandoned; Cairns's memorandum of 21 December (see below, **493**) was an attempt to
resolve the impasse thus created.

The Porte to be told that, if it was unreasonable in the matter of terms, England must withdraw and leave Turkey to her fate. We should, however, in that case probably retain our hold on Gallipoli, which would give us a vantage-ground in subsequent negotiations.

We should inform Parliament of all that we were doing; and should state that if Russia attacked Constantinople while the mediation was being attempted we should consider it free to England to take such measures as she might think it necessary.

We should of course ask for a vote of credit.

493

Cairns, Memorandum, Dep. Hughenden 113/1, fos 246–249
21 December 1877
10 Downing Street

The despatch to Ld A. Loftus agreed to in Cabinet[333] appeared likely to secure three objects.

1. It w^d., without expressing any opinion on the tone of the Turkish note,[334] or on the Russian proposals of June last,[335] shew the Porte that we considered that any business to be done, must be done on the lines of the latter, & not of the former document.

2. It w^d. shew those who placed faith in the disinterested objects of the Emperor of Russia, that his aims were not unmixed with a considerable desire for personal aggrandizement.

3. It w^d., on some points as to which Russia has latterly shewn a tendency to enlarge her demands, tend to limit her, morally, to what she originally proposed.

It now appears that the proposal of this despatch has had another very important, – though somewhat unexpected, effect. It has drawn Austria from her state of torpidity, & led her to shew a real alarm

---

[333] The draft of 19 December, intended ultimately for Loftus in Russia, sent to Vienna first, but which the Austrians had rejected. See above, **492**.

[334] See above, **489**.

[335] Shuvalov had informed Derby on 8 June 1877 of what would be the Russian conditions for peace: (1) Russian acquisition of Batoum; (2) Russian acquisition of part of Rumania down nearly as far as the Danube mouth (effectively reversing the Crimean war losses); (3) a client Bulgarian state down to the Balkans; (4) provision for the Christians in the Ottoman Empire; (5) enlarged Serbian and Montenegrin states; (6) Austrian oversight in Bosnia; (7) a rearrangement of the situation in the Dardanelles. See *DD*, 8 June 1877, p. 407.

at the proposals of the Emperor of Russia being even mentioned by England.[336]

I think every effort sh^d. be made to take advantage of this state of the Austrian mind.

It wd. I think be desirable in the first place (this was perhaps not sufficiently considered by the Cabinet) to ascertain from Turkey, categorically, whether she wishes, even tho' a joint mediation by the Powers sh^d. not be undertaken, still that England sh^d. endeavour to mediate alone. I think the Porte sh^d. be, privately, encouraged to desire to do this.

Supposing that the Porte, as is most probable, solicits this separate mediation, I sh^d. then recast the despatch to Ld A. Loftus agreed to in Cabinet.

I sh^d. leave out the enumeration of the specific conditions proposed by Russia in June last. I sh^d. simply remind Russia, as the despatch does, that the Emperor, thro' Count S[huvalov]., & Col^l. Wellesly [sic], expressed his desire to make peace north of the Balkans, & urged on England & the other Powers the propriety of their inducing Turkey to do this. I sh^d. say, generally, that certain conditions were then mentioned, but that we did not think it right to assume, after a lapse of time, & change of circumstances, that those conditions w^d. now be proposed. That we felt it to be our duty, in harmony with the tone of the Emperor's previous communications, to inform him of the application made to us by the Porte, & to state that we were ready to make known to the Porte the terms on which he w^d. now be ready to make peace.

I sh^d. then go to Austria, & say we were prepared, in deference to her wishes, to shape our communication to Russia in this way, on, substantially, the following terms. If Russia declined any mediation, or overtures of peace, we should further consult with Austria as to the protection of our common interests. If Russia, on the other hand, sh^d. state the terms on which she w^d. make peace, we w^d. confer with Austria as to how far these terms were in accordance with the common basis on which we were endeavouring to act, & w^d. express our views upon them accordingly.

[336]The news had been received on 21 December that Austria objected to Britain's proposal for mediation (see above, **492**), but was officially communicated by Beust on 22 December. With the failure of this initial proposal for mediation, Cairns's memorandum was the result of a discussion between Cairns and Disraeli, attempting to circumvent Austrian objections with a unilateral British proposal.

We should, I think, make a great point of appearing to place in abeyance a course of action which we might have been free to adopt alone, for the sake of an harmonious cooperation with Austria.

494

Disraeli to Derby, DP 920 DER (15) 16/2/3
21 December 1877
10 Downing Street

The affair is so important, & time so precious, that the L[or]^d Chan[cello]^r., & myself, think, that no Cabinet sh^d. be called, but that the matter sh^d. be left entirely to you.[337]

I send a mem[orandum]: of the joint deliberations of Cairns & myself wh: please return to me when you have copied it. It is for your consideration – As Hatfield is so near, Salisbury might be easily consulted.[338]

495

Derby to Disraeli, Dep. Hughenden 113/1, fos 243–244
22 December 1877
Foreign Office

I think we can hardly make a complete change in our method of proceeding without consulting such men as Cross and Northcote – who will have to bear the chief burden of defending whatever we do.

But we need not lose time in the meanwhile. We may ask the Porte to say whether it is willing that we should address Russia on the subject of terms of peace. So far I agree with Cairns: and the step pledges us to nothing to which we were not pledged before. We can do nothing more till we get an answer: and as that will probably not be immediate, a Cabinet called for next Friday would involve scarcely any delay.

---

[337]This was clearly an attempt to 'bounce' Derby into accepting the scheme proposed in **493**. Derby was determined not to act without the sanction of Cabinet, where he knew he could rely on the support of others. His diary recorded his resistance on this score when he had met with Disraeli that same day. See *DD*, 21 December 1877, p. 467. See also Derby's response below, **495**.

[338]A copy of the Cairns memorandum of 21 December (**493**) is then enclosed. Salisbury was by now the crucial figure in the Cabinet. Both Derby and Disraeli were well aware of this, which prompted letters **497** and **498**.

Considering how very ticklish the whole affair is – the early approach of the session – and the possibility of disagreement among ourselves in future stages of the affair, we cannot be too careful to give no colleague reason for saying that he has not been consulted.

496

Northcote to Disraeli, Dep. Hughenden 107/1, fos 137–138
22 December 1877
Pynes, Exeter

The Vienna telegrams seem very awkward. If we go forward with our communication to Russia against the remonstrance of Austria the latter will have an excuse for throwing us over; and she will at one and the same time take credit with Russia for having disapproved our efforts at mediation, and with the Porte for having protested against our giving colour to terms which are so unfavourable to Turkey. [. . .]
Would it be possible to [. . .] propose that England and Austria should make a joint (or identic) communication to the Porte recommending it to ask Russia for her terms, and promising that if Turkey would follow our counsels (and not make peace without our consent?) we would do our best to obtain favourable terms for her?

497

Derby to Salisbury, SP, fo. 95[339]
23 December 1877
Foreign Office

The more I reflect on the present situation, the more uneasiness I feel. It is difficult to give a definite reason for suspicions, however strongly one may entertain them; but I know our chief of old, and from various things that have dropped from him I am fully convinced – not indeed that he wishes for a war, but that he has made up his mind to large military preparations, to an extremely warlike speech,[340] to an agitation in favor [sic] of armed intervention (recollect that

[339] Derby regarded this letter (reproduced in Cecil, II, pp. 170–171) as 'a warning letter urging him [Salisbury] to look out for future danger', *DD*, p. 469.
[340] The Speech from the Throne (Queen's Speech) on Parliament's return.

he said in Cabinet 'the country is asleep and I want to wake it'), and if possible to an expedition that shall occupy Constantinople or Gallipoli.

Now I am not inclined to any of these things, and I believe others among us are not so either: but if we don't take care we shall find ourselves, as you said last year about the vote of credit, 'on a slippery incline': each step will make another necessary, and in the end we may find ourselves in a position which none of us either expected or would have accepted beforehand.

I have no feeling towards the Premier but one of personal friendship and good will, and would make personal sacrifices to help him out of a difficulty: but his views are different from mine, where such matters are concerned, not in detail but in principle. He believes thoroughly in 'prestige' – as all foreigners do:[341] and would think it (quite sincerely) in the interests of the country to spend 200 million on a war if the result of it was to make foreign states think more highly of us as a military power. These ideas are intelligible, but they are not mine, nor yours: and their being sincerely held does not make them less dangerous. We are in real danger, and it is impossible to be too careful. I write without any more specific object than that of general warning: but I know what the pressure of the court is on our chief, I am convinced that the Queen has satisfied herself that she will have her way (it is not disguised that she wishes for a war): and the conviction is universal among the diplomatists that she and the Premier will leave no stone unturned to accomplish their purpose.

The first thing to see to is that nothing shall be done without the Cabinet being consulted. That I can ensure, so far as diplomatic business is concerned.

The next is to keep the military preparations within bounds, and to insist on knowing exactly why they are wanted. In this we should only be anticipating the inevitable criticisms of the H[ouse]. of C[ommons].

The third is to be ready for a difference on the speech from the Throne – which as matters stand is of the greatest consequence.

Andrassy won't have our plan, and has got another to propose, which we shall know in a day or two. — I have insisted on a Cabinet before the end of this week – though it is a nuisance at this time of year. — I go to Knowsley till Wednesday or Thursday, but return on that day at latest.

---

[341]Derby was not necessarily taking a swipe at Disraeli's Jewish ancestry, as has been commonly assumed; rather, as he noted in his diary on 18 December, he regarded Disraeli's suggestion that Britain would lose out by not being consulted in any Russo-Turkish peace as 'the foreign view, which treats prestige as the one thing needful in politics'. *DD*, p. 466.

498

Disraeli to Salisbury, SP, fos 265–267[342]
24 December 1877
10 Downing Street

I enclose you a letter, which I have not shown to any of my colleagues, but which requires, & deserves, your deep attention.

When Colonel Wellesley last left England, & had his final interview with me, I advised him to impress upon the Emperor that England was unwilling to depart from her neutrality, that it wished to assist in bringing about a settlement, not only honorable [sic], but fairly advantageous, to Russia, but that I could not conceal from myself, that if the Emperor was obliged to enter into a second campaign, it wo[ul]^d be difficult for England to rest in her present inertness. The Emperor accepted this statement with confidence, & in the conciliatory spirit in which it was conceived, & he acted on it.

I have myself been convinced, both from thought & information, that a firm front shown by England would terminate the war without material injury to our interests. I hope, I could persuade you of this, but I will not dwell on the matter now. What I wish to show you is, that, if the present system of the Cabinet is persisted in, & every resolution of every council regularly reported by Count Schouvaloff, it seems inevitable, that our very endeavours to secure peace, will land us in a totally different conclusion.

I have endeavoured to arrest this evil by some remarks I made in Cabinet, & I have been told, that Lady Salisbury with the wise courage which distinguishes her, has, socially[,] expressed her sentiments to the great culprit.[343] But more decisive means are requisite.

We must put an end to all this gossip about war-parties & peace-parties in the Cabinet, & we must come to decisions which may be, & will be, betrayed, but which may convince Russia, that we are agreed & determined. You and I must go together into the depth of the

---

[342]Reproduced in M&B, VI, pp. 210–211, but without the lines about Ladies Derby and Salisbury, and apparently copied from Disraeli's notes rather than the version sent to Salisbury.

[343]Mary Derby, whose frequent meetings with Shuvalov had led to speculation that she was the source of Cabinet 'leaks'. It has been incorrectly assumed that Derby and his wife deliberately leaked Cabinet decisions to Shuvalov, so ardent was their desire for peace. Shuvalov had only to read the newspapers for reports of Cabinet dissension, but it is clear that Mary Derby was viewed by the ambassador as a valuable ally, and that she did impart significant details to him. Derby appears only to have been guilty of naivety, as far as his wife was concerned.

affair, & settle what we are prepared to do. I dare say, we shall not differ when we talk the matter over together, as becomes public men with so great a responsibility, but unless we make an effort to clear ourselves from the Canidian spells,[344] which are environing us, we shall make shipwreck alike of our own reputations, & the interests of our country.

499

Salisbury to Disraeli, Dep. Hughenden 80/4, fos 244–245[345]
26 December 1877
India Office

I return the enclosed most interesting & disquieting letter, with many thanks.

I sympathise fully in the solicitude this information causes you. Throughout the last anxious year, the apparent ease with which a knowledge of our councils has leaked out has placed us at a constant disadvantage. I hardly see in what way you, or the Cabinet as a body, can do anything to check the evil. It is a question of honour for each member of the Cabinet individually: but the public mischief of any such breach of our implied engagement as that to which you refer is enormous.[346]

I do not think Wellesley's advice 'to fight Russia now' is sound. She is exhausted in the sense, that she cannot go on fighting without great sacrifices. But she is not so exhausted as to be unable to make head against any great national danger – such as a war with England. Nor would the Turks be of any great value as allies. Enrolled as troops under our officers they would fight admirably: but such an arrangement on an extensive scale will never be permitted, so long as the Turkish government retains a shadow of independence. Under their own officers, they would be of little use. I see therefore no reason for agreeing with Wellesley that this is a good moment for seeking to bring on the inevitable collision with Russia, if it be inevitable. And there are particular circumstances in our own case that make it

---

[344] Disraeli was warning about the wiles of Lady Derby by comparing her to the sorceress Canidia, described by the Roman poet Horace. Disraeli was far too shrewd to use Lady Derby's name directly; Salisbury would have understood the reference.

[345] Reproduced in M&B, VI, p. 211.

[346] The Queen had first named Lady Salisbury, along with Mary Derby, as a possible source of the leaks.

unsuitable. Owing to financial difficulties our Indian army is in a less efficient state than will probably be the case some years hence: & the position of Cabul[347] is a difficulty. Our English army has not had time to accumulate reserves under Cardwell's system.[348] Our manufacturing industries are depressed: & profoundly averse to war. And, owing to the peculiar condition of the Continent, Austria, our natural ally in such a question, has been seduced from us at least for the moment. The national feeling here, though strongly partial to the Turk, shrinks from war; & I think with a true instinct. Of course, it is possible that events may take such a turn as to force us into war ultimately: but it will be unpopular, & unprofitable. [. . .]

500

Derby to Disraeli, Dep. Hughenden 113/1, fo. 252
27 December [1877]
Foreign Office

We must be cautious, for the sake of accuracy, as to any public announcement that we are going to 'mediate.'

As the word is understood in diplomacy, what we are now doing is not mediation.

It may be a preliminary step to mediation, but it is nothing more.

We are only asking the Russians whether they are prepared to treat for peace. The overture will probably end there, in consequence of a Russian refusal.

We should therefore be misleading foreign governments if we stated that we were 'mediating': which would imply giving advice, and the discussion of conditions of peace.

The distinction is important, for the Porte has now asked us to mediate, and if we tell the public here that we are doing so, we shall create an idea at Constantinople that we are doing more than is really the case.

You may say with truth that we are 'taking the initiative in bringing about negociations for peace.' That is an accurate statement of the situation.

---

[347] Kabul in Afghanistan.
[348] The Army Enlistment Act of 1870, introduced by Edward Cardwell, the Liberal Secretary of State for War, had dramatically reduced the time spent on active service by infantrymen, but required them to be added to a reserve force for a period thereafter. By the mid-1870s this had only had a limited time to develop.

501

Northcote to Disraeli, Dep. Hughenden 107/1, fos 139–140
4 January 1878
11 Downing Street

[. . .] I retain my opinion that it is most desirable to avoid a rupture, if it is possible to avoid it, which I think very doubtful. I believe Carnarvon intends to write to you, but I hope he may wait till tomorrow before doing so.[349] [. . .]

It seems to me that we have created for ourselves a position which we must accept; though it is a peculiar and a difficult one. It would have been simple enough to have taken our stand on treaties, and to have declared ourselves ready to fight for Turkey — The nation would not have supported us, and we should have had to give up the conduct of affairs; but we should have been understood. It would have been simple to associate ourselves with the other Powers, and to join in coercing Turkey, and claiming our voice in the ultimate settlement. Or it would have been simple to say, we will not concern ourselves with this war, but if we see Turkey going to pieces we will strike in for such arrangements as may secure our own interests. But we have rejected all these lines, knowing that if we had attempted to follow any one of them we should have disagreed among ourselves, and we have stuck out a line of our own, which may lead to a successful termination of the question if we can follow it out, but which will be rendered impossible by disunion among ourselves. [. . .]

Now I admit that Carnarvon's indiscreet speech was calculated to do harm: but I doubt whether the harm was as great as you are disposed to think it; and I feel very doubtful whether an attempt to remedy the mischief will not make it much worse. [. . .]

502

Corry to Disraeli, Memorandum, Dep. Hughenden 69/1, fos 134–135
7 January 1878
St James' Club, Piccadilly

Editorial note: In the following letter, Corry surrounded two sections with square brackets and marked them 'A' and 'B'. To avoid confusion with editorial

---

[349] Carnarvon, in a pacific speech on 2 January, had said that there was 'nobody insane enough to desire a repetition' of the Crimean War. Disraeli upbraided him in Cabinet on 3 January.

interpolations, those sections are here italicized, and – as in the original – appear in square brackets, marked 'A' and 'B'.

During the last few days I have had some private interviews with the Turkish ambassador – and, for fear of after misconception, I make a very brief note of certain points.

On Dec 27th, at the Porte's request, the Eng[lish]. Govt asked in the name of the Porte if Russia would entertain overtures for peace.

A [P. Gortchakow replied that Russia desired nothing better than peace but that, as a preliminary, an armistice must be settled [. . .]]

H.M. Govt. replied to this that they were willing to forward suggestion of an armistice to the Porte, but that it must be done in a 'form likely to produce a practical result': – and added reasons to show that negotiation between the respective governments – and not the commanders [in the field] offered such a prospect.

P. Gortchakow replied to this that he adhered to his former statement, and that the commanders were informed of the conditions on which the Govt of Russia would agree to an armistice.

To this, the English Govt have, today, replied that, this being so they were not unwilling to suggest that the Porte should send accredited persons to the Russian commanders in order to learn the conditions on wh: the Russian Govt had decided. In coming to this decision, Lord B, at least, was influenced by Lord D[erby].'s statement that the Turkish ambassador had told him that an armistice was necessary for Turkey.

On Sunday Dec 30, – before the answer wh: I have marked A. was considered by the Cabinet, I called on the T[urkish]. Amb[assado]^r to learn, for Lord B, how Turkey viewed the question of an armistice, generally. The proposal was new to Musurus Pacha [*sic*] and he gave reasons, (his own, at first sight) against an armistice, and gave a decided opinion against the conclusion of one in the mode proposed by Russia.

During the week wh: followed I saw Musurus Pacha, at his invitation, once or twice, when he read to me his own despatches to his govt, & despatches from the Porte, containing argument & suggestions which have produced no result and, already, are dead matter.

On Sunday Jan 6. he called on me, and, after communicating other telegrams – propositions wh: today's Cabinet have set aside as impracticable – he showed me a very confidential enquiry from the Porte. – B [*How did Lord B. reconcile the existing attitude of H. M. Govt, as explained to him by Lord D., with his own confidential instigation (through Musurus Pacha) that the Porte should request our mediation?*] I denied that Lord B. had held out the promise of mediation, and declared that what H.M. Govt was doing was quite consistent with – in fact was – what Lord B. had undertaken to do. The ambassador, then, decided to withhold the question, for the present: and I promised to call on him after today's Cabinet.

I saw him late this evening, and found him desponding. Lord D. had just informed him that H.M. Govt had already, since the Cabinet, telegraphed to Mr Layard to advise the Porte to instruct their commanders to apply to the Russian generals. 'Very bad' he said. I said that I was not aware that this was intended, until a reply had come from Russia to the message sent today: – and I explained that H.M. Govt would not have contemplated such a step, except on the assurance, already given, that the commanders had the instructions of the Cabinet of St Petersburg. This was new to him.

I went on to say, as to the whole question, and as to the confidential enquiry B he was instructed to make of Lord B. that his best course was not to hurry – but to wait until Parliament met on the 17th; that it would be folly, on the eve of that event, for Turkey to discard the friendship of this country, however dissatisfied with its present evidence. His excellency seemed to share this view.

503

Disraeli to Derby, DP 920 DER (15) 16/2/3
7 January 1877
10 Downing Street

Can we 'advise' the Porte to accept the armistice? Is this consistent with our neutral position? We held, that we could not give advice to Russia —

I assume, also, that the Porte is adverse [sic] to armistice — Why sh^d. we force her to a step, wh:, in the event of refusal on her part, w^d. have the appearance of disregarding her only friend?

504

Layard to Disraeli, Dep. Hughenden 70/2, fo. 179
9 January 1878
British Embassy, Constantinople

We must not conceal from ourselves that the state of affairs in Turkey is extremely critical. The Turks are greatly disappointed at what they call our 'desertion' of them, and very bitter with us for the advice we have given them to make their own arrangements with Russia for an armistice. They maintain that if we did not intend to use our influence to obtain a favorable [sic] basis for an armistice, we ought not to have led them to lose most precious time, of which the Russians have availed themselves to the utmost by occupying a considerable part of Rumelia. [. . .]

505

Corry to Disraeli, Memorandum, Dep. Hughenden 69/1, fos 136–137.
10 January 1878
St James' Club, Piccadilly

In continuation of memo: dated Jan 7.

I called upon Musurus Pacha on Jan 8 – chiefly [to] tell him what I had heard from persons lately arrived from the East as to the condition of Russia, vis à vis of the question of [an] armistice.

The testimony of Archibald Forbes – the Daily News correspondent who had just returned from Bucharest, via Petersburg; of Lt Col Parker (of the Reserve forces) who had been all the autumn in Turkey (see his letter to me): of J.S. Bowles the editor of Vanity Fair, who returned from Constantinople on the 6th inst: (these 3 names I mentioned): and of Col. Wellesley (whose name I did not mention) – all pointed to this, that an armistice was <u>necessary for Russia</u>, owing to her want of supplies and difficulties arising from the season. His excellency told me that his information pointed to the same conclusion.

He then read to me a secret despatch he had sent that day to Constantinople; in wh: he gave <u>his own</u> views as to differences in our Cabinet, which he said were the cause of its being desirable that he should not have <u>personal</u> intercourse, at present, with Lord B. Hence his interviews with me – the result of wh: (from <u>his</u> reading of what I had said, – generally correct, tho rather <u>overstated</u>–) he recapitulated. He ended by advising the Porte to keep negotiations alive, at least until the meeting of Parliament.

He regretted, much, that Lord D[erby]. had advised the Porte to apply direct by their commanders to the Russian generals for the conditions of armistice, but felt sure that the Porte would agree to do so.

I mentioned that, after all, it was most important, by whatever mode, to obtain from Russia a statement of their conditions.

But, I added, there was reason to apprehend that Russia would attempt a 'coup', and would at the same time perhaps endeavour to obtain from Turkey suddenly the acceptance of bases for <u>peace</u>. This, it was of extreme importance to guard against.

It was, besides, of great consequence that we should have the earliest information of the conditions for armistice wh: Russia might prescribe, and should, generally, be informed of what might pass.

His excellency undertook to write to his government on both these points, and to advise his being at once acquainted with what took place, promising to let me know immediately on his hearing.

I have not since heard from his excellency.

The Cabinet and the war

During this period, the Russians advanced rapidly into Turkish territory, taking Sofia, Philippopolis, and Adrianople, and being by the end of the month in sight of Constantinople. On 10 January, Layard requested that the British fleet be moved up to Constantinople. On 12 January, Disraeli proposed in Cabinet the occupation of Gallipoli, as a guarantee of the security of the Dardanelles. Derby and Carnarvon would not consent to this, but in the end the Cabinet agreed to a compromise suggested by Salisbury, whereby the Turks would be asked if an application to send the fleet into the Dardanelles would be favourably received. On 14 January, Carnarvon privately informed Derby that he would resign if the Turks agreed to this. On 9 January, Derby fell ill, and was unable to attend Cabinet between 12 January and 21 January. On 15 January, the Turks refused to allow Britain to send in the fleet as a neutral power, which was exactly the answer Derby had expected. Meanwhile, in Derby's absence, Disraeli continued his own confidential negotiations with the Austrians, in an attempt to come to an agreement with them to contain Russia.

506

Corry to Disraeli, Dep. Hughenden 69/1, fos 138–139
14 January 1878
Turf Club, Piccadilly

I met Beust at dinner.

He evidently is not aware of the Austrian communications to Petersburg and Constantinople, as to a 'direct' peace, of which we have heard;[350] but he is conscious of the vast importance, common to Austria and England, of the moment. And he hinted his great desire to see you: – since he has been told today that Lord Derby will not be well enough to see him for <u>some days</u>![351]

So I invited him to call on you tomorrow and he will do so at four o'clock, unless I write to change the appointment. I can, at present, recall nothing which stands in the way!

---

[350]The precise nature of this reference is unclear, but there were any number of rumours in circulation, of which this was evidently one. As Chapter 3 also demonstrates, Disraeli was apt to set too much store by rumour.

[351]Derby had been taken ill on 9 January. See editorial note, 'The Cabinet and the war', after letter **505**.

507

Derby to Disraeli, Dep. Hughenden 113/2, fo. 5
15 January 1878
23 St James's Square

It is vexatious in every way to be helpless in a crisis: but I am bound to tell you at once that both my doctor and my own sensations tell me that I cannot hope to appear in the H[ouse]. of Lords for the next week or ten days. I have passed most of the time since our last Cabinet in bed, and though picking up, am very weak and pulled down.[352]

After the next two or three days, I could manage to attend a Cabinet, but not to make a speech.[353]

More I think of the Dardanelles business, less I like it. Will not negociations supersede the necessity for any such step?[354]

508

Northcote to Disraeli, Dep. Hughenden 107/1, fo. 153
15 January [1878]
11 Downing Street

Are you going to take any steps to prevent Tenterden's influence over his chief from stopping the despatch of the telegram?[355] I am very much afraid of it. [. . .]

[352] Derby described his symptoms as 'a sharp bilious attack'. *DD*, 9 January, p. 482. Carnarvon later recorded that rumours were 'immediately set in circulation in the Carlton, and thence carefully disseminated through every drawing room in London, that he was suffering from drink'. John Vincent has suggested that he may have had gastric flu. See *DD*, 9 January 1878, p. 482, n. 23.

[353] He did not attend Cabinet until 21 January.

[354] Despite the Cabinet of 12 January, at which Derby and Carnarvon had resisted attempts to send an expedition to seize Gallipoli, their colleagues still wished to send the fleet to the Dardanelles.

[355] Tenterden had attended Cabinet between 14 and 16 January to advise on foreign affairs as Derby's proxy, given the latter's absence through illness. Northcote had been irritated by Tenterden's advice to the Cabinet of 15 January, advising against moving the fleet as the Cabinet desired. There is no particular evidence of Tenterden's influence over Derby; rather the reverse, in fact, given his faithful transmission of his departmental chief's wishes. The decision to move the fleet awaited a Turkish response to the earlier request sent by Derby, which the Turks then refused anyway. See note, 'The Cabinet and the war', after letter **505**.

509

Thomas Sanderson to Disraeli, Dep. Hughenden 113/2, fo. 7
16 January 1878

Lord Derby's doctor is decidedly of opinion that he could not attend a Cabinet council today without risk of a relapse —

Lady Derby thought it might perhaps be more satisfactory if Dr. Drage called himself to explain his opinion on the subject, and he is the bearer of this note.

Lord Derby is in bed, but may probably send me later with a message, unless he writes.

510

Derby to Disraeli, Dep. Hughenden 113/2, fo. 9
16 January 1878

I enclose a short minute, stating what I should have liked to be able to say in Cabinet today. I cannot put too strongly the objections which I feel to the sending up of the fleet.

511

Derby, Minute dictated to Sanderson, Dep. Hughenden 113/2, fos
11–16
[16 January 1878]

Being unable to attend the Cabinet held today I wish earnestly to advise my colleagues against the proposal to send ships to anchor within the Straits. It does not appear that the Porte will consent to a proposal of this kind so long as we accompany it with a declaration of our continued neutrality, which in practice we must do, lest we should create unfounded expectations.

If we take this step without the consent of the Porte, we do so, as I conceive, in violation of treaties, and thereby place ourselves in the wrong —

Not having heard the naval opinions, I cannot say what amount of danger to the fleet may be involved in thus sending it up. But if this danger were found or thought to be serious, it would furnish a strong argument in favour of supporting the fleet by a land expedition, in which case we should be reversing the decision come to last week, and doing that which I firmly believe Parliament would not sanction.

I have never been able to understand what the ships are to do when they get into the Dardanelles. If the Russians do not go to Gallipoli, they are useless:– if the Russians do go there, there is imminent risk of a collision. Their presence would not prevent an occupation of the coast by Russian troops, supposing that to be intended:– on the contrary the presence of Russian troops on the sea board would render their position precarious. Suppose such an occupation to take place, – the ships being there, – what would follow? Either we must bring them back – in which case the whole proceeding would be ridiculous, – or if we left them there, their presence in face of a Russian army would only show the inutility of their having been sent.

I fail to see what object, – diplomatic or parliamentary, is to be gained by sending them. From the diplomatic point of view our position is this – negotiations for peace have begun, the result of which we cannot possibly know as yet, but we know that the Porte is inclined to make peace on almost any terms, and considering the heavy losses incurred by Russia, and the attitude of Austria now becoming more decided, there seems reason to hope that the Russian conditions will not be extreme. We are acting in concert with Austria, and with her assistance we are able to exercise a real control over the conditions of peace without risk of being involved in war. I cannot see that there is anything in this situation of affairs to justify hasty or hazardous proceedings, especially when they are of a nature to irritate one Power and to be misunderstood by all the rest.

For parliamentary purposes I should have thought it was sufficient to be able to say that we adhere to the conditions of neutrality laid down in May last – that it is through our good offices that the negotiations for peace have been commenced – and that we have claimed and shall continue to claim a voice in the final settlement. Looking to the state of public feeling, I cannot conceive that more is needed to satisfy the requirements of Parliament.

I object to the proposed step as contrary to treaty, as increasing the risk of collision with Russia, as tending to irritate rather than to conciliate, and as being, so far as I can judge, useless if not dangerous in a military point of view. I see every reason to hope that if we continue on our present course we may be able in the course of the present spring to announce that a peace has been concluded which, if not in all respects such as we might have desired to make it, will be accepted by the great majority of the public as a relief from the anxieties and uncertainties of the last 18 months.[356]

---

[356]This letter is signed with a very wobbly 'Derby'.

512

Note by Salisbury, Dep. Hughenden 113/2, fo. 29[357]
21 January 1878

The continued occupation of Bulgaria by foreign troops, or of any part of the shores of the Bosphorus, the Sea of Marmora and Dardanelles, or any alteration of the rules affecting the navigation thereof are to be declared inadmissible without the consent of Austria and England.

513

Corry to Disraeli, Memorandum, Dep. Hughenden 69/1, fos 140–142
22 January 1878
St James' Club, Piccadilly

I called at the Austrian embassy, at 7.30 this evening, where, at my request, Count Montgelas read to me the telegram wh: Count Beust sent, last night, to Count Andrassy, reporting his conversation in the afternoon with Lord Beaconsfield. I afterwards saw Count Beust, and supplied some explanations and additions, which appeared necessary to convey Lord B.[']s full intentions.

I explained (there seeming to be doubt in Count Beust's mind) that the 'defensive' alliance, wh: Lord B. offered,[358] was a 'continuous defensive alliance' (specially pointing out that it was <u>not</u> 'offensive') – & not merely a 'defensive alliance' to repel invasion resulting immediately from the proposed identic note.[359] I told Count Beust that the British Govt would guarantee a loan.

And I said I was empowered by Lord B. to say that he was prepared, if England and Austria arrived at an understanding, to send the British fleet to Constantinople.

On being pressed, I told Count Beust & Count Montgelas that I was not in a position to say <u>when</u> England would so send the fleet – <u>whether on the conclusion of the agreement to send the identic</u> note

---

[357] Note at head of paper, in Corry's hand: 'Copy of a note (in Lord Salisbury's writing) adopted in Cabinet Jan. 21. 78– as a suggestion for identic note to Russia to [*sic* – presumably 'from'] Austria & England. The proposal went to Vienna the same evening. MC. Jan 22.' This had presumably been drawn up in the absence of Derby, before it was known if he would attend Cabinet.

[358] To Austria.

[359] On 21 January, Derby believed that the proposal for an alliance and loan had been postponed pending further discussion and the Austrian answer to a more general enquiry as to a joint position. *DD*, p. 488.

– or on its presentation – or on the issue of the order by Austria to mobilize.

I found both of them positive on this point, viz: that Count Andrassy would not agree to the last of the above three conditions[.]

I said that I had no reason to believe that England would insist on this, if it should appear that the end in view could be otherwise obtained. But I declined to commit Lord B. on this head, and invited Count Beust to call on Lord B. at one tomorrow to discuss the point.

My impression is that, Count Andrassy will at once conclude the alliance, provided that Lord B. will meet his views on this head.

At the moment I left the embassy – 8.20 – no answer had reached them from Count Andrassy.

The objections of Austria to mobilize, at once, are, mainly – that the act must be viewed by Russia as an act of war – that the common object we have in view can be obtained without it – that it entails a large and not necessary expenditure.

I replied that mobilization on their part was not an act of war, and quoted as a precedent the mobilization by Austria in 1854.[360]

They answered that that was an act of folly on the part of Austria, wh: their then acquired experience had taught them not to repeat.

I said that it only seemed equitable that, if England sent up her fleet, Austria, acting with us, should take some step 'pari passu',[361] – wh: could only be mobilization.

They replied that our sending up the fleet was a natural and in any case to-be-expected step, and could not be regarded by Russia as an act of war, and besides would cost us nothing[.] I did not admit all this contention: – but its force is, no doubt, great.

My opinion is that the point is not in reality material. If Austria will but agree to join us in the Note, all the rest must follow, should Russia prove obstinate.

I should add that I insisted upon instant action as 'sine quâ [sic] non'.

My general impression is that Austria desires the alliance quite as much as we do: – and that it will be concluded forthwith, on Count Andrassy's receiving the report of the above interview.[362]

---

[360] Austria remained neutral during the Crimean War, despite mobilizing at its outset.

[361] 'hand-in-hand'; or, more literally, 'with equal step'.

[362] Andrássy rejected the idea of an identic note the next day, 23 January, along with Disraeli's idea of a subsidy for the Austrian army. This latter point revealed to Derby 'that negotiations have been going on behind my back'. *DD*, 23 January 1878, p. 489.

514

Sir William Hart Dyke[363] to Disraeli, Dep. Hughenden 125/3, fos 177–179
23 January [1878]

You have always dealt leniently with any opinions I have expressed upon public affairs, and I cannot resist therefore placing before you my views upon the present crisis.

Of two alternatives – 'that of taking immediate action possibly resulting in war' – and 'that of allowing Russia to advance to a position from whence she can dictate the terms regardless of those interests which the Cabinet has pledged itself to preserve' – In my opinion if the first be adopted 'that of taking immediate action' you will find you have in the House of Commons with a few exceptions a united Party at your back – also a very considerable support from our opponents, resulting in a majority I believe more than double the actual number upon which we usually rely.

[...] Should however the second alternative be adopted I can see nothing but disaster in the future – a divided party in the House of Commons – hostile motions from members sitting behind ministers & a feeling of disgust amongst our supporters in the country generally, which must prove disastrous at every election. [...] The feeling in the House of Commons amongst our supporters is intense & is largely shared by all the younger members of your government. This is the tenth year since I first became connected with the management of your party & I claim a right to speak plainly – although the position is a grave one and even perilous – one thing only can injure the Tory Party of the future – namely if it ever can be hinted either in public or private that in a great national emergency; of two courses open – it's [*sic*] leaders forsook the brave one & preferred the timid.

515

Derby to Disraeli, Dep. Hughenden 113/2, fos 38–39[364]
23 January 1878

After our repeated discussions in Cabinet on the question of sending up the fleet to Constantinople, and the decision which was come to

---

[363] Sir William Hart Dyke (1837–1931), seventh baronet; Conservative chief whip in the House of Commons.
[364] Reproduced in M&B, VI, p. 228.

this afternoon,[365] you will feel as I do that only one result is possible so far as I am concerned.[366]

The question on which we were unable to agree is obviously one of grave importance: it is certain to be eagerly and frequently discussed both in and out of Parliament: the Foreign Secretary more than any other minister would in the ordinary course of things be charged with the duty of defending the decision taken: and as I cannot think it, or say that I think it, a safe or wise one, it is clear that no alternative is left me except to ask you to allow me to retire from the post I hold.

I deeply and sincerely regret that we should differ on any point of policy; but two considerations reconcile me in some measure to a step which is quite as painful to me personally as it can be to you. You will get on better with a thoroughly harmonious Cabinet: and you are so strong in the Lords that the loss of two colleagues will not practically affect you there. — I may add that the incessant anxiety of the last two years has made me often doubt of late – all questions of political difference set aside – whether I should long be capable of even moderately efficient service in an office which at times like these admits of no rest from responsibility and labour.

It is needless to say that whatever I can do, out of office, to support your government will be done by me, both as an obligation of public duty and from feelings of private friendship which no lapse of time or change of circumstances will alter.

516

Northcote to Disraeli, Dep. Hughenden 107/1, fos 171–172
23 January 1878
11 Downing Street

[. . .] Our position is just now one of so much delicacy that I hope you will allow me to know whatever steps you may be taking, and especially whatever communications you may be making to foreign powers, as I may by and by have to defend our course. Several of our colleagues have spoken to me as to the difficulty we shall be in, as we are without a Foreign Secretary, and as the Cabinet cannot conveniently meet, shorn of two members, till we are able to tell our whole story – I would venture to suggest that it would be important to keep Salisbury well informed — Several of us think that some kind

---

[365]That the fleet be sent to Constantinople, with or without the Sultan's consent, and a large vote of credit be sought. *DD*, 23 January 1878, p. 490.

[366]That 'result' was Derby's resignation. Carnarvon's resignation was also presented.

of communication should be made to the other Powers, as soon as the secret of the fleet's movement can be divulged, explaining the character of the act. [. . .]

517

Disraeli to Derby, DP 920 DER (15) 16/2/3
24 January 1878
10 Downing Street

I can't trust myself at this moment to make any remark on your letter just received, & would willingly let four & twenty hours elapse before I attempted to do so, but it is my urgent duty to remind you, that no explanations or statements can be made in the House of Lords till I have received Her Majesty's pleasure on yr resignation, & her permission for your remarks.

I mention this, as Lord Carnarvon, in a letter I have received from him seems inclined to make his explanation prematurely.

518

Derby to Disraeli, Dep. Hughenden 113/2, fo. 42
24 January 1878

I have no wish to make explanations at any time, and the less said at the present moment the better. I think it will be as well that I should not be in the Lords this afternoon. Pembroke can very well put off his question. I have not been in communication with Carnarvon since the Cabinet.

519

Northcote to Disraeli, Dep. Hughenden 107/1, fos 179–180
25 January 1878
11 Downing Street

I think it right to tell you that I hear alarming accounts of the effect which Derby's resignation might produce, especially on our Lancashire and Cheshire members. Dyke has not given me any names, but he says the feeling is much worse than he believed it to be when he spoke to you, and he thinks the division may be seriously affected by it.

The Home Rulers, I am also told, have held a meeting and resolved to go as a body against us. [. . .] Of course this line will be taken independently of Derby's action.

On the other hand I hear that Derby would not like to take anything but the F.O. He would look upon an exchange of office at such a moment as a descent.

Whether he would return to his old post if he had the option does not seem certain. He is very well disposed to us, and if all were suddenly to go right he would probably be willing to come back, – but then if all went right we should not want him so much, and the objections you spoke of would I suppose continue.

We on our part cannot change our policy even to get him back; and we must face the chance of a bad division – and be prepared for a possible overthrow —

Cross has been asked to call on Lady Derby in the morning; and I am thinking of calling on our friend himself, probably about 11. But I shall hardly know what to say.

If you wish to see me before I go I will come to you; otherwise I will feel my way with him as best I can and commit nobody.

520

Hart Dyke to Disraeli, Dep. Hughenden 113/2, fos 50–51
25 January [1878]

You asked me a question today with reference to the possible resignation of the Foreign Secretary — Since giving you my views I have heard much that confirms my opinion that he should at this moment be retained if possible in the Cabinet — The feeling in Lancashire is very strong & I have had many telegrams on the subject, all expressing great anxiety. The commercial element existing there, may also if thoroughly alarmed affect members in this House, & I am sure it would be well if no further change took place. The discussion in the Lords tonight was most useful in every way.

521

Derby to Disraeli, Dep. Hughenden 113/2, fo. 44
25 January 1878

I understand that you wish I should defer making any statement in the House until Monday. I cannot object to this, more especially as I have not received from you a formal announcement that my resignation is accepted.

522

Northcote[367] to Disraeli, Dep. Hughenden 113/2, fo. 54
[?25 January 1878][368]

> The personal arrangement won't work.[369]
> F.O. or nothing. He does not understand the former to be hopeless.

523

Derby to Northcote, IP, BL Add. MS 50022, fo. 164
25 January 1878 '3.P.M.'
St. James's Square

> Would it be inconvenient for you to look in here again? I have been reflecting anxiously on our conversation, and should like to renew it.

524

Northcote to Disraeli, Dep. Hughenden 107/1, fo. 181
26 January 1878
11 Downing Street

> I have had another very long conversation with him.[370] He sent to ask me to come, and raised more points than I could have imagined.

---

[367] Northcote increasingly acted as the intermediary between Disraeli and Derby in this period, given their deteriorating relationship and the 'curious reserve' between them, as Buckle, curiously, described it. M&B, VI, pp. 232–233.

[368] See following note for dating.

[369] It had been suggested to Derby, via his brother Frederick, that he should take a lesser office 'on the ground of health, [and] need of rest'. *DD*, 25 January 1878, pp. 491–492.

[370] Disraeli and his colleagues had twice sent Northcote to see Derby on 26 January, 'with a request that I should withdraw my resignation'. *DD*, p. 492. On 24 January, Layard had conveyed the news that the Porte had accepted Russian peace terms, in which case, as Derby noted, 'all this trouble of the last few days has been taken for nothing'. *DD*, 24 January 1878, p. 491. The fleet had been recalled, and thus the grounds for his resignation no longer stood.

Finally he has promised to send me an answer before dinner – I <u>think</u> he will come in, but I can't feel at all sure.

525

Derby to Northcote, IP, BL Add. MS 50002, fos 160–162
[?26] January 1878[371]
Foreign Office

I have considered carefully and anxiously the subject of our conversation today, and with the following result.

I do not conceal from you the feeling of extreme uneasiness and distrust which is created in my mind by the situation.[372] What happened on Wednesday[373] may happen again, and with worse results. What with pressure from friends in parliament and from other quarters, I feel painfully the risk in which we are placed of compromising ourselves and the interests of peace by some hasty determination.

Nor do I like the vote which you are going to take: but in that matter you have gone so far that it is impossible to recede, except under altered circumstances.

Under these conditions, I should have been well pleased if the Prime Minister had dealt with me as he has with Carnarvon.[374] But he has not done so, and I have to consider whether I am justified – the immediate cause of difference having disappeared – in persisting in an intention to retire for which the original reason is no longer assignable. On the whole I incline to believe that if I can be of use in my present post, it is my duty not to quit it without fresh cause. My doing so might lead to misunderstanding here, and possibly on the continent. I should, by withdrawing, weaken that section of the Cabinet which most inclines to pacific views; and the spectacle of internal dissensions is not one which it is desirable that we should present to Europe.

I have taken this resolution reluctantly and doubtfully, but I have taken it, and if the Prime Minister wishes me to withdraw my letter

---

[371] The letter is dated 25 January (a Friday), but it is clear from *DD* (pp. 492–493) and other accounts that this must have been written on Saturday 26 January, Northcote having spent 'the whole of Saturday in negotiation' (M&B, VI, p. 233).

[372] Derby made this letter 'purposely stiff and unconciliatory'. *DD*, p. 493.

[373] Disraeli's demand for the fleet to be sent to Constantinople and an immediate, large vote of credit.

[374] i.e. if he had accepted Derby's resignation.

of resignation, I do so. I need not add that on personal grounds it is more agreeable to me that our differences should disappear. But in face of such questions as we have to deal with, the personal aspect of the matter is not one which ought to influence a decision one way or another.

526

Northcote to Disraeli, Dep. Hughenden 113/2, fo. 52
27 January 1878
11 Downing Street

Here is the letter – now shall I telegraph anything to Osborne? I can do so in cipher —

I might say, – 'Since writing yesterday I have seen reason for much stronger alarm as to the possible effects of D[erby]'s resignation. I think it might endanger the loss of the vote and the defeat of the government.' But have you made any communication to Her of his willingness to remain?

527

Disraeli to Salisbury, SP, fos 270–271[375]
27 January 1878
10 Downing Street

I inferred from your significant remark, at yesterday's 'Cabinet', respecting Derby, that you desired his return.

I have succeeded in accomplishing that, tho' a pyrrhic victory: at least I feel I have not sufficient energy remaining to go through another such trial.

The Cabinet is called today at 5 o'[clo]ck: It is necessary for Northcote's sake, but I thought it desirable, as the most effective mode, tomorrow, of answering the rumors [sic] afloat respecting D[erby].

I must express my sense of the cordial co-operation & confidence I have received from you throughout this affair. It is a good omen for the Sovereign & the country & I can assure you, and I ought to assure

[375]Reproduced in M&B, VI, pp. 236–237.

you, that yr behavior [*sic*] at headquarters is entirely understood & completely appreciated.

528

Salisbury to Disraeli, Dep. Hughenden 92/4, fos 47–48[376]
27 January 1878
20 Arlington Street

I am very glad Derby has come back. At this juncture his secession would have exposed us to all kinds of wild suspicions, & would have much added to the difficulties which, in any case, the country will have to face.

I am very much grateful to you for your kind expressions – & to the Queen for those you have conveyed to me from her. I should have rendered with great willingness any service in my power: but I am glad to be spared the duty of undertaking a task which under the peculiar circumstances of the case I might not have been able to discharge advantageously to the country.

529

Disraeli to Derby, DP 920 DER (15) 16/2/3
27 January 1878
10 Downing Street

I have at this moment received a cyphered [*sic*] telegram from the Queen approving of y^r withdrawal of your resignation, & I have summoned the Cabinet at five o'[clo]ck: today, as there are points on wh: the C[hancellor]. of Ex[cheque]^r. wishes to consult his colleagues before his important statement tomorrow–

Y^r attendance at the Cabinet will be a sufficient reply to all rumors [*sic*] respecting yourself, & from my management, they have only been rumors [*sic*], & will do away with the necessity of explanations & 'all that'.

Carnarvon, I thought, made an ungentlemanlike speech,[377] as well as a vain, & egotistical one – I believe Salisbury much disapproved it, & was annoyed.

---

[376] Reproduced in part in Cecil, II, p. 194.
[377] In the House of Lords, on 25 January 1878: see *Parl. Deb.*, CCXXXVII, cols 436–446.

530

Derby to Disraeli, Dep. Hughenden 113/2, fos 59–60
28 January [1878]

I have your letter, and can assure you with perfect sincerity that I neither have, nor at any moment had, the wish to hurt your feelings.

There is always a certain awkwardness in the renewal of interrupted official relations: and it seemed to me that this awkwardness would be best avoided by our meeting first in Cabinet, and under such conditions as to make explanations neither necessary nor possible. I know your difficulties and will do what I can to lessen them: the difficulty of the position is this, that the question now dividing the whole political world is one which cuts across the existing divisions of parties, so that men who have always acted cordially together find themselves separated. It was the same in the Crimean time, as we both recollect. I do not despair of a solution: and will help to the utmost of my power.

I have destroyed your note, and have neither shown it nor mentioned it to any one – not even Lady D. – so that no record may exist of personal unpleasantness between us. Do the same with this.[378]

531

Disraeli to Salisbury, SP, fos 272–273
30 January 1878
10 Downing Street

Have you read Sir H. Elliot[']s tel: received by me this morning? All depends on our decision today. That will settle whether we are men or mice.

I greatly, almost entirely, depend on you.

As our ships unhappily are not in the Sea of Marmora, the Russians will certainly enter Const[antinople]:, unless, with Austria, this day we prevent it.

---

[378] An instruction that was clearly ignored.

532

Disraeli to Derby, DP 920 DER (15) 16/2/3
1 February 1878
10 Downing Street

C[oun]t Shouvaloff addressed me in the Hall of Ho[use]. of Lords yesterday evening, told me of the telegram he had just shown you, announcing appeal of Sultan to Emperor, spoke of affairs as now happily all terminated, & said that he did not think he could have borne the excitement any longer, & all that sort of thing — I cannot say his narrative quite satisfied me, & I ventured to observe, that I hoped his anticipations would be realised, but that there seemed to me some mystery in the affair wh: neither Emperor, nor Sultan, seemed to be able to control —

Last night, I received this secret information in the accuracy of wh: I believe[:]

'C[oun]ᵗ. S. will this afternoon show a tel: to Lord Derby, just received from Sᵗ. P[etersburg]. announcing appeal of Sultan to Emp: to stop hostilities as he had accepted all terms demanded &ᶜ., & favorable [*sic*] reply of Emp: virtually amounting to peace.['] This is all a comedie [*sic*] – C[oun]ᵗ. Schou:, at the same time, received two telegrams, one to show to Lᵈ. Derby, as above, & another for himself, which ran thus 'Delegates have not signed: we are in full march on Constantinople, and only 40 versts[379] distant[.]'[380]

I fear, & feel, that in a few days, & perhaps hours, we shall be the objects of general indignation & contempt, but as I have ceased to direct the Cabinet, I can only lay this matter before yourself.[381]

Punica fides![382]

I think, at any rate, Schou:, who has done so much mischief, shᵈ. receive his passports.[383] [. . .]

---

[379] A Russian measure of length, the verst was equivalent to 1.07 kilometres or 0.66 miles.

[380] There was no such telegram, and Disraeli's intelligence was false.

[381] Derby was bemused by this, noting 'an odd letter from Ld B.' *DD*, 1 February 1878, p. 497.

[382] Punic faith – an ironic reference to Carthaginian reliability, for Romans the worst form of treachery. The reference is presumably either to Russia or to Derby's own unreliability, although in what sense it could be defined as treachery is unclear, given that he had been obstinately consistent in his views.

[383] Derby thought this 'would be absurd, and a direct challenge to Russia'. *DD*, 1 February 1878, p. 497.

533

Derby to Disraeli, Dep. Hughenden 113/2, fo. 72
1 February 1878

I suppose you will be at the House, and we can talk about Schou.
It does not seem easy to prove that he is consciously lying to us. If
his employers want him to lie with effect, they probably mislead him
– they certainly did in the Dardanelles case, for he showed me the
telegram. No doubt we could send him away as a mark of displeasure:
but should we get a better in his place?

534

Salisbury to Disraeli, Dep. Hughenden 92/4, fo. 51
6 February 1878
20 Arlington Street

Very grave news indeed. The mere fact that our ambassador is
cut off, & that the Russians are still advancing, seems to require
the presence of the fleet at C[onstantino]ple. At all events a strong
remonstrance ought to go to St. Petersburg at once. But if it were
possible I should much like to move up the fleet.[384]

535

Disraeli to Derby, DP 920 DER (15) 16/2/3
6 February 1878
10 Downing Street

The last tel: of Layard is very grave.

We shall have French, & perhaps Italian, squadrons at
Const[antinopl]ᵉ. before England.

This will not look well. I believe you will see a burst of indignation
in this country, that has not been equalled since —32.[385]

---

[384] Layard reported that Russian troops had advanced towards Chataldja, on the outskirts
of Constantinople. Some of his telegrams were missing, indicating that 'the lines' had been
cut. The news caused panic in London, with the *Morning Post* reporting that Constantinople
had fallen. The Queen sent Derby a number of telegrams, 'mostly incoherent and excited'
(*DD*, 7 February 1878, p. 503). In fact, the advance had been agreed with the Porte during
peace negotiations at San Stefano, where a treaty was ultimately signed on 3 March 1878.
The date was deliberately chosen by Russia as the anniversary of the Tsar's accession, in
less auspicious circumstances during the Crimean War.

[385] That is, at the time of the Great Reform Act.

The entry of the Russians will be an act of wanton duplicity, & may lead to infinite confusion.

536

Derby to Disraeli, Dep. Hughenden 113/2, fo. 79
[6] February 1878[386]
Foreign Office

I quite agree. If the Russians go in now, without military reasons to allege, or any justification for what they know we regard as an offence, the anti-Russian feeling here will grow beyond all control.

I am telegraphing to Loftus to find out what he can. Schou. has not been here.

537

Northcote to Salisbury, SP, fo. 139
[?8] February 1878[387]
11 Downing Street

We are to have a Cabinet at 2. I am inclined to propose that we should at once, openly, send orders to our fleet to go up to Constantinople to protect life & property, and invite the other maritime powers to do the same; and I would openly announce this in the House tonight. We shall do no good by confidential communications, and shall only make ourselves contemptible.

A bold move of this sort is really the safest, for Russia cannot with any decency object, especially after the Gortshakow contradiction.

What do you say?

---

[386]Dated by Derby at the bottom as 'F.6' but another hand gives '10 Feb 76'. Given the previous letter, however, 6 February seems most likely.

[387]A note on the back of this letter dates it to 8 February, although letter **537**, dated 7 February, appears to be the response. The date in Northcote's hand on the letter is unclear, although it might be read as 5, 6, or 8. There was no Cabinet on 5 February, although Derby's diary records a Cabinet 'at 12' the following day. On 7 February, the Cabinet met at 11 am, at which it was agreed to propose to France that the fleet would be sent up to Constantinople. But the Cabinet of 8 February, as per Northcote's letter, met at 2 pm, and agreed to send the fleet. Derby duly announced this to the House of Lords that evening. Thus it seems that 8 February is the likeliest date. See *DD*, pp. 500–503.

538

Salisbury to Northcote, IP, BL Add. MS 50019, fo. 64
[?7] February 1878[388]
20 Arlington Street

I am quite of your mind. I strongly pressed the sending up of the fleet at once on the Chief last night.

539

Salisbury to Disraeli, Dep. Hughenden 92/4, fo. 53[389]
10 February 1878

I hesitate to trouble you with an expression of opinion knowing the difficulties under which you labour; but the very grave news this evening compels me to write.[390] It is the most critical moment we have yet passed through.[391]

I cannot help fearing that efforts will be made in Cabinet to <u>prevent</u> the fleet being ordered to force its way in. Yet, if, after all that has been said, the fleet once more returns to Besika Bay, our position will be utterly ridiculous. We shall disgust our friends in the country, & lose all weight in Europe. [. . .]

540

Derby to Northcote, IP, BL Add. MS 50022, fos 166–167
28 February 1878
Foreign Office

I am sorry that drafts on important foreign questions are sent round and read at dinners where necessarily others besides our colleagues are present.[392] If they are there talked over, it is easy to understand how so little of what we do or say is kept secret. — As to the subject of your note, I certainly think that the seizure of a Turkish island, in

---

[388] See above. This letter, evidently a response to **537**, may have been misdated by Salisbury.

[389] Reproduced in Cecil, II, p. 197.

[390] The Porte had refused to allow the fleet up to Constantinople.

[391] Salisbury was right, although he cannot have known it. Tsar Alexander, in response to what he saw as British provocation in sending the fleet to Constantinople, ordered his forces to occupy Constantinople. Fortunately, his orders were not carried out. At the front line, the Russian general staff, headed by the Tsar's brother Grand Duke Nicholas, often received delayed and contradictory orders from St Petersburg.

[392] This is the first reference in Derby's correspondence to the question of Cabinet leaks since letter **441**.

time of peace, without explanation or justification except that it may be a convenient port for us to hold in the event of war, would be an act so violent, and so entirely disturbing our existing relations with other countries concerned in the eastern question, that the Russian government might not unreasonably treat it as absolving them from the Gallipoli engagement. That they would treat it so is nearly certain: and I am not prepared to say that they would be wrong.

541

Disraeli to Derby, DP 920 DER (15) 16/2/3
28 February 1878
10 Downing Street

I must point out to you how insufficient, in my opinion, is the manner in wh: F.O. has expressed the resolutions of the Cabinet about the preliminaries of peace.

The enclosed tel: means, that H.M. Gov^t. wish to know, as soon as possible, the terms of the peace _made_ between Russia & Turkey. [...]

What the Cabinet wanted to know was, what are the terms, wh: Russia proposes to Turkey, & as to wh: Turkey hesitates to accept. It is very likely, that Russia will refuse to tell us, & will not allow Turkey to tell. But we can, then, say, we have asked, & have been refused.

I don't think we are justified, in the present crisis, to be sending to Russia civil messages 'We shall be obliged to you, as soon as you have made your terms with Turkey, to let us know what they are.'

I am very anxious about this matter, as the Cabinet counts, when it meets again, on a reply from Russia, on wh: they w^d. be prepared to shape their course.

Depend upon it, the uneasiness & dissatisfaction of the country on this head are great, & parliamentary action, from our own side, will be the disastrous consequence.

542

Derby to Disraeli, Dep. Hughenden 113/2, fos 98–99
1 March 1878

I have your note, which it is not now necessary to discuss, further than to say that I pressed Schou. as strongly as courtesy allowed, not to keep us in the dark. But we cannot demand as a right, according to any rule or custom of international law known to me, to be made acquainted with the terms of a treaty not yet negociated.

You will however have seen Layard's telegram just come in, in which he announces the abandonment of the demand for the Turkish fleet and other concessions. I hope this will go far to satisfy public feeling.

I did not understand that it was the desire of the Cabinet to shape their enquiry so as to bring about a refusal to answer it: nor does that seem to me good diplomacy.

543

Disraeli to Derby, DP 920 DER (15) 16/2/3
11 March 1878
10 Downing Street

I think, besides distinctly stating, that we require the treaty between the belligerents to be submitted to the consideration of Congress, we ought, at the same time, to invite the opinions of the Powers on the subject.[393]

If Russia will not agree to the proposal, she will fill Europe with suspicion — [. . .]

544

Northcote to Salisbury, SP, fo. 112
16 March 1878
11 Downing Street

I tried to get Derby to call a Cabinet today, but he would not. I inclose his note. I think it very unfortunate; but there seems no help. I don't like this appearance of slackness on our part.

545

Disraeli to Salisbury, SP, fos 277–278
18 March 1878

Schou: has got the answer, but keeps it in his pocket. It is a refusal, &, according to him, the English proposal will never be accepted.

---

[393]The proposed Congress was to include all the major powers. To this Derby saw 'no objection' (*DD*, 11 March 1878, p. 525), but the crucial point would come to rest on Disraeli's determination that Britain (alone among the powers) should press for each and every clause of the treaty to be submitted to the Congress.

A counter proposal will be offered: 'that every power shall enter the Congress free & disengaged' – whatever that may be.[394]

Russia does not believe there will be any Congress.

Schou: said to my informant, that he sh^{d}. call on L^{d}. Derby today, but didn't think he sh^{d}. give him the Russian answer – but feel his way a little.

I shd. like to talk over these affairs together, if you happen to be disengaged at three o'cl[ock].

546

Derby to Disraeli, Dep. Hughenden 113/2, fos 114–116
19 March 1878

I am compelled against my will to bring to your notice a disagreeable circumstance. Read the enclosed cutting from the Telegraph, and you will see that the decision of the Cabinet of yesterday is announced, under the obviously fictitious assumption that the news comes from Constantinople.

Now it was a condition insisted upon and agreed to in Cabinet that whatever communication we made to Russia should be kept entirely secret, in order that it might retain the character of a friendly warning, and not assume that of a public defiance.

It is certain that the D[aily]. Tel[egraph]. can only have got its information from the Cabinet. No one in the F.O. except Tenterden and Sanderson, both of them perfectly discreet, knows anything of what passed.[395]

I wish I could think that the disclosure was the result only of accident or indiscretion. But the facts point to a different conclusion. — A step is taken which if made public increases the chances of a quarrel between England and Russia: and it is at once communicated, by somebody, to a journal which though friendly does not conceal its desire that such a quarrel should take place.

---

[394] Gorchakov and the Tsar, bridling at the presence of the British Navy off Constantinople, refused to submit every clause of the Treaty of San Stefano to a Congress. Shuvalov formally delivered Russia's rejection on 25 March 1878.

[395] In fact, on at least one occasion Sanderson showed such documents to Lady Derby, whom the Queen and Disraeli suspected of leaking Cabinet secrets to Shuvalov. See B.G. Grosvenor, 'Lord Derby and the Eastern Crisis' (unpublished PhD thesis, University of East Anglia, 2009), ch. 8.

What can one infer?

What I have said does not point to any one [*sic*] personally, for in truth I have no reason to suspect one person more than another. But you will agree that business cannot be carried on where promises of secrecy are not to be relied on.

I think I ought to bring this subject before the Cabinet when it meets: but I mention it to you, as head of the government in the first instance.

547

Disraeli to Derby, DP 920 DER (15) 16/2/3
19 March 1878
10 Downing Street

[...]
[P.S.] I can throw no light on the parag[raph]: in D[aily]. Tel[egraph].

My people are perfectly innocent of newspaper acquaintance, [and] personally, I never see, or hear from, them[396] — And I don't know, now that Carnarvon has gone, any member of the Cab[ine]ᵗ. who has such weaknesses.

I always thought D.T. was devoted to you, but I suppose that's over.

548

Salisbury to Disraeli, Dep. Hughenden 113/2, fo. 118
19 March 1878

I was struck by the D[aily].T[elegraph]. extract myself. Personally I can only say that I do not know by sight any of the D.T. people – & that I tell nothing of what passes in Cabinet to my private secretary. Why should Sanderson know?

The occasion might be a fair one for protesting against the system of taking notes in Cabinet. You are never certain that they will not fall into hands for which they are not intended.[397]

---

[396]This was untrue. Corry's correspondence with Disraeli, for example, reveals regular contacts with the press.

[397]This was quite clearly directed at Derby and his habit of note-taking. In addition to the jibe at Sanderson, the implication may have been that Lady Derby was behind the leaks.

549

Disraeli to Salisbury, SP, fos 279–280
21 March 1878
10 Downing Street

I wish the Cabinet on Saturday to consider the treaty[398] – not to be put off by treaty not having arrived, or having arrived only that morning.

There is no doubt we are, substantially, in possession of the text, & might thus be prepared to decide at once on the authentic version when before us.

Lord Lyons ought to attend the Cabinet.

550

Salisbury to Disraeli, Dep. Hughenden 92/4, fos 55–58
21 March 1878

I see no difficulty about considering the treaty on Saturday as you suggest. We ought to prepare ourselves, in case there is no congress, to state which are the articles of the treaty to which we specially object.

Of course, we have a right to object to all, as all are contrary to existing treaties. But it would be doubtful policy to do so, in view of English opinion. At all events I think we should put in the forefront of our objection[:]

1. Those articles which menace the balance of power in the Egean [*sic*]:

2. Those which threaten the Greek race in the Balkan peninsula with extinction:

And that we should indicate the necessity of either cancelling, or meeting with compensatory provisions, the portions of the treaty which, by reducing Turkey to vassalage, threaten the free passage of the Straits, & also menace English interests in other places where the exercise of Turkish authority affects them.

I am, as you know, not a believer in the possibility of setting the Turkish Government on its legs again, as a genuine reliable power: & unless you have a distinct belief the other way, I think you should be cautious about adopting any line of policy which may stake England's

---

[398] The Treaty of San Stefano, between Russia and the Porte. Its terms included the creation of a large and autonomous Bulgaria, complete with Mediterranean coastline.

security in those seas on Turkish efficiency. I should be disposed to be satisfied with war or negotiations which ended in these results:

1. Driving back the Slav State to the Balkans – & substituting a Greek province, politically, but not administratively, under the Porte.

2. Effective securities for the free passage of the Straits at all times, as if they were open sea.

3. Two naval stations for England – say Lemnos & Cyprus, with an occupation, at least temporary, of some place like Scanderoon[399] for the sake of moral effect:

4. Perhaps I would add reduction of indemnity to amount which there would be reasonable prospect of Turkey paying without giving further pretext for fresh encroachments. [...]

551

Derby to Northcote, IP, BL Add. MS 50022, fos 168–169
27 March 1878
Foreign Office

You were fully authorised to say what you have said, with the one slight exception that I should not commit myself to declare that 'entry into the conference had become impossible' since one does not know what solutions might be suggested; but I am quite ready to state that in this business of the conditions of going into congress I am agreed with my colleagues, and that we could not do otherwise than maintain our objections.

As it is desirable to put on record conclusions come to, I will now ask you to place my resignation in the Prime Minister's hands:[400] and to ask him to arrange for my being able to announce the fact tomorrow in the H[ouse]. of Lords. — I shall say as little as possible, reserving all explanation till the measures are announced.

---

[399] İskenderun, on Turkey's Mediterranean coast.

[400] Following Russia's refusal to commit in advance to allowing every point of the Treaty of San Stefano to be open for review at the forthcoming Congress, Disraeli had proposed to 'issue a proclamation declaring emergency, to put a force in the field and simultaneously to send an expedition from India to occupy Cyprus'. *DD*, 27 March 1878, p. 532. This prompted Derby's second and final resignation. In response to the announcement from London, the Tsar ordered the occupation of the Turkish forts on the Bosphorus. As before, however, his orders were not carried out. More time for European negotiation was gained when the Tsar replaced his cautious brother as commander-in-chief with General Todleben, who did not arrive at the front line until 14 April. By then, the situation had cooled once more, thanks in part to the offer of mediation by Bismarck.

552

Northcote to Disraeli, Dep. Hughenden 107/1, fo. 203
28 March 1878
11 Downing Street

I will tell Derby what you have told me; but I venture to think it would be better that you should yourself write to him.

553

Derby to Northcote, IP, BL Add. MS 50022, fos 170–171
28 March 1878
Foreign Office

Thanks for your letter, which makes all clear. I shall say the very little that it is necessary or desirable to say, in the Lords, this afternoon.

I hope the Premier understands that my sole reason for treating this matter through you was the desire to avoid what can never be otherwise than a painful interchange of communications with a very old friend, to whom I owe much, and of whom I shall never think otherwise than with kindness.

It is needless to speak of personal regrets; but one cannot break through political ties of long standing (even temporarily) without so much of pain and annoyance as far to outweigh whatever satisfaction there may be in freedom from anxiety and responsibility.

My wish is to rest for the present, and take no more part in public business than is forced upon me.

If I can be of any use to my successor I am at his orders. [. . .]

554

Disraeli to Derby, DP 920 DER (15) 16/2/3
28 March 1878
10 Downing Street

I have avoided writing on matters which infinitely distress me – & I thought a dragoman might have done, but to prevent misunderstandings, I send this to say, I have received the Queen's acceptance of yr resignation & H.M's permission for yr making, as a privy councillor, such statement as you, in your discretion, in which the Queen has entire confidence, may think fit.

BIOGRAPHICAL APPENDIX

Entries are ordered alphabetically according to the name most commonly used in the correspondence in this volume. If individuals' roles changed during the four Conservative administrations covered, the month in which the change took place (where known) has been listed. The biographies are not intended to be comprehensive guides to individual lives, but to contextualize roles during the particular administrations considered.

Aberdeen, George Hamilton-Gordon, fourth Earl of (1784–1860), Conservative Foreign Secretary, 1828–1830 and 1841–1846; Prime Minister, Whig–Peelite coalition, 1852–1855.

Addington, Henry Unwin (1790–1870), permanent under-secretary at the Foreign Office, 1842–1854.

Albert, Prince (Francis) Augustus Charles Emmanuel of Saxe-Coburg-Gotha (1819–1861), married Queen Victoria 1840; Prince Consort 1857.

Albert Edward, Prince (1841–1910), Prince of Wales, 1841–1901; as Edward VII, King of the United Kingdom of Great Britain and Ireland, and Emperor of India, 1901–1910.

Alexander II (1818–1881), Tsar of Russia, 1855–1881.

Andrássy, Count Gyula (1823–1890), Foreign Minister of Austria-Hungary, 1871–1879.

Antonelli, Giacomo (1806–1876), Cardinal Secretary of State, Vatican, 1848 and March 1852–November 1876.

Apponyi, Rudolf, Graf Apponyi von Nagy- (1812–1876), Austrian minister in London, 1856–1860; Austrian ambassador, 1860–1871.

Augustenburg, Christian August, Duke of (1798–1869), representative of the cadet branch of the Danish royal family; claimed to rule over Schleswig and Holstein, 1848; renounced claim, 1852. His son, Frederick, claimed the duchies in the 1860s.

Azeglio, Victor Emmanuel Taparelli, marchese d' (1816–1890), Sardinian minister in London, 1850–1864. To distinguish him from his uncle Massimo, also the Marchese d'Azeglio, he was sometimes known as 'Minimo'.

Barron, Henry Page Turner (1824–1900), paid attaché at Turin, temporarily at Florence, 1851 and 1852. Transferred to Berlin in June 1852. Despite Malmesbury's irritation with his conduct, he remained in the service and retired as Minister Resident at Stuttgart in 1890.

Bernstorff, Albrecht, Graf von (1809–1873), Prussian envoy to Naples, 1852–1854; Prussian minister in London, 1854–1862 (and informal intermediary between Britain and Naples while the two nations had no diplomatic relations); ambassador, 1862–1867; ambassador of the North German Confederation, 1867–1871; ambassador of the German Empire, 1871–1873.

Beust, Friedrich Ferdinand, Baron (from December 1868, Count) (1809–1886), prime minister of Saxony, 1853–1866; Austrian foreign minister, October 1866–February 1867; prime minister and foreign minister, February 1867–December 1867; lord chamberlain and foreign minister of Austria-Hungary, December 1867–1871; Austro-Hungarian ambassador to Britain, 1871–1878.

Bismarck, Otto Eduard Leopold (1815–1898), created Prince, 1871; Prime Minister of Prussia, 1862–1873 and 1873–1890; Chancellor of Germany, 1871–1890.

Bloomfield, John Arthur Douglas (1802–1879), second Baron Bloomfield and first Baron Bloomfield of Ciamhaltha; minister in Prussia, 1851–1860; ambassador to Austria, 1860–1871.

Bourke, Robert (1827–1902), Baron Connemara from 1887; parliamentary under-secretary at the Foreign Office, 1874–1880; younger brother of the murdered viceroy of India, Lord Mayo (formerly Lord Naas); the fifteenth Earl of Derby's fellow Conservative MP for King's Lynn, 1868–1869.

Brünnow, Filip Ivanovich, Baron (later Count) (1794–1875), Russian minister in London, 1840–1854 and March 1858–1861; ambassador, 1861–July 1874.

Bulwer, (William) Henry Lytton Earle, later Baron Dalling and Bulwer (1801–1872), minister in Tuscany, 1852–1855; commissioner to the Danubian principalities, 1856–May 1858; ambassador to the Ottoman Empire, May 1858–1865.

Bunsen, Christian Karl Josias von (from 1858, Freiherr) (1791–1860), Prussian minister in London, 1842–1854.

Buol-Schauenstein, Count Karl Ferdinand (1797–1865), Austrian minister in London, 1851–April 1852; Austrian minister-president and foreign minister, April 1852–August 1859.

Cairns, Hugh McCalmont, first Earl Cairns (1819–1885); Solicitor-General, 1858–1859; Attorney-General, 1866–1868; Lord Chancellor, February–December 1868 and 1874–1880.

Cambridge, Prince George, Duke of (1819–1904), Commander-in-Chief of the Army, 1856–1895.

Canning, Stratford, Viscount Stratford de Redcliffe (1786–1880), ambassador to Constantinople, 1841–February 1858.

Carnarvon, Henry Howard Molyneux Herbert, fourth Earl of (1831–1890), parliamentary under-secretary for the Colonies, 1858–1859; Colonial Secretary, 1866–1867 (resigning over reform) and 1874–1878.

Cavour, Camillo, Count Benso di (1810–1861), Prime Minister of Piedmont-Sardinia, November 1852–July 1859 and 1860–1861.

Clarendon, George William Frederick Villiers, fourth Earl of (1800–1870), Whig Viceroy of Ireland, 1847–1852; Whig Foreign Secretary, 1853–1858; Liberal Foreign Secretary, 1865–1866 and 1868–1870.

Colloredo-Wallsee, Count Francis (1799–1859), Austrian ambassador to Britain, 1849–1851 and again, after Buol's elevation, 1852–1856.

Corry, Montagu William Lowry, Baron Rowton (1838–1903), Disraeli's private secretary and confidant from 1866 until Disraeli's death in 1881.

Cowley, Henry Richard Charles Wellesley, first Earl (1804–1884), ambassador to France, 1852–1867.

Crampton, Sir John Fiennes Twistleton (1805–1886), second baronet; minister in the United States, 1852–1856; in Hanover, 1857–1858; in Russia, March 1858–1860; and in Spain, 1860–1869.

Cross, Richard Assheton, first Viscount Cross (1823–1914), protégé of the fifteenth Earl of Derby; Home Secretary, 1874–1880 and 1885–1886; India Secretary, 1886–1892; Lord Privy Seal, 1895–1900.

Danilo II, Petrović Nejegoš (1826–1860), Prince of Montenegro, 1851–1860.

Decazes, Louis Charles Élie Amanieu, duc (1819–1886), French foreign minister in the governments of MacMahon, de Broglie, Cissey, Buffet, Dufaure, and Simon, November 1873–November 1877.

Derby, Edward Geoffrey Stanley, fourteenth Earl of (1799–1869), Chief Secretary for Ireland, 1830–1833; Colonial Secretary under Grey (Whig), 1833–1834; Colonial Secretary under Peel (Conservative), 1841–1845; leader of the Conservative party from 1846; Prime Minister, 1852, 1858–1859, and 1866–1868.

Derby, Edward Henry Stanley, fifteenth Earl of (1826–1893), parliamentary under-secretary at the Foreign Office, 1852; Colonial Secretary, 1858; India Secretary, 1858–1859; Foreign Secretary, 1866–1868 and 1874–1878. Subsequently served under Gladstone as Liberal Colonial Secretary; later, a Liberal Unionist. Generally referred to in letters from his father and Malmesbury as 'Edward' or 'Stanley'.

Derby, Mary Catherine Stanley, Countess of (1824–1900), neé Sackville-West; formerly married to the second Marquis of Salisbury; after being widowed in 1868, she married the fifteenth Earl of Derby in 1870.

Disraeli, Benjamin, first Earl of Beaconsfield (1804–1881), Chancellor of the Exchequer, 1852, 1858–1859, and 1866–1868; Prime Minister, 1868 and 1874–1880.

Drouyn de L'Huys, Édouard (1805–1881), French foreign minister, 1848–1849, 1851, July 1852–1854, 1855, and 1862–September 1866.

Edward, *see* **Derby, Edward Henry Stanley, fifteenth Earl of**

Eglinton, Archibald William Montgomerie, thirteenth Earl of, and first Earl of Winton (1812–1861), Lord Lieutenant of Ireland, 1852 and 1858–1859.

Elliot, Sir Henry George (1817–1907), minister in Denmark, March 1858–1859; in Naples, 1859–1863; and in Italy, 1863–1867; ambassador to the Ottoman Empire, July 1867–December 1877; and to Austria-Hungary, December 1877–1884.

Erskine, Edward Morris (1817–1883), British minister in Greece, 1864–1872.

Fane, Julian Henry Charles (1827–1870), first secretary and acting chargé d'affaires, Paris; subsequently ran the embassy after Cowley retired, until Lyons arrived as ambassador. Stanley admired his work as protocolist during the Luxembourg conference.

Fitzgerald, William Robert Seymour Vesey (1816/1818–1885), parliamentary under-secretary of state for the Foreign Office, 1858–1859; Governor of Bombay, 1866–1872.

Friedrich Wilhelm IV (1795–1861), King of Prussia, 1840–1861.

Gladstone, William Ewart (1809–1898), President of the Board of Trade (as a Conservative, under Peel), 1843–1845; Secretary for War and the Colonies, 1845–1846; in 1851, published a denunciation of misgovernment in Naples and Sicily (thereafter he maintained a close interest in Italian affairs); Peelite Chancellor of the Exchequer under Aberdeen, 1852–1855; commissioner extraordinary to the Ionian Islands (appointed by the fourteenth Earl of Derby), 1858–1859; Chancellor of the Exchequer under Palmerston in the first Liberal government, 1859–1866; Liberal Prime Minister, 1868–1874, 1880–1885, 1886, and 1892–1894.

Gorchakov, Prince Aleksandr Mikhailovich (1798–1883), Russian foreign minister, 1856–1882; vice-chancellor, 1862; chancellor, 1867.

Granville, Granville George Leveson-Gower, second Earl (1815–1891), Whig minister in various offices, 1848–1866; Colonial Secretary, 1868–1870 and 1886; Foreign Secretary, 1851–1852, 1870–1874, and 1880–1885. Led the Liberal Party in the Lords, 1859–1891, with a short break in the 1860s after Russell's return to the premiership.

Grey, General Charles (1804–1870), son of the reforming Prime Minister; private secretary to Prince Albert, 1849–1861, and to Queen Victoria, 1861–1870.

Hammond, Edmund (1802–1890), permanent under-secretary at the Foreign Office, 1854–1873; created Baron Hammond of Kirkella, 1874.

Harcourt, George, marquis d' (1808–1883), French ambassador to Britain, 1875–1879. Sometimes confused with his namesake and predecessor, Bernard Hippolyte Marie, Comte d'Harcourt (1821–1912), French ambassador to Britain, 1872–1873.

Hardinge, Henry, first Viscount Hardinge of Lahore (1785–1856), master-general of the ordnance, March–September 1852.

Hardy, Gathorne Gathorne-, first Earl of Cranbrook (1814–1906), parliamentary under-secretary to the Home Office, 1858–1859; President of the Poor Law Board, 1866–1867; Home Secretary, 1867–1868; Secretary for War, 1874–1878; created Viscount Cranbrook, 1878, when he also adopted the extra Gathorne (Earl, 1892).

Hornby, Sir Geoffrey Thomas Phipps (1825–1895), vice-admiral; cousin to the fifteenth Earl of Derby; Commander-in-Chief of the Mediterranean fleet, January 1877–1880; it was he who would take the fleet through the Dardanelles in February 1878.

Howard, Henry George (1818–1879), secretary of embassy in Vienna, 1851–1853; chargé d'affaires during Westmorland's absence, 29 July–7 September and 8 November–23 December 1852.

Hudson, Sir James (1810–1885), minister in Piedmont-Sardinia, January 1852–1861; ambassador to Italy, 1861–1863.

Hunt *see* **Ward Hunt, George**

Ignatiev, Nikolai Pavlovich, Count (1832–1908), Russian ambassador at Constantinople and a leading Pan-Slav.

La Tour d'Auvergne-Lauraguais, Henri Godefroy Bernard Alphonse, Prince de (1823–1871), French ambassador to Britain, 1864–1869; served two brief terms as foreign minister in 1869 and 1870.

La Vallette, Charles Jean Marie Félix, marquis de (1806–1881), acting French foreign minister until Moustier returned from Constantinople; later his successor as foreign minister, December 1868–1869.

Layard, Austen Henry (1817–1894), ambassador to Madrid, 1869–1877, and thereafter to Constantinople, 1877–1880.

Leopold I of Saxe-Coburg (1790–1865), King of Belgium, 1831–1865.

Loftus, Lord Augustus William Frederick Spencer (1817–1904), minister in Austria, March 1858–1860; in Prussia, 1860–1863; and in Bavaria, 1863–1866; ambassador to Prussia, February 1866–March 1868; to the North German Confederation, March 1868–1871; and to Russia, 1871–April 1879. Disraeli and the fifteenth Earl of Derby nicknamed him 'Don Pomposo Magnifico'.

Lyons, Richard Beckerton Pemell (1817–1887), second Baron Lyons 1858, Earl Lyons 1887; special mission to Naples to resolve *Cagliari* affair, 1858; minister in the United States, 1858–1865; ambassador to the Ottoman Empire, 1865–1867; appointed ambassador to France by Stanley in 1867.

MacMahon, Marie Edmé Patrice Maurice de (1808–1893), duc de Magenta, President of France, 1873–1879. His peerage followed his victorious leadership of the French forces at the Battle of Magenta in 1859, during the Second Italian War.

Malmesbury, James Howard Harris, third Earl of (1807–1889), Foreign Secretary, 1852 and 1858–1859; Lord Privy Seal, 1866–1868 and 1874–1876.

Manners, Lord John, seventh Duke of Rutland (1818–1906), finally succeeded to the dukedom in 1888; Commissioner of Woods and Forests, 1852; First Commissioner of Works and Public Buildings, 1858–1859 and 1866–1868; Postmaster-General, 1874–1880.

Manteuffel, Otto (Theodor), Freiherr von (1805–1882), Prussian foreign minister and minister-president, 1850–November 1858; a constitutional conservative and negotiator of the Olmutz Punktation.

Montgelas, Rudolf Ernst Emil Simeon Maria Franz von Sales, Count de Garnerin de la Thuille von (1843–1915), a younger son of the third Count Montgelas and Elizabeth Jemima Watts-Russell; secretary at the Austrian Embassy; central to the erratic secret negotiations between Disraeli and Andrássy in late 1877 and early 1878; transferred to Constantinople; subsequently dismissed in scandalous circumstances, 1880.

Moustier, Lionel, marquis de (1817–1869); French foreign minister, September 1866–December 1868; previously served as French ambassador in Constantinople.

Münster-Ledenburg, Count Georg Herbert zu (1820–1902), German ambassador to Britain, 1873–1885; subsequently ambassador to France; created Prince, 1899.

Musurus, Constantine (1807–1891), variously described by contemporaries as Musurus Bey or Musurus Pasha; Turkish minister in Austria, 1848–1851; minister in London, 1851–1856; ambassador to Britain, 1856–1885.

Naas, Lord, Richard Southwell Bourke, sixth Earl of Mayo (1822–1872), known from 1849 until 1867 by the courtesy title of Lord Naas; Chief Secretary for Ireland, 1852, 1858–1859, and 1867–1868; Viceroy of India, 1868–1872 (assassinated).

Nesselrode, Count Karl Robert Vasilyevich (1780–1862), Russian foreign minister, 1817–1856; vice chancellor, 1828; chancellor, 1845.

Northcote, Sir Stafford Henry (1818–1887), first Earl of Iddesleigh; President of the Board of Trade, 1866–March 1867; Secretary of State for India, March 1867–1868; Chancellor of the Exchequer, 1874–1880; Leader of the House of Commons, February 1877–1880; briefly Foreign Secretary (as Iddesleigh) under Salisbury, 1886–1887.

Northumberland, Algernon Percy, fourth Duke of (1792–1865), First Lord of the Admiralty, 1852.

Pakington, John Somerset (1799–1880), first Baron Hampton; Secretary of State for War and the Colonies, 1852; First Lord of the Admiralty, 1858–1859 and 1866–March 1867; Secretary of State for War, March 1867–1868.

Palmerston, Henry John Temple, third Viscount (1784–1865), Whig Foreign Secretary, 1830–1834, 1835–1841, and 1846–1851; Home Secretary, 1852–1855; Prime Minister, 1855–1858 and (in first Liberal government) 1859–1865.

Pélissier, Aimable Jean Jacques, duc de Malakoff (1794–1864), Persigny's replacement as French ambassador to Britain, 1858–1859; French commander-in-chief in the latter part of the Crimean War. A popular figure in Britain.

Persigny, Jean Gilbert Victor Fialin, comte de (duc, 1863) (1808–1872), French ambassador to Britain, 1855–1858 and 1859–1860.

Pius IX, Giovanni Maria Mastai-Ferretti, Pope (1792–1878), 'Pio Nono', 1846–1878.

Prussia, Prince of, *see* **Wilhelm I**

Raglan, *see* **Somerset, Lord FitzRoy**

Richmond, Charles Henry Gordon-Lennox, sixth Duke of (1818–1903), President of the Board of Trade, 1867–1868; Lord President of the Council, 1874–1880.

Russell, Lord John, first Earl Russell (1792–1878), Whig Prime Minister, 1846–1852; Leader of the House of Commons, 1852–1855; Foreign Secretary, 1852–1853 (held with the leadership of the House); again Foreign Secretary, 1859–1865; Liberal Prime Minister (as Earl Russell), 1865–1866.

Russell, Odo William Leopold (1829–1884), first Baron Ampthill, Britain's unofficial envoy to the Vatican, November 1858–1870; ambassador to Germany, 1871–1884.

Salisbury, Robert Gascoyne-Cecil, third Marquis of (1830–1903), India Secretary, 1866–1867 (as Viscount Cranborne) and 1874–1878 (as Salisbury, his title inherited in 1868); Foreign Secretary, 1878–1880; Conservative Prime Minister, 1885–1886, 1886–1892, and 1895–1902.

Sanderson, Thomas Henry (1841–1923), later Baron Sanderson, private secretary to the fifteenth Earl of Derby, 1866–1868 and 1874–1878, and to Earl Granville, 1880–1885; Permanent Under-Secretary, Foreign Office, 1894–1906. John Vincent speculates that he 'may have been the son Derby and Lady Derby never had' (*DD*, p. 9).

Scarlett, Peter Campbell (1804–1881), secretary of legation in Florence, 1844–1855; minister in Tuscany, December 1858–1860.

Schwarzenberg, Felix Fürst zu (1800–1852), Austrian minister-president and foreign minister, 1848–April 1852.

Schouvaloff, *see* **Shuvalov Pyotr Andreyevich, Count**

Seymour, Sir George Hamilton (1797–1880), British minister in Russia, 1851–1854; envoy to the Vienna peace talks in 1855.

Shuvalov, Pyotr Andreyevich, Count (1827–1889), Russian ambassador to Britain, 1874–1879.

Smith, William Henry (1825–1891), newsagent and Conservative politician; Financial Secretary to the Treasury, 1874–1878; First Lord of the Admiralty following George Ward Hunt's death in 1877 (until 1880).

Somerset, Lord FitzRoy (1788–1855), Baron Raglan from 18 October 1852; lieutenant-general; military secretary to the Commander-in-Chief of the Army, 1827–1852; Master-General of the Ordnance, September 1852.

Stanley, *see* **Derby, Edward Henry Stanley, fifteenth Earl of**

Stratford, *see* **Canning, Stratford, Viscount Stratford de Redcliffe**

Tenterden, Charles Abbott, third Baron (1834–1882), permanent under-secretary at the Foreign Office, 1873–1882.

Thouvenel, Édouard Antoine de (1818–1866), senior French diplomat; ambassador to Constantinople, 1855–1860; foreign minister, 1860–1862.

Turgot, Louis Félix Étienne, marquis de (1796–1866), French foreign minister, 1851–July 1852.

Van de Weyer, Sylvain (1802–1874), Belgian minister in London, 1831–June 1867.

Victor Emmanuel II (1820–1878), King of Piedmont-Sardinia, 1849–1861; first King of Italy, 1861–1878.

Victoria (1819–1901), Queen of the United Kingdom of Great Britain and Ireland, 1837–1901; proclaimed Empress of India, 1877.

Wales, Prince of, *see* **Albert Edward, Prince**

Walewski, Alexandre Florian Joseph Colonna, comte de (duc, 1866) (1810–1868), French ambassador to Britain, 1851–1855; French foreign minister, 1855–1860.

Walpole, Spencer Horatio (1806–1898), Home Secretary, 1852, 1858–March 1859 (until his resignation over reform), and 1866–May 1867 (until his resignation over the handling of the Hyde Park reform meeting), after which he remained in Cabinet as minister without office.

Ward Hunt, George (1825–1877), Financial Secretary to the Treasury, 1866–1868; Chancellor of the Exchequer, 1868; First Lord of the Admiralty from the formation of the Conservative government in 1874 until his death on 29 July 1877.

Wellesley, Frederick Arthur (1844–1931), lieutenant-colonel, 1875; military attaché at St Petersburg, 1871–1878; made aide-de-camp to Queen Victoria, January 1878; secretary of embassy, Vienna, April 1878–August 1879; retired from army, 1881.

Westmorland, John Fane, eleventh Earl of (1784–1859), ambassador to Austria, 1851–1855.

Wilhelm I (1797–1888), second son of Friedrich Wilhelm III; younger brother of Friedrich Wilhelm IV; Prince Regent of Prussia, October 1858–1861 (in October 1857 he took over royal duties on a 'temporary' basis as his brother's physical and mental state had deteriorated); Wilhelm I, King of Prussia, 1861–1871; Emperor of Germany, 1871–1888.

Wood, Charles (1800–1885), first Viscount Halifax, senior Whig politician occupying a series of ministerial roles; preceded Pakington as First Lord of the Admiralty, 1855–1858.

INDEX

Index created by Meg Davies (Fellow of the Society of Indexers)